Computers and Learning

A Reader edited by
Oliver Boyd-Barrett and Eileen Scanlon
at The Open University

Addison-Wesley Publishing Company

Wokingham, England · Reading, Massachusetts · Menlo Park, California
New York · Don, Mills, Ontario · Amsterdam · Bonn · Sydney · Singapore
Tokyo · Madrid · San Juan · Milan · Paris · Mexico City · Seoul · Taipei

in association with

The Open University

Cover design by David, Charles & Co. and
printed by The Riverside Printing Co. (Reading) Ltd.
Typeset by Longman Malaysia.
Printed and bound in Great Britain by Mackays of Chatham PLC, Kent.

First printed 1990. Reprinted 1991.

British Library Cataloguing in Publication Data
Computers and Learning.
 1. Schools. Training. Applications of computer systems
 I. Boyd-Barrett, Oliver II. Scanlon, Eileen
 371.334

 ISBN 0–201–54411–3

Computers and Learning

This volume of readings has been prepared for the Open University course, Computers and Learning (course code: EH232). Other components of the course include correspondence texts, audio and video tapes, computer software and personal tuition. The course may be studied either as a second–level course within the Open University's degree programme, or it may be studied on a one-off basis within the associate student programme. Further details about either of these programmes may be obtained from the Central Enquiry Service, The Open University, PO Box 71, Milton Keynes MK7 6AA.

The editors wish to acknowledge the help of the course team and its consultants in the compilation of this Reader. Opinions expressed herein are not necessarily those of the Open University.

Editors' Introduction

Computers and Learning is the course reader for the Open University's course of the same title, coded EH232, and produced by a collaborative team that includes staff of the University's School of Education and its Institute of Educational Technology. The main themes of the volume closely reflect those of the course of which it is part. Appreciation and understanding of the contents of this Reader are not dependent, however, on study of the course, and the editors believe that these papers will be useful to a great many teachers throughout education who have already adopted computers into their classroom teaching or would like to do so.

The course, Computers and Learning, was first presented in 1991. It replaced an earlier course, Educational Computing (EH221). In the period of time separating the production of these two courses, there had been significant changes in educational context. In the early 1980s when the government launched the Microelectronics Education Programme which ran from 1981 to 1985, the political objective was still largely about placing at least one computer in every school. In the early 1990s it is more relevant to ask how long it will take before there is a computer in every classroom, perhaps even for every pupil. In the early 1980s, some educationalists wondered whether computers in education might prove to be a mere fashion, perhaps following the path of programmed learning into relative oblivion. This has not happened: computers have arrived in schools, are being used in a great variety of ways for teaching and for educational management, and the probability is that they will continue arriving in greater numbers, diversity and complexity. In the early 1980s the concerns of many of those involved with in-service training (INSET) in the area of educational computing were primarily to introduce computers to teachers, allay anxieties, explain what computers were, what they could do, and perhaps provide some elementary prac-tice in simple programming. These are still relevant objectives, but now that many schools and colleges have accumulated experience of computing that reaches back over a decade, the identification of teaching and learning needs has grown more varied and sophisticated. There is now much greater interest, for example, in such issues as: understanding and learning to manage the deployment of computers and software in schools; relating software to processes of children's learning both as individuals and in groups; learning to evaluate new software; uses of subject-independent applications as well as subject-related drill-and-practice and simulation software; understanding the challenge of artificial intelligence and its relevance to schools; making interconnections between computing and other technologies such as interactive television and communication networks.

These questions frequently draw on multidisciplinary approaches, that include the psychology of education, curriculum theory, information technology, and artificial intelligence as well as the various subject disciplines which have adopted aspects of the new technology. A continuing problem is the lack of sufficient integration of these approaches, and in this volume we have brought together teachers and researchers from different backgrounds to help achieve a more holistic appraisal of the field.

The course of which this volume is part is not addressed to the study of computers in isolation, but to the study of *learning*. More specifically, it is about how computers can assist, and sometimes impede, the learning of subjects in all areas of the curriculum and at all stages of the educational system – primary, secondary, colleges and universities. The course looks at learning and the ways in which computers affect learning. It examines the relationships of computing to educational curricula and looks at how information technology affects the role of teachers, and the ways in which the computer can promote, enhance and interfere with learning. Examples throughout the course relate to various topic areas including language, humanities, science and mathematics. The course team wanted to avoid too narrow a focus on only one or two topic areas, or too diffuse a focus which embraced all and any educational objective. But it felt that the examples chosen have a broad relevance across the curriculum: they illustrate the variety of uses and approaches that are possible, and relate them to issues about classroom management, and the relations between teachers, learners and software that are of universal significance within education. Methods of analysis employed in the course include historical, socio-political, evaluative, theoretical and case study.

The structure of this volume reflects the structure of the course of which it is a component. Part 1 has to do largely with the political, resource and pedagogic rationales which have informed the introduction of computers into education, and the variety of uses and applications in education to which computers are put. Part 2 analyses the assumptions built into different kinds of software about how children learn. It asks how computing should relate to the cognitive development of children. It explores how the interaction of learners with computers is influenced by factors such as teaching styles, classroom discourse and gender and by the organization of learners into groups, pairs or single individuals.

The third and final part has to do with specific applications of computing, for example, hypertext or computer conferencing, or the relevance of computing to specific groups of learners, including those with special needs.

A substantial part of the reader reflects a central preoccupation of the course. This has to do with the perception that the educational significance of computing to a significant extent may reside, not in machines, but in the ways in which teachers and learners interact with them, and in doing so, the ways in which teachers and learners interact among themselves. There are differences of view among the various authors as to the extent to which computers facilitate new forms of interaction or simply stimulate more of the same, the desirability of any new interaction and for what purposes, and what needs to be done to inspire desirable forms of interaction.

Behind this central preoccupation there lies a more fundamental value position, which is made explicit in some of the chapters, and is shared by most. This is that educational computing should represent something more than a didactic machine-mediated transmission of knowledge from expert to novice. There may be a place for software which seeks to 'stand in' for teacher, and which, as in drill-and-practice programs, takes over some of the more laborious and repetitive of traditional teaching tasks, but it should not be the dominant role. Software of this kind is sometimes modelled on theories of teaching and learning which were out of date even before the advent of the micro. Were this kind of use allowed to become too prevalent, it would certainly seem, within this perspective, that education was being enslaved and dehumanized by the machine. That would represent an appalling failure of imagination. The authors of this volume are mostly engaged in a struggle to escape just such a fate: they are looking at the ways in which computing can be used to give learners more autonomy, to engage them in new ways of conceptualizing processes and problems, and new ways of interacting with their teachers and fellow learners. For these authors the preferred rationales for educational computing are most likely to be either what Hawkridge in Paper 1.2 calls the **pedagogic** and the **catalytic** rationales: that is to say, educational computing is valued either for the ways in which it can improve the teaching and learning process within traditional subject areas, or more dramatically, the ways in which it can transform how educators conceive of education and its provision.

As some of the important themes of this volume also cut across its formal structure, it is useful to summarize what the central themes are. The volume cannot do complete justice to every theme, but it can help put them on a conceptual map, as it were, of approaches to this applied subject area and perceived issues within it. The questions that follow are examples of issues, not an exhaustive list of issues actually dealt with in the volume:

(1) *Use*. How are computers typically used in educational institutions? How do they relate to the curriculum? How do they extend the curriculum?

(2) *Rationale*. What are the rationales governing the use of computers in education? How convincing are these? How do they differ as between politicians and educators, and between different subjects and levels of education?

(3) *Deployment*. What is required, what has to happen if computers are to get into schools and if they are to be deployed effectively once they do arrive? What environmental factors of management, staff training and commitment, resource allocation, etc, are relevant to effective deployment?

(4) *Software*. How do teachers get to know what kinds of software are available? How can they assess the likely utility of particular software and evaluate its uses?

(5) *Gender.* Is there an association between computer performance and gender? What are the causes of any such association? What can be done to reduce gender differences?

(6) *Cognition.* How does effective use of computers relate to what is known about the cognitive development of children and models of learning? What can observation of learners at work with computers tell teachers about cognitive processes?

(7) *Learner autonomy.* Can computers meaningfully enhance the autonomy of learners in a way that gives them more control over what they learn, how they learn and how effectively they learn?

(8) *Pedagogy.* How do uses of computers relate to teaching objectives, pedagogic strategies and other teaching media? What is the relevance of computers for the roles of teachers and learners, and what is the significance of having learners in groups, pairs or as single individuals?

In compiling this volume, as in preparing the course, we have started on the assumption that most teachers who use computers in some way in their teaching, or who are seriously thinking about doing so, are familiar with at least one kind of machine and one or two types of application. They are not necessarily needing or wanting a technical 'how to do it' manual. But they may be unsure about why there has been so much outside interest in the use of computers in education and its justification, about the range of applications open to them, and about the educational effectiveness of such applications in relation to what different categories of learner most need. It is to these kinds of question that this volume is addressed. In such a fast-changing field, we can certainly not claim anything final, but we believe this book will help establish the relevance of a multidisciplinary approach to educational computing which emphasizes the relationship between teacher, computer and learner.

Oliver Boyd-Barrett
Eileen Scanlon
August 1990

Contents

Part 1

Learning through Computers

This part is largely concerned with the contextual factors which influence the effectiveness with which computers are used in schools. Boyd-Barrett in Paper 1.1 focuses primarily on the role and significance, within the UK context, of central government promotion of computer use in education, and argues that there has been a gradual sharpening of centrally articulated rationale for educational computing over the past decade which favours the use of computers for learning across the curriculum. The importance of coherent and convincing rationales is taken up in Paper 1.2 by David Hawkridge who turns to the Third World for a comparative analysis of different rationales. Third-World countries sometimes have a clearer idea of what they want to do with computers in the classroom than the developed countries. Hawkridge establishes a typology of rationales. Among these he identifies a *social* rationale, which focuses on the desirability of fitting pupils to the demands and needs of the wider society, and a *vocational* rationale which is more specifically concerned with preparing pupils for the needs of the external job market. Quite a different rationale is the *pedagogic*: here, computers are seen as relevant to education because they seem to enable pupils to learn and teachers to teach better than they would without computers. A more radical rationale is the *catalytic*, which is premised on the view that computers can usefully transform the whole educational process, reducing the stress on memorization and individualization in favour of information handling, problem solving and collaboration. Applying Hawkridge's typology to the earlier paper by Boyd-Barrett suggests that in the United Kingdom there has been a shift away from a mixed social and vocational rationale towards a pedagogic and, to a much lesser extent, catalytic rationale.

The following papers look at some of the various ways in which computers are actually used in education. There are various approaches to distinguishing the major educational roles of computers: Anderson in Paper 1.3 employs the concepts of tutor (didactic mode), tutee (interactive mode) and tool (enabling mode), but other authors variously employ a range of different concepts which include

1

drill-and-practice, tutorial, simulation, artificial intelligence and content-free applications. While the focus of many writers on the limitations of a didactic perspective may be persuasive to liberal minded and child-centred educationalists, it should not blind us to ways in which computing can fulfil a didactic role very effectively, especially when the educational contexts of curriculum and classroom organization are carefully integrated with the software. This aspect is explored in White and Horwitz's analysis in Paper 1.4 of computer microworlds, or interactive simulations which are designed to teach very specific concepts. Laurillard, in Paper 1.5, distinguishes between communication and didactic models of computer teaching. In the former, knowledge is seen as negotiable, while the latter is about what she calls preceptual knowledge, that is, knowledge of precepts. Communication models, she argues, respond to the likelihood that students are better than teachers at directing their own learning, but these models are rather limited for the task of inculcating preceptual knowledge. She looks at these models in relation to the degree of student control over learning strategy, the manipulation of learning content and the description of content.

Effectiveness of educational computing is also related to the integration of the content and context of computing with the characteristics of the learner. A particular example of the problem of integration is raised by the issue of gender. Culley in Paper 1.6 looks not only at how computing has come to be defined by many girls as essentially a masculine activity which is not for them, but shows how the organization of schooling can reinforce this perceived bias: for example, through male-dominated teaching of computing, linking computing with mathematics, and housing computers in maths or science areas.

If an important key to effective computing in education lies in classroom organization and integration of computing with both the demands of the curriculum and the needs of the learner, then it is important for teachers to develop a clear understanding of the potential and pitfalls of particular pieces of software. But just how practical is it for teachers to acquire this kind of knowledge in advance of use, and what does it take for them to develop it for themselves? Hawkridge in Paper 1.7 looks at the range of relevant information that teachers can generally expect to find in software reviews, and contrasts this with what they need to know. Full evaluation of educational computing, however, involves much more than analysis of software, as Anita Straker shows in Paper 1.8, and incorporates such factors as school computing policy, classroom organization, staff development, resource management, and assessment of the full range of outcomes. Integration of software specifically with the processes whereby children learn is another aspect of evaluation which is picked up in Part 2.

Paper 1.1

Schools Computing Policy as State-Directed Innovation

Oliver Boyd-Barrett

■ Introduction

The decade of 1980–90 was one of great importance for educational computing. The outstanding feature of the first half of the decade was the Microelectronics Education Programme (MEP), which ran from 1981 to 1986. This period may be described as one of relatively open-ended exploration. In the second half of the decade, by contrast, there was a sharpening of policy goals and a move towards curriculum compulsion. In this paper I have three objectives. First, I will look at the major strengths and weaknesses of MEP and of provision of educational computing in its immediate aftermath, and will attempt to identify factors that account for these. Secondly, I want to consider how far the Government's approach to educational computing in this period can be considered effective in terms of innovation strategy. Finally, I will ask in what ways developments of the 1980s are likely to influence developments into the 1990s.

■ Government as driving force

An evaluation of the offer to schools from the DTI (Department of Trade and Industry) (1981–84) of a 50% subsidy towards their first acquisition

Reprinted by permission of J.O. Boyd-Barrett. Originally published in *Educational Studies*, 1990, **16**(1), Carfax Publishing Company, Abingdon.

of computers, concluded: 'The DTI Scheme undoubtedly played a major role in promoting the acquisition throughout the '80s of greater numbers of micros and associated software, courseware and accessories' (CARE, 1988). No other educational technology, save perhaps the book, has been the object of so much political concern.

In this section I advance the view that it was the intervention of government, first and foremost, that constituted the driving force of computer adoption in schools and consider what significance this may have for ways of thinking about top-down models of educational innovation.

The literature on educational innovation is replete with accounts of the failure of centrally generated and imposed curriculum innovations, especially where these have had only a 'pump-priming' character, but more generally where they have not been able to carry the understanding and commitment of practising teachers (Becher and Maclure, 1978). There has been a scepticism in the literature about 'top-down' or 'centre–periphery' approaches to educational change. All too often such approaches have been under resourced, badly understood or simply unpopular at institutional or classroom levels. Alternative models favour innovations that address grassroot needs as articulated at the grassroots, and which facilitate initiative at this level.

Cynics may say that teachers are seldom motivated or able to articulate needs and mount grassroot initiatives, and are likely to change, if they change at all, only in response to central initiatives. There is also arguably a tendency among those who favour grassroot or periphery–periphery models of innovation to assume that the innovation process is necessarily a good thing. There is a problem about what is meant by 'grassroots' and how this should be regarded: an initiative may come from the grassroots, yet be unrepresentative of grassroot sentiment, unpopular, founded on wrong premises, or not be suitable for wider adoption.

Development of interest and practice in educational computing certainly had a grassroots flavour in the 1970s, and at least one pressure group (Microcomputer USers in Education – MUSE) exerted significant influence on government thinking. Involvement of the government seemed at first to be an economic solution in search of an educational problem. The DTI's main objective was to foster an indigenous IT economy, and the main aim of MEP was to prepare children for it (Fowler, 1988). Was there more to it than reducing the balance of trade deficit in IT products, establishing a domestic industry and enhancing Britain's international competitiveness? Should there have been more? Looking at the late 1970s and the early 1980s, in short, one can find evidence both of grassroot initiative representing relatively small numbers of teachers, and of central intervention driven by economic motive – not the most propitious combination.

Enthusiastic teacher supporters of educational computing, inevitably, were in the minority, based typically in maths and science departments, nearly all of them young men. Their immersion in computer culture, with its jargonistic allusions to indigestible trade names, numbers and peripherals sometimes proved more of a barrier, even a repulsion, than an invitation to the uninitiated. Effective 'change agents' in innovation theory ideally should be high in status and popularity.

More widespread teacher interest in computing (as in many other subjects) was too often dampened by the reality of existing curriculum and examination constraints, especially at secondary level. Early trials of micros in the classroom often proved frustrating and off-putting to those teachers new to computing but nevertheless brave enough to try their hand: frequent equipment or system crashes, difficulties in getting started (as with cassette loading for the original BBCs), disappointing or even embarrassing software. All of this occurred at a time of severe restraint on educational expenditure, and of demoralization of a teaching force caught in an unusually protracted, ultimately unsuccessful industrial action. Many teachers felt that any available capitation was better spent on books, pencils and rubbers than on expensive new computers of which there would be too few to give children more than a few minutes familiarization a week – if they were lucky and the teachers sufficiently resolute.

If grassroots support was sketchy and often disillusioned, why then has educational computing survived? If the central innovations that fail to address experienced need do not survive, why does educational computing appear still to grow? The contribution of government finance in this can scarcely be overestimated. While state support for an innovation is often insufficient in itself for the survival of that innovation, few if any educational innovations with significant resource implications can survive without support from the top. One other crucial ingredient, a relatively late development in this saga, is the power of curriculum compulsion.

The original MEP and DTI schemes did end as planned, in the mid-1980s, but were soon succeeded by further sources of funding: DTI grants, Microelectronics Education Support Unit (MESU), Training and Vocational Educational Initiative (TVEI) money, commercial sponsorship and centrally ear-marked Education Support Grant (ESG) money, channelled through local authorities. I venture to suggest that none of these would have been very influential were it not for the background general influence of transatlantic media-talk of how computers were already beginning to transform society, work and family life, together with startling predictions of the future rate of change. When not under pressure from the state, therefore, teachers had to respond to growing parental expectations. A significant level of uptake of home computers (even if many were soon to be relegated to the attic), everyday experience of computer-driven change in high street banking and office word-processing all helped reinforce the message that computers were happening, were important and were going to get more important.

A study of the emergence of educational computing policy serves to highlight not just the importance of grassroot initiative and the limitations of state intervention, but also some of the problems of depending on grassroots experience as a guide to wider practice, and some of the benefits that follow from government involvement. State intervention can vary from the exercise of influence to out-and-out control or regulation. In the case of educational computing during the 1980s there was a discernible movement from grassroots initiative, to a state strategy of influence, then towards a state strategy of control. This then raises the question of how far the effectiveness of the control strategy is related to the effectiveness of the preceding strategy of influence.

■ Antecedents

Government promotion of schools computing may be traced back at least as far as a 1969 Scottish initiative, the interim Bellis report of the Computers and the Schools Committee which advocated the use of computers across the curriculum. By 1970, a number of local centres had been established jointly by local authorities in Scotland and the Scottish Education Department to develop software and software application. Scotland was one of the first countries to have a national policy on the use of computers in schools (SED, 1987).

Prior to the DTI scheme for England and Wales 1981–84, 'computers were thin on the ground, especially in primary schools. The pattern was uneven, reflecting individual (LEA, school, teacher) enthusiasms and histories' (CARE, 1988), and 'piecemeal, with wide local variations' (Gwyn, 1987, p. 40). State involvement was largely indirect. During the 1970s, the Schools Council (funded by the DES and the LEAs, but largely teacher controlled) produced materials in five subject areas based on interactive computer programs. Through the DES-funded Council for Educational Technology (CET), the Government established the National Development Programme in Computer-Assisted Learning (NDPCAL, 1973–77) a £2.5 million project restricted to higher education. The roles of the Schools Council and NDPCAL have been described as a 'typically British form of central support function with no central control' (Gwyn, 1987, p.10). Closure of the Schools Council in 1982, reflected government disappointment with the take-up of its many curriculum projects.

This model of development allowed a range of experiments, some of which were promising. Innovations were often spearheaded by and bore the personal imprint of individual enthusiasts whose departure or promotion they were unlikely to survive, and which were sometimes counter-productive in their effects on the attitudes of other teachers. Many such pioneers were self-taught and their programs amateurish. LEAs adopted a variety of different and incompatible hardware and there were marked regional variations in the level of support available, a problem exacerbated by expenditure constraint. Variations in exam board syllabuses and the lack of systematic links between teacher training and IT development in the classroom can also be cited as further consequences of the absence of a national policy.

■ MEP and micros in schools

In 1978, as MEP director Richard Fothergill later recollected, a government advisory body, the Council for Educational Technology (CET), 'prepared several persuasive documents urging the DES to launch further projects to ensure that microelectronics was exploited at all levels of education' (Fothergill, 1988). Later that year, still under a Labour government, CET was able to announce a £12 million scheme designed to remedy national backwardness in microelectronics. This did not actually come to fruition until the launch of MEP under the Conservative government in 1980. Also in 1978, the DTI launched the business-oriented Microelectronics Awareness Programme (MAP). This took the form of training workshops, funding of college courses and of the Open University's course on the Microelectronics and Product Development, in 1979.

MEP was launched in 1980 by the DES on a reduced budget of £9 million, although the project was later extended by two years to 1986 and spent a total of £23 million in the course of its life, including LEA contributions (Thorne, 1987). Its early life ran in parallel with the DTI hardware finance scheme, and the effects of the two initiatives are almost inseparable. This two-pronged approach on the part of the DES and DTI was to characterize the promotion of educational computing over the next decade. Sources differ in their assessment of this duality, the extent to which it was seen to be coordinated or uncoordinated, useful or a hindrance.

The final MEP blueprint did not appear until April 1981. It was organized in the form of a small national directorate and 14 regional centres (whose boundaries were determined by groupings of the 104 LEAs participating in the management of the scheme). This 'avoided the centralized direction which would be unacceptable in the U.K. and also overcame the intense localization of development which is the norm' (Gwyn, 1987, p. 47). One may doubt whether the same sensitivity to central direction would have been evident in the late 1980s, by which time the 1988 Educational Reform Act had effectively changed the educational system from one of partnership between central government, local government and teachers to one of compliance with central control. MEP was controlled by the DES in consultation with an advisory committee, through a programme director and a small central staff. CET provided the administrative services and dispensed the funds, but on the instructions of the DES.

MEP priorities were the dissemination of information, teacher training, curriculum and software development with reference to specified subject areas. It covered special educational needs, to which approximately one-fifth of its budget was committed. Its overall brief was both to promote micros in schools and to develop teaching in micro-electronics. The second of these objectives was overshadowed by the first. MEP INSET activities were directed towards teacher leaders and advisory teachers so that these could train others – the 'cascade' model, a strategy which was deemed to have failed by most respondents to a retrospective survey conducted by CARE in 1988.

In effect, therefore, government intervention did not so much define a policy as provide the means whereby activity would be generated of a sort that could lead to a policy or series of policies. In this respect MEP continued the soft-nose, pluralist approach to curriculum development, previously favoured by the Schools Council (the official advisory body charged with curriculum development and examinations review, 1964–82). While its specific effects may be hard to detect some years later, MEP helped establish considerable, persistent pressure on the educational system in general to take microelectronics seriously and to integrate it into the curriculum. This might not have been the case were earmarked funds not also available.

These came with the DTI's Micros in Schools scheme, 1981–84. (The DES had little power at that time to direct LEA expenditure outside the margins of statutory obligation.) DTI offered 50% finance towards the purchase by schools of their first microcomputer. (If they already had one, they were not eligible.) The offer was independent of school size. Schools had to find the other half of the money from whatever source they could tap, together with the cost of any extras, such as a printer. The aim was to get one micro into every secondary school by the end of 1982. The scheme was extended to primary schools in July 1982. For secondary schools, choice was limited to either Research Machines' RML380Z or Acorn's cheaper but less powerful Model A BBC Micro. Primary schools could choose between the 48K Spectrum, the 32K BBC Model B or the RML 480Z. All the machines were British. Schools opting for the more expensive machines benefited from a larger grant, but in fact most went for the cheaper options. In 1984, 73% of all primary schools had a BBC B. The next most common machine, acquired by 19% of primaries was the RML 480Z, followed by the ZX Spectrum (14%) and the RML 380Z(4%). Among secondary schools the most popular machine was also the BBC B (78%), followed by the RML 380Z (62%), ZX Spectrum (18%) and RML 480Z (17%) (Moore, 1986).

In Scotland, the Scottish Microelectronics Development Programme (SMDP) collaborated with the MEP to produce software, to act as an information centre and to conduct research and development. SMDP merged with SCET in 1983, the new unified body reporting to the Microelectronics Education Committee of the Scottish Education Department.

■ Towards a policy, post-1986

MEP came to an end in 1986. It was succeeded by MESU, which did not become operational until January 1987. The main functions of MESU were to exploit the potential of successful MEP programmes, promote the curricular integration of information technologies via LEAs and teacher-training establishments, and set up curriculum development projects. MESU retained MEP's structure for work in the area of special educational needs. In Scotland, SMDP continued in existence, collaborating with MESU as it had done with MEP. In 1988, MESU was integrated with CET to form the National Council for Educational Technology (NCET).

Following the demise of Micros in Schools, the DTI continued as a funding agency, in particular for education and training in microelectronics, for which it disbursed a total of £21 million per year, primarily through IT centres set up jointly with the MSC (reporting to the Department of Employment) for 16–17-year-olds. £45 million was provided to create additional engineering and technology places in higher education. A three-year, £3.5 million project, Software in Schools, which offered grants to schools towards the purchase of software, and a similar £1.5 million project, Modems in Schools, were both launched in 1986. DTI's software subsidy was extended to 1989 with a view to encouraging the purchase by local authorities of 16- and 32-bit software.

Further funds for IT were channelled to education through the MSC via its Youth Training Scheme (YTS) for 16–17-year-olds, TVEI to influence the curriculum of 14–18-year-olds at school, and City Technology Colleges (the first of which started in 1988). Other sources of funding have included GCSE equipment funding, private industry, local authority INSET budgets and Education Support Grant (ESG) money.

In the mid to late 1980s, government involvement and direction showed signs of renewed vigour in both monetary and policy terms. In 1985, the Scottish Microelectronics Education Committee published a national plan advocating the setting up of Regional Development Units, and the specification of programmes by local subject groups. The report in 1987 of HMI on Learning and Teaching in Scottish Secondary Schools:

the Use of Microcomputers, identified aspects of best practice and suggested ways forward for more concerted developments – as did a later HMI report, *Information Technology from 5 to 16* (DES, 1989b)

Also in 1987, the UK Government circulated LEAs with proposals for New Technology for Better Schools. The title was significant, reflecting the stated central aim 'to harness the potential of IT for enhancing the quality of teaching and learning across the curriculum'. The centre of government focus, in other words, had shifted from preparing children for the information society to helping them learn in general. The document promised more money for hardware (£8.5 million), the training of 700 advisory teachers (£10.5 million) – training was undertaken by MESU and completed by the summer in 1988 – and continued software support. It identified criteria for the selection of hardware. There was continuing lack of support for the purchase of non-UK machines: LEAs were required to seek permission if they wished to buy anything other than Acorn or RM. But the criteria emphasized open design, access to MS-DOS operating systems and relevant software. A coordinated cross-curriculum policy was encouraged, linking computing with other sources of funding.

The proposals heralded the start of a five-year plan, the first two years with guaranteed funding. LEAs were required to bid for funding from Education Support Grant (ESG) money, taking into account: what they already had and from what sources; what they needed and for what purposes; how their scheme would fit into an overall county policy and link with other support services; and whether they would be consorting with other local LEAs to establish a larger support service.

The document was a good example of a government influence strategy on local policy, linking funding to approved procedures for decision making that promised optimal use of resources. It is also important because it suggests a process of greater clarification at central level of the educational rationale for the promotion of educational computing. The economic arguments of the inclusion of computing in the curriculum, after all, were not invincible: Computers were de-skilling many jobs and, in effect, reducing employers' requirements of school-leaver skills. While computer manufacture was a rapidly growing industry, it would employ only a very small proportion of all school leavers. Because computing technology was changing so fast, arguably, computer education or training was best left to employers. In *New Technology for Better Schools* the DES was clearly taking the line that computers in education were important because they could improve both the delivery and above all the quality of education. This was not an unassailable argument, but at least it was an educational argument, one with a better chance of convincing teachers.

New Technology for Better Schools provided a major resource fillip, but still not the compulsion to use computers, and certainly not across the curriculum. An element of compulsion began to emerge in the wake of the 1988 Education Reform Act. For the first time since 1944, and for the first time ever in such detail, England and Wales were to be subjected to a national curriculum with attendant programmes of study, attainment targets and attainment testing at 7, 11, 14 and 16. Information technology did not appear as either a core or as a foundation subject, but it was an integral part of all programmes of study and many attainment targets, including even the English Language curriculum which sported many references to word processors and information retrieval (DES, 1989d).

■ MEP and its aftermath: a critique

Evaluations of the MEP and the parallel DTI subsidy scheme have been mixed at best, scathing at worst:

> 'Britain's IT policy was centrally generated; it did not grow out of the demands or needs of pupils or teachers ... The policy also failed to stimulate the production and distribution of good educational software. It concentrated on hardware but did not standardize on one machine or software system ... ' (Kirkup *et al.*, 1987, p. 27)

> '(The MEP) was a short-term ephemeral initiative, part of a growing tradition in British government technology policy. A problem was identified, a political posture was struck, a programme was launched, a public relations victory was scored, a limited scale and duration budget was committed. Underneath little may have changed, or the change may have been for the worse.' (Ennals, R. 1987, p. 194)

> 'DTI intervention was decisive in promoting computer awareness across the board. It was widely welcomed as an enabling measure, but widely criticised as rushed, ill thought out and coercive. The scheme forced the pace and direction of change ... The DTI scheme undoubtedly played a major role in promoting the acquisition throughout the '80s of greater numbers of micros and associated software, courseware and accessories. The across the board strategy of funding, although it spread the funds too thinly to support rapid curriculum development, is widely regarded as having been the best choice for whole system development, even though the need for models of good educational practice was, and still is, acknowledged.' (CARE, 1988)

Assertiveness is no guarantee of accuracy: one may query whether the first quote is fair to suggest that IT policy had no relation whatever with grassroot demand, or whether in stressing the limited duration of

MEP, the second too conveniently ignores subsequent programmes of support. More generally one can ask by what standards of achievement is MEP being compared? This was a five-year programme at the beginning of which there were hardly any computers in schools or teachers to use them. Drill-and-practice software had its use in the early days simply as a means whereby teachers and children could develop familiarity with the machines before becoming more adventurous (DES, 1987*a*). In reviewing problems which MEP was unable to resolve, therefore, the purpose is not so much to draw attention to inevitable limitations of a 'new frontier' programme, but to examine a legacy which does much to define the context in which educational computing is still developed.

This analysis centres on four evaluative criteria: need or demand; control and dissemination; provision and quality of hardware and software; and effect. By the close of this period, the nature of government intervention had undergone profound shifts which are likely to characterize the 1990s, and in three major directions: greater clarity and focus of objective (namely, the improvement of teaching); more persistent attention to resourcing and training; more direct control over the curriculum.

■ The problem of demand

One considerable difficulty was the initial absence of widespread teacher perception of need, despite the enthusiastic lobbying of special interest groups such as MUSE. Arguably, therefore, it was much to the government's credit that it made the resources available. But these were in part motivated by considerations of national economics, not education as such. The programme attempted to compensate for the problems inherent in a 'top-down' approach: for example through the MEP regional structure – a 'star system' (Fothergill, 1987) of innovation, supporting promising developments at grassroot level; regional curriculum projects; and regional small budget activities. For many teachers, unfortunately, location of a support unit in a regional centre which may still have been many miles away, was no more useful than had it been in London. Furthermore, as Gwyn (1988) points out, while some regional centres were very active, not all of them were. The 'cascade' model, focusing on teacher leaders and advisers who were expected to pass on the benefit of their training and enthusiasm, did not guarantee the involvement of heads and department heads, whose attitudes to any innovation are important factors in its adoption and effectiveness (Chandra *et al.*, 1988). The involvement of other agencies reflected the open, democratic character of MEP, but underlined the lack of direct MEP access to schools, and the attendant problems of communication and information dissemination. Its non-prescriptive developmental character cloaked a damaging absence of a coherent and consensual rationale for computers in education, and this legitimized a 'wait-and-see' or even a 'do-nothing' attitude among the most cautious. On the other hand, perceived urgency (at least as seen from the centre) of the need, set against the length of time it takes to steer innovation through a decentralized system, favoured a 'suck-it-and-see' approach which was to yield a wealth of insight.

With the introduction of the National Curriculum at the end of the decade one might argue that the government had solved the problem of demand by creating a condition of permanent need. Through the inclusion of information technology as a component part of all foundation subjects, there is now a statutory requirement on schools to reach a certain minimal level of proficiency in educational computing that no longer depends on teacher perceptions of usefulness or cost-effectiveness. The National Curriculum may also help to break the tendency at secondary level for computing to be confined mainly to computing and business studies. At the same time, improvements in hardware and software, both in what they can do and in user-friendliness will have made computing a more attractive proposition to at least some of those teachers as yet relatively unfamiliar with computing technology. Another factor which has greatly propelled the infusion of information technology into schooling has been the recently introduced system of local management of schools (LMS). In the period 1990–94, LMS will affect all secondary schools and half of all primary schools. These will receive a *per capita budget* from the local education authority out of which they will have to meet their costs, including salaries. LMS will require a new computerized management information system in every school, and most will need new computers to run the system. The government in 1989 was already providing three times as much money to buy computers to run schools' administration than to buy computers for the classroom (Lewis, 1989 b), and spending nearly three times as much on training heads and governors to use computers to run their schools than on training teachers to use computers in the classroom. There may be scope for putting some of this investment to educational use, and if heads and senior teachers are to receive training in the administrative uses of computers this may have some carry-over effect on their attitudes to uses of computers in teaching.

■ The problem of control

MEP initiatives have been criticized (Kirkup *et al.*, 1987) for being too isolated: what was needed was a system, an integrated approach to pedagogic objectives, funding, machine purchase and replacement, software design and teacher training. This in turn suggests the prior need for a coherent and agreed educational philosophy, for as Curtis (1988) points out in relation to individual schools, a chosen approach to educational computing depends very much on prior assumptions about what education is all about. This kind of criticism is all too easy with hindsight; it pays scant regard to the uncertainties and compromises of political process, and draws comparison only with absolute perfection.

Talk of a system seems to suggest some guided, accumulative process travelling more or less in a set direction. One practical drawback has been the difficulty of evaluating what was being achieved and hence lack of certainty about future direction. MEP's director, Richard Fothergill (1987) refers to the impossibility of sustained evaluation in a climate of constant hardware change and development. He further argues that it is difficult to compare like with like when attempting to assess whether instruction in one medium is as effective as another: a new medium invokes new kinds of learning and is properly exploited when set to achieve things which were not generally possible with pre-existing media. These difficulties tended to reduce evaluation to case studies and subjective experience, whose conclusions were often ambivalent and vulnerable on methodological grounds.

The two-headed charge by DTI and DES in retrospect still remains a curiosity. Were the initiatives rationally coordinated, was there departmental rivalry, or was there simply a lack of coordination? Fothergill's account (1988) suggests that the DTI's subsidy programme, first mooted by Kenneth Baker before he was appointed minister for information technology, definitely followed in the wake of MEP (which was established, though not active, one year earlier) and was designed to do something about the absence of hardware in schools, without which much of MEP's work would be useless. A condition of DTI subsidy was that at least two teachers in each receiver school should acquire relevant training: Thorne (1987) suggests this placed a somewhat unwelcome obligation on MEP to provide such training at an early stage of its development. MEP's successor, MESU, suffered a similar fate when required in its infancy to cope with the training of new advisory teachers.

By the end of the decade there were clear signs that mechanisms for control of progress of educational computing in school have been put in place: greater clarification of the philosophy informing government promotion of educational computing; establishment of guidelines for hardware purchase, and the linking of grants to compliance with guidelines; encouragement of local authority and school-wide computer policies to ensure coordinated policies for purchase, use and cross-curricular applications; greater control of content of educational computing through the National Curriculum. The main outstanding problems, however, were resources, and the availability and training of teaching staff. The level of hardware provision in schools at the end of the 1980s was still relatively modest, and to equip all schools to the standards envisaged in the National Curriculum, together with funding for in-service training, was expected to involve increased resourcing over the 1990s, but this promise of increased resourcing was clearly vulnerable to changes in the wider economic context. There were teacher shortages in several subject areas, particularly in inner-city areas and areas affected by the property boom where few young teachers could afford to live. There were also clearly potential problems about teacher training.

■ The problem of hardware

The DTI can be criticized for failing in the first half of the decade to specify a more precise choice of hardware, making it difficult to establish an effective network of software support. What it did do was link software development to a particular range of hardware. Had the initiative been geared solely to educational need then arguably the DTI's starting point would have been to specify the quality of software it required and on that basis to recommend the hardware needed to run such software (Kirkup *et al.*, 1987). Ennals (1987) states quite simply that DTI tied educational computing in schools to obsolescent hardware. But obsolescence in computer technology is difficult to avoid. Ennals also argues that DTI's imputed aim to protect and to promote British manufacturers was inequitable and futile: many British manufacturers were excluded; some of those included later collapsed; and it is doubtful whether in the long run much has been done to stem the penetration of foreign machines. There is a continuing problem (Roper, 1988) that neither Acorn nor RM machines are widely used in business, nor widely used outside of the United Kingdom. This then restricts the market for software for these machines, exacerbating difficulties faced by UK software publishers.

CARE's survey (1988) concludes that the scheme forced the pace and direction of change but not necessarily in the right direction, for example the choice of cassette over disk drive was 'a turn-off for teachers, demanding more commitment than most were prepared to give ... The evident inferiority of the printer ... made many users feel they were having to do a difficult job with the additional burden of shoddy merchandise'. Not only was the initial software 'educationally retrogressive, thus raising questions of justification about the diversion of educational resources from cheaper, traditional alternatives', but as Fothergill (1987) complains, MEP software, when it became available, was outpaced by hardware developments (for example WIMP environments). Conversely, some schools may have hung on to obsolescent hardware so they could continue to exploit obsolescent software.

Hardware provision remained inadequate anyway throughout the life of MEP, with only one machine for every 60 secondary pupils and one for every 107 primary pupils even as late as 1986. Inadequate provision exacerbated problems of inequality. Schools in wealthy catchment areas were more likely to benefit from funds raised by parents, although there was later a significant reduction in the proportion of funds coming from parents which fell from 33% to 27% at primary level, and from 19% to 9% at secondary, between 1985 and 1988 (DES, 1989c); government financing accounted for 60% of primary computer expenditure, and 80% of secondary in 1988. The DTI did opt for an across-the-board strategy of support, in preference to developing centres of excellence or a phased introduction. This decision 'is widely regarded as having been the best choice for the whole system development' (CARE, 1988). But Ennals (1987) argues that the government dampened teacher expectations (and hence resource demands) by withholding funds to improve the flow of information to schools until late in the programme.

There can be no doubt that together the MEP and DTI programmes directed computers into almost all schools and helped establish some degree of computer use, but it is doubtful whether the average number of computers per school was even close to adequate by the end of the decade. A 1988 DES survey found one micro for every 67 pupils in primary schools and one for every 32 in secondary schools. This is a significant improvement on 1985, but it is envisaged that if the objectives of the National Curriculum are to be met, the ratio will have to improve to about 1 in 20 in both cases by the year 1996. At the end of the decade there was an existing stock of nearly 200 000 machines (Lewis, 1989a). Of existing stock, 79% in primary schools and 57% in secondary schools were still BBC Bs or Masters. This gives some indication of the scale of pending obsolescence and of the investment which will have to be made to replace stock and to add the estimated (Lewis, 1989b) further 150 000 machines necessary to meet the improved ratios required by the National Curriculum.

■   The problem of effect

It is to MEP's credit that it was able to make any progress, at a time of reduced resources for education, industrial disruption and poor morale, a time when several innovations competed for teacher attention, in a period of major structural reform such as GCSE and the move towards a National Curriculum. It also made possible the development and dissemination of some remarkably good software, such as Newsroom and Mary Rose, which helped show the way forward from drill-and-practice to exciting simulation functions appropriate to cross-disciplinary theme work. HMI commented that such packages 'encouraged the development of many worthwhile skills, requiring co-operative group work and the evaluation of evidence' (DES, 1987b).

This kind of computer application was more palatable to teachers in the United Kingdom than mainstream US software, and there was evidence that MEP products could have positive implications for change in teaching and learning styles, especially among more experienced users or where INSET was closely involved. The Microelectronics For All (MFA) course for secondary schools reached one-fifth of secondary schools in the country with some considerable success. The MEP-funded Investigations on Teachings with Microcomputers (ITMA) established an innovatory trail towards classroom-based software evaluation (Phillips, 1988).

Direct MEP influence on the classroom was judged disappointing by some commentators. HMI considered that 'in the bulk of schools visited MEP did not seem to affect the quality of accommodation for IT and its use nor the deployment of human and material resources on IT-related work' (DES, 1987a). The most positive outcomes, possibly, were the least easy to quantify: model examples of how to relate software to conceptions of good teaching practice; expertise that was to be available for later initiatives; encouragement to publishers (although many withdrew after disappointing sales in small markets). Gwyn (1988) considers that in its production, or promotion of the production of software (over 1000 programs as early as 1984) MEP was successful. Fothergill (1987) considers that material production was especially good in CDT and practical subjects. But HMI (DES, 1987a) found that many MEP products were never developed to the point where they were satisfactory for general use, and that other suffered from delays in getting projects approved and up and running.

Several commentators (DES, 1987a, Gwyn, 1987, CARE, 1988) consider that progress was much greater than expected at primary level but disappointing at secondary. Constrained by subject boundaries and examination syllabuses, secondary computing was all too often confined to computer studies, maths and business studies. The CARE report notes a breakthrough in primary schools after 1986, with a move away from drill-and-practice towards more innovatory practice. Secondary computing seemed less promising, even though more machines were available. In the DES 1988 survey, significant computer usage was reported by 84% of staff in computer studies, and 60% in business studies, but only 35% in CDT and 34% in maths, while other departments indicated lower percentages.

MEP courses reached 120 000 teachers, not including those who attended courses provided by LEAs. INSET provision related to the DTI scheme is described by the CARE survey (1988) as 'totally inadequate'. Overall, Gwyn (1987) considers it appropriate to register disappointment: relatively few teachers had developed an awareness of the real potential of IT and for this reason there were relatively few applications. Teacher training could not keep up with the development of programs. Nevertheless the international visibility and reputation of the programme was high, and MEP helped create a supportive environment for teacher initiatives.

> 'In 1988 it is clear that a beachhead in the schools has been established, but no more. The basic need, for more and better machinery, remains a priority. ... Improving the quality of use depends upon the provision of training, advice, technical and psychological support ... It is important to note that the 'critical mass' at which point radical changes in teaching, curriculum and school organization would become apparent, has not been achieved as yet.' (CARE, 1988)

The problem of teacher training continued to be highly visible to the end of the decade. A working group set up by the Secretary of State for Education and Science reporting in 1989 concluded that most initial training courses failed to give instruction in even the minimum of skills new teachers need to cope with the rapidly growing demands of computers in the classroom (DES, 1989a). In 1988, approximately half the teaching force had still to benefit from relevant INSET, and of the rest some 25% had received no more than initial awareness training (DES, 1989c). A study by Cox and Rhodes (1988) reports that at the end of such courses many teachers said they were unable to implement computer use in the classroom and several teachers said that they needed more training and time to practise their newly acquired skills. Implementation of the new National Curriculum would clearly require considerable INSET provision, for which it is doubtful whether sufficient expenditure has been envisaged. The Financial Memorandum to the Education Reform Bill allowed £33 million a year for all aspects of implementation, yet the TGAT (Task Group on Assessment and Training) document states that it would require over £20 million to provide one day's INSET for every teacher where this involved absence from teaching.

■ The problem of software

John Foster (1988), chief executive of MESU, stated in the *Times Educational Supplement* (*TES*) that at the start of MESU operations in January 1987 the majority of teachers were not using computers. He blamed poor programs that were difficult to use, trivial in content and not meeting perceived needs. Teachers had received little or insufficient training, feared the unknown, and were ill-prepared to deal with the implications for classroom management and styles of teaching. There were too few computers, yet too many different kinds of computer.

Prospects for a general improvement in software design and supply have been dampened by problems facing the software industry. These were addressed by Noel Thompson in the *TES* computer supplement of 18 November 1988, where several contributors seriously questioned the viability of the UK market. There were 300 educational software publishers averaging only modest turnover, yet the development of good quality software was costed at between £10 000 to £100 000 over periods ranging from one to five years for development and marketing. Avis (1988) calculated that the commercial marketplace could support only 10–20 new software packages a year. The sheer diversity of models merely compounded the difficulties. 'Versioning' or adapting software to suit different machines added to development costs. Clients had little idea of the actual cost of software, for they were not accustomed to paying 'real' prices, cushioned as they had been by DTI subsidies. One contributor concluded 'The market is too small, cannot afford the true cost of the products and is fragmenting as a result of the increasing range of hardware' (Chapman, 1988). DTI encouragement of a shift towards 16- and 32-bit software might have a negative effect by creating a wider lag between hardware and software capabilities. Noel Thompson, chief executive of NCET considered that there was no way forward so long as the market was seen in the context of the UK alone. But Bill Tagg, director of the Advisory Unit at Hatfield was sceptical about overseas sales, given language and culture problems.

Many educationalists in the late 1980s believes that the future lies with generic or content free software. This is thought to give the teacher more freedom to adapt software to specific curriculum contexts. Generic software is also suited to a broad range of commercial and educational uses, and is consequently much more profitable for developers to produce. But Fothergill (1988) warns that generic software can be likened to the provision of books without content. He believes that a more likely future scenario is a mix of generic and subject-specific software.

Compatibility of software across different machines is of considerable importance to teachers who have acquired libraries of valuable software but are faced with the problem of hardware obsolescence, or who simply want to make the best they can out of a diverse range of equipment. Emulators are increasingly available to make one machine work like another. A major problem is that graphics are generally not transferable in this way, although development work on a portable graphics package is described by Thorne (1989).

Driscoll and Govier (1989) point out that the most commonly used programs in primary schools are still drill-and-practice and word processors. The 1988 DES survey reports that in both primary and secondary schools, the younger age groups use software primarily for practice exercises and puzzles, while word processing is the most common use among the older age groups. Yet software of the kind envisaged by National Curriculum applications requires far more learning on the part of the teacher and may demand a change in classroom practice. The educational demands on the software industry therefore may increase, alongside the need for more sophisticated teacher training.

■ Conclusions

The main weaknesses of MEP were consonant with what might have been expected of any 'frontier' educational development programme Teachers were not necessarily convinced. It was difficult, though by no means impossible, to reach beyond the already converted. Available hardware and software were often rudimentary. There were wide variations of resource. The general level of training provided was relatively low. Yet had MEP died abruptly and schools been left to decide for themselves how to handle the challenges posed by information technology, there can be little doubt that further progress would have been very patchy indeed: brilliant in a few cases, mediocre to non-existent in most. Subsequent government promotion and policy, particularly related to the National Curriculum, appears to have rescued educational computing from such a fate. The dangers of a 'top-down' strategy for the promotion of an educational innovation do not appear in themselves to have seriously impeded progress. The widely accepted significance of information technology in contributing to wider social changes has lent it status, influencing the expectations and perceptions of teachers, parents and pupils. For all its weaknesses, the legacy of MEP and its aftermath for the longer term can be seen as largely positive: commitment of system funds at almost all levels to the purchase of computer equipment, a pool of skill and talent in the teaching profession, an active – if troubled – supply industry, widespread understanding of the case for challenging and imaginative use of software. Problems of rationale and resources persist. Almost all primary and three-quarters of all secondary pupils have now had some 'hands-on' experience with micros (DES, 1989c). But the value of this experience is not yet clear in relation to subject learning, attitudes to schooling, or future jobs. There is still a need to define more clearly what is wanted of information technology in schools and to ensure that adequate resources exist to provide what is needed.

■ References

Avis Peter (1988). Strategy, in Computers in Education, *Times Educational Supplement*, 18 Nov., p. 64.

Becher Tony and Maclure Stuart (1978). *The Politics of Curriculum Change*. London: Hutchinson.

CARE (University of East Anglia) (1988). DTI Micros in Schools Support 1981-1984. An Independent Evaluation.

Chandra P, Bliss J. and Cox M. (1988). Introducing Computers into a School–Management Issues, *Computer Education*, 12(1), 57-61.

Chapman Alan (1988). Subsidy, in Computers in Education, London, *Times Educational Supplement*, 18 Nov., p. 62.

Cox M. and Rhodes V. (1988). Training Primary School Teachers to Use Computers Effectively in the Classroom. An Investigation into Inservice Provision. In Collins, Ester and Walker (eds). *Proceedings of the Fifth International Conference on Technology in Education*, Edinburgh. Vol. 2. pp. 80-83.

Curtis Chris (1988). *The Impact of IT on Education*. Institution Focused Report, M.Ed. (mimeo).

DES (1987a). *Aspects of the Work of the Microelectronics Education Programme*. Report by HM Inspectors, London, DES.

DES (1987b). *New Technology for Betters Schools*.

DES (1989a). *Information Technology in Initial Teacher Training*.

DES (1989b). *Information Technology from 5 to 16*. No. 15 of Curriculum Matters, an HMI Series, London, HMSO.

DES (1989c). *Survey of Information Technology in School*. Statistical Bulletin 10/89, London, DES.

DES (1989d). *English for Ages 5 to 16*. London, DES.

DTI (1982). *Information Technology: The Age of Electronic Information*. London, HMSO.

Driscoll Maggie and Govier Heather (1989). Handle with care, *Times Educational Supplement*, 16 June, p. B28.

Ennals Richard (1987). Difficulties in Managing Innovation, *British Journal of Educational Technology*, 18(3), 194-198.

Foster John (1988). Justification, in Computers in Education, London, *Times Educational Supplement*, 18 Nov., p. 61.

Fothergill Richard (1987). The Director's View. *British Journal of Educational Technology*, 3(18), 181-193.

Fothergill Richard (1988). *Implications of New Technology for the School Curriculum*. London: Kogan Page.

Fowler William S. (1988). *Towards the National Curriculum*. London: Kogan Page.

Gilbert L.A. (1985). The Distribution of Microcomputer Software to Education, CET Working Paper, No. 26, London, Council for Educational Technology.

Gwyn Rhys (1987). Information technology and education: the policy in England, Wales and Northern Ireland. In *Educational Computing* (Scanlon Eileen and O'Shea Tim, eds). London: John Wiley and Sons.

Gwyn Rhys (1988). Information technology and education in the UK: a survey of recent developments. in *Education for the New Technologies, World Yearbook for Education* (Harris D., ed.), pp. 95-118. London: Kogan Page.

Kirkup Gill, Laurillard Diana, Stannett Charles and Bates Anthony (1987). Computer-Based Learning, Block 4A, Unit 2 of Introduction to Information Technology, DT200, Milton Keynes, Open University Press.

Lewis P. (1989a). Heads of the queue *Times Educational Supplement*, 16 June, p. B18.

Lewis P. (1989b). Battle of the PCs for the lucrative schools market. *The Independent*, 22 May, p. 16.

Moore P. (1986). *Using Computers in English*. London: Methmen.

Phillips R. (1988). ITMA's approach to classroom observation, in Jones A. and Scrimshaw P. (eds) *Computers in Education 5–13*, pp.249-254, Milton Keynes: Open University Press.

Roper Christopher (1988). Working it out, in Computers in Education, London, *Times Educational Supplement*, 18 Nov., p. 62.

Scottish Educational Department (1987). *Learning and Teaching in Scottish Secondary Schools: The Use of Microcomputers*. A Report of HM Inspectors of Schools. Edinburgh: HMSO.

Tagg Bill (1988). Long Term, in Computers in Education, London *Times Educational Supplement*, 18 Nov., p. 64.

Thompson Noel (1988). Into Europe, in Computers in Education, London, *Times Educational Supplement*, 18 Nov., p. 61.

Thorne Michael (1987). The legacy of the Microelectronics Education Programme, *British Journal of Educational Technology*, **18** (3), 165–181.

Thorne Michael (1989). All for one ... *Times Educational Supplement*, 16 June, p. B16.

Paper 1.2

Creative Gales and Computers in Third World Schools

David Hawkridge

Are computers needed in developing countries, and, in particular, are computers needed in their schools? Both questions are important. Neither has a simple answer. Information technology is the latest 'creative gale of destruction' sweeping industrial countries, which are educating people to deal with and benefit from it. Developing countries cannot shelter from this gale.

■ Are computers needed in developing countries?

Are computers needed to satisfy the social and economic needs of developing countries? It is certainly true that governments of many of these countries have decided that computers are essential. Computers entered the economies of industrial nations very rapidly. Are developing countries merely being forced to follow suit, or do they have their own reasons for using computers?

'Creative gales of destruction' are sweeping the economies of industrial countries, according to Schumpeter's (1939) classic study. These storms are accompanied by radical and pervasive changes, particularly in the technological foundations of industry and commerce. The latest gales to batter industrial economies are those of information

This is an abridged version of Chapters 1 and 2 of *Computers in Third World Schools*. Originally published in Hawkridge, D., *et al* (1990) *Computers and Third World Schools*. Reprinted by permission of Macmillan, London and Basingstoke.

technology, a combination of developments based on computers but including communications. Information technology is pervasive: it penetrates all sectors of these economies, creates new jobs, destroys others, obliterates many activities and enhances many. It requires less energy than older technologies and uses new materials. Such changes demand changes in organizations and structures throughout the economy: if problems of adapting to new conditions can be overcome, there are opportunities for employment-generating investment as well as labour-saving productivity gains. So runs the theory.

Information has always been a source of power and control, but never more so than in the modern world. Individuals and governments are using it to gain political and economic advantage. Industrial countries are seeking, through information technology, to exert greater control over their competitors and over developing countries. All countries are being obliged to respond by stepping up their capacity to access and process information, to protect their own interests. All governments are developing policies with the aim of maintaining or gaining a competitive position. Governments of many industrial countries are assuming that a principal source of economic development will be production and consumption of information, which will significantly increase demand for higher levels of skills. Computers are at the heart of this revolution because they are very fast information processing machines.

As industrial countries survive these gales and prosper, almost all have undertaken a drive to teach their children about computers, to make them aware of the new technology and its implications for their lives. Must governments of developing countries follow the example of industrial ones? In a poor country with many illiterates, few skilled people, high unemployment, disease, malnutrition and even starvation, should scarce foreign exchange be spent on importing computers? If that country also suffers from uncertain electricity supplies, a humid or dusty climate and a chronic shortage of spare parts for anything electronic, is money spent on computers wasted because they will be out of order in a few months? In such a country, is it not likely that computers will be simply the smuggled playthings of an elite, of little or no value to the nation? Consider the words of Elmandjra (1985):

> Experience has taught us that technological breakthroughs have to be examined with attention and even suspicion – they never generate freedom, democracy or justice on their own. In fact they create a whole host of new problems.

Nationally, and internationally, much is at stake. Can developing countries afford to employ information technology? Can they afford not to? Are they untouched by the 'creative gales of destruction'? Information technology is essential to developing countries if they wish to modernize their infrastructures, survive in economic terms and compete internationally, and if they wish to be in electronic communication with each other and other countries for such purposes as trade. This view was taken by the Organization for African Unity, meeting at Addis Ababa in 1981, although its members were wary of increasing dependence on industrial countries. In all sectors, including agriculture, industry, commerce, health, education, defence, local government, transport, energy and water, the technology offers opportunities which are being seized in the Third World, according to a report from an *ad hoc* panel set up by the US National Research Council (Ruskin, 1986). Foreign aid programmes may now require it, and certainly recommend it. Conversely, countries which neglect it widen the technological gap between industrial countries and themselves.

■ Training people

The greatest problem in exploiting computers in developing countries is the shortage of trained personnel, often due to the passive role played by governments. Few of these countries are able to train all the technicians, programmers and system analysts they require to operate computer-based systems, even supposing that the hardware has been provided. Robertson (1988), in commenting on the shortage of trained people in Kenya, sees the main problem as being lack of those who can manage multi-user systems. Computers may be installed with the help of foreign aid, but they are under-used because of lack of staff. In some cases, they are abused because staff capable of using them commit fraud, being inadequately supervised by others who do not understand computers. Not only computer personnel need training, but also managers must be trained so that they understand how computers can be used properly in running businesses or government departments. Managers who are unsympathetic to computers, possibly because they fear or simply do not understand them, hold back their enterprises.

Should such training be undergirded, as in industrial countries, by 'computer education' of large numbers of children? Should the next generation of workers in developing countries include a significant cadre of those who lost their fear of computers because they used them at school? Schools may have an important role to play in transfer and integration of computer technology. Ideally, national policy on computer technology should be taken into account in policy guiding the introduction of computers into Third World schools, and vice versa.

■ Do schools in developing countries need computers?

It is clear that almost all Third World governments are considering, often against a background of immense economic difficulties, what policy is required with regard to information technology. But what are computers used for in schools and do schools in developing countries need them? What are the main rationales?

Large numbers of, but certainly not all, students, teachers and administrators in schools in industrial countries use computers. Students use them in schools, and school-based computer clubs, for four main purposes:

(1) To become aware, at a basic level, of the uses and limitations of computers.

(2) To learn computer programming, usually in BASIC but sometimes other languages such as Pascal or LOGO.

(3) To learn the correct use of 'applications' programs, for word processing, spreadsheet analysis, graphics, process control and information retrieval from databases.

(4) To learn selected topics from school subjects right across the curriculum, with the computer either complementing or temporarily replacing the teacher.

Of these four purposes, the first is by far the most common in schools that have computers. Teachers, of course, use computers to teach students these aspects of knowledge. Some teachers also use them to improve their own administrative efficiency, whether by preparing examination papers with a word processing program or by setting up students' marks using a spreadsheet. Computers are also used now in a great many schools in industrial countries to support managerial and administrative functions, such as record keeping, scheduling and financial accounting.

Terminology in this field can be confusing, therefore a few definitions are necessary:

- **Computer education**, the broadest term, covers teaching about computers or use of computers, and teaching of other subjects with computers.

- **Computer studies** covers teaching about computers and computer languages, whether at a basic level (**computer awareness**) or at a slightly more advanced level involving applications (**computer literacy**) or at the most advanced level in school (**computer science**).

- **Computer-assisted learning (CAL)** is the term reserved for learning about other subjects through a computer. North Americans often call this **computer-assisted instruction** (CAI).

■ Four popular rationales

Why do Third World countries want to put computers into their schools? One reason offered is that children should be aware and unafraid of how computers work, because computers are pervading industrial societies and are likely to be important in all countries. Since schools prepare students for life, they should prepare them to deal with computers, which ought to be de-mystified. Many politicians feel that modernization of schooling involves bringing in computers. If children need to become literate and numerate, they need also to know something about computers. This is the **social rationale** because it deals with students' place in society. It leads ministries of education to provide classes or extra-mural clubs where children learn the principles on which computers work, including some elementary programming, but gain only a little hands-on experience. They usually face no examination of their achievement.

A second reason offered is that children should learn to operate computers, at least at a basic level. Teaching them programming gives children some confidence in their ability to control computers, and possibly lays the foundation for a career in computer science. Teaching children how to use applications programs gives them skills that may be useful to them as students and when they move into jobs. At school, runs the reasoning, boys and girls should take courses in 'computer literacy', 'computer studies' or even 'computer science', quite often aimed at preparing them for an examination. This is the **vocational rationale**: computer education should be related to future jobs, says the Minister of Planning.

A third reason advanced is that children will learn physics, art or any other subject through computer-assisted learning. This is the **pedagogical rationale**, calling for improved teaching and learning, and may well be the one that commands greatest support among educators. In the United Kingdom, the Minister of Education speaks of computers-across-the-curriculum.

A fourth reason given is that schools can be changed for the better by the introduction of computers. Teaching, administrative and managerial efficiency may be improved. Computers require students to do less memorizing of facts and more information handling and problem solving. Computers encourage students to learn by collaborating rather than competing with other students. Computers are seen as catalysts, enabling desired change in education to occur. This is the **catalytic**

rationale. Teachers will adopt 'more relevant' curricula and bring educational opportunities to a larger number of children. Even administrators will change the way they manage schools – for the better, of course.

The information technology industry rationale, backed by the industry itself, favours placing large numbers of locally made or assembled computers in the schools, at government expense, in the hope that this will bring down the average cost of hardware. It calls for the building up a highly skilled workforce of data-entry operators and programmers, capable of undertaking contract work for customers from this and other countries.

The industry bring pressure to bear on ministries of education to prescribe the models they sell. Once the machines are in the schools, they expect the vocational rationale to prevail and have little interest in the others. This rationale is market driven, without doubt, under the guise of serving the national interest.

The cost-effectiveness rationale commands little support, but its proponents argue that computer hardware and software can substantially replace teachers, and be more cost-effective. Some possibly draw their evidence from industrial and commercial training, where computers *are* cost-effective in certain settings. Others suggest that, in real terms, prices of computers are falling, whereas salaries of teachers are rising. They have little confidence in the abilities of teachers in developing countries, and believe that educational software from industrial countries can do the job as well, if not better than the teachers can. They ignore the socializing and other humanistic roles of schools, which parents take for granted and will not sacrifice. They dismiss the very high cost of developing and marketing culturally appropriate educational software, and the problem of obsolescence. They have no hard evidence to support their rationale, because no cost-effectiveness studies have been done.

■ Scrutinizing the four popular rationales

It is not enough merely to point out what computers can be used for: the ideology behind each must also be considered. Does the social rationale have its roots in liberal thinking which urges free access for all children to computers, the wonder machines of our age, so that the citizenry will be more fully developed as individuals? If so, industrial countries are far from providing free access for all, though there are some signs of computers aiding individual development of a very small minority of students. Or do its supporters take the socialist utilitarian line of the greatest benefit for the greatest number, in the service of society? That would mean at least avoiding the development of elites. Or is it technology driven, in the sense that people fear lest their children should be unable to cope with these new monsters, which must be demystified? Yet it is well known that children cope with them better than adults do! Or is the social rationale put about by politicians in league with capitalist financiers and manufacturers who see great profits to be made out of widespread acceptance of computers? Schools in industrial countries may have been stampeded into teaching computer education by the technological hype, generated by giant multinational companies selling information technology and information itself. Or is the social rationale merely a piece of 'after-the-fact' justification for the rather low level of what has happened so far in many schools? Some educators argue that using computers in this way, to generate computer 'awareness', is a waste of resources, because computers are potentially very powerful educational tools.

The vocational rationale has a commercial ring to it: computers help students to prepare for jobs in the marketplace. But in industrial countries political parties of varied hues have declared that computers are vital to our economy and children should learn how to use them. Arguments arise instead over whether school is the right place for vocational training. Because the vocational rationale calls for far more time to be spent on computer education than does the social rationale, the question of curriculum priorities comes up. What should computers displace? Because computer-related jobs are changing fast, Ministries and schools adopting this rationale may be uncertain about the course content. Worse, will the lack of well-trained teachers mean that programming is poorly taught, and that students must later unlearn what they learned at school, once they are in jobs or post-secondary education? There is also real doubt about what computer-related skills will be required by workers once the creative gale has blown itself out. Will they need no more than computer literacy, or should they be trained in programming? The former seems more likely than the latter.

The pedagogical rationale is not fundamentally flawed, even if enthusiasts exaggerate a little. But the means of following it through may be lacking, as countries struggle to develop educational software. Much research is going on to realize the potential of computers in helping children to learn. There are already examples of what computers can teach that teachers alone cannot. Computers are being used by teachers as tools, by learners as resources. Using computers at school for monitoring and sensing within science, for data logging, robotics and computer-aided design, and for information retrieval in the humanities, is far more satisfactory educationally than using them for drill-and-practice and games. By varying inputs and observing results, students can learn much from simulations on computers. They can achieve important National Curriculum objectives in language with the help of word processing, and in mathematics with spreadsheets and statistical programs. Regrettably, it is still the case that more often than not computers are being used by students to learn what teachers can teach better. Ideologically, advocates of the pedagogical rationale are seldom radical or revolutionary. They expect others to adopt computers because of what they themselves perceive to be demonstrable improvements in teaching and learning.

Of these four rationales, perhaps the catalytic one has the most hidden power, but it also promises a somewhat Utopian future. There are even suggestions that schools, with the help of computers, will move away from an educational system dominated by nineteenth-century values and traditional subjects. Somehow, say supporters of the catalytic rationale, teachers will adopt 'more relevant' curricula and bring educational opportunities to a larger number of people (Commonwealth Secretariat, 1987). King (1984) challenges the view that poorer schools will benefit, saying that it seems likely that elite schools will 'use computers to develop problem-solving skills (that is, students programming computers)' while poor schools will 'principally use computers for drill-and-practice (that is, computers programming students)'. Market-oriented politicians also use the catalytic rationale, but in a different sense. They call for cost sharing in education, that is to say, they want schools to depend on sources other than government for part of their funding. This actually strengthens the rationale for having computers in the school office. Schools under such politicians face having to raise funds and control expenditure, to say nothing of teaching more students with fewer qualified staff. Computers are already helping to bring about this kind of change. But this is a case of computers following the law, rather than the law following computers. In administration, computers are sometimes the catalyst, sometimes the cause of change. Only a blind optimist would use the catalytic rationale to justify expenditure on the basis of what has changed so far.

■ Rationales in developing and industrial countries

National policy on putting computers into schools depends to a large extent on the dominant rationale. The social rationale does not lead to the same policy as the vocational one. For example, if a government wants to teach computer awareness in secondary schools, it may try to introduce rather low-cost microcomputers into a large number of schools. It will expect every school to have several teachers who, between them, can teach all students for 2–3 hours a week in, say, the second year. But if a government strongly influenced by the vocational rationale wants to introduce computer literacy or computer science courses, possibly as examination subjects near the end of secondary schooling, medium-priced microcomputers will be needed, teachers will have to be much better trained, and probably only selected classes of students will be able to take the course. In fact, the government will probably decide to limit hardware and software provision to a minority of secondary schools in the country, on the grounds of shortage of resources and only a small national requirement for school graduates with computer science.

Governments influenced by the pedagogical and catalytic rationales must face a far larger bill for hardware, software and training. The cost of developing and marketing suitable educational software is so high that very few countries have attempted it. The rest are importing software or doing without it. Those importing it are usually unhappy with what they get, for educational and cultural reasons. Those doing without it are escaping from these two rationales: they are giving up hope and may indeed be very sceptical of trials elsewhere.

Developing countries advance similar rationales to those given by industrial ones, most placing greatest emphasis on the vocational rationale, and much less on the social, pedagogical and catalytic. For example, China, which committed about £50 million in 1984 to support its policy on computers in schools, selects students to study computers, and expects them to proceed to computer science at university, or to be useful to their employers, because it perceives computers as an essential part of its drive towards modernization. India, in launching its massive CLASS project, while indicating its determination to de-mystify computers for as many students as possible also signalled its determination to give selected students a chance to take degrees and get jobs in computer technology. Pakistan, on a much smaller scale, is doing the same, in a pilot project aided by an international bank. Tunisia's national project has avowedly vocational goals and students will focus on learning programming and applications while gaining some knowledge of computer 'architecture', that is, the design and inner workings of the machines on which they work.

Six South-East Asian countries have planned for a computer literacy class for all secondary students, with elective computer studies courses for upper secondary students, but hardly any CAL to serve the pedagogical rationale and no mention at all of the catalytic one. Of the six, some have resources to implement the plan in full, others not. Among these countries, Singapore decided some years ago that software development, in particular, would be a very important part of its economic future, The Ministry of Education requires every secondary school student to take a 20-hour computer familiarization course, and subsidizes computer clubs in many of the schools. Mauritius and Sri Lanka are taking a similar social and vocational line, with undertones of the information technology industry rationale. Could these islands, with their well-educated peoples, become software suppliers for Asia and

Africa? Might they be forced to become software sweatshops for industrial nations?

Western Hemisphere island nations, Fiji, Jamaica and Trinidad and Tobago, found that their desire to follow the pedagogical rationale was frustrated because British origins of their curricula clashed with the US origins of the software, bought to run on US machines. In Kenya, with the Ministry's blessing but not run by it, there has been a well-founded, but not entirely successful, attempt to follow the pedagogical and catalytic rationales as well as the social and vocational. Kenyan demand for computer-related skills is very small as yet, therefore it can be met by students from only a few secondary schools.

Ministries of education without a policy on computers in schools are waking up to the fact they need one, based on a clear rationale. The trouble is that computers reach schools anyway, whether through donations or by purchase out of non-government funds. Without a policy computers arrive in uncoordinated fashion. Teachers are not trained. Software is scarce. Hardware is incompatible. Spares, repairs and maintenance barely exist. Expensive private schools probably survive best, with a network of foreign contacts, quickly widening the gap between their students and the rest. Ministries of education with a policy, backed by a rationale or rationales, may still lack the resources to do all they want to, of course, and they may be unable to give computers high priority. But at least they are able to take important decisions, within the policy. For example, should they allow their schools to accept donations of hardware, particularly of obsolete hardware? Should they require schools to have at least one properly trained teacher before obtaining a computer? Should they set up a centre for support services and possibly to develop educational software? What degree of dependence on other countries can they tolerate? The social and vocational rationales are gathering strength in developing countries, with a few espousing the pedagogical rationale like their richer industrial neighbours. The catalytic rationale, noble as it is, remains in the background.

■ Who decides?

The question of whether or not schools in developing countries need computers has been raised at the highest levels of government. Politically speaking, computers have a high profile, and so do schools. For example, ministers of education from Commonwealth countries, meeting in Cyprus in 1984, asked the Commonwealth Secretariat to provide advice. A set of policy guidelines was published (Commonwealth Secretariat, 1987), following a meeting of experts (Commonwealth Secretariat, 1986). UNESCO has called regional meetings to consider the same question, resulting in papers and reports to governments (for example, UNESCO, 1984a, 1984b, 1985; Anderson *et al.*, 1986; Carnoy and Loop, 1986; Carnoy *et al.*, 1987) and leading up to an International Congress in Paris in April 1989 on Education and Informatics.

Policy in this field is usually developed by ministries of education, although ministries of industry, trade and finance may well have a role too, if only because this revolution is so strongly technology and commerce led. Ministry of education officials advise their ministers in the light of conditions in the education system and, to a large extent, draw on experience in other countries. Ministers' decisions are influenced very strongly by political, commercial and fiscal factors, but as Jennings-Wray and Wellington (1985) point out in discussing whether or not Jamaica needs computers in its secondary schools, the rhetoric of technology 'tends to mesmerise educational planners in Third World countries into thinking the introduction of technology [from the developed world] into their educational systems will act as a panacea for whatever ills are being experienced'. If a minister decides that the introduction of computers into schools is justified, this policy, when announced, is usually backed by an apparently convincing rationale.

■ The process of adoption

Rogers (1983) defines diffusion as the process by which an innovation is communicated through certain channels over time among members of a social system. Diffusion of the innovation of using computers is at an early stage in schools in the Third World, and cannot be said to have reached take-off (the stage when roughly 25% of potential users have adopted the innovation) even in industrial countries. Indeed, so far as computers in schools are concerned, the majority of the Third World educators, and their ministries, are at the first step of Rogers's five-step innovation–decision process: knowledge, persuasion, decision, implementation and confirmation. Among them are few innovators and even fewer adopters of computers for education.

It is clear that few countries, industrial or developing, have seen computers arrive in their schools solely through a single rational decision-making process centred on the Ministry of Education. According to Carnoy *et al.* (1987), even in the United States, where there are, in 1990, about 5 million computers in schools, it was private schools and commercial enterprises that led the way in the 1960s and 1970s, not the education authorities, local, state or federal. Adopting computers as valuable tools in education seems to be rather haphazard. How, then, are computers getting into schools in developing countries? Are they arriving because of government policy to adopt them, or despite the lack of it? Who is pushing them?

Where ministries are slow to develop policy, computers arrive in schools anyway, though in small numbers. Take the case of Zimbabwe. In the absence of central policy in the early 1980s, schools bought hobbyist microcomputers from their own money or received them as donations from foreign companies, parents and well-wishers. By 1986, the Zimbabwean Ministry of Education's Curriculum Department Unit had a part-time adviser on computers in schools, who reported after a survey that there were about 150 machines installed, most of them with only small memories and no disk drives. Schools with computers ran clubs for interested students, teaching them computer awareness and simple programming. By 1988, the adviser had resigned to teach at a private school, which, through a benefaction, installed 24 Amstrad machines with disk drives. The school designed a computer studies course leading to an examination, and obtained recognition from the Computer Society of Zimbabwe, and then from the Ministry of Education, for the certificate it gave to students who passed.

Zimbabwe is but one example of specific practice coming before general national policy. The Kenyan government agreed to experiments in a few schools under the Aga Khan Computers in Education Project, using computers donated by an American company, Apple Computer. In Malawi, an enterprising young teacher who had taken a course in Britain returned to introduce computers into the teaching of mathematics in a few schools and to create computer awareness, with the support of his principal and through donations of a few machines by foreign companies (Bajpai, 1988; Ngwale and Bajpai, 1988). In Tunisia, computers donated by several foreign governments and companies were the first to arrive in two selected pilot schools. In India, a stimulus was provided through a gift of 250 Acorn BBC-B computers from the British government. In Pakistan, an international bank helped to set up the first project. Even in China, where government agencies have now done a great deal to foster computer studies in secondary schools, the first computers arrived in schools through a Hong Kong benefaction. In the Philippines, out of 65 public secondary schools surveyed in 1987, 23 had acquired computers through donations and fund-raising efforts of the parents and students, while in Brunei Darussalam almost all the computers in schools in 1987 were donations from Shell, the international oil company (Pak and Punyapinyophol, 1988).

It seems that some ministries are obliged to develop policy to follow and regulate practice. Elsewhere, ministries have taken the lead, usually through controlling the flow of funds for provision of hardware, software and teacher training, and often by announcing a firm policy, backed by a rationale, and by setting up structures to implement that policy. China, Singapore and Sri Lanka are three notable examples. China's State Education Commission developed a policy through national conferences, and announced a syllabus for computer studies in 1987. This announcement roughly coincided with the arrival in key secondary schools of many microcomputers, paid for by the Commission and other more local education authorities. In Singapore, the Ministry ruled that Advanced Level Computer Science should be offered in all the junior colleges (upper secondary schools) and subsidized provision of computers in these schools and for computer clubs in all lower secondary schools (Wong *et al.*, 1988). In Sri Lanka, a Computer Education Programme was established as early as 1983, with a firm policy, and the Ministry of Education paid for microcomputers in over 100 schools. Of course, in many countries, industrial and developing, declared policies do not match precisely what is happening in schools.

In contrast, Akinyemi (1986) reports on a 1984–85 Moroccan government-backed pilot experiment. He says, 'The primary school environment in Morocco had no history of technological introduction, therefore the computer ... was seen as "intruder in the school system". Teachers killed the idea, " ... some new technology coming from outside, therefore superfluous and useless".'

■ Preparing for computers in schools

For the process of adoption to succeed, each category of people in the education system must be prepared. Ministries cannot afford to neglect any one of these categories, if they want their policies to be successful. Are the policy makers themselves ready? Whether politicians or officials, they should give a strong lead through being fully aware of the issues. Nothing is worse than a strong lead based on ignorance! They should have had at least a little hands-on experience themselves. They should understand the benefits and dangers of seeking foreign aid, whether as hardware, software or expertise. Even more so, they should be aware of the educational issues that will arise. If they are then convinced that computers should be brought into the schools, are they willing to provide resources for training teachers and support staff? Will the country have a 'computers in schools centre', offering educational and technical back-up, and possibly advising the policy makers? Is there, or should there be, a curriculum (and an examination, with a certificate) for computer studies courses? These are just a few of the questions for policy makers if the country is to be prepared for computers in its schools.

Are the project leaders ready? If the country is to bring computers into its schools through a national project, perhaps initially through a pilot project, does it have suitably trained and experienced people to be project leaders? Are these people aware of national needs and strategy? It is important that those chosen to lead do not install and direct a project which is merely an end in itself. The leaders must be in tune with the rationale behind the project and understand its educational implications.

Are principals ready? If so, they will have considered the rationales for introducing computers into their schools, and will understand the implications for them, their staff and their students. Are they satisfied that there is sufficient culturally relevant software for their students? Will they make space in the schools' timetables for these lessons? What about providing proper accommodation for the machines? Or should they be on trolleys, moving around the school? Who should they select to be trained? Will the computers become the 'property' of the mathematics or science department? Who will do the maintenance and repairs? Where will computers fit into administration and management? How will they change the school? Is it all worth it? Principals cannot be blamed for sometimes wishing that computers had never been invented.

Are teachers ready? Do they perceive the benefits (and the snags) for themselves or the students? Have they received adequate training, including hands-on experience, and will there be further updating each year? Are they getting for their schools the kinds of hardware and software with which they became familiar during their training? Are they ready to change their roles to some extent, because computers do challenge the traditional role of teachers? Or will they merely challenge back, asserting that computers are irrelevant to proper education? Where teachers perceive 'proper education' as a traditional curriculum based on factual knowledge and requiring of the students detailed recall for examination purposes, they may fiercely resist computers. Without teachers' support, Ministerial policies are certain to fail.

Are students and their parents ready? What do they think about computer studies? Do they understand why computers are being introduced? Do parents fear that their children will be diverted from serious study, necessary to pass examinations? Do students perceive computer studies as being of vocational value? Are there cultural factors to be taken into account in preparing the students?

This paper began by asking questions about whether Third World countries need computers, and, if they say they do, why computers are introduced into schools. It offered some comparisons between rationales in developing and industrial countries. It dealt with the question of who decides, and examined briefly the process of adoption. Because many countries are still developing policy on computer education, tracing this process of adoption in each country in more detail, describing students' experiences and evaluating the computers' effectiveness in educational terms, can be extremely interesting. To do so for even part of the Third World requires a whole book – Hawkridge *et al.*, 1990!

■ References

Akinyemi K. (1986). Micros and children in developing countries. *Programmed Learning and Educational Technology*, 23,2.

Anderson Jonathan *et al.* (1986). *Developing Computer Use in Education: Guidelines, Trends and Issues.* A report of the Expert Planning Meeting on Use of Computers in Education, Bangkok, 2-7 December 1985. Bangkok: UNESCO Regional Office for Education in Asia and the Pacific.

Bajpai Avi C. (1988). The use and implications of new information technologies for STME in developing countries: an overview. *CASTME Journal*, 8, 3.

Carnoy Martin and Loop Liza (1986). *Computers and Education: Which Role for International Research?* (Report of) the Stanford/UNESCO Symposium, 10-14 March 1986. ED.86/WS/86. Paris: UNESCO.

Carnoy Martin, Daley Hugh and Loop Liza (1987). *Education and Computers: Vision and Reality*. Paris: UNESCO.

Commonwealth Secretariat (1986). *Microcomputers in Schools.* Report of a Commonwealth meeting of specialists. Edmonton, Alberta, 15–17 May 1986. London: Commonwealth Secretariat.

Commonwealth Secretariat (1987). *Microcomputers in Schools: Policy Guidelines.* London. Commonwealth Secretariat.

Cumming C.E. and Quickfall M. (1987). *Micros in Africa: Policy Issues for Education.* A report to the Overseas Development Administration. Edinburgh: Moray House College of Education.

Elmandjra M. (1985). Communication, informatics and development. *Development*, 1,1. (Quoted by Papagiannis George and Milton Sande (1987). Computer literacy for development. *Prospects*, XVII, 4).

Hawkridge David, Jaworski John and McMahon Harry (1990). *Computers in Third World Schools.* London: Macmillan.

Jennings-Wray Zellyne and Wellington P.I. (1985). Educational technology utilization in Jamaica's secondary schools: present problems and future prospects. *British Journal of Educational Technology*, 16, 3.

King Kenneth (1984). Computers in schools: propositions, assumptions and an agenda for research. Notes for a lecture given at a Symposium on New Developments in Science Education, Bombay, November.

Ngwale Matthews and Bajpai Avi C. (1988). Innovation in the use of software in the teaching of mathematics. *CASTME Journal*, 8, 2.

Pak Leong Yong and Punyapinyophol Kittiporn (eds) (1988). Final Report of the Second Seminar on Computers in Education Project, Penang, 5-8 April, 1988. Penang: SEAMEO Regional Centre for Education in Science and Mathematics.

Robertson Edward L. (1988). Pitfalls for Kenya's computerisation. *Computers in Africa*, July-August.

Rogers Everett M. (1983). *Diffusion of Innovations*, 3rd edn. New York: The Free Press.

Ruskin F.R. (ed.) (1986). *Microcomputers and their Applications for Developing Countries.* Boulder (Colorado) and London: Westview Press.

Schumpeter J.A. (1939). *Business Cycles: A Theoretical, Historical and Statistical Analysis of the Capitalist Process.* New York: McGraw-Hill.

UNESCO (1984a). *Consultation Regionale sur l'Application de l'Informatique dans l'Education en Afrique*. Rapport Final. Bureau Regional d'Education pour l'Afrique, Dakar.

UNESCO (1984b). *Computers in Education*. Final Report of the (Third) Asian Seminar on Educational Technology, Tokyo. Bangkok: UNESCO Regional Office for Education in Asia and the Pacific.

UNESCO (1985). Premiere Reunion Consultative d'Experts sur les Applications de l'Informatique dans l'Education dans les Etats Arabes. Bureau Regionale de l'UNESCO pour l'Education dans les Etats Arabes, Damascus.

Wong Khoon Yoong, Lim Yoke Seng and Low Khah Gek (1988). *A Report on Computer Education and the Use of Computers in Singapore Schools and Institute of Education*. Singapore: Curriculum Development Institute of Singapore.

Paper 1.3

The Computer as Tutor, Tutee, Tool in Reading and Language

Jonathan Anderson

The microcomputer has been described as 'an imagination machine', an 'almost anything machine' (*Computer Solutions*, 1981, **2**(2)); and the range of ways that micros are beginning to be used by reading and language teachers testifies that the computer is the most versatile of inventions. At the same time, however, criticisms are made that many computer programs, especially in reading and language, are somewhat limiting. How are these different views to be reconciled?

Recently, I was looking for a particular disk when a young student said, 'The computer's not much use without floppy disks, is it?' How right she was. A microcomputer without programs, or software, as these are often called, is rather like a car without wheels. The purpose of this overview is to focus on software and the applications of microcomputers in reading and language classrooms, on the assumption that what is under the bonnet, referred to as hardware, is not of vital concern to the user. Paradoxically, much of the debate in schools, at least in Australian schools, revolves around what hardware to purchase. More sensible considerations would be how computers are to be used in schools and then, as my young friend said, what disks or programs are available.

Reading teachers know that language development is best nurtured if based on plenty of student talk, listening, reading and writing, and that language development goes hand in hand with growth in students' thinking abilities. In considering the applications below, then, we should try to determine the extent to which talk, listening, reading, writing and thinking are promoted by the use of particular

First published in *Reading*, 1984, **18**(2), 67–78, published by Basil Blackwell. Reprinted with permission of the United Kingdom Reading Association.

computer software. It is these aspects that should be foremost in evaluating software, rather than the user-friendliness of programs or the attractiveness of screen presentations, important though these are.

■   How computers are used in schools

A useful framework for discussing computer applications in the classroom is that of Taylor (1980), who suggested that all uses of computers in schools can be accommodated in one of three modes: tutor, tool or tutee. When the computer functions as tutor, students' behaviour is essentially governed by the computer: that is, material is presented, students respond, responses are evaluated, leading either to further presentations or a branch back to a previous item. By contrast, when the computer functions as tutee, students are in the driving seat (to continue our earlier analogy) and direct the computer, thereby assuming greater responsibility for their learning. As a tool, the computer is used by the students and teachers primarily as an aid, having been programmed to carry out certain useful tasks.

■   The computer as tutor

Possibly as much as 95% of commercially available computer software in reading and language is of the sort where the student is drilled, taught or managed by the computer. This type of software is easy to produce and may be useful in certain teaching situations. On the other hand, software of this kind fails to utilize the full potential of the microcomputer and generally adds little to learning that cannot be provided by more traditional, less expensive, means.

□   Drill and practice

One of many examples of drill-and-practice computer programs is *Microcourse: Reading* (Houghton Mifflin, 1983). It is rather easy to believe the claim made that this course may be the most comprehensive of its type, for practice is provided in some 330 skills. The course comes on 114 disks, with pre-tests, practice exercises and post-tests for each skill. Characteristic of this kind of computer software is that students know immediately whether they are right or wrong, the microcomputer is ever patient, and the task of record keeping for teachers is made easy. The majority of programs, however, are dreadfully dull and run counter to the philosophy of reading espoused by many teachers.

☐   **Tutorial**

Tutorial programs differ from the drill-and-practice variety in that a teaching component is included. An example is *Word Attack* (Davidson and Eckert, 1983a), which aims to develop students' receptive vocabulary. The teaching component consists of presentations of new words with meanings and sentences illustrating usage. Follow-up exercises provide practice using a variety of formats: multiple choice, sentence completion and arcade-style game. Perhaps the most useful feature of this program, and one that makes it more valuable than purely drill-and-practice programs, is that teachers are able to enter their own lists of words. Thus the program might find useful application in remedial work, in teaching ESL students, or in teaching specialized vocabulary in various content subjects.

☐   **Management systems**

Most of the major publishing companies in the United States have developed what are called management systems to accompany their basal reading programs. CLASS (Holt, Rinehart and Winston, 1983), for instance, an acronym for computerized learning and scoring system, is designed to accompany a basal reading scheme. This and similar systems usually test mastery of objectives in reading, score and analyse these tests, and print reports showing students' strengths and weaknesses, ways to group students who need help on specific objectives, individualized lesson plans, and so on. Claimed advantages for such systems are the immediate feedback provided and the consequent freeing of teachers from tedious testing. The style of teaching implied by such management systems may, of course, be alien to many teachers. And not all teachers would want to lock themselves into using a single reading scheme or series.

■   The computer as tutee

Usually included under the mode of computer as tutee is computer programming. This is a large topic, and limitations of space prevent discussion of it here. The following program, however, may give a flavour of what is involved when students play a more active part in learning than is allowed in the computer software so far described. The program also illustrates how imaginative software designers can turn a drill-and-practice program into a learning experience where students 'teach' the computer.

The aim of *Shrink 'n' Stretch* (Education Department of Western Australia, 1983) is to provide practice with contractions and their expanded forms (for example, 'I'd' for 'I would'). The program is presented in the form of a game with two cartoon characters, Shrink and Stretch, respectively asking students either to contract an expanded form or to give an expanded form of a contraction. Thus far the program does not differ from countless similar drill-and-practice programs. The innovative aspect comes when, alternating with the computer, it is the student's turn to ask Shrink or Stretch a question. Suppose the student asks Stretch to give the expanded form of 'can't'. The computer checks its store of expansions and contractions, and if this contraction is not recognized, asks the student to teach it. And so the computer 'learns' and 'improves', not unlike the familiar computer game, Animal. The game is highly motivating, students delighting in searching for questions to stump the computer. This involves discussion, reading and thinking, some of the criteria suggested above for evaluating reading software.

■ The computer as tool

The versatility of the microcomputer is best seen when it is used as a tool. For reading and language teachers, there is arguably more scope for the microcomputer than in any other subject area. The following applications, by no means an exhaustive list, suggests some of the possibilities.

☐   Modelling handwriting

Lally and Macleod, from the Department of Engineering Physics at The Australian National University, have explored in a systematic fashion over a number of years the use of the computer to model handwriting. More than 60 papers have come from their multidisciplinary research unit. Initially working with minicomputers and with severely retarded students as subjects, these researchers found that the computer was effective in providing immediate feedback of incorrect movements, in allowing guidance to be varied through partial cues, and in emphasizing the process in handwriting. More recent work of the unit (Lally and Macleod, 1983) has been to transfer from mini- to microcomputer and from the clinic into the classroom.

☐   Reading aid

Also working with Lally and Macleod is Grocke, whose special interest is reading. In a recent article (Grocke, 1983a), she describes how the computer can be used as a reading aid, prompting the student as necessary. Text is displayed on the screen; then, if any word is not known, the student may press HELP, indicating the word in question, and a moderately successful spoken rendition is given by the computer. Quite extensive experimental trials have been completed (Grocke, 1983b), showing the effectiveness of the computer as a reading aid with students of limited skills. As with the handwriting trials, microcomputers with speech synthesizers attached are now being given trials in regular schools.

☐   Efficient reading

A program that demonstrates the versatility of the microcomputer as tool is *Speed Reader II* (Davidson and Eckert, 1983b). At one moment it simulates a tachistoscope, exposing letters and words for brief intervals; at another it is like an elaborate slide projector for controlling the speed of text display; at yet another it is a pace reader for varying reading rate; and elsewhere it acts as a stopwatch. At the same time, the program has an optional sound feature and offers a choice of printing styles, regular and bold.

Accompanying computer exercises are designed to increase eye span, widen peripheral vision, increase reading speed, compute reading rate and comprehension level – the kinds of activities included in many efficient reading courses. Again, the usefulness of this program, as in *Word Attack* described above, is the provision of a general purpose editor that allows teachers to enter their own selected materials to meet the needs of particular students.

☐   Simulations

Simulations are programs that approximate some aspect of the real world. In *Archeology Search* (Snyder, 1982), for example, the computer simulates, first, the surface examination of a particular area of ground; at later stages, it simulates probes beneath the surface, laboratory examinations and expert assessment of specimen findings. The students' task is to try to deduce who formerly occupied the site. Classroom activities include group discussion (speaking and listening), keeping logs (writing), locating information (reading), making and testing hypotheses (logical and critical thinking) and sessions at the keyboard. A strong feature of this particular computer program is the way it integrates a number of important language skills. It is available for the Apple and TRS-80 computers.

A different kind of simulation is *Gold Dust Island* (Gare, 1984), written for the Apple and BBC microcomputers. Whereas *Archeology Search* promotes cognitive outcomes, Gare's program promotes affective outcomes. In this simulation game, the computer simulates the maintaining of water supplies, the building of a boat and the search for gold. What makes this game different from other similar games is that it is largely left to the players to determine even what the goals are, to explore interpersonal relationships and to aim for group cohesiveness. Indeed, working only for oneself in this game is a losing strategy, leading usually to death by dehydration. By the same token, other players are worse off as a group if one of their number dies. Here is a stimulus, then, for much discussion, discussion geared towards formulating goals, determining strategies and learning to trust other people. *Gold Dust Island* is one of a new series of software, demonstrating the potential of microcomputers to improve learning and to achieve, as here, educational objectives that are often hard to attain.

☐   Information retrieval

An application of microcomputers spanning across subject areas, and with obvious implications for reading and study skills, is to retrieve information from databases. A database is simply a collection of information, perhaps names, addresses and telephone numbers as in telephone directories, or the kind of information collected in a census. If the database is stored on computer and a query language is available, information can be retrieved much more easily if the information is in book form. Coburn *et al.* (1982, pp. 43–44) note that 'imaginative educators are beginning to devise ways of adapting the data processing capabilities of computers to enhance learning'.

One such example of imaginative teaching is the work at Fox Primary School, ILEA. Ross (1982) describes how information gathered in the 1971 census for residents in the local street was stored in the school's 380Z Research Machines Limited microcomputer. Students then interrogated the database to 'sort and retrieve original data in powerful and thought-provoking ways', thus developing their understanding in history. Using the computer as tool, students become historians or, in the case of other databases, they become scientists, demographers, and so on. Keeling (1982) describes similar teaching programs in which the teacher (and students) develop their own databases, for instance of personal information – name, date of birth, gender, brothers, sisters, height, weight, colour of hair and eyes – to interrogate and analyse. Activities such as these effectively involve students in reading, writing, speaking, listening and thinking, all in a very meaningful context.

☐   Text analysis

Microcomputers may also be used as tools to furnish indices of language use. Programs are available to analyse text in terms of number of words, average length of words, number of sentences, average sentence length, percentage of syllables and polysyllables, or even use of adjectives, adverbs, prepositional phrases, subordinate clauses and so on. Such analysis can be particularly useful if applied to students' writing, for it provides 'valuable information about student language production' (Kuchinskas, 1983, p. 13).

☐ Readability analysis

From analysing students' writing it is a small step to analysing the readability of text. For example, I have developed a program for the Apple IIe microcomputer based on the Rix index (Anderson, 1983). Rix is useful in that it may be used with foreign language material as well as English, it is suitable for easy to adult reading texts, and it is one of the few measures that may be used with shorter texts. The program provides an indication of the relative contributions to readability of word difficulty and sentence complexity, as well as an approximate grade level of difficulty.

☐ Word-based games

A wide variety of word-based games is available for microcomputers. An excellent tool for generating crossword puzzles, for instance, is *Crossword Magic* (Sherman, 1981). One way to use this program is for the teacher to generate crossword puzzles and for students to attempt these, either on the screen or in printed form. The program takes the tedium out of making crossword puzzles for it automatically interconnects words, holding any words temporarily that cannot be fitted immediately; it is easy to operate and puzzles may be stored for subsequent retrieval. A more powerful educational tool, according to Hyde (1983), is when students use the program to make crossword puzzles themselves, that is be author rather than player. An illustrated example is given of students generating puzzles based on the plays of Shakespeare. Of course, a program such as this could be used in any subject as a powerful tool for learning.

A rather different kind of puzzle is a simple one of my own called *Friend or Foe*, based on a game readers may recognize. It is a game of logical thinking, though it could serve as an introduction to artificial languages and formal grammars where the following 'rules' apply:

my friend's friend	=	my friend		
my foe's foe	=	my friend		
my friend's foe	=	my foe		
my foe's friend	=	my foe		
enemy = antagonist	=	opponent	= ... =	foe
pal = mate = buddy	=	comrade	= ... =	friend

Players are invited to test the computer with any questions they choose. They might, for example, ask: Is my foe's chum's pal's mate's comrade my friend or my foe? Students enjoy testing the computer and seeing it formally apply the rules above. A useful addition to the game might be to ask students to define as 'friend' or 'foe' any words not recognized by the computer (for example, critic). As in *Shrink 'n' Stretch* above, this would allow students to teach the computer.

☐ Text-based games

A game described as 'a significant teaching tool' and one allowing 'children to read in a new way' (Govier, 1983) is *Tray*, being developed as part of an MEP project. Called *Tray* because text is initially hidden, rather like an undeveloped photo, the students' task is to make the text progressively appear in a developing tray. Govier's full description of how this program might be used in the classroom suggests the potential of this new teaching tool. Students work in groups and this generates useful discussion about language. At different points in the 'development' of the text, they are invited to write a telegram saying what they think the text is about. The game thus links reading, writing and thinking.

The *Tray* concept is one of the more exciting I have seen for it involves students 'in a process of deep text analysis'. As Govier (1983, p. 49) continues, the process requires 'the simultaneous application of analytic, convergent thinking as well as creative thought'.

☐ Cloze generator

Reading teachers today are, in general, quite familiar with cloze procedure, both as a teaching and a testing technique. Numerous studies attest to its usefulness as a means of developing vocabulary, of assessing comprehension and of gauging readability. While it is not difficult to generate cloze tests over selected passages, the microcomputer makes the task even easier. *GAP Maker* is a general-purpose teacher's tool developed at Flinders University, and it enables the user to specify various formats – for example, standard-length or exact-length gaps, numbered or unnumbered gaps, varying deletion rate, single or multiple versions, random start or lead-in. Cloze tests may then be printed, with deleted words in a separate numbered list.

☐ Cloze tester

Closely associated with *GAP Maker* is *GAP Taker*, a program for administering cloze tests. A spelling algorithm is incorporated so that spelling errors are not penalized. Here, then, is another tool that may prove useful to reading teachers. Both programs are written for the Apple IIe microcomputer.

☐ GAP analysis

A useful introduction to the concept of textual cohesion may be found in Chapman (1983a) while some of the background to the OU longitudinal research project is described in Chapman (1983b). GAP analysis was developed as a means of quantifying students' perception of cohesive ties. Among several indices that are computed is a measure of consensus which has proved sufficiently sensitive to detect differences in reading development.

Thus far, GAP analysis has been developed on minicomputers and largely in a research context. In view of the increasing availability of microcomputers in schools, it would be a useful project to make GAP analysis also available on microcomputer. The additional insights into reader–text interaction afforded by this computer program should be welcomed by teachers of reading.

☐ Word processing

Word processing programs are tools in the same way that pencils and rubbers, biros and liquid paper, and typewriters are tools. But computers are much more versatile than these other tools since they can store students' text for subsequent retrieval, to revise, to polish and to print. The biggest impact of word processing programs in many classrooms is on the process of writing itself. This is well illustrated in a delightful article entitled 'Learning about reading, writing and fish with the help of a word processor' (Smith and Gray, 1983)

In an extended review of computing in schools (Anderson, 1984), I have highlighted some of the innovative work being done with word processors in many schools, particularly in primary classrooms. Among trends noted were for students to write more copiously, for this increased length to reflect a wider variety of syntactic structures, for more enthusiasm for writing and for a willingness to revise. An interesting observation made by one teacher was that students were better able to note errors in their writing, particularly spelling errors, when using a word processor.

☐ Spelling aid

Other programs that work in conjunction with word processors can provide assistance with spelling. The *Spell Handler* (Silicon Valley

Systems, 1983), for instance, a spelling checker for the Word Handler word processor for the Apple microcomputer, contains a 90 000 word dictionary. It can check documents for spelling and typographical errors, marking these in the text appending the mismatches located. Not all English teachers will approve of writing aids of this kind; there was resistance, too, by mathematics teachers when calculators initially appeared in classrooms. Advantages of such aids, however, are an increased awareness of patterns in spelling and of language usage. A disadvantage, especially of *The Spell Handler*, is the use of American spelling. A useful project will be the development of a spelling checker based on the Oxford Dictionary to work in conjunction with, say, *View* or *Edword* on the BBC microcomputer.

☐   Writing aid

Electric Webster (Cornucopia Software, 1983), available for the TRS-80 and IBM microcomputers, is yet another writing aid. In addition to checking spelling, this program contains a number of punctuation checks. It can also check for pompous and awkward phrases, for slang and obsolete words. Other checks are for word repetitions, double negatives, excessive use of the passive, and overly long words, phrases or sentences. Has a program like this a place in the classroom? Teachers, and certainly professional writers, would definitely love it.

☐   Creative writing

Some highly innovative programs, developed at the Department of Artificial Intelligence at Edinburgh University, conclude this sampling of applications of the computer as tool in reading and language. Sharples (1983) describes 'a construction kit for language' consisting of a suite of programs, each of which allows students to experiment with written language. Thus program *POEM* is a child's version of generative grammar for creating silly stories. Using the library of story patterns, Sharples says that students can deepen their understanding of parts of speech and of the way sentences combine together to form texts.

Another program called *WALTER* (contraction of Word Alterer) goes beyond traditional word-processors in allowing students to see what happens if – if, for instance, active is changed to passive voice throughout a story, or if sentences are combined using relative clauses. As Sharples (1983, p.55) notes, '*WALTER* is one step towards a computer-based "writer's assistant"'. It seems an exciting step and the wider availability of these programs is awaited with interest.

■   An imagination machine

In this overview, some 20 different uses of the microcomputer in reading and language are considered briefly. There are other applications; and still further possibilities will suggest themselves in the future as the use of computers in schools becomes more widespread, for the micro-computer is indeed an imagination machine.

Whether the microcomputer will usher in new modes of learning, as some would assert, changing the very way students think, will depend largely on the kind of software teachers choose. As was suggested above, the choice currently is too often between the 95% kind and the 5% variety. On a purely chance basis, then, the probability that the computer will fulfil its potential to modify learning appreciably is small – statistically non-significant. The onus is thus on reading teachers to search for those applications that might, in conjunction with other appropriate classroom experiences, promote language and cognitive development.

■   References

Anderson, J. (1983) Lix and Rix: variations on a little-known readability index. *Journal of Reading*, 26, 490-496.

Anderson, J. (1984) *Computing in Schools: An Australian Perspective*. Melbourne: Australian Council for Educational Research.

Chapman, L.J. (1983a) *Reading Development and Cohesion*. London: Heinemann.

Chapman, L.J. (1983b) Cohesion: an overview for the teacher of reading. *Australian Journal of Reading*, 6, 5-11.

Coburn, P., Kelman, P., Roberts, N., Snyder, T.F.F., Watt, D.H. & Weiner, C. (1982) *Practical Guide to Computers in Education*. Reading: Addison-Wesley.

Computer Solutions (1981) *Zardax Word Processor*. Brisbane: Computer Solutions.

Cornucopia Software (1983) *Electric Webster*. Walnut Creek, CA: Cornucopia Software.

Davidson, J. & Eckert, R. (1983a) *Word Attack*. Rancho Palos Verdes, CA: Davidson and Associates.

Davidson, J & Eckert, R. (1983b) *Speed Reader II*. Rancho Palos Verdes, CA: Davidson and Associates.

Education Department of Western Australia (1983) *Punctuation* [includes *Shrink 'n' Stretch*]. Perth: Education Department of Western Australia.

Gare, R. (1984) *Gold Dust Island*. Brisbane: Jacaranda Wiley.

Govier, H. (1983) Primary language development. *Acorn User*, 10, 45-51.

Grocke, M. (1983a) Computers in the classroom: how can they teach reading? *Australian Journal of Reading*, 6, 175-185.

Grocke, M. (1983b) *Computer-based Instruction for Disabled Readers.* Unpublished doctoral thesis, Australian National University.

Holt, Rinehart & Winston (1983) *CLASS (The Reading Computer Management System).* New York: Holt, Rinehart & Winston.

Houghton Mifflin (1983) *Houghton Mifflin Microcourse Reading.* Hanover, NH: Houghton Mifflin.

Hyde, H. (1983) Switched on to crosswords. *Australian Journal of Reading,* 6, 193-198.

Keeling, R. (1982) Program listing: PQUERY. *Micro-scope,* 6, 16-19.

Kuchinskas, G. (1983) 22 ways to use a microcomputer in reading & language arts classes. *Computers, Reading and Language Arts,* 1, 11-16.

Lally, M.R. & Macleod, I.D.G. (1983) The promise of microcomputers in development of basic skills. In J. Megarry, D.R.F. Walker, S. Nisbet & E. Hoyle (ed.) *World Yearbook of Education 1982/1983, Computers and Education.* London: Kogan Page.

Ross, A. (1982) Learning history with the help of a microcomputer. *Micro-scope,* 6, 10-14.

Sharples, M. (1983) A construction kit for language. In D. Chandler (ed.) *Exploring English with Microcomputers.* Leicester: Council for Educational Technology.

Sherman, L. (1981) *Crossword Magic.* Sunnyvale, CA: L & S Computerware

Silicon Valley Systems (1983) *The Spell Handler.* Belmont, CA: Silicon Valley Systems.

Smith, J. & Gray, J. (1983) Learning about reading, writing and fish with the help of a word processor. *Australian Journal of Reading,* 6, 186-192

Snyder, T.F.F. (1982) *Archeology Search.* New York: McGraw-Hill.

Taylor, R.P. (ed.) (1980) *The Computer in the School: Tutor, Tool, Tutee.* New York: Teachers College Press.

Paper 1.4

Computer Microworlds and Conceptual Change: A New Approach to Science Education

Barbara White and Paul Horwitz

■ Introduction

Research has demonstrated that students can succeed in high school and even college physics courses, while still maintaining many of their misconceptions and without acquiring an understanding of the physical principles addressed in the course (Caramazza *et al.*, 1981; Clement, 1982; diSessa, 1982; Larkin *et al.*, 1980; McDermott, 1984; Trowbridge and McDermott, 1981; Viennot, 1979; White, 1983; and many others). For example, they make incorrect predictions about what will happen to the motion of a ball when it emerges from passing through a spiral tube (McClosky *et al.*, 1980). Such questions do not call for computation or the algebraic manipulation of formulas; rather, they require understanding the implications of the fundamental tenets of Newtonian mechanics. Students' failure to answer such questions correctly reveals a deficiency in their knowledge of the causal principles that underly the formulas they have been taught.

We believe that students need, at an early age, experiences that will enable them to acquire accurate causal models (Bobrow, 1985; Gentner and Stevens, 1983; White and Frederiksen, 1986a, 1986b) for how forces affect the motions of objects. This will inhibit the development of misconceptions and foster the type of understanding

First published in Ramsden (ed.) (1988) *Improving Learning*. London: Kogan Page. Reprinted with permission.

that older students appear to lack. In contrast to our view, many cognitive and educational theorists believe that attempts to teach children physics will inevitably fail (see, for example, Shafer and Adey, 1981). They argue that understanding physical principles requires formal operational thinking (Piaget and Garcia, 1964), and that many students have not reached this stage of cognitive development at high school or even college level, let alone at elementary school level. Consequently, such students cannot be expected to master physical principles. We have found this not to be the case. This paper will describe an instructional approach that enabled sixth graders to understand important aspects of Newtonian mechanics. Further, it will illustrate how they also began to learn about the nature of science – what are scientific laws, how do they evolve, and why are they useful? For the interested reader, this approach to science education is more fully described in the research report by White and Horwitz (1987).

■   The progression of microworlds and subject matter

The objective was for students to evolve a mental model of sufficient sophistication to enable them to analyse projectile motion problems (that is, problems involving motion under a constant, uniform gravitational force). The desired model would incorporate such fundamental concepts of Newtonian mechanics as force, velocity, and acceleration, as well as causal principles, such as *forces cause changes in velocity*. In order to enable students to acquire such a causal model, we created a progression of increasingly complex microworlds. Associated with each microworld is a set of problem-solving authorities and experiments designed to help the students discover the laws governing the microworld. These microworlds gradually introduce the full set of principles needed to analyse projectile motion problems. All of them require students to control the motion of a computer-generated graphic object via the application of forces. Within these simulations, the complications introduced by friction and gravity can be selectively eliminated, allowing students to encounter first simpler situations obeying Newton's first law (objects do not change their velocity unless a force is applied to them), and later to analyse more complex situations in terms of such basic laws. In addition, the microworlds incorporate a number of different representations for the application of forces and for the motions of objects. For example, there is the datacross (see Figure 1), which is essentially a pair of crossed 'thermometers' that register the horizontal and vertical velocity components of an object via the amount of 'mercury' in them. Also, there are wakes (also shown in Figure 1) that

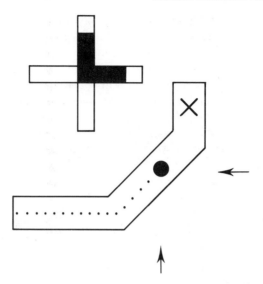

Figure 1 The representation of motion within the microworlds. In this game, one must control the motion of the dot so that it navigates the track and stops on the target X. The shaded circle in the middle of the angled path is the dot. It represents a physical object which may be given fixed sized impulses in the left–right or the up–down directions. In this figure the dot has been given the (optional) property of leaving 'wakes' in the form of little dots laid down at regular time intervals. These denote, by their position and relative separation, the past history of the motion. The large cross in the middle of the figure is the 'datacross' – a device for displaying the instantaneous values of the X and Y velocity components. Here the datacross is depicting a velocity inclined at +45 degrees to the horizontal. The arrows at the bottom and right side of the figure continually point to the dot, unless it leaves the screen, in which case they 'get stuck' at the edge of the screen. They represent the X and Y coordinates of the dot's position, and are useful for determining its location to within a quadrant when it is off the screen. Their motions, while the dot is on the screen, dynamically illustrate the X and Y components of the dot's velocity.

provide a record of an object's past speed and direction of motion by leaving a mark on the screen at fixed time intervals. These representations allow the effects of forces on an object's motion and velocity components to be directly observed, and thereby facilitate students' attempts to formulate the principles governing these causes and effects.

Microworld 1

At the beginning of the curriculum, we introduce a simple one-dimensional microworld which has no friction or gravity. In this world, students try to control the motion of an object (referred to as the 'dot') by applying fixed-sized impulses to the right (→) or to the left (←). The students observe that whenever they apply an impulse to the dot, it causes a change in its speed: if the impulse is applied in the same direction that the dot is moving, it adds to its speed; applied in the opposite direction, it subtracts from the speed. In this way, the students discover that a formalism they learned in second grade, scalar arithmetic (for example, $3 - 2 = 1$), will enable them to make predictions about the effect that a particular impulse, or sequence of impulses, will have on the motion of the dot. As part of this process, the students have discovered a corollary of Newton's first law – whenever you apply an impulse to an object, you change its velocity.

Microworld 2

Next, the students are given a two-dimensional microworld. Again, there is no friction or gravity. In this world, the students can apply impulses up or down, as well as to the left or right. Through carefully designed problem-solving activities (see, for example, White, 1984), the students discover that the law they developed for the horizontal dimension applies equally well to the vertical dimension of the dot's velocity. Further, they learn that these two components of the dot's motion are independent of one another – for instance, if you apply an upwards or downwards impulse, it has no effect on the horizontal velocity of the dot[†]. Finally, they acquire the foundation for an understanding of vector addition – they learn how the vertical and horizontal velocity components combine to determine the speed and direction of the dot's motion.

Microworld 3

The next step is to provide students with a microworld where the rate at which they can apply impulses can be varied. The purpose of this microworld is to introduce students to continuous forces via a limit process. The students can repeatedly double the frequency with which they can apply impulses, while at the same time, the size of each impulse is halved. At the end of this process, the students are applying very small impulses closely spaced in time. In this way, the students learn to think of continuous forces, like gravity, as a lot of small impulses applied one after another. This enables students to apply their causal model, learned in the simpler microworlds, to understand the effects of continuous

---

[†] This is learned by giving one student the capability to apply only horizontal impulses to the dot and another the capability to apply only vertical impulses. The first student is then given a task that requires controlling the arrow whose motion represents the dot's horizontal velocity, and the second student has to control the arrow whose motion represents its vertical velocity. They discover that the other student's impulses have no effect on the motion of their arrow.

forces. For example, they are asked to think about what happens when you throw a ball up into the air. They discover that gravity is constantly applying an impulse that continually adds a small amount to the vertical velocity of the ball in the downwards direction. This causes the ball to go upwards at a slower and slower rate until it finally stops, turns around, and accelerates downwards. By analysing such problems, the students develop an understanding of acceleration and of $F = ma$ where the mass and the force are constant. In other words, they learn a simpler causal form of $F = ma$, that is, $F \rightarrow a$.

Microworld 4

Finally, the students are presented with a microworld in which gravity is acting, and they can again apply impulses to the left and right, as well as up and down. In this world, in the absence of other forces, motion is characterized by constant acceleration in the vertical dimension and constant speed in the horizontal dimension. The students are given problems of the form: 'Imagine that you give two balls a horizontal push off the side of the table. One ball gets a soft push and the other ball gets a hard push. Both balls are pushed at the same time. Which ball hits the floor first?' Working on this microworld thus enables students to make connections to some interesting real-world situations. Solving such problems requires the students to apply the causal model that they learned from interacting with the prior microworlds.

■ The instructional approach

The set of microworlds we have created focuses on, simplifies and makes concrete certain aspects of Newtonian mechanics. The challenge was to devise instructional techniques, centred around the microworlds, that would facilitate students' acquisition of the desired mental model. A central aspect of the approach that we developed is to synthesize the teaching of subject matter with teaching about the form, evolution and application of scientific knowledge. Students are given a variety of laws that have been proposed for a given microworld, and are asked to determine which laws are correct and which laws are incorrect (that is, demonstrably false). Then, for the correct laws, they have to devise a criteria for deciding which laws are better than others. Finally, they have to apply their laws to real-world contexts and thereby discover that the laws are general and enable one to make predictions about a wide range of physical phenomena.

Within each of the existing four modules of the curriculum (corresponding to the four microworlds described above), instruction was divided into four distinct phases:

The motivation phase

In the first phase, students are asked to make predictions about what they think will happen in simple real-world contexts. For example, in the first module of the curriculum, the teacher asks the students: 'Imagine that we have a ball resting on a frictionless surface and we blow on the ball. Then, as the ball is moving along, we give it a blow, the same size as the first, in the opposite direction. What will be the effect of this second blow on the motion of the ball?' The teacher simply tabulates the different answers and reasons for these answers without commenting on their correctness. This process demonstrates to the students that not everyone holds the same beliefs. For instance, some think that the second blow will cause the ball to turn around and go in the opposite direction, others think that it will make the ball stop, and yet others believe that it will simply cause the ball to slow down. Since not everyone can be right, students are motivated to find out who has correct explanations and who has misconceptions. Further, since the predictions are about the behaviours of real-world objects, this phase sets up a potential link between what happens in the computer microworld and the real world.

The evolution phase

In this phase students solve problems and perform experiments in the context of the computer microworld. For instance, one of the problems in the first module requires the students to make the dot hit a stationary target while moving at a specific speed. Once the student succeeds, the dot returns to its starting location and a new target speed is specified. By attempting to solve this problem, the students learn how impulses affect the speed of the dot. As described in the previous section, the computer microworld increases in complexity with each new module of the curriculum. The problems and experiments are designed and sequenced to build upon the students' prior knowledge and to enable them to induce increasingly sophisticated concepts and laws relevant to understanding the implications of Newton's laws of motion.

The formalization phase

In this phase the students are asked to evaluate a set of laws formulated to describe the behaviour of objects within the microworld. Examples of such laws are:

(1) *whenever you give the dot an impulse to the left, it slows down;*
(2) *if the dot is moving, and you do <u>not</u> apply an impulse, it will keep moving at the same speed.*

Initially students are asked to sort the laws into two piles: Those that they can prove wrong and those for which they cannot find a counter example. Then, for the subset of 'true' laws, they are asked to pick the rule they like best: 'if you could only have one of these rules in your head to base predictions on, which one would you pick and why?' This activity typically engenders discussions of:

(1)   the precision of a rule's predictions;

(2)   the range of situations to which it applies;

(3)   its simplicity and memorability.

The transfer phase

In this phase the objective is to get the students to appreciate how the rule they have selected applies to real-world contexts. In the first stage of this process, students apply their rule to the predictive question that they were asked at the beginning of the instructional cycle. They then compare the answer that the rule generates to the set of answers generated by the class. For answers that differ, students go to the microworld and experiment, for example by putting friction and/or gravity into the microworld, to see which of their 'wrong' predictions can become correct predictions under these more complex circumstances. In the second stage of the transfer process, students conduct experiments with real-world objects, or design their own experiments to illustrate how the rule they evolved in the microworld context holds in these real-world contexts.

■   Experimental results

The curriculum was implemented by a teacher who taught five science classes in the sixth grade of a middle school located in a middle class Boston suburb. One of the five classes was used for a pilot trial of the first two modules of the curriculum. Of the remaining classes, two were used as a peer control group (containing 37 students), and the other two were given the ThinkerTools curriculum (containing 41 students). The curriculum took two months to complete. During this period, the students had a science class every school day for 45 minutes. The ThinkerTools curriculum occupied the entire class period. Students in the control classes received the standard curriculum which, at this point in the year, was devoted to a unit on inventions. All students had completed a physics unit earlier in the year which included material on Newton's laws.

In addition to the control group of sixth grade students, a second control group was employed, consisting of two classes of high school physics students (containing 41 students) drawn from the same school system as the sixth graders. These students had just completed two-and-one-half months studying Newtonian mechanics using the textbook *Concepts in Physics* (Miller, Dillon and Smith, 1980).

We utilized a variety of evaluation instruments to help us determine the effectiveness of the ThinkerTools curriculum. During the course we observed numerous classroom sessions and kept videotape and audiotape records of certain sessions. At the end of the course we administered three written tests measuring: (1) ability to translate between the alternative representations of motion (datacrosses and wakes – see Figure 1) employed within the curriculum; (2) subject matter knowledge in the computer microworld context; and (3) transfer of the underlying principles to real-world contexts. This third test was also given to the two control groups. In addition, following the administration of the written tests, seven of the ThinkerTools students were interviewed on an individual basis. These protocols allowed us to explore in depth the nature of the mental models they had acquired.

Since the first two tests were given only to the experimental subjects, we will focus in this limited space on the results of the third test. The findings will be discussed with respect to the two primary objectives of the course: (1) understanding the principles underlying Newtonian mechanics; and (2) learning about the form and evolution of scientific knowledge.

☐ Understanding Newtonian mechanics

The experimental students did well in the first two tests, with one-third of them getting more than 90% of the questions correct. Protocols of high scoring students reveal that their pattern of correct answers was produced by the consistent application of the desired mental model for reasoning about force and motion problems. This is in marked contrast to the inconsistent and misconception fraught reasoning that sixth graders display prior to instruction (White and Horwitz, in preparation), and that high school physics students exhibit following a traditional physics course (White, 1983).

The third test, administered to the experimental group and two control groups, measures students' understanding of Newtonian mechanics in real-world problem-solving contexts. It is composed of questions used by other researchers in studying misconceptions among physics students (Clement, diSessa, McClosky, McDermott, Minstrell, White). The particular questions used are simple predictive questions to which high school and college students frequently give wrong answers. They all require reasoning from basic principles, rather than constraint-based, algebraic problem solving.

In the first analysis of this transfer test, we compared sixth graders who had the ThinkerTools curriculum to those who did not. A three-way between-subjects analysis of variance was carried out with:

(1)   treatment (experimental versus control);

(2)   gender;

(3)   ability (low, middle, and high, based upon California Achievement Test (CAT) total scores)

as the three factors. With this design we could assess the effectiveness of the experimental curriculum for subjects of each gender and ability level. There was a highly significant main effect of instructional treatment ($F_{1,62}$ = 62.9, $p<0.0001$). The average number of questions correct for the experimental subjects was 11.15 out of 17, while the average for the control subjects was 7.56. In addition, there was no significant interaction of gender with treatment ($F_{1,62}$ = 0.219, p = 0.64), or ability with treatment ($F_{2,62}$ = 0.834, p = 0.44). Thus, the ThinkerTools curriculum was equally effective for girls and boys as well as for students of different ability levels as measured by the CAT.

With respect to the ThinkerTools students, the questions on the test can be classified into two categories:

(1)   Those that involve the application of a principle taught in the course and that the students have applied in a context similar to the one presented in the problem.

(2)   Those that involve a principle addressed in the course but that the students have never applied to the particular context presented in the problem.

An item analysis revealed that the experimental students did better than the control students on both types of problems. This suggests that the ThinkerTools students not only learned the principles focused on in the course, but also could apply them to unfamiliar contexts.

Finally, it is noteworthy that the ThinkerTools students also did significantly better on this transfer test than the high school physics students (t_{80} = 1.7, $p<0.05$), who were on the average six years older and had been taught about force and motion using traditional methods. An item analysis revealed interesting differences between these groups. The ThinkerTools students performed better (in some cases dramatically better) than the high school physics students on problems that involved analysing the effects of forces in terms of velocity components. The high school students, however, performed better on problems that involved constraint forces (such as a fixed length string constraining the motion of a pendulum bob). This latter result is not too surprising, since constraint forces were not dealt with in the ThinkerTools curriculum.

☐   **Acquiring scientific enquiry skills**

In addition to teaching students principles underlying Newtonian mechanics, we had the symbiotic goal of helping them learn about the form, evolution and application of scientific knowledge. In evaluating our success with respect to this second major objective of the curriculum, we relied partly upon observations of students' classroom performance. For instance, we examined the quality of the laws and experiments that they formulated for themselves, as well as the sophistication of the discussions they held when they were attempting to select the best law. In addition, we looked at the results of the written tests, particularly the transfer test, to aid in this aspect of the evaluation.

Understanding the form of scientific knowledge

Knowing the characteristics of a useful scientific law is an important aspect of understanding the form of scientific knowledge. The instructional technique we developed was to present students with alternative laws for each microworld, and have them select the best law. We observed that when students were evaluating these sets of laws, they spontaneously engaged in discussions concerning the simplicity of a law, the precision of its predictions, and its range of applicability. The set of laws was carefully constructed to elicit such discussions and this approach thus appears to have been highly successful.

Developing scientific enquiry skills

It is important to understand that falsification is part of the process by which scientific knowledge evolves. For a rule to be a potential scientific law, it must be capable of being proven wrong. Being able to develop and reason from counter evidence is an important scientific enquiry skill. We observed that when the students were evaluating the sets of laws given to them, they were adept at designing experiments that would falsify a particular law.

When we went on to look at what the students did when they formulated laws for themselves, there were clear limits to their scientific enquiry skills. For example, one group of students discovered the 'linear friction law'; in the microworld the effect of friction is linearly proportional to the speed with which the object is moving. The consequence is that when a sequence of impulses is applied to the dot, it does not matter whether the impulses are applied one right after the other or whether they are separated, the dot will come to rest at the same point. The students discovered this fact, but they did not fully explore its implications, nor did they go on to investigate whether it was true for the kind of real-world friction that affects, for instance, rolling balls or sliding hockey pucks.

If one looks at our instructional approach, this limitation in their enquiry skills is understandable. We gave the students activities to help them induce the laws, as well as sets of possible laws to evaluate, and real-world activities that enabled them to see that the laws generalized. Towards the end of the course they were asked to formulate their own laws and to design real-world activities that illustrated the laws. This was clearly too abrupt a transition, and an important area of our future research will be the development of bridging activities that enable a more gradual transition to independent scientific discovery.

Acquiring scientific problem-solving skills

Students need to understand that the laws they are evolving are of increasing general applicability, and they need to be able to apply them in new contexts. Based upon classroom observations and the results of the transfer test, we see that the students were indeed able to generalize principles derived from the microworld contexts to a variety of simple real-world contexts. This was achieved by a process of abstracting what they learned from the computer microworld into a set of laws and then learning how to map the laws on to different real-world problem-solving situations.

The general conclusion is that the ThinkerTools students learned that a useful scientific law is a concise principle that enables predictions across different contexts. In addition, they developed skill at designing experiments to falsify or show the limitations of a law, and applying a given law to a variety of different domains. This view of scientific knowledge and these enquiry skills are an important component of understanding what science is all about.

◼ Discussion

The design of the curriculum was based upon extensive protocol studies of sixth graders' reasoning about force and motion problems. Based upon this research, we determined which aspects of their prior knowledge we could build upon, and which misconceptions we could use to motivate their learning about Newtonian mechanics. The progression of increasingly complex computer microworlds was then designed to correspond to the desired evolution of the students' understanding of the phenomena. Further, the design of the microworld made abstractions, such as Cartesian components of displacement and velocity, into concrete observable data objects, and introduced simplifications, such as quantized impulses, that enabled students to learn and make concrete what are normally regarded as abstract and difficult concepts.

Another aspect of the instructional approach that we believe was crucial to its success is the process of reification – students were asked to consider alternative descriptions of what they learned from the computer microworld in the form of a set of laws, and had to evaluate the properties of the various laws. This enabled the students to develop a concept of what it was they were trying to learn, for example rather than learning a set of facts, they were trying to induce a set of laws and learn about the properties of scientific laws. Further, the process of getting students to apply the laws they induced from the microworld to real-world contexts was important both for their understanding of Newtonian mechanics and for their perception of the nature of scientific knowledge. They learned that their laws apply in a wide range of contexts and they gained experience in transferring what they learned in one context (that is, the computer microworld) to another context (that is, particular real-world situation). We conjecture that these formalization and transfer phases of our curriculum are responsible for the ThinkerTools students being able to apply their knowledge to unfamiliar contexts – a result which is rarely obtained in educational research.

■ References

Bobrow D.G. (Ed.) (1985). *Qualitative Reasoning about Physical Systems*. Cambridge, MA: MIT Press.

Caramazza A., McCloskey M. and Green B. (1981). Naive beliefs in 'sophisticated' subjects: Misconceptions about trajectories of objects. *Cognition*, **9**, 117–23.

Clement J. (1982). Students' preconceptions in elementary mechanics. *American Journal of Physics*, **50**, 66-71.

di Sessa A. (1982) Unlearning Aristotelian physics: a study of knowledge-based learning, *Cognitive Science*, **6**(1), 37-75.

Gentner D. and Stevens A. (eds.) (1983). *Mental Models*. Hillsdale, NJ: Lawrence Erlbaum Associates.

Larkin J.H., McDermott J., Simon D.P. and Simon H.A. (1980). Expert and novice performance in solving physics problems. *Science*, **208**, 1335–42.

McCloskey M., Caramazza A and Green B. (1980). Curvilinear motion in the absence of external forces: Naive beliefs about the motion of objects, *Science*, **210**, 1139–41.

McDermott L.C. (1984). Research on conceptual understanding in mechanics. *Physics Today*, **37**, 24–32.

Piaget J. and Garcia R. (1964). *Understanding Causality*. New York: Norton.

Shafer M. and Adey P. (1981). *Towards a Science of Science Teaching*. London, England: Heinemann Educational Books.

Trowbridge D.E. and McDermott L.C. (1981). Investigation of student understanding of the concept of acceleration in one dimension. *American Journal of Physics*, **49**, 242–53.

Viennot L. (1979). Spontaneous reasoning in elementary dynamics. *European Journal of Science Education*, **1**, 205–21.

White B. (1983). Sources of difficulty in understanding Newtonian dynamics. *Cognitive Science*, 7(1), 41–65.

White B. (1984). Designing computer activities to help physics students understand Newton's laws of motion. *Cognition and Instruction*, **1**, 69–108.

White B. and Frederiksen J. (1986a). *Progressions of Qualitative Models as a Foundation for Intelligent Learning Environments*. BBN Laboratories Report No. 6277. Cambridge, MA. (To appear in *Artificial Intelligence*.)

White B. and Frederiksen J. (1986b). Intelligent tutoring systems based upon qualitative model evolutions. In *Proceedings of the Fifth National Conference on Artificial Intelligence*. Philadelphia, PA.

White B. and Horwitz P. (1987). *ThinkerTools: Enabling Children to Understand Physical Laws*. BBN Laboritories report No. 6470. Cambridge, MA. (To appear in *Cognition and Instruction*.)

White B. and Horwitz P. (in preparation). *Multiple Muddles: Novice Reasoning about Force and Motion*.

Paper 1.5

Computers and the Emancipation of Students: Giving Control to the Learner

Diana Laurillard

■ Introduction: models of teaching and learning

Any attempt to clarify the pedagogical principles associated with the design of educational media has to begin with some consideration of an underlying educational model. In this paper I want to consider two possible models for education, which I will label for convenience the 'didactic' model and the 'communication' model, and then use these to analyse the pedagogical principles inherent in the design formats of educational media such as CAL.

The main difference between the two models is in the kind of knowledge with which they are concerned. Within the didactic model subject matter knowledge is what I have termed 'preceptual knowledge'– to distinguish it from the perceptual knowledge we acquire through perception, and from the conceptual knowledge we acquire through social interaction and experience (Laurillard, 1987). 'Preceptual knowledge' is knowledge of precepts, of givens, of what is 'definitely known' in a subject. The dictionary refers to 'preceptive' as 'mandatory, didactic, instructive'. Thus, the student is not learning about the world, as they are in learning about perceptual and conceptual knowledge. In learning perceptual knowledge, they are learning about descriptions of

First published in *Instructional Science* (1987) **16**, 3–18 © Martinus Nijhoff Publishers (Kluwer), Dordrecht. Reprinted by permission of Kluwer Academic Publishers.

the world. They are not learning about what happens when they throw a ball in the air; they are learning about Newtonian mechanics, which is a form of description. Descriptions of the world have been constructed for the student. It follows that the teacher's aim must be to transmit this constructed knowledge to the student. The teacher has control over what is taught, and how.

By contrast, within the communication model knowledge is not a given body of facts and theories, but a 'negotiable commodity between teacher and pupil' (Esland, 1971). It is not regarded as something static and unchanging. There is no such object as a 'precept'. Knowledge is not, therefore, something that can be given from one person to another. The student constructs their own descriptions of the world and the teacher's aim is to facilitate the student's development of their own perspective on the subject. A corollary of this is that students take more responsibility for what they learn and how they learn it. The student is given control over what the content can be, as well as control over their access to and experience of it.

Education as communication is an important and valuable model, but ironically, in the age of communication, it is not an appropriate description of what usually happens in education. As distance learning methods are more widely used, and as, even on the traditional campus, there are more educational media in evidence, so the direct face-to-face communication between teacher and student decreases. The value of the 'communication model' is that it gives greater credence to the student's view of the world, and allows an interaction between the two participants in which it is acknowledged that the student may not be the only one who learns. When teachers play only an indirect and absent role in the teaching process, as they do with educational media, they necessarily relinquish the opportunity for the kind of negotiation that face-to-face communication provides. Does this mean that educational media such as CAL necessarily operate within the didactic model?

As one way of tackling this question, I want to consider the two models of education in terms of three aspects of control, that is, the extent to which a student has control over (a) learning strategy, (b) the manipulation of learning content, and (c) the description of learning content. Learning strategy refers to whether the student can make decisions about the sequencing of content and learning activities. Manipulation of content refers to the way a student experiences the domain being learned, that is, whether or not this is by direct manipulation of it. Description of content refers to whether the student constructs their own perspective of the subject. In a pure didactic model the teacher will control them all; in a pure communication model, the student will control them all. The following three sections discuss the application of these aspects of control to various forms of CAL.

■   Student control of learning strategy

There are two aspects of conventional tutorial program design where it is easy to give control over learning strategy to the student: the sequence of presentation of content, and the sequence of learning activities.

Control over the sequence of content means providing facilities such as

(1)   index of content;

(2)   content map;

(3)   escape at any time to index or map;

(4)   skip forward or back a chosen amount;

(5)   retrace chosen route through the material.

These are conceptually straightforward facilities for a programmer to provide, although they require careful planning and some storage space. Unfortunately they are still rare, as many designers prefer to dictate the optimal route through the material, and allow no deviation from it, as though students were incapable of deciding which section of the content they needed to study at a particular time. It is worth remembering that the primitive technology of a book provides all of the above facilities, and we are still a long way from making CAL as easy to study from as a book.

Nonetheless, students' ability to cope with this degree of freedom has been questioned, and some studies gave credence to it (Fry, 1972), suggesting that it led to insufficient learning, while others (Hartley, 1981) showed that under the right conditions, learner control is more effective than program control. This issue was further investigated in a more recent study of students learning from an interactive video cassette program. They were given complete freedom to decide how to work through the nine sections of material. Of the above facilities, only (1), (3) and (4) were provided. Even so, the freedom this gave meant that students were able to exhibit a wide range of routes through the same material. Some began by looking at what they already knew, others by looking at the most unfamiliar topics. Some worked through systematically, others left an exercise to look at another section, and then returned to the first exercise ... it was clear that the imposition of a program designer's 'optimal' route would have seriously constrained the students' own optimal routes (Laurillard, 1984).

The second aspect of control of strategy concerns learning activities, that is, control over when and whether to:

(1)   see examples;

(2)   do exercises;

(3) receive information;

(4) consult glossary;

(5) ask for explanation;

(6) take test.

Again, this kind of control is conceptually easy for a program designer to provide. It requires only standard programming techniques, with careful organization of the program structure. In the study referred to above, student control over (2), (3) and (6) was also provided, with the result that, again, a wide range of strategies was exhibited. Some students began with the test, then studied those exercises where they had done badly. Others began with relevant information on a topic, then practised the exercises, and only later took the test (ibid.).

There is no well-established reason to suppose that a program designer, whether teacher, researcher, or programmer, knows better than the student how they should learn. Therefore when we are designing materials for a medium that is capable of providing an unusual degree of individualization via student control, it seems perverse not to take advantage of it, and allow students to control both the sequence of content and their learning activities. Moreover, this is an improvement that is easily incorporated even into conventional tutorial designs, that requires none of the sophisticated techniques of intelligent tutorials, and that makes all forms of CAL much less forcefully didactic than they normally are.

■ Control of content manipulation

Student control of learning strategy is relatively easy to implement, and requires only intention and commitment on the part of the program designers. But this is not the most critical aspect of control. More important, and more difficult to implement, is the student's control over the manipulation of the subject matter.

What are we trying to get the computer to get the student to do, in designing a teaching program? We need some model of the optimal learning situation to emulate. The one-to-one tutorial is not appropriate for a medium where the teacher is necessarily absent. The focus is not going to be student–teacher, but student–subject. A paradigmatic learning situation that could act as a model for this is Popperian scientific method (Popper, 1963). As the scientist learns about the real world, so the student learns about the world modelled by the computer. To what extent real students are capable of acting like the ideal scientists we want to emulate is an arresting question, but let us remain in the realm of the ideal for a while.

Progress in scientific knowledge occurs, if we assume a Popperian account, when the scientist erects an hypothesis, tests it, and obtains a confirmation or disconfirmation. Each stage involves intricate reasoning about the domain and the relationships between its parts; the hypothesis must be meaningful and testable, the experiment must test the hypothesis and contain no irrelevant artefactual effects, the data must be interpreted in terms of the hypothesis, and so on. The scientist needs the real world in which to set up the experiment, and nature does the work of confirming or disconfirming the hypothesis. By analogy, the student can develop personal knowledge by erecting hypotheses which are testable in the simulated world of the computer program, with the computer model doing the work of confirming or disconfirming the student's hypotheses.

A computer program that supported an environment of this type would allow the student to manipulate the objects in the domain, and obtain feedback about the behaviour of the system in terms of the results of their manipulations.

Given these considerations, it follows that some of the pedagogically desirable features a CAL program should have are the following:

(1)   The student should have direct access to the object domain – the object domain is an algorithmic description of how the domain behaves, such as a mathematical model of a physical system.

(2)   The program should have operational knowledge of the domain, that is, it should be able to carry out any manipulations the student requests.

(3)   The program should be able to give intrinsic feedback – intrinsic feedback refers to results of the student's operations in terms of the system's behaviour, that is, the program can operationalize the match to the present goal.

(4)   The program should make the goals of the exercise explicit – these goals may be defined either by the student or by the program.

If these define a desirable learning environment, how far do the standard forms of CAL program live up to them?

Consider the following extract from a conventional tutorial on NMR (nuclear magnetic resonance) spectra, in which, as in later examples, student input is underlined (Morris and Archer, 1977):

> What group (or type) of protons is responsible for the signal at 14.1 delta?
>
> 2 COOH
>
> Correct. COOH would explain the low field proton(s).

This leaves: 4 C 8 H to be accounted for.

What group (or type) of protons is responsible for the signal at 1.23 delta?

CH$_3$

You are on the right lines. However, this arrangement would not account for 6 protons.

Please reconsider your answer and try again.

If we interpret the four features listed above in terms of this tutorial, we find:

(1) The student has no direct access to the object domain – they cannot choose to carry out operations on the domain, such as building a molecule. They may only answer the questions posed.

(2) Knowledge of the domain is encoded explicitly in program statements – the explanatory statements are a series of PRINT statements with variables (or expressions) evaluated by referring to DATA statements for the particular problem, that is, they put values into a template, they are not logically or semantically interconnected as they would be in a model of the domain.

(3) Feedback is extrinsic – it is an evaluative comment on the match between the student's input and the goal, as in 'Correct', and 'You are on the right lines'. It may appear to be intrinsic, as in 'would not account for 6 protons', but this statement relies on the programmer having predicted this mistake, and having explicitly programmed this form of response, with the '6' being evaluated from the data on the problem. Feedback that is apparently intrinsic would probably be sufficient from the student's point of view, except that it is always limited to the expected inputs; it cannot be available for the unexpected inputs the student might make.

(4) There are no explicit goals – the student has no choice but to follow the route chosen by the program, and the program goals remain implicit in the dialogue, namely to get the student to give correct answers to its questions.

Teaching programs of this type can be very effective when the likely student errors are well understood, and when the teaching strategy is known to be successful for what it is attempting to achieve – in this case a practised familiarity with the solution procedure for NMR spectra. There is no sense in which the student has control over the manipulation of the content, however.

Compare the format of that conventional tutorial with an intelligent tutorial on the same topic (O'Shea & Self, 1983):

' ... Choose appropriate groups from those remaining.

Join O corresponding to peak (0,0)

No

Explain

We will now attempt to build such a molecule.

No peaks left in the spectra. Spectrum of molecule is

$((3,2)(2,5)(2,4)(2,2)(0,0)(2,3)(3,2))$.

Molecule built was $CH_3CH_2CH_2CH_2OCH_2CH_3$.

Spectra still to be explained is nil.

Remaining molecular formula C.

Search was unsuccessful.

Join CO corresponding to peak (0,0)

Correct.'

In this case the interpretation of the four features is as follows:

(1) The student has access to the object domain – via instructions to the program, as in 'Join O corresponding to peak (0,0)', and through this operates directly on the object domain.

(2) The program has both operational and descriptive knowledge of the domain – it can carry out operations such as attempting to build a molecule, and can describe what it does in doing so.

(3) Feedback is both intrinsic and extrinsic – as in 'Search was unsuccessful', and 'Correct'.

(4) The program can support both program goals and student goals – this style of 'mixed-initiative' dialogue allows the program to state explicit goals such as 'Choose appropriate groups', and also allows the student to interrupt with a request of their own, such as 'Explain'.

Thus the intelligent tutorial conforms to all the pedagogical conditions defined for it, and therefore allows the student total control over the manipulation of content.

Now consider the format of a simulation program. A simulation program contains the following elements:

(1) A model of the domain.

(2) Options to select program-defined goals.

(3)   Options to select operations on the domain.

(4)   Results of these operations displayed in relation to the goal.

Figures 1 to 3 illustrate a simple version of this type of program. The objective is for the student to understand the concept of the period of a waveform. As this example shows, the simulation mode does not apply only to large-scale systems or experiments, but can also be used for concept acquisition. The program provides a goal for the student, who uses their conception of 'period' to generate an hypothesis about how to attain that goal. They then test it out and the feedback the program gives shows the result of that input and its relation to the goal, thus giving the student information about the behaviour of the model and suggesting how they might modify their hypothesis. By the end of the series of interactions, it should be possible for the student to have established the correct relationships, and acquired the intended conception. To show how this might happen, a continuation of the program is sketched in Figure 4, where, for each frame, I have suggested the kind of reasoning process such a program could engender in a student who was unfamiliar with the concept of 'period'.

If we interpret the pedagogical features defined above for this program in comparison with the intelligent tutorial, we find that:

(1)   The student does have access to the object domain, but only through program-defined commands, not through natural language descriptions of the operations to be carried out.

(2)   The program's knowledge of the object domain is confined to operations on it, in the sense that it possesses an algorithmic description of its behaviour for given input, but has no alternative descriptions of its behaviour.

(3)   The feedback it gives is intrinsic in the sense that it shows the results of the student's input in terms of the resultant behaviour of the system. Any extrinsic feedback it provides has to be explicitly programmed, as it is for the conventional tutorial.

(4)   The program provides explicit program goals, in the form of options to change a variable, but cannot support student goals or a mixed-initiative dialogue – all student choices have to be handled via menus of predefined options.

The advantage of this kind of goal-oriented manipulation is that it gives the student direct access to and control over the critical relationships and mechanisms in the domain. It allows the student to come close to what it means to 'act like a scientist'. The hypotheses that are posited by the student in the course of the program are simple, each one is meaningful to them at the time, and each one is testable. Moreover, the

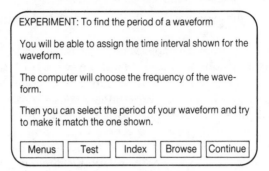

Figure 1   Simulation program introduction

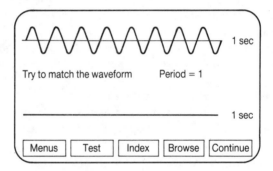

Figure 2   Simulation program: student chooses period of 1 sec

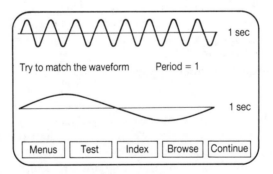

Figure 3   Result of student's input is displayed

Student input for period and interval	Computer output	Student response
11		That gives fewer curves. So to get more curves I must make the period less than 1. Try 1/2.
12		It's in the right direction, but should be smaller still. Try 1/4.
1/4		So 1/2 gives 2 curves, 1/4 gives 4 curves. So 1/11 should give 11 curves.
1/11		That's now correct. Try another exercise with a 2 sec interval
2 sec		This time it has 6 curves.
1/6		Why doesn't it work this time? The time interval is 2. I need fewer curves, so make the period larger.
1/3		OK, so now if I choose a time interval of 100...
100 sec		The period should be the time interval divided by the number of curves, so the period is 10.
10		That's correct. So the period is the length of one curve (cycle).

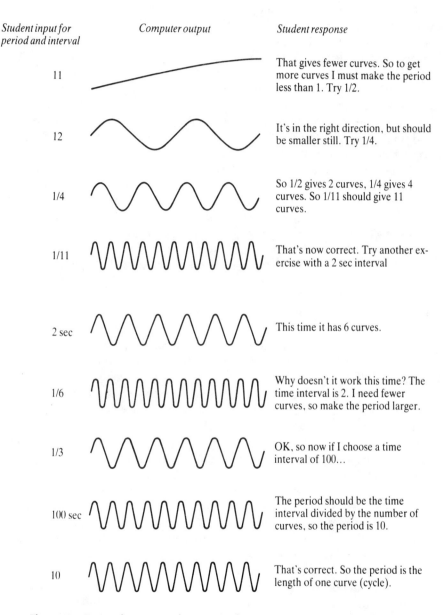

Figure 4   Trace of an extract from a simulation program with putative dialogue.

feedback is meaningful. It is interpretable in terms of both their original hypothesis, and the goal they are aiming for. In each case, the feedback gives them information which helps them get closer to the goal, but without telling them how. It forces them to reason about the relationships involved. That is what makes intrinsic feedback preferable to the purely extrinsic form.

Whether the students actually carry out such a logical analysis of the results is an empirical question. The design of the simulation is based on Popperian scientific method, but Popper described the logic of scientific discovery, not the history of it. The fact that scientists do not, and even cannot, follow Popper's procedure has been persuasively argued, for example, by Feyerabend (1970), and we must assume that students are likely to exhibit all the irrational expediencies that real scientists are subject to. Simulations are a good model of the optimal learning situation, therefore, but this does not guarantee that they will always use this opportunity to its fullest advantage. The extent to which they do will depend, as Feyerabend would argue for scientists, on the context within which they are operating.

There are three ways in which the simulation is a pedagogical advance on the conventional tutorial form: (a) it gives the student direct access to the domain model, rather than mediating this through dialogue; (b) because of this, the explanations are implicit in the behaviour of the model, giving the student experience of its behaviour, rather than being articulated through a verbal description, which only tells about the behaviour; and (c) the student has complete control over the solution path.

The simulation mode is a compromise between the conventional and the intelligent tutorial systems. It is clearly a pedagogical improvement on the former; it is clearly not as helpful as the latter, principally because its only form of feedback is intrinsic, so that the student has to determine purely from the behaviour of the system what they should do next, and they have no help in interpreting the meaning of its behaviour, although it is to be expected that students will often need such help. In terms of student control of operations on the domain it is a good match for the intelligent tutorial. In terms of student demands for help, it cannot cope as well as the intelligent tutorial, because it possesses no descriptive knowledge of the domain.

As with both tutorial forms, it is still essential for the simulation designer to define the expected categories of error, as these are what determine the 'experiments' to be made available to the student. Not all experiments will decide between the model answer and the student's misconception in the way that the example above does. The experiment has to be (Popper's phrase) the 'crucial experiment'. For the program designer to be able to define which experiments should be included, they need to know both the model answer, and the predicted categories of errors, each one of which may require a different crucial experiment to help the student pinpoint the flaw in their own conception. For example, the designer only knows that the 'period' program will work if they know that students might have that particular misconception, that is, that the period is the length of the waveform shown. The crucial experiment is important because it occupies a unique position, arbitrating between the model answer and the misconception (between theory A and theory B). Its outcome should be capable of demonstrating that one is confirmed and the other disconfirmed. The importance to the student is that it not only shows that their conception was wrong, it also gives them a new fact to be explained, a cognitive motivation to change their way of thinking about the phenomenon. And because of the unique nature of the crucial experiment, the new fact to be explained will require the postulation of the correct conception. This is similar to the process di Sessa has called 'genetic task analysis', the process of 'finding or imagining the essential phenomena that may conspire to produce an understanding of the subject' (di Sessa, 1986) [...]

Simulation programs cannot support student goals, and cannot provide advice, but they serve two other very important pedagogical features that conventional tutorials cannot: they can give the student direct access to the behaviour of the object domain, and they can give intrinsic feedback on their experiments within it. This is the kind of experience a student needs if they are to develop their own conceptual understanding of a domain, because it gives them direct contact with the environment they are trying to understand, be it the domain of numbers, or waveforms or theories about societies. If they have already developed inappropriate conceptual constructs, then they need experiences of the behaviour of those domains that allow them to see that their conception is inappropriate, which is far more powerful than telling them that it is wrong. If we can provide students with this kind of control over their interaction with the subject matter, that will be a considerable advance beyond the tedious and unimaginative programs that abound in conventional CAL at the moment.

The intelligent tutorial program provides control over both strategy and manipulation of content, but is an improvement on both conventional tutorials and simulations because it can support student-defined goals and requests for help with much greater flexibility.

■ Control of domain description

With all these forms we are still operating within the didactic model of teaching, however. The goal is still conceptual change in a particular direction, to assist the student to learn the 'givens' of their subject, the 'precepts'. By virtue of the fact that the program is supplying a model of an environment, it is embodying the fixed and immutable givens of that domain. It is therefore not supporting the pure communication model, where the teacher's role is to facilitate the student's development of their own perspective on the subject, rather than to give them the received knowledge. But human teachers find this hard enough; could we expect computers to do it?

Given the epistemological framework of the communication model, the computer's role has to be very different from its role within the didactic model. In the latter, as surrogate teacher, it has to be capable of either dialogue about the domain (tutorial mode), or operations on the domain (simulation mode), or both (intelligent tutorial), in order that the student learns the behaviour of that domain, as modelled. The definition of the teacher's role within the communication model means that, as surrogate teacher, the computer has to support the student's own description of the domain. The theoretical framework that best encompasses this idea is conversation theory (Pask, 1976), within which students can develop their own knowledge representation explicitly by acting as an author, and can compare and contrast it with that of the teacher's both through computer-mediated dialogue about their respective representations, and through models of them represented as simulations. Thus the teaching program embodies no pedagogic theory beyond that implicit in its structure as a 'conversation' between two individuals.

An intelligent tutorial program is similar to this except it is usually less democratically organized, because the system embodies a teaching strategy whose job it is to direct the student towards purposeful behaviour if the monitoring of their inputs suggests that they need help. Pask's 'CASTE' system (Pask, 1973) also takes a more didactic line of this sort, not allowing the student to attempt goals for which they have not already mastered the prerequisites. However, the basic design of the underlying theoretical framework of Conversation Theory gives equal status to teacher and student goals. The superimposed teaching strategy is optional.

The Conversation Theory framework gives a more democratic teaching program than most, because it can support total student control over the development of their knowledge domain, over consultation with the teacher, over their learning strategy, and over their manipulation of the knowledge in terms of testing its application in the object domain. But to support a pure communication model of the teaching process the student must have control over the object domain against which their representation is tested, which, this being a computer, is itself a theoretical construct, a set of precepts about the world, rather than the real world itself. In so far as the program's object domain is arbitrating between two knowledge representations, the teacher's and the student's, it will always have an in-built preference for its author's, whoever that is.

It is, therefore, never possible for a computer teaching program, no matter how democratic it is, to support the pure communication model of teaching just as it is not possible to achieve equal status between teacher and student. The face-to-face tutorial can, because here the world is the final arbiter. Within a computer teaching program, the final arbiter always has to be someone's theoretical construct.

The only way a computer program can support the student's control of the description of the domain is by allowing the student to act as program author, but that gives the teacher lower status than the student in negotiating knowledge. This is the approach taken, in part, by those who advocate 'microworlds', computer simulations that students can construct for themselves in order to manipulate and explore the behaviour of that world (Papert, 1980, pp. 120–34). The idea of microworlds is a powerful and attractive idea because it is designed to bring all the heuristics of learning about the world, so successfully mastered by all of us, to bear on the learning of the teacher's particular microworld, typically mastered by so few – the usual example is Newtonian physics. Papert's is a liberal approach, certainly within the communication model, that allows students to create Aristotelian micro-worlds (the child's personal beliefs about motion are ' ... in many ways closer to Aristotle's than to Newton's', ibid., p. 123) on the grounds that ' ... by trying many different laws of motion, children will find that the Newtonian ones are indeed the most economical and elegant for moving objects around' (ibid., p. 129). However, the Scholastics were not complete fools, and spent some time being perfectly able to describe the world in Aristotelian terms without having to invent Newton's conception of force. Why should students do any better? Perhaps they will have the advantage of being advised that a Newtonian microworld is available for them to try out – but why should it be preferred? How will they discover that it is 'most economical and elegant'? They need the kind of evidence that convinces physicists that Newton's conception of force is preferable to the more intuitive Aristotelian idea that force is the cause of continued motion (see, Crombie, 1959, pp. 61–4). But the reasons are quite subtle, and may well not be discovered by students, and are certainly never covered in modern physics textbooks, no doubt because of their philosophical complexity. The classic problems with the Aristotelian conception, discussed by Aristotle himself, concern instantaneous velocity, initial velocity and acceleration in freely falling bodies. It requires a crucial experiment (or in this case, a 'thought experiment') to decide between the two: such as Aristotle's own admission that while velocity is proportional to force/mass, this formulation breaks down in the case of a man trying to move a ship (Hope, 1961, p. 142). That is the kind of essential phenomenon that will produce understanding of the importance of the Newtonian idea of force, but students will have to be led to it – they will not discover it.

What computers offer is not a specialized environment 'more flexible and precise in crafting experiences that lead to essential insights' (di Sessa, 1986, p. 224). They have to be more didactic than this implies, and a lot less flexible. The pedagogic challenge has to be the same as it is for all didactic learning – to discover empirically the forms of misconception, and to deduce logically the forms of crucial experiment that will motivate a change in conception to the preferred form. Computers offer an individualized teaching program (assuming that the misconceptions can be reliably diagnosed) and a learning activity that is genuinely active in the sense that the student can control the experiments on offer. But if we allow the student to design those experiments, as Papert and di Sessa seem to allow, they are never likely to hit on the crucial experiments they need to enable them to choose the right form of conception. These have to be provided, and the students have to work through them in order to experience the necessity of changing their original conception. Thus the program becomes relatively didactic in character, and flexible only in the sense that students can have control over strategy and manipulation of the content within the experiments provided. If we allow the student to be the author, there is little hope that they will learn Newtonian physics. It is in the nature of the communication model that you cannot control what students will learn. What they do learn from Papert's microworld may be something much more important, such as the idea that facts and theories are interdependent, or that they too can be physicists; and that is what makes the communication model pedagogically valuable. But if you want them to learn some specific perceptual knowledge, then the more didactic mode, making use of devices such as the crucial experiment, will be unavoidable.

Both Pask and Papert have envisaged ways in which students may control the description of the domain they manipulate, but as the student becomes tutor, so the status of the teacher is necessarily diminished, and the essential communicative aspect of the communication model is lost. Where computers are used to facilitate communication between students and teachers, for example, in a computer network, then perhaps they can be said to support a communication model. But CAL aspires to make the computer the teacher, not a mere communication tool.

■ Conclusions

To summarize: the pure didactic model of teaching and learning allows the student no control over learning strategy, nor content manipulation, nor description of the domain; these are the teacher's responsibility. The pure communication model gives more responsibility to the student and allows them to control all of these aspects of the learning situation. The three principal forms of CAL discussed here are the conventional tutorial, the simulation and the intelligent tutorial. Of these, all are capable of allowing the student considerable control over their learning strategy; both the simulation and the intelligent tutorial can support student manipulation of the content domain; the intelligent tutorial is more flexible in its responses to the student than the other two.

I have argued that student control over learning strategy is relatively easy to provide. The simulation format is well understood in training applications, but as a teaching program for conceptual change it is not so straightforward. The development of this kind of program requires research into the common student misconceptions in the topic concerned, and the derivation of the crucial experiments necessary to help students decide between their conception and the received knowledge. The style is preceptual, the students are learning the 'givens', but the design of the teaching strategy will be more scientific, and is likely to be more effective, if it incorporates this analysis of the relation between what a student knows and what they need to know. The analysis requires no special techniques beyond those already practised by educational researchers of the phenomenographic school (see Marton *et al.*, 1984), namely the empirical derivation of categories of description of students' conceptions. The derivation of the crucial experiment requires the kind of logical analysis that every practising scientist has to learn.

The conceptual problems with this approach are surmountable, and are achievable now. There is no need to wait for AI (artificial intelligence) techniques to bear fruit before CAL can be pedagogically respectable. The teaching philosophy implicit in this still has to be accepted, however: that students can, and should be enabled to 'act like scientists', but within a simulated world, rather than the real world.

The point of trying to emancipate students from the conventional program-controlled tutorial is that educational research is not in a position to define the kind of deterministic model of teaching that computers as purely didactic tutors require. Students are still likely to be better than teachers at directing their learning. Therefore we should be harnessing the power of the computer to provide a closer approximation to the communication model. That means giving them maximum control over learning strategy and manipulation of content. We cannot aspire to the pure communication model because of the limitations of the medium, but CAL can be significantly less didactic than it has been so far.

■ Note

1. Throughout this paper, I use 'they', 'their', 'them', for the third person singular as it seems to me the only reasonable solution to the absence of a non-sexist third person singular pronoun. The practice is given grudging approval by

the Shorter Oxford: 'used instead of "his or her" when the gender is inclusive or uncertain (regarded as ungrammatical)', supported by quotations from such eminent persons as Thackeray, 'A person can't help their birth', and Shaw 'It's enough to drive anyone out of their senses'.

■ References

Crombie, A.C. (1959). *Augustine to Galileo* 2. Harmondsworth: Penguin.

di Sessa, A. (1986) Artificial worlds and real experiences. *Instructional Science*, **14**, 207-227.

Esland, G.M. (1971). Teaching and learning as the organization of knowledge, in M.F.D. Young, *Knowledge and Control*, Collier-Macmillan.

Feyeraband, P. (1970). Against Method. *Minnesota Studies in the Philosophy of Science*, 4.

Fry, J.P. (1972). Interactive relationship between inquisitiveness and student control of instruction. *Journal of Educational Psychology*, **63**, 459-465.

Hartley, J.R. (1981). Learner initiatives in computer assisted learning, in J. Howe (ed), *Microcomputers in Secondary Education*. London: Kogan Page.

Hope, R. (1961). *Aristotle's Physics*. University of Nebraska Press.

Laurillard, D.M. (1984). Interactive video and the control of learning. *Educational Technology*, **23**, 7-15.

Laurillard, D.M. (1987). The different forms of learning in psychology and education, in J. Richardson, M. Eysenck & D. Warren Piper (eds), *Student Learning*. Guildford: SRHE.

Marton, F., Hounsell, D. & Entwistle, N. (1984). *The Experience of Learning*. Edinburgh: Scottish Academic Press.

Morris, H. & Archer, D. (1977). *The interpretation of NMR spectra*. CALCHEM, Department of Physical Chemistry, University of Leeds.

O'Shea, T. & Self, J. (1983). *Learning and Teaching with Computers*. Brighton: Harvester Press.

Papert, S. (1980). *Mindstorms: children, computers and powerful ideas*. Brighton: Harvester Press.

Pask, G. (1973). CASTE: A system for exhibiting learning strategies and regulating uncertainties. *International Journal of Man-Machine Studies*, **5**, 17-52.

Pask, G. (1976). Conversational techniques in the study and practice of education. *British Journal of Educational Psychology*, **46**, 12-25.

Popper, K.R. (1963). *Conjectures and Refutations*. London: Routledge & Kegan Paul.

Paper 1.6

Girls, Boys and Computers

Lorraine Culley

Despite tight educational budgets, the number of microcomputers in British schools has increased dramatically over the last five years, aided by two schemes funded by the DES and the Department of Industry. A recent survey carried out by the Department of Education and Science showed that virtually every secondary school has at least one micro-computer, with an average of 13.4 computers per school. Most schools now present pupils with some element of 'computer awareness' and many offer examination courses. According to the DES survey 20% of headteachers said that micros had made a significant contribution to teaching in their schools (DES, 1986). Entries for computer studies GCE 'O' level and CSE exams have risen sharply from nearly 7000 in 1974 to nearly 121 000 in the summer of 1985.

Many commentators have stressed the importance of teachers gaining the technical expertise necessary to use the hardware made available under government backed schemes and to develop interests and skills in their pupils. There is, however, also a need for an awareness of the possibility of gender inequalities in the computer classroom. Schools and teachers need to develop strategies to ensure that girls participate more fully in opportunities available to them to acquire skills in computing.

In 1985 girls were approximately 30% of total candidates in computer studies 'O' level and 18% of 'A' level computer science candidates (a fall from 21% in 1984). While this degree of gender differentiation is not as marked as in some other subjects the imbalance

Reprinted by permission of L.A. Culley. Originally published in *Educational Studies* (1987) **14**(1), 3–8, Carfax Publishing Company, Abingdon.

between males and females is significant and has caused concern in several quarters. There are general educational arguments for both girls and boys to receive a 'balanced' curriculum in our schools and it is felt by most educationalists that neither sex should be excluded from important areas of knowledge. This has been clearly and forcefully argued in the case of scientific knowledge by HMI (1980) and it is no less important with respect to the new and fast growing area of new technology.

My research into sex differences in the take-up of computing opportunities in secondary schools has highlighted some of the ways in which computing may become defined as an activity more appropriate to the masculine gender than the feminine gender. In assessing the extent and nature of gender differences in participation in computing courses, the research examined in detail the organization of computing in eight secondary schools in three LEAs. It examined the staffing of computing courses; the location of computing facilities; the use of computers across the curriculum; options schemes and careers guidance; classroom interactions and the views of computer studies teachers on gender differences (Culley, 1986). The research explored the reasons why male and female pupils chose to take or not to take computer studies examination options and examined the career aspirations of 974 fourth and fifth year pupils. Further information was obtained on some of these issues from a larger number of schools (238) who responded to a postal questionnaire.

The study examined the differential access of male and female pupils to computers both in the school and at home. In most schools fewer girls than boys participate in optional computer activities such as computer clubs, where girls were less than 10% of regular attenders. Computer rooms in most schools were regarded as male territory and girls reported being made to feel very uncomfortable by the attitudes and behaviour of boys. Several schools had recognized this problem and responded by establishing certain times as 'girls only'. Such schemes were only partly successful, however. The tendency was for the open sessions to become effectively the *boys'* sessions and thus reduce even further the access of girls to computers. In one school the 'open' sessions were overseen by a male computer teacher, while the girls-only session was staffed by a female who had no computing expertise.

The research identified several aspects of the *organization* of computing in secondary schools which often make computer-related activities less attractive to girls. Important in this respect is the perceived link between computing and mathematics. There is research evidence to suggest that boys show a greater liking for mathematics than girls and are more confident in their mathematical ability (Cockcroft Report, 1982). The manner in which computers have been introduced into most schools has tended to link computing with mathematics. The majority of teachers of computer studies in the schools visited were also teaching mathematics as part of their timetable, despite the fact that in most cases separate departments of computer studies or computer education had been formally established. In the schools replying to the postal questionnaire, responsibility for computing was allocated to computer studies departments in 39% of cases and allocated to mathematics departments in 37% of cases. The siting of computers also tends to emphasize a link between computing and mathematics or science. In the majority of schools the computers were housed in the mathematics or science areas of the school. However, these were not the only ways in which computers were linked with mathematics. Possibly even more important was the fact that in the majority of cases the mathematical background of teachers of computing came across quite strongly in the content of the courses they were teaching. In several schools the computer awareness courses presented to children reflected the mathematical interest and expertise of their teachers. Computer games and other programs devised by teachers to demonstrate the capacities of computers were very often based on mathematical concepts, processes and examples. Word games, word processing and graphic design applications were much less commonly used.

Computers are not only linked with mathematics, they are also closely associated with men. The vast majority of teachers of computing are male. Not only are specialist computer studies teachers much more likely to be male than female but so are the teachers of other subjects using computers as a learning tool. In the schools responding to the postal questionnaire over 70% of teachers using computers in their teaching were male. To some extent this reflects the fact that the most common users of computers are science and mathematics departments, both often having a majority of male teachers. An association between computers and men is also enhanced by the content of commonly used school textbooks. One analysis of textbooks for computer studies shows a consistent sexist flavour to such books. Women are seen handling input/output media or as 'operators' while men make decisions. A typical photograph shows a woman typing in data with a man leaning over her in a supervisory role. Most computer personnel are referred to as 'he'. When females are referred to they are invariably 'girls' (EOC, 1983).

As many other researchers have argued, pupils' perceptions of subjects, and their behaviour in relation to them, are an effect of wider social forces as well as the organization of schooling. The career aspirations of pupils are significant influences on subject choice and the evidence from this study is that very few girls are attracted to careers in computing. The research found that the career aspirations of pupils were very highly differentiated according to gender and that careers in computing played very little part in girls' hopes for their future occupational roles. Working with computers was a significant aspiration for a high proportion of boys, however. Careers material on jobs in computing produced for schools often portrays a gender differentiation of tasks along stereotyped lines. In most of the schools studied careers guidance proper did not begin until the fourth year, after subject option choices have been made. The schools varied in terms of how they organized the choice of optional subjects in year three. Where subjects were grouped to form blocks of mutually exclusive subjects, option schemes tended to require pupils to choose between computer studies and subjects which are traditionally popular with girls such as typing, history, geography and modern languages.

The marketing of the home microcomputer as a machine for men and boys is a significant factor in the process of sex-typing of computing. Boys have much greater access to home computers than girls. Of the 974 fourth and fifth year pupils surveyed, 383 had a computer at home. Only 107 of these were girls. Very few of these girls (14%) reported that the computer had actually been bought for the girl herself whereas 85% of the boys with a home computer said that it had been bought for themselves or another male member of the household. The research has shown that most home computers are used solely for playing games and many girls and women are not interested in this kind of activity. It has also shown that while many fathers use home computers, very few mothers use them.

The fact that computers are used at home for particular purposes by particular members of families, has consequences for the way in which many girls and boys approach computers in school. Girls are less familiar with computers than boys and consequently they feel less confident in handling them at school, at least initially. Because of the uses to which home computers are generally put, many girls do not see computing as having much to do with their interests. Boys themselves tend to assume a lack of interest, knowledge and competence on the part of girls. Boys are able, through their greater familiarity with computers and their general physical and social power, to secure for themselves a greater share of resources and teacher attention than girls.

Most teachers make no effort to accommodate girls' interests in devising curriculum materials. Classroom observations showed that very little effort was made to counteract the tendency of boys to dominate lessons. The research included observations of 25 individual classes of pupils taking exam courses in computing and 17 computer awareness or appreciation classes. In the discussion part of lessons boys dominated the lesson, consistently asking more questions of the teacher and making more comments on the content of the lesson. Girls were also marginal to the classes in a physical sense, often seated in groups at the back or sides of the room. In the practical part of lessons boys would typically acquire the newest computers, those with disk drives and *colour* monitors. Often girls would be elbowed out of the way and left standing in the rush, without access to a computer at all.

The interviews with teachers of computer studies, revealed that teachers saw boys as more noisy and demanding than girls. Boys were not always sufficiently motivated towards written presentation of work but they were frequently regarded as more interested in computing, and more rewarding to teach than girls. Even when girls did all that was necessary, followed instructions carefully and presented their work well, they were still seen by some teachers as less interested and as having less 'flair' for computing. Some teachers clearly had a 'hobby' interest in programming similar to that of their male pupils.

It is common for teachers and other educationalists to play down the importance of processes within the school in determining the attitudes of children generally, and the existence of sex stereotyping in particular. Several teachers and headteachers interviewed during the research sought to explain gender differentiation in school subject choices by reference to social assumptions and processes which were seen as having their origin outside school in family socialization, media images and so on. There is, it was implied, little that schools can do against the power of such outside influences. It is not suggested, here, that the practices of schools and teachers are the only factors involved in gender differences in schools in general and the sex-typing of computing as a 'masculine activity' in particular. They are, however, of some significance. Schools are part of 'society', what goes on in school interacts with 'outside' forces and is itself part of the creation of social relations, attitudes and assumptions.

The relevance of the attitudes, approaches and curricula of schools in relation to girls and computing is further illustrated by the experiences of pupils in girls-only schools. Two of the schools visited were single sex girls' schools and the evidence from this research suggests that in such schools there is no shortage of enthusiasm for computing. Computer studies was a popular option and computer clubs thrived. A similar level of interest and a high level of participation in computing activities was reported from the girls' schools in the postal survey. Since outside social influences are unlikely to be radically different for girls attending single-sex schools, the processes involved in the organization of teaching with and about computers in a coeducational setting must be significant.

■ Recommendations for action

The most favourable circumstances for change in gender divisions in school computing are likely to exist where approaches to computing are underpinned by a 'whole school policy' on equal opportunities, coordinated by the headteacher and senior members of staff and supported by teachers and parents. In the context of such a policy, specific strategies relating to the use of computers within secondary schools should include the following.

(1) Schools should monitor gender differences in participation and performance in computing courses.

(2) Schools should examine option schemes to ensure that it is not made especially difficult for girls to take computer studies.

(3) Schools should consider ways of breaking the link between mathematics and computing. This might involve consideration of the distribution of teaching responsibilities as well as the physical location of computer facilities.

(4) Mathematical and technical bias should be eliminated from computer awareness courses by more careful and balanced choice of course material. Teachers should consider what aspects of work with computers appeal to girls and make efforts to represent these more fully in computer awareness and computer studies classes. Published materials should be checked for sexist bias.

(5) Careers guidance and careers literature should be carefully examined for sexism. Dissatisfaction with careers material should be expressed to those responsible for publication. Care should be taken in the way that careers in computing are presented in careers lessons and at careers conventions.

(6) Schools should encourage more use of computers across the curriculum and especially in subject areas where there are many female teachers. Female staff should be especially encouraged and assisted to take in-service training in the use of computers.

(7) All initial teacher training courses and in-service courses in school computing should include discussion of the complex and often subtle processes of gender differentiation. Particular emphasis should be placed on examining the tendency of boys to dominate computing lessons and on the development of teaching strategies to overcome this problem.

(8) All computer clubs should be supervised by staff at all times. Girls-only sessions should be available, well publicized and attended by staff competent in computing.

(9) Schools should give consideration to 'positive action' in the form of single-sex classes in computing. This is a sensitive issue both for teachers and for pupils but some schools may wish to consider experimenting with single-sex classes. It is important to consider the content of lessons and the style of teaching as well as the sex structure of classes.

(10)   Teachers need to develop an awareness of the ways in which boys come to dominate lessons. Having a colleague observe the patterns of interaction in their class could prove a fruitful cooperative exercise. Teachers need to develop sensitive strategies to involve girls more centrally in classroom discussion. They need take more positive steps to ensure equality of access to discussion and to facilities.

■ References

Cockcroft Report (1982) *Mathematics Counts* (London, HMSO).

Culley, L.A. (1986) *Gender Differences and Computing in Secondary Schools* (Loughborough, Dept of Education, Loughborough University of Technology).

DES (1986) *Statistical Bulletin* 18/86 (London, HMSO).

Equal Opportunities Commission (1983) *Information Technology in Schools* (Manchester, EOC).

HMI (1980) *Girls and Science* (London, HMSO).

Paper 1.7

Software for Schools: British Reviews in the Late 1980s

David Hawkridge

■ Introduction

'So you'd like to know what's the best software to use in your school! That's a good question. Well, we find HATS is excellent. Marvellous colour graphics and the kids love it. Oh, sorry, you say it isn't being marketed any more, the supplier went bust. But you might be able to find a copy.'

'Er, no, I don't know anywhere you could go, not round here, where you could look at all the geography programs for 11-year-olds. London, maybe? But most of them are no good anyway, I'm told. Have you seen the Apple catalogue – oh, you have BBCs.'

'Perhaps you'd better tell me what you want it for, then I'll see if I can help – sorry, the line's crackling. You say you're just interested in seeing what there is for use with the National Curriculum in Design and Technology. How much time have you got? No, time, not money. Time to look at everything.'

These imaginary telephone conversations give the flavour of problems facing anyone who wants to find good quality educational software, whether for use at school or at home. People know what works for *them*, but may judge it on criteria you don't accept, or their favourites may no longer be available. There is no place you can go to for a comprehensive overview, but if there were, the task of searching for a program that satisfies your needs (assuming you know what these are) and meets your criteria (yes, assuming you know those too), is daunting. No wonder most of us rely on hit-and-miss approaches – and perhaps then complain that we can't find the good programs. Just imagine going to your doctor for treatment and being told that the drugs he or she asked you to take had seldom been publicly tested and that there were few reviews, or none at all, of those trials.

Educational programs are like films or television broadcasts: you don't really know how good or bad you think they are until you've seen them in action, but you may be influenced a good deal by the reviews, assuming you can find them. You should approach reviews of educational software informed about what to look for. This paper tackles three questions:

(1) How has software, developed in this country for use in our schools, been reviewed in journals, magazines, newspapers, newsletters and catalogues since 1985?

(2) What kinds of opinions were being passed in these publications of the late 1980s, by whom and on what evidence?

(3) Were there enough published reviews, and if not, what types were missing?

◼ Reviews in the late 1980s on software developed for use in British schools

Reviews in the late 1980s on software developed in Britain for use in British schools (you'll notice that for the moment foreign software is excluded) range all the way from straight descriptions to proper evaluations. So far as the author knows, nobody has tried to categorize them, but probably all of them would fit into four broad categories: descriptions, analyses, critiques and evaluations.

Table 1 Four broad categories of British reviews of software developed for use in our schools

Category	Distinguishing features of these reviews
Descriptions	Briefly describe programs, mentioning at least their content and approach, but offering little or no hint or assurance of their effectiveness.
Analyses	Analyse programs in detail, leaving the reader in no doubt about their objectives, content, approach, and hardware requirements, but still offering little or no assurance of their effectiveness.
Critiques	Analyse and criticize programs in detail, commenting on their internal quality and coherence, mentioning potential problems in using them and offering opinions on and simple anecdotal evidence of their effectiveness.
Evaluations	Provide a full analysis and critique, supplemented by qualitative and quantitative data on the programs' effectiveness, based on actual use by an appropriate sample of students.

☐   **Descriptions**

If you pick up an educational software distributor's catalogue, you probably expect to find out each program's content, the intended audience, roughly how long the program takes a student and how much it costs. These are 'facts', you hope, based firmly on the designer's intentions and the results of tests with students. You may also find details of the 'bells and whistles', those special features that make a program particularly worth buying. You may be told that it's ideal for low-achieving students. The program may be in colour, or there may be a claim that it serves the National Curriculum in a specific way, or even that it has won a prize. And there will be technical details, of course, so that you know whether the program will run on your computer.

Have a look at this example, taken from the National Council for Educational Technology (1989) catalogue, and note what is missing. Is there anything extra that might make you think it was an analysis or even a critique (using my four categories)?

Example 1

Pipistrelle

1 disk (40 track); BBC (B, Master); 10 activity sheets; 7 factsheets; teachers' notes, 1988.
ISBN 1 85379 019 2
£17.50; £11.50; £10.35

Pipistrelle is a simulation program which provides an experience of one night in the life of a bat. The aim is to allow children to explore problems in bat life: the use of sounds to recognise objects and to navigate, finding food and the importance of weather conditions. The program helps children to establish links between the individual elements of the environment, to develop aural discrimination and to see, select and accurately record events.

Like many programs for schools, this one has accompanying print, for children and the teacher. The three prices reflect educational discounts. The short description does little more than simply describe the program content: it also makes a few unsubstantiated claims for the program's potential. There is no statement about the intended audience or how long the program might take. Instead, you may say, teachers are expected to know where such a program would be useful, and how much time could be spared for it in class. As for quality, you have only the assurance that the Council would not include a dud program in its catalogue. If you want to know more, you will have to look elsewhere.

Similarly, the catalogue of the Scottish Council for Educational Technology (1987) contains short descriptions. A typical one appears below:

Example 2

Drover

5.25" – £15.00	*Upper primary / secondary*
BBC B, B + & Master	*History simulation*
	Worksheet included and off-computer activity suggested

Droving was one of the steps in the move from subsistence farming – once practised throughout the world – to that which we know today in developed countries. It was a method of generating income from the sale of cattle at a central market, but it also imposed severe physical and financial risks.

This program simulates such 18th Century droving. Pupils assume the role of a drover taking a herd of cattle from his farm on an island to a market town many miles away. Problems have to be solved and decisions taken to ensure the success of the trip. Hazards are inbuilt and if the pupil is not careful, some or all of the cattle may be lost. Finally, a financial statement is given on the sale of the cattle.

The package encourages decision-making and focuses on historical and environmental issues. A well-illustrated background booklet is included.

For me this description has the air of low-key advertising copy. I find it interesting and quite informative. It makes me want to have a look at the program, but it also leaves me with many unanswered questions. If it 'focuses on historical and environmental issues', what is its ideology? If it encourages decision making, in whose favour – the community's or the drover's or some landowner's? Beyond such questions, I wonder how successful it is in simulating the complex geographical and social environment of those times. At that price, and running on a BBC B, can it exploit the power of computers to do what I, the teacher, could not do as well or better? The questions proliferate.

Perhaps that is all we should expect from catalogue entries: that they should be accurate descriptions that make us want to know more, rather than providing a basis for ordering programs. Both these suppliers ought to let you try a program and return it if it doesn't suit your needs.

☐   **Analyses**

In my search for published British reviews I found few that were analyses, that is, listing objectives, content, approach and hardware requirements but offering little or no assurance of effectiveness. It seems as though reviews prefer to offer a critique, with their opinion of likely effectiveness, if they go beyond mere description. Here is one from the magazine of Microcomputer Users in Education, *Information Tech-*

nology and Learning (**11**(4), July 1989), which I might call an analysis, rather than a critique:

Example 3

Stock Pack

For middle school upwards, for use by teachers and learners.
Nimbus Topologika (Box 39 Stilton PE 7 3 RL) £24.95

This is a PC program with PC emulator on the disk (and is also available for Acorn machines). It's a thorough implementation of stock control and accounting, marketed as a content-free package able to act as a basis for GCSE projects.

The installation instructions aren't too easy to work through, while the Guided Tour booklet, though excellent, was written for the BBC. Once you've sorted out these problems, though, the software is a pleasure to use – flexible routines, thorough yet straightforward. Validation routines are included.

The system works with two files – clients and stock items – and there are eleven main options on the menu. The accounting procedures are sophisticated enough to include VAT, so there's no reason why this product couldn't be used for real.

Indeed it's valid for GCSE work, though one shudders at the thought of working with a whole class on this software alone. Maybe a better approach is to fit the software with sample files and let learners explore it that way for general background purposes.

In my opinion, this rather brief analysis is written for teachers of accounting who already know the context. If you happen to be from another discipline, it may not mean a great deal to you because it is so concise about objectives, content and technical details. I certainly have the feeling that the reviewer has tried the program, but not that he or she has tried it with a class. The language is quite cautious, with little to assure users that the program will be effective in the hands of the teacher. There isn't even a claim that this program is good value for the money – though it probably is.

☐   **Critiques**

If you are a teacher, with precious little cash to spend on educational software, you probably *do* want more details. A critique of the program might help you to make up your mind whether to buy it. Here is Zalie Wright's (1988) account, published in *The Chiltern Courier* (newsletter of The Advisory Unit in Hatfield), of her experiences of using a program in a Stevenage junior school.

Example 4

Nature Park Adventure

I've been with eight year olds (first-years Juniors) as they work through this program in groups of three. The game involves rescuing large blue butterflies from the Trogg and his two glob monster helpers. On the way you meet approximately 12 different animals or insects and have maths problems to solve. The game is in three parts.

The overall presentation is very good. A lot of reading is involved and the lettering is excellent. The vocabulary is suitable – except I've been amazed to find that not many children know the meaning of 'rare'. The graphics are good – colourful and interesting, but simple. Only the odd hiccup, a conker as red as a hollyberry so that one child would not believe it was meant to be a conker, and a green kingfisher – why not use a green woodpecker both from the colour point of view and also children are more likely to see or at least hear one.

The program is good for reading, teamwork and cooperation, oracy and following instructions. The children love the game and some get very involved, talking in whispers near the sleeping Trogg. The program also helps children to use their eyes. A butterfly is no longer just a butterfly but a peacock or tortoiseshell, and so on. However, they need access to identification charts for the butterflies, birds and trees. The program can also stimulate the imagination – what does the Trogg look like (you never actually see him), what next, and so on.

I feel the maths section is not up to the same high standard as the rest to the program. A lot of good ideas but ...

(1) Some suffer from lack of explanation, for example there is a crane which has to be used to break a wall. The program just asks for any number between 1 and 30. How is one to know that 30 is the length of the arm and that the crane will drop a weight on the wall? I have tried keeping silent and letting the children enter a number and see what happens. They realize they need a bigger/smaller number and find it by trial and error. I'm convinced they don't do any estimating. I have also tried explaining before they enter their first number that the crane arm is 30 units long, and we also talk about how the crane might work and what might happen. These children make a reasoned estimate, which I feel is far more valuable.

(2) Some suffer from too much explanation, for example the four-colour problem. If you make a mistake you have to go through four screens of explanation and start again. All the children I have watched have understood what to do and have only pressed the wrong key by mistake.

(3) Some suffer from lack of logic! For example the frog is not allowed to jump on to certain floor tiles because they are loose,
but in fact he has to land on them to reach the firm one.

(4) Some suffer from being confusing! For example the shape
problem is confusing visually. The shapes are falling down the
screen and it is quite difficult to spot the difference between a
hexagon and an octagon.

Enough – I could go on!

Overall, a very good program, which could make a very good basis
for a topic for a class. All aspects of the curriculum could be
involved. The pack comes with a teacher's book full of ideas, work
cards, and so on. It is good to see children working with a
computer. I've had some surprises regarding who takes the lead,
and their speed of understanding and ability to solve problems. It's
not always those who shine in the classroom who shine on the
computer.

Let's ask a few questions about this critique, which is longer than
most you will find.

- Does it include any statement of objectives that gives you a sound
idea of what students will be able to do after studying the
program? Why are they rescuing butterflies from monsters?
- Is there a commentary on whether the 'bells and whistles', such as
use of colour and the game-like format, improve the program's
ability to motivate students?
- Can you tell from the review whether the program's level of
vocabulary is appropriate for this age group?
- Do you get the impression that children can use the program
without frequent help from the teacher?
- Can you tell whether the program is an appropriate length for the
intended audience? Young children usually need shorter programs
than older ones.
- What does the review say about logical breaks in the program?
Does the student have to start the program all over again on
returning to it?
- Is the screen well formated, with a clutter of labels or unnecessary
or distasteful use of colour? Does the use of colour take into
account colour blindness in males?
- What other learning materials (such as booklets) go with the
program and how is it integrated with them?

You may feel that I am expecting too much of a critique, yet I'm fairly
sure these are the kinds of questions teachers ask when they are

considering whether to use a new program. Such questions arise both from their experience of what children need and from teachers' and children's criticisms of inadequate programs they have seen. Even critiques written by teachers like Zalie Wright don't usually cover the ground quite well enough, though clearly she could have told us more, given the space.

To press home this point, let me give you another example, probably written by a teacher member of Microcomputer Users in Education (MUSE), a society open to all interested in using computers in education, for the MUSE magazine, *Information Technology and Learning* (**11**(3), April 1989).

Example 5

Spell Master

For primary school upwards, for use by learners and teachers.
Z88 ROM Computer Concepts (Gaddesden Place Hemel
Hempstead Herts HP2 6QZ).

Z88 users will use this impressive spelling checker chip even if they don't find (as some do) that laptop work on the move makes mis-spelling more common.

The chip is easy to install and to remove (if that extra drain on the battery causes concern); it's very easy to use, being closely compatible with the BBC micro version of Spell Master and with the Z88's existing routines. There are two methods of use, each appearing at the end of the Z88 index menu.

QuickEdit is a simple word processor, simple at least in not having Pipedream's columnar format. It's actually a pretty good word processor with, in comparison to Pipedream, more standard handling of ENTER and TAB. QuickEdit can be used for text creation, therefore, and you can also import into it files from Pipedream and from BBCs and PCs.

In this context, though, it's the spelling checking aspect that's of interest. Access this from the last (and why not the first?) entry on the QuickEdit menu and obtain the same features as BBC Spell Master (check all text from cursor, marked block or continuously) plus check current word. On querying an unrecognized word, the system offers ignore, add to user dictionary, guesses, retype and browse. The retype option is better than in the BBC version in allowing you to enter a non-dictionary word or to retype with a space.

The second style of usage is 'Word Finder'. This pop-down facility offers browsing, anagrams, matching, and 'crossword' word seeking. This last offers single and multi-character wild cards.

A crucial aspect of spelling checkers is the user dictionary. Z88 automatically creates a user dictionary for each document unless you load a previously saved one. You can merge such dictionaries, and, when browsing, you'll find the current dictionary merged on

> screen with the 60 000 words in the chip.
>   This is a powerful, versatile program that sits well in a powerful, versatile computer.

This reviewer leaves you in no doubt about his or her expert opinion: *Spell Master* is apparently without fault. (Does this make it an analysis, rather than a critique, I wonder?) The language of the review is rather technical, including comparison with another version for the BBC. If you know about spelling checkers already, you will appreciate the finer points. If not, would you buy it, relying on the reviewer's enthusiasm? As a careful buyer for your school, what questions would you ask first?

☐   **Evaluations**

If you look back at the table 1 on page 89, you'll see that I suggested that evaluations would provide a full analysis and critique, supplemented by qualitative and quantitative data on the program's effectiveness, based on actual use by an appropriate sample of students. Such evaluations might demonstrate that students could achieve the stated objectives for the program, by using it, or perhaps that the program taught the topic better than an alternative method used to teach a comparison or control group. That sounds like the 'scientific' way of going about reviewing software, whereas the descriptions, analyses and critiques seem much more like reviews of books, videos or plays.

In fact, I failed to find *any* such reviews in the British educational literature of the late 1980s. You may be able to guess why: is it because British universities don't go in for that sort of research? Is it because setting up such experiments, with pre- and post-tests, seems too artificial? Is it possible to control all the variables in experiments that compare computer-assisted learning with other 'ordinary' methods? Or is it simply because nobody wants to pay for such evaluation?

Of course, in the United States the ethos is different, with children taking quite a few standardized tests during their schooldays. Although this paper is mainly about British reviews, I would like to tell you a little about what has happened in the United States, where thousands of programs have been reviewed, mostly in the form of descriptions or critiques. The interest in reviews was so strong in the early 1980s that Apple Computer Inc., which had and still has a large share of the US education market for both hardware and software, started *The Apple Journal of Courseware Review.*. The editors set strict standards, with the result that some of the most comprehensive reviews ever published appeared in the two issues (yes, Apple closed it down after that, for reasons not revealed). These reviews came very close to evaluations, in my opinion, but not quite. See what you think. Here is one example, written by David McCarthy (1982), a university researcher, not a teacher, which you may like to compare with Example 5, *Spell Master*. I have abridged it slightly to bring it down to a reasonable length for this article. My comments follow.

Example 6

Compu-Spell

Edu-ware Services, Inc., P.O. Box 22222, Agoura CA 91301.
32K Apple II or Apple II Plus, with disk drive and monitor
Disk plus user guide, $29.95

Compu-Spell, a technically sophisticated, computer-managed sequence of spelling drills, contains thousands of words for students in grades 4–8 and those at a 'secretarial' level. For the teacher, it maintains a record of each student's location and progress within the system. *Compu-Spell* contains extensive provisions for modifying its contents, but the documentation is not designed for teachers who have little or no training in the computer field. The directions contain confusing terminology such as 'booting', 'initialization', and 'routines'. Some attempt has been made to give directions on proceeding through the various menus, sub-menus, and sub-sub-menus. For example, selecting the choice 'view/change general options' from the 'main menu' takes the user to a sub-menu that lists six other choices: drives, printer, password, mode, post-test display, passing score. Some kind of structural map needs to be provided, as in the introductory guide to Applesoft BASIC. Computers-in-education is a novelty for nearly every teacher: software designers have got to simplify their directions.

As a student, I am presented with a 'page' containing a series of sentences (Figure 1).

The box around a word represents 'inverse' (black-on-white) printing. When I press the space bar, the word disappears and the

Figure 1

Figure 2

inverse block remains. My task is to type the first word, 'armor'
(American spelling, of course!), in the blank block (Figure 2).

When I have correctly spelled the word, the inverse representation disappears and I proceed to the next word. If I enter any
letter that is not part of the correct spelling of the word, the letter
will not appear. If I do make an error in typing 'armor', it remains
in inverse form on the screen, and I will have to type it correctly
again before I can exit this lesson – whether my error was in typing,
spelling, or because I forgot 'armor' and substituted 'helmets'. In
the sentence, 'There is a __ in this town', literally thousands of
nouns could fit in this blank, but I had better remember 'curfew'
(Figure 3). That's what I am learning to 'spell' (?). I can, however
press the ESCape key and have the word presented.

After working my way through the complete list of words, I
proceed to the post-test. Here the program prints one sentence at
a time, with the spelling word deleted. The sentence 'Knights wear

Figure 3

heavy _____ ', appears. The program will accept anything I type into the blank, and then replace it with the correct word. Hence, if I type 'hats' or 'shoes' or 'armour' (British spelling) all of which are correct in both logic and spelling, I have missed it. By the time I get near the end of the drill, I am quite likely to have forgotten that there is a 'curfew' in this town. There is a river, a park, a fountain, a school, a university. There isn't a curfew, but, once again, I'd better remember what the sentence requires. I consider myself a fair speller and a relatively competent typist, but I was not able to progress through any of the four sample drills and post-tests I tried without making errors in typing, cognate substitutions, or logical substitutions. Finally, since I've made errors, I must repeat the entire post-test. The program does offer the option 'quit for now?' and I'll confess I took it.

The designers of *Compu-Spell* say that it is based on an 'instructional model'. They contend that 'spelling is memorization' and that, although many teachers teach it as a rule-generating strategy, most learners do not follow such a strategy in learning to spell. The authors seem to deal entirely with visual, and perhaps kinaesthetic (movement) memory, since their program does not allow for either speech or audition. They claim that the 'vagaries and ambiguities' of English necessitate the memorization.

One problem with this approach is that spelling, like human learning in general, is acquired through the senses. It is multi-sensory, multi-motor, using vision, speech, touch and audition. Thus, the child develops the ability to speak and write a language after hearing it. S/he speaks by selecting appropriate phonemes (sounds) for the construction of words and applies a motor response for pronunciation. The act of writing and spelling is basically one of encoding phonemes into graphemes. If the English language is full of "vagaries, ambiguities and inconsistencies", it would, indeed, be counterproductive to ask the learner to develop such structures. However, studies have shown the relative regularity of grapheme– phoneme correlation in American English. Roughly 80% of the phonemes in words comprising the traditional spelling vocabulary of elementary-school children approximate the alphabetic principle in their letter representations. About 75% of vowel phonemes do not represent significant spelling problems, and 82% of consonant clusters have only one spelling. These facts suggest that it is valuable to teach sound-letter concepts, and some spelling rules.

The authors assume correctly that students do not *learn* to spell by applying 'rules'. Rather, they learn inductively. The strength of inductively derived concepts lies in the individual's ability to use them. The mechanical memorization of a rule is of little use. But inducing a principle through examining specific instances is not the same thing as 'rote memorization'. I think the authors are confounding the two principles. In the sample lesson previously shown (Figure 1) the authors are apparently dealing with the 'schwa' sound. This is probably the most difficult sound to learn to spell, since it can be constructed using any of the five vowels. Hence, the -er in 'observe', the -ur in 'curtain', the -ear in 'earned' and the -our in 'journey' all have the same sound. These spellings need to be memorized. Not only is there no rule to apply, there is not even one to be induced. The authors are right in teaching this sound the way they do. Another sample lesson contains the following words: controlled, equipping, crestfallen, remitted, propelling, roughneck, transferring, ninety, nineteen, benefited, forfeited, hairbrush and interference. The general principle that may be induced is that of doubling a final consonant when adding a suffix. If that is the case, it might be useful to use regular words (controlled, remitted, and so on) to induce the principle and present exceptions (benefited, forfeited) to be memorized.

The other premises upon which the authors design this program are valid: words need to be written in the context of surrounding words; learning behaviour should parallel perform-ance behaviour, so the best way for students to practise spelling is by writing. The authors also distinguish between register memory, short-term memory and long-term memory of taught materials. The goal of instruction should be to have information remain in the long-term memory. True. But the question is what should remain in the long-term memory: how to spell the word 'curfew', or that 'curfew' belongs in the blank?

Lastly, the authors contend that they 'precisely accomplish' behavioural shaping by making it impossible (for the students) to be presented with incorrect reinforcements. They are referring to the fact that, during the drill phase of their lesson, the blank will show only letters that are the correct ones. However, response made is response learned, whether this is translated into visual representation or not. It would be easy to imagine the student typing (and reinforcing) a letter several times, waiting for the machine to respond. The authors might more 'precisely accom-plish' their shaping of behaviour by being more certain that errors made by students were fewer, and the result of misconceptions of concepts being taught, rather than misunderstandings of words being sought.

Compu-Spell represents a classic example of the frequent mismarriage between technology and pedagogy. Technology says, 'Since we can do things, using slide tapes or videodisks or disappearing words, let's use them to teach.' The process should be reversed. Education should say, 'This is what we know about how to teach spelling, reading, maths, and so on. How can technology facilitate the process?'

Compu-Spell is of some value. With proper documentation, probably many of the lessons could be used to teach particular types of words, such as words that are basically learned visually, to certain students who are having trouble with those words. It might be used as a drill to teach irregular words, also. It would, however, need to be integrated selectively into an entire language-arts curriculum that would include saying a word, examining it for graphemic correlations or irregularities, writing the word, checking its accuracy, identifying errors and restudying difficult words. Its record-management system, once fathomed, may be of little use in such a case. Compared with complex language-arts subjects like reading comprehension or writing, spelling is a relatively simple learning process to analyse and teach.

Although this is a strong, long and interesting critique, McCarthy doesn't appear to have tried the program with children, does he? His reasons for doubting its effectiveness are theoretical as well as practical, but not based on actual use. In my opinion, his review is different from rather than better than the best British reviews. The program, based on Skinnerian principles, seems quite obsolete to us now, because hardware and software developed a good deal during the 1980s.

Have there been no hard-nosed evaluations, anywhere? Yes, a few. For example, Mike Thorne (1989) summarizes one apparently important US evaluation. IBM markets the *Writing to Read* software, which has young children typing in words, reading while listening to stories, and listening to words designed to teach the basic phonemes, all words being spoken in digitized speech. The software was used in 35 schools, and the result compared with those from 25 other comparable schools. Over 7000 children were given standardized tests. The results showed that *Writing to Read* users scored significantly better in writing than the controls up to and including first grade level, but not thereafter. The reading and spelling results showed no significant differences. The *Writing to Read* users actually spent more classtime learning to read than their controls, thus making the results even harder to interpret.

■ The Microelectronics Education Programme evaluation checklist

Only a few years ago, the Open University (1985) published an evaluation checklist in one of its packages for introducing teachers to microcomputers. Perhaps the checklist, developed by the Microelectronics Education Programme (MEP), was ahead of its time, because it suggested criteria which few programs could then meet and which few reviews have covered since. It had six main sections, plus a summary. All judgements about a particular program were to be made on a rating scale, with space for additional comments. Let's have a look at each section in turn, starting with the criteria for educational documentation, and see whether British reviews of the late 1980s take them into account.

(1) Educational documentation

 (a) Statement of aims and objectives
 (b) Information about the content and background
 (c) Statement of intended type of use and audience
 (d) Suggestions of ways to use the program
 (e) Pupil activities and worksheets
 (f) Instructions for running the program
 (g) Presentation of a typical run
 (h) General impressions

The educational documentation is the equivalent of the 'blurb' on the jacket of a book, plus perhaps parts of the preface. You read this, but you don't run the program. By the time you have read it, you expect to be able to have a good deal of information about the program. The authors of the checklist picked eight items, dealing with purpose, content, audience, use, activities, instructions and a typical run. You'll notice that this section omits 'Problems anticipated', therefore it could not yield a complete critique, still less an evaluation (to use my categories again). From the examples you have looked at already, you know that descriptions never include all of these eight items, but the best analyses may do. On average, I'd say that British reviews of the late 1980s tell us only a few of the things suggested by this section.

 The second section of the checklist goes further, however, being about achievement of aims:

(2) Achievement of stated aims (as far as you can tell without actually using the program with a class)

 (a) Aims/objectives
 (b) General impressions

Among British reviews, analyses offer minimal assurance here, perhaps by including a bland statement that primary schoolchildren enjoy using the program. What you want is a critique, or better still, an evaluation, with qualitative and quantitative data on the program's effectiveness, based on actual use by an appropriate sample of students. Qualitative data might consist of teachers' and students' variegated opinions. Quantitative data might include results of tests taken before and after using the software, or marks given for a student project requiring its use.

The third section of the checklist is deceptively simple. It is actually very important.

(3)   Appropriateness of the micro and program

(a)   For teaching this topic
(b)   For the suggested audience and type of use (for example group, whole class)
(c)   General impressions

The reason why it is important is that you certainly don't want to pick the wrong tool for the job. Maybe the criteria are stated *too* succinctly. What you should be thinking about as you read the documentation is whether a computer program is the best tool for the job you have in mind. Could you teach the topic, to this particular group, as easily without the computer? Is the computer the best way? Does the program take advantage of what the computer provides? The example the checklist authors give is that of rotating a three-dimensional diagram, something which they say could not have been shown in any other way. If you look back at the examples I have given, or at others you know, you'll find very few from which you can be certain that the program is teaching in a way unique to the computer, or that the computer program is the best tool for the job. Clearly, you are going to have to take risks as you select programs.

The fourth section deals with basic screen presentation:

(4)   Screen presentation

(a)   Use of graphics
(b)   Use of colour and animation
(c)   General impressions

Here you really must run the program. You simply cannot judge the screen for yourself without doing so, even if there are a few prints of screens in the documentation. Even descriptions often contain a comment on the graphics, however, and you can expect graphics to receive attention in most analyses, critiques and evaluations. Why is this so, when so many other criteria are frequently neglected? I would say that it is because we all expect a high standard of screen design, through our experience of print and television. 'Graphics' under 4a includes text on screen, and text is very frequently criticized: the older programs used only upper case and the program authors squeezed too many words on to the screen, while the more recent programs sometimes use violent and unsuitable colours for no apparent reason.

The fifth section is an assessment of user-friendliness:

(5)   Friendliness and flexibility of the program

   (a)   Helpful messages to correct user errors
   (b)   Help to pupils in understanding the program
   (c)   Versatility so that the user can control what the program does
   (d)   Feedback to pupil
   (e)   Program adapts to pupils' performance
   (f)   Record of pupils' performance kept by program
   (g)   Program model accessible to pupil
   (h)   Suggestions or help for teacher to modify the program
   (i)   General impressions

Reviews do touch on all these matters. By working through the program, a reviewer may be able to find out what 'help' is available, but only by asking learners to work through it, probably making a wide range of errors, can the reviewer really discover how helpful the 'help' is. This argues, yet again, for testing programs with learners before buying them, yet how seldom that is possible! Critiques seem to have little to say about the helpfulness of help.

None of the reviews I have quoted touches on user control. Assessing whether the user can control what the program does probably also requires testing with learners, although you may be able to conduct some tests yourself, bearing in mind that you may be outside the target audience for the program.

Most programs give the learners some feedback, and you can check on this the moment you run them. At the very least, they indicate right answers in some fashion. At best, they adapt to learners' performance as well as indicating whether the answer was correct. Perhaps reviews seldom deal with feedback because provision of it is expected, and adaptive programs are now the norm. In British schools you would have to look hard to unearth the old 'linear' type of software which takes learners along a single route, as B.F. Skinner, the American behaviourist, had advocated back in the early 1960s at the start of programmed learning.

Keeping a record of pupils' performance may be unnecessary and even educationally undesirable in a few cases, but is probably rather useful for student and teacher in many more. Much educational software does not include this facility, and it is seldom commented on in reviews. Equally, giving the learner access to the program model would probably be valuable, but is seldom built in. None of the reviews I have quoted mentions it, either.

There are circumstances under which it is vital for the teacher to be able to modify a program, yet it is very unusual for reviews to deal with this point. For example, modifications may be needed to make the software available to children with special needs.

Finally (not counting the summary section), the MEP checklist has a section on technical documentation.

(6) Technical documentation
- (a) Information about machine requirements
- (b) Information about the model used
- (c) Information about the program structure
- (d) Listing and readability of the program code
- (e) Portability, that is ability to transfer program to a different computer
- (f) General impressions

This is the section where many reviews seem best. Perhaps the 'technologist' in the reviewer comes out: machine requirements are clearly stated, including details of the model (though the item could be misinterpreted as meaning the program's model, not the model – BBC Model B – of the hardware). Even comments about the program structure are not uncommon. Reviews are less likely to contain a listing of the program code, but may comment on the software's portability, particularly whether it can be used on more recently released and more advanced machines, such as the BBC Master and Archimedes. Look back at the examples I have given to check on this.

To summarize, then, we could say with some truth that British reviews of the late 1980s do not tell us as much about software for schools as the MEP checklist would like us to know. In a few cases this is because some of the criteria simply do not apply to those particular programs, but in most cases it is because reviewing has been unsystematic. If you want to find the 'best buys', don't expect too much from the consumer reports. But even if reviewing were systematic, under some new central government edict, would that guarantee that your learners would succeed if you bought only the 'best' for them?

▪ Evaluation and replication

In the commercial life of our nation, it seems accepted that consumer reports play an important role determining the saleability of products and services, whether they be washing machines or holidays to Morocco. A great deal of money is spent on preparing these reports and on drawing positive findings to the attention of the great buying public. Needless to say, the underlying assumption is that products and services that are judged successful by a large set of customers will probably be successful for others too.

In education, it is tempting to follow this market model. Let's discover what works, and spread the good news about it so that other children, other teachers, other schools can benefit in the same way. Is this true for educational programs?

The answer I would give is a heavily qualified Yes. Washing machines do not always meet the purchasers' needs, and holidays in foreign parts are not always a success. Consumer reports draw attention to shortcomings as well as strong points. Critiques and evaluations of educational programs do the same, where they are available. There are some serious difficulties in applying the market model, however, and you should be aware of them.

- Written educational objectives are notoriously weak controllers of what happens in the classroom. Therefore, matching program objectives to lessons will not necessarily guarantee successful learning.

- Program content cannot keep pace with changing lesson content, even where curriculum reform is slow, therefore obsolescence is common.

- For many reasons intended audiences, based on field trials, will be different in some respects from what the program authors had in mind; therefore, the learners will respond differently.

- Program use will seldom parallel the original use in field trials, as teachers and students introduce variations, for their own reasons.

If that sounds a gloomy forecast, I am merely trying to emphasize that it is a mistake to think that exact replication is possible in education. A computer program may sound as though it is capable of producing the same successful results in every case: after all, in most cases doesn't the learner have to work through it in a predetermined way (hence all these complaints about computers programming the child)? In fact, such a program is only one element in a complex teaching and learning process. To increase your chances of selecting a winner, you need to understand the context in which it will be used. If you think the pharmaceutical companies have problems, consider how much better they can secure successful replication of results than can companies selling educational software! Replication of learning cannot be guaranteed, no matter how good the evaluation. Maybe that's the chief reason why so few evaluations are available to us among British reviews in the late 1980s. I am inclined to agree with Derek Blease (1986), who, after writing his book on evaluating educational software, came to the conclusion that you only understand the potential of software once you have explored it with learners. Experience gained in using software is probably the best way to qualify as an expert selector of educationally effective programs, though it certainly helps to know what to look for.

■   So where should I look?

It may surprise you to know that British academic journals simply do not carry evaluation reviews of educational software. They review books, but not programs. Occasionally you will find in one of them the story of how a particular program was designed and developed. Quite frequently they feature articles about principles of design and use. They are most helpful if you want to know about recent experiments in teaching children through LOGO or some other programming language, or through new applications such as Hypercard.

For mere descriptions, look at catalogues like the ones I have mentioned, and at commercial publishers' catalogues (for example, *ESM Software for Schools*). *Educational Computing*, a teachers' magazine, only carries very short critiques. You could turn to other magazines such as *Information Technology and Learning*, from which I took some of my examples. The best source of critiques is the *Times Educational Supplement*, which has a regular column devoted to reviewing computers and information technology, including educational software. Its reviewers are critical and well informed. Another sound but less accessible source of critiques is the *Journal of Computer-Assisted Learning*, which started in 1985 and from its first issue has carried 'Previews'. These 500–800 words organized under the headings of : educational content, printed material, preparation time, ease of use/ flexibility, software and classroom potential. The editor's original intention was that brief evaluations of the programs in use would then appear a year later, as 'Reports', but in fact only a few have been published, in 1985 and 1987.

A good set of critiques, including several dozen programs suitable for schools, is in the *Courseware Directory,* produced by the Further Education Unit (1988). The reviews are usually written by college staff and some of their remarks are relevant to use of the programs by older students only. You can read the same critiques, plus updates, by accessing the NERIS (National Educational Resources Information Service) database.

What about software libraries? Do they exist and how do they help? One example is the software library of MUSE, at Felsted School in Essex. If you want to check what is available in the library, you can look at viewdata pages describing the software, provided you know how to access the Communitel database on 031-820790. As you may know, viewdata pages don't contain a great many characters, so the descriptions are brief. Or you can read the printed catalogue (MUSE, 1989), from which this is a typical entry in the 'Maths Senior' section:

'Pythagtest   *R. Murphy*

Demonstrates and tests Pythagoras's Theorem. The program includes a visual "proof" of the theorem and limits on its use. The tests require a student to enter an expression for the unknown

side with the option of also calculating the result. A demonstration
of each test is available. Econet compatible.
BBC-B   £5.00   [B0351/Mar 85]'

Whose programs are they and how did they get chosen for the
library? Most of them were written by MUSE members and evaluated as
suitable for learning purposes by panels set up by MUSE. In July 1989
there were just over 100 programs in the library, mostly for BBC
machines but some for the Nimbus. The cost of a copy varied from £2.50
to £15.00. Some programs were already six years old, raising the
question of who decides when a program should be dropped.

Maintaining such libraries is not without cost, although a small
one like MUSE's cannot be very expensive. The MUSE panels are made
up of unpaid volunteers. A private school like Felsted can often afford to
welcome such a collection without charging MUSE for the space. In this
case, a member of Felsted's staff looks after the library in his spare time
and makes copies for buyers.

To summarize, that was the situation regarding (mainly) British
reviews of educational software in the late 1980s. Perhaps it will have
changed by the time you read this. On the whole, the marketplace, not
evaluators, determines what survives and what disappears. Good luck in
your search for high quality programs! If you find something that works
with your students, spread the news.

■ References

Blease D. (1986). *Evaluating Educational Software*. London: Croom Helm.
Further Educational Unit (1988). *Courseware Directory (Issue 2)*. London: The
    FE Unit.
McCarthy D. (1982). Compu-Spell: an electronically-assisted spelling bee. *The
    Apple Journal of Courseware Review*, Issue 1.
MUSE (1989). *Information Technology and Learning Software Catalogue*.
    Leicester: Microcomputer USers in Education.
National Council for Educational Technology (1989). *Software Catalogue*.
    Coventry: The Council.
Open University (1985). *Educational Software: Activities Book Troubleshooting
    Guide*. Appendix 6, BBC Model B edition. Milton Keynes: Open University
    Press.
Scottish Council for Educational Technology (1987). *Software Catalogue:
    Creative Software for Education*. Glasgow: Scetlander Ltd.
Thorne M. (1989). The way ahead: an American study of technology has
    important lessons for Britain. *Times Educational Supplement*, 2 June.
Wright Z. (1988). Nature Park Adventure. *The Chiltern Courier*, October 1988.

Paper 1.8

Evaluation and Assessment

Anita Straker

Information technology has now established itself both in society and in education. Before the DTI hardware scheme few people would have imagined that computers would become commonplace in primary schools. When the equipment first arrived in classrooms teachers were excited, but they were also uncertain about the prospective role of the new technology. The last decade has been a period for trial and for experimentation, for sharing good ideas and for rejecting those which seem less profitable. The computer is becoming established as a resource for learning across the primary school curriculum and, through this approach, is providing children with a broad appreciation of its versatility. As a consequence, it will be possible to start the next decade with a clearer idea of what can be achieved.

Both old ideas and new ones need to be evaluated by those who are trying them out. Self-appraisal involves asking questions about what is being done and why it is being done, deciding whether it is being done well, or whether the school should be doing something different. Some evaluation is taking place all the time as teachers look critically at their own work, but there is also a need for the staff as a whole to take stock of what has been achieved, so that plans for the future can be reviewed and crystallized.

This chapter suggests questions which the staff of a primary school could consider. The questions are not intended to be used as a blueprint, or to be followed in their entirety. The level of resourcing and of in-service provision, and the consequent level of achievement, will in any case vary considerably from one area to another. An individual school could base a discussion upon one or two of the listed questions, and could talk through some of the issues raised in the discussion with a member of the LEA advisory service. Groups of teachers from different schools might consider the broad headings at an in-service course, and evolve their own sets of questions to suit their local circumstances.

First published in Straker, A (1989) *Children Using Computers*. Oxford. Basil Blackwell. Reprinted with permission.

■ The curricular policy and classroom practice

The school's aims and its curricular policy are the foundation stones on which developments can be built. Each school needs to consider the value of its policy as well as its effectiveness.

☐ **Policy**

- Are the school's aims for the use of information technology clear to everyone: staff, governors, parents, children?
- How do the children in the school learn about the computer itself and the significance that it is likely to have in their lives?
- Can teachers in the school describe occasions when the computer has been used in a way which gives children opportunities to:
  - exchange ideas through discussion;
  - suggest and then test hypotheses;
  - organize and analyse information;
  - experiment with and express creative ideas;
  - pose and find solutions to their own problems;
  - develop methods for themselves;
  - sort out their own mistakes?
- Do any teachers consider that they have used the computer to:
  - help them to cope with the varied demands of the primary classroom;
  - help them to develop new teaching styles;
  - focus on how children learn rather on what they learn;
  - give better insight into children's thinking?
- Has there been any debate about the possible advantage of concentrating computer use throughout the school on one or more of the major applications: adventure games and simulations, word processing and text management, information handling, programming in LOGO, control technology, graphics or music?
- To what extent has it been possible to review the school's curriculum guidelines for, say, language, mathematics and science in order to take information technology into account?

☐ **Continuity**

- How do teachers know which software the children have used previously:
  - in another class;

- at home;
- in a previous school or playground?

● How do teachers in the school prevent unnecessary repetition of work with computers? What ways are there of ensuring that the children's experiences are progressively more challenging?

● Are staff aware of the ways in which other primary schools in the area are making use of their computers?

● What has been done to ensure that the children's future secondary school teachers are familiar with their computer experiences at the primary school level?

☐ **Classroom organization**

● When the use of a computer has been allocated to a particular class or group of children, what are the advantages or disadvantages of
   - positioning the computer within the classroom or work area;
   - using a corridor or a special computer room?

● How frequently, and for what purposes, should:
   - a teacher use a micro to work with a small or large group of children;
   - a small group of children work at the keyboard, with the occasional but not constant presence of their teacher;
   - a child work individually with the computer?

● For each class, what proportion of time with the computer is spent by children on
   - basic skill practice;
   - extending their skills of listening, talking, reading or writing;
   - solving problems;
   - organizing, interpreting or presenting information;
   - creative or imaginative work?

● What organizational strategies do teachers use so that children can have time away from the micro to
   - plan and to follow up their computer work;
   - to exchange ideas and explain their work to others?

■ People

Curriculum innovation of any kind needs to take into account the needs, skills and sensitivities of all the people concerned. In the case of computers, the pressure on schools to adopt them can sometimes ma

Figure 1

the adults feel insecure, whereas children seem to be able to use the new technology with great ease.

☐ **Children**

- How are children encouraged to feel that they have a part to play in the care of the hardware and the software?
- Is it necessary for the staff to take any special steps to encourage particular groups of children: for example,
    - children for whom English is a second language;
    - children who do not have a computer at home;
    - girls?
- What do teachers do if they discover children who know more about computers than they do?
- Should there be occasions when the children in the class can use their own initiative in deciding to use the computer, without asking permission or being directed to it by the teacher?
- Should there be occasions when the children themselves decide which piece of software it would be appropriate to use?

☐ **Parents and the community**

- What opportunities are there for parents and governors to gain an active understanding of what the school is trying to do? Are there workshops for parents and/or governors? Are they invited into the school to watch or participate? Is there any information in the school brochure about the role of the computer?

- Are there other ways in which the involvement of parents and others in the community could be extended?
- What advice does the school offer to parents who are thinking about buying a computer for their child, or who want to know which programs to use at home?
- How many girls and boys have access to a computer at home? What do they use it for? Are there implications for what should happen in school?

☐   Staff development

- Are all the staff encouraged to take the computer home for preparation?
- What strategies have been used to share expertise among the staff in the school? Has it been possible to:
  - double up classes so that one teacher can help another;
  - have workshops after school;
  - discuss successes or failures in the classroom;
  - compare the work done by two age groups who have used the same piece of software;
  - use some video film as a basis for discussion?
- When teachers attend courses, what arrangements are made for them to share their new knowledge and skills with colleagues?
- What arrangements are made to support:
  - probationary teachers;
  - student teachers;
  - teachers who are new to the school;
  - teachers who are using a new piece of software for the first time in the classroom;
  - any staff members who feel they lack the skills needed for computer use?
- Which teachers should take priority:
  for attending out-of-school courses or conferences;
  for visiting other schools to see what they are doing?
- What are the duties of the teacher/s who take overall responsibility for the management of the computer? Are all staff aware of these duties? Are the duties reviewed from time to time?

- What steps are being taken to ensure that:
  - the female staff are as involved as the male staff;
  - the older staff are as involved as the younger ones?

☐   **Support services**

Local authoritie vary in the support which they are able to offer their primary schools. What is important is that all primary teachers are aware of the facilities which exist, and make maximum use of them.

- Could the school make more use of the facilities and support provided in the locality? For example, by
  - a computer centre or a teachers' centre;
  - a software viewing or lending library;
  - colleges, universities or polytechnics?
- Could more use be made of the help which has been or could be offered by any advisory teachers?
- What procedure is there to draw the staff's attention to suitable courses?
- How is any information sent to the school by the LEA or publishers made known to each member of staff?
- Could the school make more use of the journal, software and local events provided by MAPE?

■   Resource management

The way that resources are managed in a school is one of the key factors in determining the success of any curricular innovation. Resource management will need to take into account the hardware and software, the use of time, and financial planning.

☐   **Hardware**

- How many computer systems does the school need?
- Is the present hardware well organized and well maintained? Are the staff generally satisfied with the arrangements?
- Is there a need to review the school's present policy:
  - for the use of existing equipment;
  - for the purchase of new equipment?
- Are there any ways in which changing the location of any of the existing computer systems would ensure that it is used more effectively?

☐ **Software**

- Is there an efficient system for storing the software and its documentation? Is the system working effectively? How satisfied are the staff with the arrangements?
- Do staff have an easy means of knowing what software is available in the school?
- Which programs should form the core of the school's software library?
- What is the system for reviewing the software library? Has any inappropriate software been discarded?
- Does the school need to purchase more software? Why?
- When a new piece of software arrives in school what arrangements are made for each member of staff to appraise it and become familiar with it?
- Do the school's curricular guidelines for core subjects refer to appropriate pieces of software? If not, how could appropriate references be incorporated?

☐ **Time**

- Would there be any advantages in using the computing resources with just one group of children for a substantial period of time?
- Are there other ways in which a reallocation of computer time would ensure that it is used more effectively?

☐ **Financial considerations**

Financial support for schools wishing to buy computing equipment varies considerably from one local authority to another. As well as any support provided by the LEA, parents' associations are often willing to raise funds for computers. Sometimes there are local trusts or businesses which will help. Occasionally there are special projects, initiated either by the LEA or by others, which can provide funds.

- Do financial plans cover:
  - insurance and security arrangements;
  - maintenance;
  - future purchases and/or replacements;
  - installation, including storage, furniture and any new wiring?
- Does the school have other important needs which should take priority over expenditure on additional computing equipment and software?

	6 months	1 year	2 years
Hardware			
Software			
INSET			
Curriculum			
?			

Figure 2

■ Questions for individual members of staff

The staff as a whole will be involved in the discussion of the questions listed above. Indeed, the discussion of some of the questions may involve others from outside the school: governors, parents, the local authority advisory service. But each individual member of staff will also need to appraise his or her own role.

☐ Questions for those in posts of responsibility

The headteacher, the deputy headteacher and any curriculum coordinator for information technology will of course play a major part in the consideration of the general set of questions. As they consider their own particular roles, it might be helpful to ask more specific questions:

- Are the staff likely to feel that I am interested in and concerned about the development of computer use in the school, and that it is high on my list of priorities?

- In the last month, how often did I set out to observe computers being used? Did I spend time talking to the teachers and/or children about my observations? Did I make it clear to them when I was pleased with what I saw?

- To what extent did the ways in which I observed the computer being used match the school's general aims for learning?
- What are the most/least exciting uses of computers I have seen so far? How do these uses compare with what I hear from colleagues in other schools?
- How often did I myself teach the children by making use of the computer?
- What time did I give to discussing computing policy individually or in groups with:
  - members of staff;
  - parents or governors;
  - colleagues in other schools?
- What should our priorities for action be in the next six months/ one year/two years? To what extent is my view of the necessary priorities shared by others?
- What constraints are there which could stand in the way of developments? Are there ways of overcoming these constraints in any way?
- Who can or should initiate any necessary action?
- Do we need any outside support and advice? If so, what?

☐   **Questions for individual class teachers**

As well as making a contribution to the overall evaluation by the whole staff, each individual class teacher will need to appraise his or her own role.

- Would the children in my class view me as someone who is enthusiastic about computer work?
- When the computer is available for my class to use, do I:
  - plan and prepare adequately;
  - spend enough time observing children who are using the computer;
  - remember not to intervene when children are trying to solve a problem for themselves;
  - allow time for children to mull things over;
  - spend sufficient time listening to and talking with the children about their work with the computer?
- Could I improve the integration of the use of the computer with other classroom activities?
- Am I sure that the programs which my class have been using are flexible enough to match the needs of each individual child?

- Have I checked that each child gets an equal amount of time with the computer, and that particular children do not dominate within a group?

- How should I assess and keep a record of the children's progress with their computer work?

- Which piece of software should I next learn to use so that I can introduce it to my class? What plans do I need to make to achieve this?

■ Assessing outcomes

The outcomes of the school's planning and provision for work with computers determine what the children gain from it. Assessing a child or group of children through observation and questioning takes time, and is not easy. It involves considering the children's attitudes, observing them in the way that they set about their work, listening to what they say, and looking at what they produce.

There is a need to sit back and watch how children approach their work, whether they enjoy it, whether they persevere with it, whether it challenges them, what they do when they get stuck, how they organize themselves, and so on. There is a need for questioning which asks children to justify what they have done, to explain their methods, and to attempt to give reasons for their results. As well as observing them at work there is a need to have open discussions with the children about how they see their own progress.

☐ Assessing children's attitudes

- Do all the children enjoy their work with the computer? How does their enjoyment of computer work compare with their enjoyment of other aspects of classroom work?

- Are all the children equally confident about their computer work? Do the girls think that they are as good as the boys?

☐ Watching children as they set about their work

- Are all the children able to operate both hardware and software without help?

- Are the children well organized? Are they working systematically, and keeping any necessary notes in an appropriate way?

- Are all the children prepared to persist with a piece of computer work, over several sessions if necessary? How does their persistence with computer work compare with their persistence with other work?

- How do children react when what they are doing with the computer does not turn out as they had anticipated? Do they make a careful check of measurements they have taken, the sequence of the commands which they have used, or the way that they have entered data? Do they try to analyse the reasons for an unexpected result?

- Is each child learning to listen, to have respect for the contributions of others, to cooperate or to take responsibility within a group?

☐ **Listening to children working at a computer**

- Do the children merely repeat the information which they see on the screen, or do they help each other to interpret, make sense of and absorb what they see?

- When they talk to each other, are they able to describe or explain a situation to give information or instructions, or justify a decision, in a clear manner?

- Are they using logical connectives to reason with each other: if then, otherwise, because, and either, or ... ?

- Are they considering in advance the possible outcomes of their decisions, and predicting the results which they expect to obtain, or are they trying things out without forethought?

- Does their conversation reveal that they are looking for relationships: for example, do they use phrases like 'that's the same as ...', 'that's less than before', 'it should go in front of ...', 'they seem to be going up together ...' ?

- Are they using unexpected mathematical skills or ideas: for example, large numbers, negative numbers, mental arithmetic ...? If so, what are the implications for their mathematical work away from the computer?

- When questioned, can they explain and justify their strategies? Can they describe and give possible reasons for their results?

☐ **Looking at recorded work**

- To what extent does the children's recorded work (handwritten notes, printouts) reflect the quality and totality of what was said and done at the keyboard? If not, does this matter?

- How does the recorded work compare with the children's non-computer recorded work?

- If the recorded work is sketchy, what would be gained by encouraging the children to extend it into a more complete description of their methods, strategies and conclusions?

- How do the children feel about their recorded work? Would they like to take it home to show parents, have it displayed for others to see, placed in a folder to add to later on ... ?

☐   **Using a framework of attainment targets**

Proposals for the National Curriculum will specify attainment targets (objectives for what children should know, understand and be able to do). These attainment targets should help teachers to plan children's work, and assess the progress which children are making.

■ Conclusion

The questions about evaluation and assessment which have been raised in this paper show that both the problems and the possibilities which have stemmed from the introduction of information technology into schools are much the same as those which present themselves when other aspects of the primary school curriculum are considered. Nevertheless, the questions should help to clarify objectives and priorities for the use of information technology, to identify strengths or weaknesses in the school's current work, and to highlight the actions which need to be taken for the future.

Part 2

Computers, Cognition and Communication

This part includes papers on the use of computers in the classroom and how computer use interacts with processes of teaching and learning. In Part 2, there are papers analysing the assumptions about children's learning that are built into different kinds of software. There is a discussion of how computers are used in such a way as to relate to the cognitive development of children, and also a discussion of other factors which might influence the interaction of learners with the computer and with each other. Ridgway (Paper 2.1) deals with an examination of Intelligent Computer-Assisted Instruction (ICAI) and asks if it is likely to de-skill teachers' jobs and pupils' tasks, and to direct attention away from human interactions. He allows that the issues which ICAI attempts to tackle are important, for example, how knowledge is represented and how learning experiences are arranged. He puts forward the notion of transparent ICAI systems which would allow students to reflect on their own knowledge. However, Self in Paper 2.2 provides a damning indictment of software produced with no attempt at intelligent interaction. He describes the program Climate in some detail in order to examine how to answer the question of what it is reasonable to expect from educational software. One of his main criticisms is the lack of geographical knowledge contained within the program.

An important issue for the teachers is how to manage the learning process in terms of a balance of emphasis between pupil autonomy and interpersonal exchange. The paper by Crook discusses the challenge presented to teachers of primary school children by the uses of computers in the classroom, and how they might affect this balance and the psychological processes relating to it. The paper discusses the Ragitian and Vygotskian frameworks for discussing these processes and is optimistic about the trend for cultivating collaborative work with computers. He defends this trend *not just* as a way of replacing the interpersonal contact which might be threatened by the increased use of computers.

Paper 2.4 by Sheingold and colleagues proposes a framework for the interaction of computers with the social life of the classroom and illustrates this framework using three examples: the introduction of a database management system into schools; the use of a navigation simulation called Rescue Mission; and the use of LOGO in elementary and middle school classrooms. The paper also raises methodological issues about the way in which questions about the 'social effects' of the introduction of microcomputers to the classroom could be studied.

Edwards, in Paper 2.5, also concentrates on the classroom setting and draws upon some new developments in the social psychology of 'discourse' and 'rhetoric' and in the study of classroom education. Like Crook, Edwards discusses Vygotsky's approach which emphasizes the importance of communicative social action in learning. Another new approach in social psychology is the shift towards the study of language, especially towards conversation discourse and text. Studies of the discourse of classroom education itself are also described, in particular the account by Edwards and Mercer (1987) of classroom discourse. He illustrates these ideas by discussing some extracts of a transcribed video recording of a lesson on computer graphics for nine-year-olds.

Paper 2.6 (Fraser *et al.*) describes the analysis of detailed observations of 174 mathematics lessons and discusses how the various roles assumed by the participants relate to the activities.

Paper 2.1

Of Course ICAI is Impossible ... , Worse, Though, it Might be Seditious

Jim Ridgway

This paper will argue that current attempts at ICAI are seriously deficient in the pedagogical and epistemological assumptions implicitly made. Problems faced by ICAI in the domain of mathematical education are considered, to focus discussion. Contrasting examples are chosen: understanding the skills of subtraction; and fostering problem-solving skills. DEBUGGY is criticized because it takes no account of pupil descriptions of process, and ignores idiosyncratic methods; it implicitly divorces algorithm from application; and, by diagnosing, takes over an intellectual task which may well be of value to pupils and teachers. Efforts to model the processes of pupils who attempt to solve more open problems are judged to be impossible in principle, for several reasons: the paucity of cues available to the program; problems of multiple representations by solvers, switches of representation, and changes in the operators used as the solver proceeds; and current naive views of the nature of expertise. Provision of help to the user is also judged to be problematic.

Current educational ambition seeks to de-emphasize the learning of technique, and to focus more on its application on open-ended problem solving, practical work, group work and discussion. None of these is well suited to ICAI which seems to be focused on individual tuition for technical mastery.

First published in Self, J. (ed.) (1988) *Artificial Intelligence and Human Learning: Intelligent Computer-Aided Instruction*. London: Chapman and Hall. Reprinted with permission.

ICAI might be seditious too, if it acts to de-skill teachers' jobs and pupils' tasks; if it directs attention away from human–human interaction; if it directs attention away from creative activities and the investigation of open problems, by focusing on technical mastery; if it presents a view of knowledge as the assembly of atoms of technique; and if it reinforces current societal views that, for every conceptual challenge (for example 'education') there is a quick technological fix.

The issues which ICAI attempts to tackle are important. How is knowledge represented? How should learning experiences be arranged? What misconceptions do learners have? and so on ... The paper concludes that 'transparent' ICAI systems should themselves be objects for study by pupils and teachers, rather than the educational activities that ICAI systems themselves might produce.

■   Introduction

All attempts to educate make assumptions about the nature of expertise and the nature of the learner, and also contain a set of epistemological assumptions. Sometimes these assumptions are explicit; more often they are implicit. In the domain of ICAI, researchers have offered a rich variety of accounts in each of these domains, and so no simple descriptions can be offered of the approaches taken within this energetic field. Nevertheless, there does appear to be a set of core assumptions which can be challenged.

In addition to the conceptual problems which ICAI faces, there are a range of pragmatic issues which few researchers have begun to tackle. These involve a consideration of current educational needs, the level of computer provision, teacher expertise and issues concerning the processes of innovation in education.

As well as these conceptual and practical issues, ICAI might be associated with broader social attitudes to education, and indeed to the nature of humanity, which may prove to be seditious. Considered under this heading will be: ICAI as a panacea for the ills of education; and possible associations between ICAI and anthropomorphic views of computers. To leaven criticisms offered throughout the paper, a suggestion will be made about an approach to ICAI which might side-step or defuse some of the criticisms raised earlier.

☐   Disclaimer

Many of the comments made in this paper will be critical of ICAI. It is appropriate to begin, therefore, by making some positive remarks. The purpose of the paper is not to be dismissive of past achievements and future potentiality, but rather to help to shape the direction in which research into ICAI might go.

Some of the virtues of ICAI are:

- It has obvious surface plausibility. Clearly the idea of injecting intelligent help into learning systems appears sensible; the development of systems which adapt to users' needs might plausibly be of benefit in education.

- AI/ICAI has a good track record in domains in which: money poses no problems for development, or for running costs; students are highly motivated; material is heavily factually based, and where these facts can be accreted in quantity.

- ICAI is great fun, exciting, poses a range of intellectual challenges for researchers, irrespective of the inherent educational utility of these challenges.

- ICAI/AI has had a great influence on both psychology and computer science and has encouraged researchers to talk to each other, to build models of processes, and to be explicit about such terms as 'knowledge representation', 'heuristics', and the like, in a way which was impossible before the advent of powerful computers.

Panegyrics on the benefits of ICAI and AI can be found elsewhere (Boden, 1977). Here we will tackle the issue of the likely successes of ICAI both in principle, and in practice.

■ Problems for ICAI in mathematical education

It is rather hard to describe the potential benefits and hazards associated with the development of ICAI across the whole framework of education. To limit the scope of the discussion and to provide concrete, illustrative examples, the discussion will be restricted to the problems which ICAI faces in the domain of mathematical education. Even within this domain, comments will be restricted to school-based education; the potential contribution of ICAI at a tertiary level will not be considered. The range of criticisms which can be levelled at ICAI approaches will be illustrated by considering two themes: the first concerns approaches to the modelling of user misconceptions in their use of algorithms, taking DEBUGGY as an example; the second involves the potential for ICAI techniques to support students who are engaged in open-ended problem solving. In the latter case there are no exemplars available for criticism, and indeed it will be argued that such exemplars are impossible in principle.

☐   **Problems with DEBUGGY**

DEBUGGY (Brown and Burton, 1978) considers the errors which pupils make when they solve subtraction problems. One might assume that errors in subtraction arise simply from computational errors which occur at random. Closer analysis of the performance of individual pupils, however, reveals some systematicity in patterns of errors, which can lead one to draw inferences about specific errors which are implicit in the underlying subtraction algorithms. Errors can arise either from bugs within the algorithms, or from omissions. (Such error analyses are well known to the education fraternity, and can be traced back at least to the 1930s.)

The general insight that errors can arise from systematic misconceptions, and that these misconceptions can be diagnosed and remediated is a valuable one. If nothing else, this framework can encourage teachers to look hard at patterns of errors, and to devise methods for remediating their pupils' misconceptions, by the wide variety of means available to them. (Especially by finding realistic situations such as giving change, or counting sweets, which can be devised so that pupils themselves notice computational errors when their subtraction algorithms give rise to answers which clash with their experientially based expectations.)

DEBUGGY describes 110 primitive bugs which can be assembled into more complex bugs. It contains a lattice model of subtraction skill which is subdivided into about 58 subskills.

On the basis of the computer model of subtraction skills, pupil responses to subtraction problems can be fed into DEBUGGY, which can then provide a diagnosis of the pupil's current knowledge about subtraction processes. This can then be the basis for appropriate tutoring (as provided by DEBUGGY). Before we criticize this approach, it might be appropriate to try an example of understanding the processes involved in subtraction.

Figure 1 consists of four different methods for carrying out subtraction. Method A is commonly used; the other three methods are quite unusual. None of these methods contains any errors. Please try to explain how each method works, then say why the method works. You will find this a non-trivial task.

Now review your explanations of why the methods work.

You are likely to have deployed a variety of representations of the problem, including some algebraic methods and perhaps some diagrams which involve number lines.

What criticisms of DEBUGGY (and related approaches) are suggested by your experiences with this example?

A	1225	B	1225	C	1225	D	1225
	876		876		876		8775
	349		226		1459		876
			123		349		9651
			349				349

Figure 1 Four methods of subtraction.

- A variety of idiosyncratic methods and approaches can be taken to the task of solving subtraction problems. DEBUGGY has no access to the huge variety of individual methods which might conceivably be used.

- DEBUGGY has no means of access to pupil accounts of how they solve problems, and therefore cannot begin to learn about the possible range of such idiosyncratic methods.

- The knowledge involved in debugging algorithms which you – as a sophisticated subtractor – have brought to bear, reveals the rich interconnections between different domains in mathematics.

- When a range of pupil solutions to subtraction problems is considered, DEBUGGGY fares no better than a human teacher. It seems reasonable to predict that DEBUGGY would fail completely to debug errors in the idiosycrantic methods presented in Figure 1 (since teachers find it hard).

- One might reflect on the benefits of offering human teachers skills in debugging algorithms, rather than on devolving such tasks to a machine. Further, one might argue that the pupils themselves should be the major agents in the debugging process, since they are the ones who have most to gain from it. The notion of debugging as an intellectual task which might have great educational value is largely unexplored despite strong advocacy (e.g. Papert, 1980).

Divorcing algorithms from applications is a device of very doubtful pedagogical value. Subtraction should not be viewed as a self-contained topic which is separate from 'mathematical thinking'. It should be viewed as an integral part of mathematics and mathematical thinking, and teaching should focus on extending and strengthening links with other areas of mathematics. Many of the ways in which mathematics is currently taught have been strongly criticized (Cockcroft, 1982) because of their focus on technical success rather than understanding. DEBUGGY seems to reinforce such a view. Considerable problems are associated with divorcing algorithms from practice; most obviously, that algorithms can be quickly forgotten, but more importantly, that the contexts in which algorithms can usefully be deployed remain unlearned. Pupils find major problems in knowing when to deploy particular algorithms (for example *when* to multiply or divide or subtract) when faced with realistic situations. DEBUGGY is implicitly supporting this split between algorithms and application.

If our goals are to foster subtraction skills which are robust and useful to pupils we need to:

- encourage the exploration of idiosyncratic methods, rather than insist that pupils learn other people's algorithms;

- expose pupils to a wide variety of situations in which subtraction tasks are presented;

- offer pupils insight into the functioning of their own algorithms, and ask them to explain why they work and to identify faults for themselves;

- emphasize the role of estimation, since algorithms do sometimes go wrong because of simple (random?) errors. It is important that pupils have some sense of the likely size of the answer when they begin a computation, rather than simply possessing a carefully polished algorithm which occasionally produces disastrously wrong results.

☐   **Problems with open-ended problems**

Problem solving is not an activity which is the exclusive property of mathematics; nevertheless, it is a topic which frequently emerges within the mathematical domain. For example, problem solving was chosen as the theme for the 1980s by the National Council of Teachers of Mathematics. There is a very large academic literature on the subject of problem solving to which AI researchers have made significant contributions. We will begin this discussion by sketching out a default model of problem solving to which many people subscribe. Some headings to be considered are shown in Figure 2.

Knowledge base refers to a whole range of facts, skills, relationships, and techniques, which the solver brings to bear on a particular problem. This might be viewed as an intellectual tool-kit.

Control refers to the way in which these resources are deployed. Solvers have a range of ways of tackling novel problems both at the heuristic level (for example, 'try simple cases', 'think of a related problem', 'work systematically', 'make a table') and at a more strategic

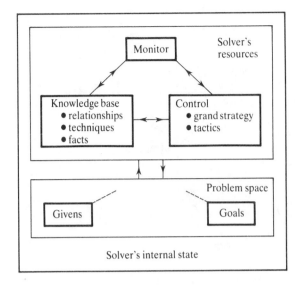

Figure 2   Minimum requirements for a model of human problem solving.

level (for example, 'choose different representations', 'plan out a solution path before you work on the details'). When dealing with a familiar problem users can recognize the problem type and can recall specific strategies, tactics and resources in order to solve it. When faced with unfamiliar problems, solvers must take active control over their problem-solving processes and should be made aware of the need to think strategically and tactically about the way they tackle the problem and about the resources they will bring to bear on the problem.

Monitor: relatively recently attention has focused on the need for problem solvers to monitor their own performance. Concepts such as metacognition, reflection, and self-awareness all refer to the need for problem solvers to emerge from the solving process at regular intervals in order to assess their progress.

The problem space: as well as this rather static description of the skills which a solver has at his or her disposition which might be of help when solving problems, one can also describe the dynamic state of the solver during problem solving. Here we need recourse to a story about the problem space, which will include a description of the elements within the problem space, together with a description of the kind of operators that the solver chooses to use; some description of the problem goals as the solver judges them; and a story about the intellectual flow between elements within the problem space, as mediated by the problem solver's resources, control system and monitoring system.

i. How many cubes are needed to build this tower?

ii. How many cubes are needed to build a tower
like this, but 12 cubes high?

iii. Explain how you worked out your answer to part ii.

iv. How would you calculate the number of cubes
needed for a tower *n* cubes high?

Figure 3   Skeleton Tower.

This sketch should not be viewed as a prescription for a particular
architecture for problem solving. For current purposes, it makes little
difference if *control* is described as being part of the *knowledge base*, or
if *monitor* is subsumed under *control*, or if more explicit connections
are made between the problem space, the world outside the solver, and
the solver's knowledge base. The reader will probably have already
noticed how much of this vocabulary has been derived from the AI
literature; and how this model in its current descriptive state can be
represented by a number of currently existing architectures.

This description appears quite familiar to members of the AI
fraternity, so how can one justify the assertion that modelling this
process in an individual is impossible in principle? Again, perhaps we
should begin by an illustration of your own cognitive processes as you
attempt to solve a straightforward but, hopefully, unfamiliar task. Please
attempt the problem shown in Figure 3. Don't throw any of your notes
away: you will find it useful to reflect on them after you have solved the
problem.

What problems might emerge for ICAI systems that attempt to facilitate human problem solving?

(a) *Cues* Understanding the processes that someone else goes through as they solve problems is hard for a human observer (even for observers who have set out to invent paper and pencil notations for just this purpose, for example Ridgway and Mansell, 1985). One of the main problems which human observers face is that they are presented with a multiple parallel stream of cues about internal processes such as: diagrams; writing – odd notes, doodles; speech – often in fragmentary form; odd analogies and slang expressions; and a range of gestures such as pointing to different parts of the figure or gazing towards particular pieces of written work; social cues which yield evidence of understanding, ignorance, frustration, withdrawal, and the like. Each of these cues can have some relevance to the problem-solving process. None of them is accessible to the computer. If you review your work on skeleton tower in Figure 3 you are likely to find a set of disconnected elements which relate to your early attempts to solve the problem. If you reflect on the process you went through during the solution of this problem you are likely to tell a rich story about cues you were able to make use of in the figure, fragments of knowledge and half-remembered ideas that later proved to be relevant, and the like. The process of giving this range of cues to the computer is overwhelmingly difficult.

(b) *Representation* Polya (1962) advocated that solvers should choose multiple representations when they begin to solve a problem. For skeleton tower, for example, one might choose a geometric representation, an algebraic one, or one might simply build up tables of numbers which correspond to towers of different sizes. It is also rather natural for humans to switch between these stages and states. This will prove to be rather problematic for computers to follow. Consider the different methods of internal representation which humans bring to bear. These include words, numbers, all sensory states; motor representations (indicated by gesturing such as hand-waving); varieties of imagery; spatial representations, and even algebra. While some translations between these states are possible, many such translations feel artificial and strange and fail to capture the essential quality of the representations. (For example, the efforts of writers to capture the essential qualities of music, art, or food and wine, in words can be a source of considerable mirth to readers.) From the viewpoint of user modelling, it is hard to see how a computer could keep track of multiple representations and the various degrees of transfer between each.

(c) *Changing representations* Characteristics of solving unfamiliar problems are that one changes representations quickly; one changes the

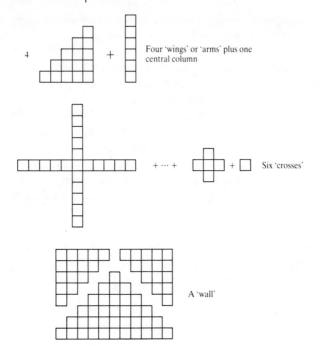

Figure 4   Pupil methods

primitives which one chooses to work with; one changes the operators used as work progresses.

For example, in an early attempt to solve skeleton tower, one might well consider a block to be a fundamental unit. However, Figure 4 illustrates a variety of pupil solutions which involve the construction of a whole range of larger scale primitives and a range of different operators.

One pupil has pulled the tower apart and considered it to be four 'wings'; another has pulled off two 'wings', inverted them, and put them on the remaining structure to create a 'wall'; another views the skeleton tower as a set of crosses and so on.

So human problem solvers change representations qualitatively as they solve problems, and change the primitive elements within their problem space, as well as the operators quite dramatically. They also use idiosyncratic labelling systems, which depend on a lot of analogizing and forging relations with real-world knowledge. Examples are labels such as 'wings', 'wall' and 'cross'. All these changes are hard for humans to track, even given that humans have access to a large range of shared real-world knowledge (and in the case of trained observers, have access to knowledge of a large number of different solution attempts). I will conclude, therefore, that modelling on-going problem solving in real time is impossible for ICAI systems.

(d) *Machine-human interaction*   If the human solver is required to input details about problem-solving efforts, during solution, this activity of self-monitoring is quite likely to interfere with ongoing problem-solving processes and is likely to have negative effects on the outcome of the problem-solving session. Questioning strategies might fail because students can know how to do things without being able to describe their knowledge.

Drawing inferences about control and monitoring processes from written or keyed responses is extremely difficult. In our work, we often adopt the device of setting pupils to work on problems in pairs. We have found this to offer a natural way of eliciting control and monitor remarks from pupils. Since pupils feel obliged to explain to each other why they are embarking on particular problem-solving tracks, they experience pressures to explain idiosyncratic representations, and quite spontaneously generate monitoring remarks, such as 'I'm stuck!' and 'Why are we doing this?' A second major role, played by pairs, is that they naturally interrogate each other and demand explanations. It is hard to imagine machine dialogues which can be as responsive and helpful as a fellow pupil.

(e)   *Problems with current attempts at user modelling*   '... at present there are not even any established techniques of user modelling, as such. All that exists is a collection of promising prototypes ... ' (Ross *et al.*, 1986). User modelling is a major target of many efforts in ICAI. These efforts are usually based on the assumption that there exists a rather small set of naive models which can be readily diagnosed. We have already seen in the domain of subtraction that the range of naive models is in fact very large. As the domain gets increasingly complex, the range of possible naive models also increases dramatically. It seems highly likely that no exhaustive set of naive models will ever be produced in a complex domain. To be crudely pragmatic, is the effort to compile an exhaustive list of naive models itself worth while? Humans are rather good at understanding explanations which others propose; many teachers have sophisticated skills for unpicking interesting conglomerations of naive models, and misconceptions. In many cases, the pupils themselves have these skills.

At a more principled level, if we take the view that the machine is there to explore the user's naive model and to provide some diagnosis and subsequent remediation, then we are assigning an important learning task to the machine which could be performed by either a fellow pupil or by a teacher. From the learner's viewpoint this may be of no consequence. However, from the fellow pupil's or the teacher's viewpoint, it may have undesirable consequences in that they will thereby lose the opportunity to engage in a form of learning situation of considerable complexity and potential value. It seems a rather strange proposition that one should write computer programs which impoverish the potential for learning by teachers or by other pupils.

(f)   *Domain specificity*   A well-known criticism of ICAI systems is that they focus on a particular narrow domain (for example chemical analysis, fault location in particular equipment, arithmetic, diagnosis of chest diseases ...). Knowledge is more than a repertoire of skills intended to perform some particular tasks. An intended outcome for education is that pupils will generalize their learning to a range of contexts. In order to make such generalizations, they must experience similar skills embedded in a variety of contexts. One educational device we employ is to involve pupils in activities which lead to the integration of mathematics and their everyday lives and experiences. So, many activities involve the use of objects such as counters, cups, cards, dominoes, beer mats and the like. Many of the mathematical activities involve them in shifting representations between written language, graphs, symbols, verbalizations, movement of objects, and so on. Our overall approach might be said to be to attempt to enrich the semantic network of mathematical concepts by extensive elaboration, as well as the more obvious goals of introducing pupils to process and monitoring skills. Unless pupils elaborate their knowledge as they work they will be unable to generalize their learning experiences. The focus of ICAI on the performance of specific tasks (necessary because of the problems representing semantically rich domains) can therefore be seen as a move towards a restricted educational environment, rather than towards an enriched one.

(g)   *Helping students*   Choosing appropriate guidance for pupils who are experiencing difficulties can be problematic. We have developed modules for use in mathematics lessons which are intended to foster problem-solving skills in pupils aged 14–16 years (Ridgway *et al.*, 1984c; Shell Centre for Mathematical Education, 1984, 1986). Each module supports about four weeks of mathematics lessons, and consists of: photocopying masters for pupil worksheets: dumb CAI (suitable for use with groups, or the whole class, as well as with individuals); teacher support in the form of a video; and a teacher workbook which offers lesson plans, and explicit guidance to teachers about the kinds of help which are, and are not, appropriate for people who are learning to solve problems (as well as advice on marking schemes, and a full set of solutions to problems!). The modules recommend strongly that pupils be encouraged to struggle with problems. This might seem somewhat perverse. We argue, however, that since our major goal is to facilitate pupils' acquisition of control skills and self-monitoring, they must be placed in situations where they have the confidence to exercise these skills. One cannot exercise these skills if one deals exclusively with familiar problems or if someone else reduces the strategic load and the need to monitor one's performance by giving help ill-advisedly. Our

When pupils learn to solve problems, they have to learn how to decide *what* to do and *when* to do it. If someone always tells them what to do, they *won't* learn these skills for themselves.

Aim to provide less and less guidance as you get further into the course.

Use freely any hints that make children think about the way they are tackling the problem:

> 'What have you tried?'
> 'Well, what do you think?'
> 'What are you trying to do?'
> 'Why are we doing this?'
> 'What will we do when we get this result?'

Use sparingly, particularly later on, hints about which strategies they should use:

> 'What have you found out so far?'
> 'Have you seen anything that is like this in any way?'
> 'How can we organize this?'
> 'Let's draw up a table of results.'
> 'Can you see any pattern?'
> 'Have you tried some simple cases?'
> 'What examples should we choose?'
> 'How can we start?'
> 'Have you checked if that works?'

Avoid any hint referring to the particular problem:

> 'Do you recognize square numbers?'
> 'Explore it like this.'
> 'Why don't you try using three counters?'

Figure 5   Checklist for the teacher.

helping hierarchy is shown in Figure 5.

We offered this advice to teachers having seen several examples in class where the pupil was able to 'drive' the teacher to the position where the pupil's task was made trivially easy. 'Teacher driving' begins by asking for advice on how to tackle an unfamiliar problem. Here is an invented dialogue between an unsophisticated teacher and a sophisticated child.

P: I don't know what to do, miss.
T: What have you tried so far?
P: Nothing really, miss; I don't know how to start.
T: Why don't you try a simple case?
P: How do you mean, miss?
T: Well, you could look at a much smaller tower.
P: How do you mean, miss?

T: Well, how many blocks would there be in a tower one cube high?

P: … just one, miss?

T: And how many would there be in a tower two cubes high?

P: … um … would there be six, miss?

T: So we can make up a table like this (draws) and count up the number of cubes in towers of different heights, then look for a pattern. You do that and I will come back and see you in a minute or two.

In this invented dialogue, the pupil faced with a difficult intellectual challenge, has successfully engineered the situation where the teacher has done all the strategic work and has left the pupil with a simple, clerical task of counting cubes and recording results. It is easy to imagine how this dialogue will proceed when an appropriate number of cases has been built up and the task proceeds on to spotting patterns and looking for algebraic relationships. It is rather harder to imagine any educational benefit for the pupil.

It has been clear from our classroom observations that handling discourse with pupils, and the assessment of appropriate levels of help which students should be offered requires careful judgement. Certainly a whole range of social cues are available to the teacher; so is an extensive memory of past pupil behaviour in different circumstances as well as detailed knowledge of the pupil's learning history. None of these sources of information will be available to an ICAI system, and so provision of help will be made on the basis of an impoverished set of information.

In educational terms this could well lead to pupils driving ICAI systems to present them with intellectually trivial tasks, rather than presenting pupils with the more challenging tasks which the ICAI designer had intended.

(h)   *Individual work*   Since a major focus of ICAI involves the development of user models, the paradigm is usually for one pupil to interact with one machine. This has a number of disadvantages. In our work in problem solving, we have been keen to foster collaborative work for a number of reasons.

- Pupils are often called upon to explain to partners their reasons for choosing particular styles of attack.

- Pupils are more likely to engage in monitoring remarks.

- Trivial errors, for example in simple counting or elementary computation, are far fewer when pairs work together, and are detected far quicker. (In tasks such as finding algebraic descriptions of number patterns, the difficulty level rises dramatically if the number pattern contains some error.)

Is there scope for using ICAI to support group work? The task of monitoring the cognitive processes of two problem solvers, in conjunction with an attempt to monitor their corporate problem-solving space seems difficult, and compounds the problems of monitoring a single user's problem-solving processes. It will be argued later that a focus on one-to-one tutorial work goes against current movements which are setting out to foster more collaborative work in mathematics classrooms.

(i)   *The expert problem solver* A common misconception is that the novice deviates from the expert in some simple way. For example, the novices might be viewed as having too few routines, and needing to add more to their repertoire; or they might be viewed as having some misconceptions, bugs, or mal-rules. Both of these simplistic views are wrong. There are major differences between novices and experts which are not so readily remedied. Another common misconception is to talk about *the* way that an expert solves the problem. A major characteristic of experts is that they can solve the same problem in a variety of ways. Experts can also translate between representations and can relate and reconcile different approaches, and different modes of representation. Attempts to tutor pupils into *the* expert's methods are therefore fundamentally misguided. They also limit the kinds of educational activities which might be pursued.

■ The needs of mathematical education

So far, oblique references have been made to educational goals in mathematics; perhaps these should be articulated more clearly so that the potential contribution of ICAI to mathematical education can be evaluated. A clear summary of these goals is provided by the Cc᠄ᵏᵗcroft Report (1982). Paragraph 243 states:

> mathematics teaching at all levels should include opportunities for
> > exposition by the teacher;
> > discussion between teacher and pupils and between pupils themselves;
> > appropriate practical work;
> > consolidation and practice of fundamental skills and routines;
> > problem solving, including the application of mathematics to everyday situations;
> > investigational work.

Where do current models of ICAI fit into the scheme of things? They certainly fit in rather well with the exposition–consolidation and practice aspects. However, surveys in schools (for example Her Majesty's Inspectors of Schools, 1979) reveal that these are predominant in classroom activities anyway. The 'missing' activities of discussion, practical work, problem solving, and investigation, seem ill-suited to current ICAI approaches. Certainly dialogue strategies available on machines are extremely impoverished. It is hard to see how practical work can be facilitated, given current limitations on computer interfaces. Problem solving has been the subject of the earlier section where it was argued strongly that current conceptions of ICAI are quite unsuited to the fostering of problem solving. Investigational work probably poses even greater problems than does problem solving, since the thrust of an investigation is to take a simple mathematical seed and to explore its implications in some domain of the pupil's choice. It is clear that to monitor and facilitate investigational work one needs an extensive and elaborate knowledge base in the domain of mathematics and mathematical processes. The problems of representing extensive knowledge domains, including real-world knowledge, via computers, are well-known, and at present can be judged impossible.

Paragraph 207 of the Cockcroft Report reads 'the fundamental criterion at all stages must be the extent to which any piece of software offers opportunity to enhance and improve work in the classroom'.

We have no evidence of any sort about the impact of ICAI techniques within the classroom. Given our reservations about the things that ICAI is likely to be good for, one might make the gloomy prediction that ICAI will focus on conservatism and a rather old-fashioned view of the nature of mathematical knowledge, and, if implemented, will become a barrier to innovation rather than an agent for the enhancement of mathematical curricula.

☐ **Missing activities**

(1) *Pupil explanations* both to fellow pupils and to the teacher are essential aspects of mathematical learning. In our work we encourage pupils to explain things clearly in words before they attempt to write down their explanations. It is not clear how this can be done using ICAI systems.

(2) *Group work* has many advocates because of its role in eliciting control and meta-cognitive remarks; because of studies which show social facilitation (that is group performance which excels that of the best individual within the group); and because group work is an inherently valuable skill (that is the ability to work well in a group is in itself an educational objective, since such skills are likely to be useful outside the classroom). It is not clear how ICAI can facilitate group work.

(3) *Reflection.* The general topic of meta-cognitive skill, self-description and self-evaluation is both fashionable and relevant to

individual development. ICAI does not seem a terribly good vehicle for fostering reflection.

☐ The new curriculum

Concerns over the nature of school mathematics and the ways in which it should be taught are the focus of a good deal of debate, internationally. In the United Kingdom, for example, debates are taking place about the nature of mathematics and the way it should be taught. The NCTM Conference on the Impact of Computing Technology on School Mathematics discussed the needs for the development of new curricula and new instructional methods. It was suggested that there should be a de-emphasis on mechanical and manipulative skills, and a corresponding increase in the emphasis and attention paid to the development of concepts, the establishment of relationships between mathematical structures, problem-solving and investigational skills. Again, we can view this as a move away from the kinds of intellectual activities which ICAI seems able to support.

More radical approaches to curricula have been brought about, somewhat paradoxically, by advances in AI. These are analogous to changes promised by ready pupil access to calculators. The calculator has caused a good deal of debate about the kinds of mathematics which is appropriate to learn. Few people now would argue that pupils need high levels of technical proficiency in such tasks as long multiplication, long division and the calculation of square-roots by hand.

Rather, emphasis has shifted towards mental arithmetic on small numbers, estimation skills about an approximate size of answers, a focus on the meaning of operations and knowledge about when to deploy particular operations, and, of course, skills in using calculators. The computer provides analogous challenges, since packages such as MUMATH can perform most of the technical mathematical tasks that pupils might need up to their first year at university. The mathematical community has begun to address the problem of deciding which aspects of mathematics should be taught and how they should be taught. If a machine can perform a task faster more reliably than a student, and can also perform it for a wider range of cases, which of these skills should be taught and to what extent should students be required to master them?

Current educational goals are in a state of flux. As computers can take on more and more tasks that hitherto were the domain of expert humans, the definition of the range of tasks which humans should perform is changing. One can summarize this by saying that, as we try to meet current educational goals using ICAI we are actually shooting at a moving target. Worse than that, the movement of the target is controlled in some non-obvious way by the extent of our success to hit it.

■ Computers in education?

The role of computers in education could well be quite profound. Early explorations into language learning (for example LOGO, PROLOG), the use of graphical packages, statistics packages, simulations, modelling packages, spreadsheets, word processors, and the like, have barely begun. (For a review of research frontiers for IT in education, see Ridgway, 1986.) Our own studies have shown that the introduction of a computer programmed for use in whole class teaching can have dramatic effects on the social dynamics of the classroom, and can facilitate role shifts by the teacher which are notoriously difficult to achieve using other means (Fraser *et al.*, in press). Earlier criticisms about the challenges for stimulating problem solving, investigational work, discussion and group work which ICAI seems unable to meet *can* be met by dumb CAI and appropriate teaching (Ridgway *et al.*, 1984a).

The spirit of the times currently advocated by professional groups both in the United States and in the United Kingdom is towards a shift in teacher roles, away from an all-knowing expert, towards a facilitator of pupil learning. In this role, teachers will, we hope, foster collaborative learning, and act as models for problem-solving styles. From a student viewpoint, pupils will be expected to operate mathematically in more open environments, to acquire skills of discovery and skills for the acquisition of knowledge. The general concern in this brave new world is to integrate mathematical knowledge into general world knowledge, to be able to talk sensibly about mathematical processes and to know when and how to deploy one's skills. The major thrust of much current ICAI work adopts old frameworks which relate to the acquisition of formal algorithms.

☐ Practical constraints

Despite the widespread belief that computers are readily available in schools, a number of recent surveys have shown rather low levels of machine provision, although these levels are rising steadily. For example, Becker (1984) conducted a survey of 1600 schools which used micro-computers in the United States; he obtained replies from 1082 such schools. The survey was conducted in the period 1982–83. This survey found that less than 20% of secondary school teachers had access to eight or more micros at a time and that typically even with eight computers ' ... students may spend as much as three-quarters of their time waiting for their turn at the computer'.

In the United Kingdom Esterson (1985) reports a survey conducted in 1984 by BBC/MEP of UK secondary schools which reported that on average there were 10 microcomputers per school.[1]

Given the dependence of ICAI on one pupil to one machine, there are considerable practical barriers to implementation. Of course this blanket assertion about the number of computers ignores the nature of the machines. These are almost invariably 8-bit machines with rather limited memory capacity, quite unsuited for running the large ICAI programs currently being developed.

☐   **Teacher resistance**

Issues of reliability of hardware and software are often to the forefront of teachers' minds. Members of the computing fraternity have a certain tolerance for software foibles and even for the idiosyncracies of hardware. This tolerance does not necessarily extend to the teaching profession where the baseline for reliability is not another computer system that works even less well, but is a piece of chalk and a blackboard. Reliability of chalk is generally rather high; even when it fails, repair or replacement is rarely problematic.

All use of CAI in classrooms requires teacher training. We ask teachers to acquire new skills, both in handling machines and in reorganizing their classrooms. This can be associated with a range of practical problems, even when the application is rather straightforward dumb CAI (for example Ridgway *et al*., 1984b). If we are talking about the provision of ICAI these problems are likely to be amplified. At a higher level of concern, teachers may well have conceptual objections to ICAI that they do not have to CAI. Examples of such worries might be: If the program can do more maths than I can (for example, MUMATH) is it not a threat? If the computer can diagnose pupil errors better than I can, is it not a threat? One may well wonder whether teachers will be enthusiastic to use programs which appear to be more sophisticated in their mathematical knowledge (and of course in other domains) than they are.

If we reflect on surveys by Bialo and Erikson (1985) about the uses to which CAI is put, we can draw gloomier lessons than the most obvious ones that much software is of poor quality and that teachers are relatively untrained to choose or use it. Clearly, not all software is of poor quality. For example, there are commercially available packages such as spreadsheets and database management systems, which work robustly. Educational uses of such packages can readily be found (Catterall and Lewis, 1985). So the problem is not simply one of poor software but is more deeply ingrained in teacher views of the appropriate use of CAI in education. The strongest version of this argument is that the technology has been absorbed into the social values of the educational system. That is to say that rather than the technology offering ways of bringing about qualitative improvements in the educational process, and therefore being the focus of intense activity by the educational community, one might argue the converse: namely, that the computer is seen to be a potential threat which should be rendered impotent by trivializing its uses in class. If this fate befalls competent and robust dumb software, which has relatively modest educational goals, and offers rather little in the way of 'threat' to teachers, what fate is likely to befall ICAI, with its promise to be more sophisticated than the teacher in several areas where professional pride is at stake?

■   Can ICAI be seditious?

- ICAI can be seditious if expertise is taken from the hands of teachers and placed in the hands of machines. Teachers need to learn how to teach and need to extend their knowledge of their subject specialism, in just the same way that academic researchers spend their lives learning more and more about their own particular subject specialisms. Removing major vehicles for teacher self-education (such as debugging skills and remediation) can be seditious.

- ICAI can be seditious if it acts to devalue communication between human beings, such as discussions between pupils, and discussions between pupils and teachers. It will be seditious if it draws attention away from the importance of group work, the importance of explanation, the importance of open-ended investigation, the importance of problem-solving activities, and the importance of reflecting on one's own mental processes.

- ICAI can be seditious if it increases a view that academic subjects should be viewed as consisting of atoms of technique which are divorced from applications and from each other.

- ICAI can be seditious if it is offered as a panacea for the ills of education. Of course no member of the ICAI community would make such bold claims, but who needs to? – they have already been made by others. For example:

'Consider for a moment a computer system that stores the knowledge, judgement, and intuition of the country's best educational diagnosticians. From this system, the information can be called up at any time to assist you, step-by-step in the assessment of your students ... These programs are called *expert systems*.' (Hasselbring, 1984)

'It is a simple step to turn an expert system into an excellent educational stimulation; and, by combining the knowledge of all top experts, it becomes a superior instructional device.' (Foster, 1984)

- ICAI can be seditious if it supports the view that there is a quick technological fix for every conceptual problem. At present we live in a society which seems to believe that technological answers can be found to conceptual problems. In the domain of international relations we see Star Wars as being offered as a 'solution' to the problems of international diplomacy. Safe generation of nuclear power is simply a question of developing good technology, and so on.

- ICAI can be seditious if the links between artificial intelligence and cognitive psychology lead us to devalue aspects such as open-ended problem solving, creative writing, musical composition, just because they are hard to describe within existing intellectual paradigms.

- ICAI can be seditious if it is associated with anthropomorphism. Imbuing machines with 'intelligence' and discussions about what the machine might be 'thinking about' are associated with risks that we devalue biological intelligence, thinking, feeling, and the like. This is not a necessary consequence of the development of ICAI systems, as Boden (1977) has illustrated; nevertheless, we should be aware of the potential risks. If people are like computers and computers are machines like motor cars and motor cars get old and are scrapped when they cease to function efficiently, then ...

■ Suggestion: Transparent ICAI systems

The overriding concern that has been expressed in this paper is that the intelligence in ICAI is being used for the wrong purpose. There is little need for intelligent machines whose purpose is to tutor techniques; rather, pupils and teachers need to be made more aware of epistemological issues, and to reflect on their own knowledge, and ways of acquiring knowledge. ICAI systems may well have a valuable role to play here.

ICAI systems usually possess, either explicitly or implicitly:

- A specification of the knowledge to be acquired (with some implicit epistemology).
- A set of teaching techniques (with some implicit theory of teaching).
- Rules to structure teaching sequences (with some implicit pedagogy).
- Descriptions of possible user states (with some implicit development theory).
- Beliefs about the current state of the user.

Users could be given access to some, or all, of this information. Of course, some information may be represented internally in ways which are quite opaque to the user, for example as tables of conditional probabilities, or as groups of production rules (and possible mal-rules). However, re-describing these states in ways intelligible to the user may have considerable advantages. In particular, if users are allowed to explore the knowledge domain in any way they choose (including being guided by the machine) then the teaching system might be able to offer differential support for users with different learning styles, such as Pask's (1976) wholists and serialists. Examining knowledge structures to be acquired before learning begins might offer benefits claimed by Ausubel (1968) for advance organizers. At a higher level of abstraction, one might expect some benefits to accrue simply by engaging in these meta-cognitive acts. Reflecting on the different ways in which knowledge can be represented, one's own preferred learning styles, devices to overcome misconceptions, and the like, is likely to have benefits outside the immediate learning environment, and will, we hope, transfer to other learning contexts. One might argue that these sorts of activities (exploring knowledge representations, teaching styles, user models, implicit philosophies) would be most beneficial to users who already possess a good deal of knowledge about the specific domain of interest. So transparent ICAI (TICAI) systems might have a useful role to play in fostering meta-cognitive skills, irrespective of their virtues as tutors within specific knowledge domains.

Making ICAI systems transparent to users is also likely to de-mystify their operation. Most systems have remarkably impoverished epistemologies and pedagogies, which users should be made aware of.

Offering the user a view from the machine about the user's state of knowledge may well have dramatic outcomes – either in terms of user outrage and rejection of the tutoring system, or perhaps as a stimulus for the user to update the machine model directly (either by demonstrations of competence in terms which the machine can recognize, or via statements of knowledge) or perhaps as a challenge to the user which increases motivation, then learning, dramatically.

How do TICAI systems relate to currently conceived ICAI systems? Surely, a competent ICAI system must precede the development of a transparent one? For most of the purposes here (notably ones concerned with fostering meta-cognition), TICAI systems need not function particularly well, since the user's task is to use the TICAI system to think about knowledge representation and acquisition – so impoverished systems will be quite adequate. For ICAI to work well, all the conceptual and practical problems described earlier need to be resolved. So the development effort needed for TICAI may well be less than that for functioning ICAI.

TICAI systems also have a role to play in teacher education. The ideas which underpin many ICAI programs – namely, that user models need to be understood, that one needs a clear story about the nature of the knowledge to be acquired, that a story about a logical sequence of knowledge acquisition should be developed, that misconceptions need to be explored, unravelled, diagnosed and remediated, are all viewpoints which can cause teachers to reflect upon their own teaching practices. Their own analyses of conceptions and misconceptions might usefully be compared with those of the machine. Any device which causes one to reflect on one's current practices and actions is likely to be beneficial. While ICAI seems an extraordinarily expensive way of fostering teacher reflection, it may nevertheless prove to be an effective one. Offering TICAI systems may also help to diffuse teacher anxieties about the role of computers in education, when they see the rather impoverished set of constructs which are available to machines, compared to constructs which they possess, and which their pupils can readily be brought to possess.

■ Editors' note

[1] By 1988, DES figures show, there were 2.5 micros per primary school and 23.2 per secondary school. BBC Acorn and Acorn Master accounted for 74% of micros in primary schools and 65% of secondary micros. (DES, 1989, *Survey of Information Technology in Schools*, Statistical Bulletin, 10/89. London: DSE).

■ References

Ausubel, D.P. (1968) *Educational Psychology: A Cognitive View*, Holt, Rinehart and Winston, New York.

Becker, H.J. (1984) School uses of microcomputers, *Journal of Computers in Mathematics and Science Teaching*, Summer, 24–33, Fall, 38–42 and Winter, 42–9.

Bialo, E.R. and Erikson, L.B. (1985) Microcomputer courseware: characteristics and design trends. *Journal of Computers in Mathematics and Science Teaching*, Summer, 27–32.

Boden, M. (1977) *Artificial Intelligence and Natural Man*, Harvester, Brighton.

Brown, J.S. and Burton, R.R. (1978) Diagnostic models for procedural bugs in basic mathematical skills. *Cognitive Science*, 2, 155–92.

Catterall, P. and Lewis, R. (1985) Problem solving with spreadsheets. *Journal of Computer Assisted Learning*, 1, 167–79.

Cockcroft, W.H. (1982) *Mathematics Counts*, Her Majesty's Stationery Office, London.

Esterson, D. (1985) The management of computing resources in schools. *Journal of Computer Assisted Learning*, 1, 134–48.

Forster, D. (1984) Simulation in tomorrow's schools. *Computers in the Schools* **1**, 9, 81–9.

Fraser, R. Burkhardt, H., Coupland, J. *et al.* (1986) Human-human-machine interactions, *Abacus* (in press).

Her Majesty's Inspectors of Schools (1979) *Aspects of Secondary Education in England*. Her Majesty's Stationery Office, London.

Pask, G. (1976) Styles and strategies of learning. *British Journal of Educational Psychology*, **46**, 128-48.

Polya, G. (1962) *Mathematical Discovery,* Wiley, New York.

Ridgway, J. (1986) Research needs for educational uses of information technology, I.T.E. Occasional Paper 9, Economic and Social Research council.

Ridgway, J and Mansell, K. (1985) Fostering and observing problems solving in mathematics classrooms, Shell Centre for Mathematical Education, University of Nottingham.

Ridgway, J., Benzie, D., Burkhardt, H. *et al.* (1984a) Investigating CAL. Computers and Education, 8, 85–92.

Ridgway, J., Benzie, D., Burkhardt, H. *et al.* (1984b) Conclusions from CALtastrophies. *Computers and Education*, **8**, 93–100.

Ridgway, J., Swan, M., Haworth, A. and Coupland, J. (1984c) Innovations in mathematical education – the TSS approach, in *Proc. Fifth International Congress on Mathematical Education* (ed. M. Carss), Birkhauser, Boston.

Ross, P., Jones, J. and Millington, M. (1986) User modelling in intelligent teaching and tutoring, in *Trends in Computer Aided Education* (eds R. Lewis and E.D. Tagg). Blackwell, Oxford.

Shell Centre for Mathematical Education (1984) *Problems with Patterns and Numbers*, Joint Matriculation Board, Manchester.

Shell Centre for Mathematical Education (1986) *Language of Functions and Graphs,* Joint Matriculation Board, Manchester.

Paper 2.2

A *Critical Evaluation of Educational Software: 'Climate'*

John Self

Teachers are enthusiastic about the use of micros and will vouch for their educational effectiveness. And yet, while watching several lessons and looking into many more educational software products, I have become increasingly uneasy. Not only is most existing educational software of poor quality, as is generally conceded, but there are, in my opinion, deep problems with even the best programs. Worse still, this is not a passing phase, a consequence of our transitory ignorance of how to use computers effectively to aid learning.

One symptom of malaise is the general eagerness to form superficial judgements of educational software products. Another symptom is a reluctance to look for general messages from programs outside one's own specialism. While there are of course differences in the design of software suitable for four-year-olds and for 40-year-olds, there are also similarities. Most educational software products are more expensive than textbooks and they should be critically examined in the same way – only more so! because we have not yet learned what it is reasonable to expect from educational software. Let us begin by taking a close look at the **Climate** program.

Climate presents the user with data for mean monthly temperature and rainfall and, through a series of multiple-choice questions, leads the user to a conclusion about the type of climate under consideration. According to the accompanying documentation, Climate may be used for both classroom demonstration and by an individual pupil.

First published in Self, J. *Microcomputers in Education: A critical appraisal of software* (1985) and reprinted with permission of Harvester Wheatsheaf.

Table 1

Questions	Possible answers
Which hemisphere?	northern, southern, equatorial
Which thermal belt?	cold, cool, warm, hot
Which latitudinal belt?	Arctic, cool, warm, tropics
Comment on rainfall	very light, light, moderate, heavy
Comment on distribution	rain all year, drought, summer rain, winter rain, summer max, winter max

Let us imagine a pupil using Climate on his own. The five multiple-choice questions which the program asks the pupil are shown in Table 1, together with the possible answers for each question. If the pupil answers a question incorrectly, a graphical hint is given. After answering all five questions correctly, the pupil has to try to classify the climate as one of 14 types.

The Climate program has access to data from 56 weather stations but only 28 of these are significantly different from one another. I have summarized some of these data in Table 2.

Our first question must be: What is the pupil expected to learn from this program? The documentation says that pupils find difficulty 'when encountering the disciplines of causality and identification for the first time. This program is designed to provide them with practice in these important disciplines'. What does this mean?

The pupil is faced with a classification task, and as in any such task

Table 2

Station number	Answers to the 5 questions	Classification
1	northern, hot, tropics, very light, drought	Hot Desert
4	southern, hot, tropics, very light, drought	Hot Desert
5	equatorial, warm, tropics, heavy, rain all year	Modified Equatorial
8	northern, hot, tropics, heavy, rain all year	Tropical Marine
.	.	.
.		.
.		
46	northern, cold, Arctic, light, summer max	Taiga
49	northern, cold, Arctic, very light, drought	Taiga
50	northern, cold, Arctic, light, summer max	Tundra
53	northern, cold, Arctic, very light, drought	Tundra
54	northern, cold, Arctic, very light, drought	Polar

there are several subtasks which have to be mastered. These are:

(1) To identify the relevant features (such as temperature, rainfall distribution, and so on).

(2) To 'evaluate' those features (for example, to work out what the rainfall distribution is).

(3) To use known rules based on these features to derive a classification (for example, to infer that anywhere which is both hot and dry is a 'Hot Desert').

(4) To discover new rules for new situations (for example, to induce the definition of 'Taiga' from the examples seen).

Let us consider each of these in turn. First, with Climate the pupil does not have to identify the relevant features: the program asks five questions (always the same five and always in the same order) and there is a strong implication that all and only the five features identified in these questions are relevant. Secondly, Climate does provide practice at evaluating these features, but this is really quite straightforward since the pupil has only to know the (somewhat arbitrary) definitions built into the program – for example, that 'moderate' rainfall means 500–1000 mm of rain a year. A mistake leads the program to give a graphical representation of this definition (always the same, regardless of which particular mistake the pupil has made or how many). Thirdly, if Climate is intended to give practice using previously learned classification rules, then it seems odd that the program does not acknowledge the existence of such rules. It does not, for example, give any sort of hint or comment, other than a blunt 'incorrect', if the pupil mis-classifies the climate. Fourthly, imagine that a pupil does not know what a Hot Desert is and is using this program to find out. The only two stations which relate to Hot Desert are the first two entries in Table 2. So what is the rule? Does it have to be in the tropics? Must it not be on the equator? There simply is not enough information from which to generalize. Of course, you probably already have a good idea about what a Hot Desert is, but what about Laurentian and Taiga?

In short, it is not clear what the program is designed to teach. In part, this confusion arises because the designers have not stated their assumptions about the knowledge built into the program.

Consider, for example, the implication that all and only the five features identified in the questions are relevant. It is obvious that not all five questions have to be answered in order to derive a classification – there are 1152 (i.e. $3 \times 4 \times 4 \times 4 \times 6$) possible ways to answer the five questions, but only 28 of these sequences arise. So, for example, if the answer to the fourth question is 'very light' then the fifth question need not be asked, for the answer must be 'drought'. Similarly, whatever the

Table 3

Station number													
5	rainfall	99	112	142	125	137	143	120	130	69	112	97	79
	temperature	15	15	16	15	15	15	15	15	16	15	15	15
	equatorial, warm, tropics, heavy, rain all year → Modified Equatorial												
28	rainfall	200	196	250	230	240	230	200	225	250	220	200	205
	temperature	26	26	27	26	26	26	26	26	27	26	26	26
	equatorial, hot, tropics, heavy, rain all year → Equatorial												

answer is to the second question then in 27 cases out of the 28 the answer to the third question corresponds (that is the answers occur in 'pairs': cold–Arctic, cool–cool, warm–warm, hot–tropics).

Imagine a pupil who does not know the difference between 'thermal belt' and 'latitudinal belt': is he to conclude that they are the same thing? Even the clues that Climate gives after incorrect answers to these two questions are the same. The one case where these two answers differ occurs with station 5, which we can compare with station 28 (Table 3). Why is station 5 considered to be in the tropics, when Climate's own clue says it should be considered warm? Well, the answer is presumably that station 5 is at an altitude of 2880 m, whereas station 28 is at 49 m. I say presumably because Climate makes no comment on this apparently anomalous result (although, to be fair, the altitude is shown in the initial presentation of the data). But imagine a pupil who does not notice this fact – there is nothing in the questions to suggest that he should take any notice of altitude.

So, the five features which climate identifies are *not* sufficient to classify climates even with these artificial data (the data are not from real weather stations but 'theoretical' ones): we have found a sixth: altitude. Climate's five features are not independent, and not necessary or sufficient to classify climates. In fact, it is obvious from Table 2 that answering the five questions correctly still did not give the pupil sufficient information to classify the climate.

Look at stations 49, 53 and 54: exactly the same sequence of answers leads to three different classifications. Why? Altitude is not the reason this time, for all three stations are at sea level. Table 4 gives the data for these three stations. A pupil unsure of the difference between Taiga, Tundra and Polar will look in vain for help from Climate – Climate will, apparently arbitrarily, label some of his classifications as 'incorrect', and that is all. A pupil may be inclined to accept such unquestionable

Table 4

Station number													
49	rainfall	2	4	0	1	11	13	20	17	8	7	8	4
	temperature	−40	−38	−32	−22	−12	4	12	8	5	0	−20	−35

northern, cold, Arctic, very light, drought → Taiga

53	rainfall	11	21	9	16	16	16	18	18	14	9	15	22
	temperature	−24	−20	−9	−5	3	5	8	6	4	0	−11	−17

northern, cold, Arctic, very light, drought → Tundra

54	rainfall	0	0	10	8	0	12	13	11	20	11	0	4
	temperature	−40	−30	−20	−15	−9	−2	0	−4	−7	−17	−28	−37

northern, cold, Arctic, very light, drought → Polar

dogmatism, but we may question whether Climate's answers are themselves 'correct'.

On consulting various standard texts on climatology, I found first a classification due to Strahler (see Barry and Chorley, 1982). He also gives 14 climate types: Wet Equatorial, Trade Wind Littoral, Tropical Desert, West Coast Desert, Tropical Wet–Dry, Humid Subtropical, Marine West Coast, Mediterranean, Middle Latitude Desert, Humid Continental, Continental Sub-Arctic, Marine Sub-Arctic, Tundra and Icecap. Only two climate types are the same as Climate's! Why should a pupil unfortunate enough to have learned Strahler's classification system be categorically told that his answers are incorrect? Moreover, Strahler's system is not the only one: there are many others, some based on quite sophisticated mathematical formulas. Climatology is, it seems, a very complex science.

Why, we might ask (and it would be a good question for a pupil to ask), bother to classify climates at all? Climate types unlike, for example, insect types do not have precise boundaries. In one sense, all classification schemes are devised for the sake of convenience. It helps to have a word or a phrase which can be used instead of a long definition. So we use the word 'desert' expecting everyone to have at least a rough idea of what is meant. Sometimes we use such a word to avoid having to say exactly what it means. Just how dry does a desert have to be to count as a desert? A precise answer, such as 'less than 25 mm rain a year', leads naturally to the response: 'Why 25 mm and not 30 mm?'

It is in asking such why questions that we begin to see the real point of classifying climates. It is not just to give us a convenient shorthand, but to provide a system which helps us to explain and understand different climates. So, a word like 'monsoon' is useful not just as a label but because it conjures up a picture of the *cause* of the climate: a particular combination of wind, sea and temperature. We can see this explanatory role of classifications by looking at the increasingly complex schemes created by climatologists.

First of all, there are schemes based directly on vegetation. These will say, for example, that a climate is tropical if its coldest month is hot enough to allow certain (tropical) plants to grow; that is, the mean temperature of the coldest month is at least 18 °C. This, then, explains one otherwise arbitrary definition used by Climate. Similarly, such a scheme will distinguish between Taiga and Tundra by vegetation (the former is a pine forest and the latter is treeless). But, of course, whether or not trees grow is determined partly by rainfall and temperature (it usually requires at least three months with temperatures above 6 °C for trees to grow). The second kind of classification scheme is based on 'moisture budgets' and thus tries to explain vegetation. These schemes make use of formulas involving temperature, rainfall, distribution, length of day, soil, and so on. Thirdly, we have 'genetic' classifications, which seek even more explanatory power by relating climates to wind regimes and air masses. Often rainfall and temperature do not appear explicitly in such schemes: Strahler's scheme is of this kind.

Most readers will probably not be very interested in climatology, but the point is that while a good geography teacher will know all this and much more, Climate does not, in any significant sense, know any of it. In order to design and to judge a program like Climate it is necessary to know the subject matter. We have said nothing about climate's use of graphics or its 'user-friendliness' (both of which are of a relatively high standard) because these are literally superficial: they are a gloss to cover a lack of substance. Climate cannot answer any of the questions which a pupil ought to ask.

Is this criticism fair and, if so, does it matter anyway? Any criticism has to be balanced against the aims and philosophies of those responsible for the product. According to the managing director of the team which developed Climate (*Computing*, 1983), the style of program is such that 'the computer is ... neutral. It presents information but does none of the teaching.' Well, the 'information' presented by Climate can be summarized on one A4 sheet – it is Table 2, and the definition of the terms therein. If it were simply a matter of presenting information, a sheet of paper would seem perfectly adequate. In fact, since Climate does not use real data it scarcely presents 'information' at all. No, the merits of Climate lie not in the information it presents but derive precisely from the fact that the computer can contribute to teaching and, more importantly, to learning.

In what sense could one say that Climate 'does none of the

teaching'? To answer this is desirable, of course, to try to say what 'teaching' is. According to Hirst (1971):

> 'A teaching activity is the activity of a person, A (the teacher), the intention of which is to bring about an activity (learning), by a person, B (the pupil), the intention of which is to achieve some end state (for example knowing, appreciating) whose object is X (for example a belief, attitude, skill).'

It is not, I think, reasonable to insist that the teacher, A, be a person for an activity to qualify as teaching: it is the activity which matters, not who, or what, performs it. Presumably, the designers of Climate intended learning to occur to achieve some object X, even if they did not say explicitly what X would be, and so the rest of the definition seems to hold. In fact, the main reason for disqualifying Climate from the teaching ranks is that the activity is not one which we willingly picture a good human teacher carrying out. To see why, we need look no further than the two conditions which, according to Hirst, teaching activities must meet.

The first is that 'the activity must, either implicitly or explicitly, express or embody the X to be learnt, so that this X is clearly indicated to the pupil as what he is to learn'. Climate certainly does not explicitly express X, and if it is implicit it is not clear to me, for one, what it is. Climate makes no attempt to ensure that the pupil understands what he is to learn and does not justify, explain or demonstrate the X in any way.

The second condition is that the activity 'must take place at a level where the pupil can take on what it is intended he should learn'. Climate takes no steps to ensure that this is so. It does not adjust the level to suit the pupil. It will respond in exactly the same way, regardless of the pupil's ability in learning X. Of course, when Climate is used as a classroom demonstration, the teacher will do what he can to ensure that these two conditions are met.

So Climate does not itself teach X (although one could imagine a differently programmed version of Climate which might be said to teach); but is it 'neutral'? An automatic washing machine may perhaps be said to be neutral in that it doesn't make any difference what clothes are put in: they will all get swirled round and come out clean. A washing machine, however, reflects its designer's view of the needs of its users, and there is a consensus about what these needs are, Similarly, Climate is neutral in that it does not matter what users type in, they all receive the same responses – and come out brainwashed (?). But Climate, too, reflects its designer's view of the needs of its users. In this case, however, there is little consensus. Various assumptions are built into Climate and to the extent that these are questionable Climate is not neutral. For example, Climate discourages pupils from asking questions (there is simply no mechanism for them to do so); it suggests that these sorts of problems can be solved by memorizing a small set of questions to ask; it assumes that a successful teaching strategy is to ask short questions which must be successfully answered; it assumes that displaying information on a computer screen rather than on, say, overheads, helps pupils to learn. In other words, while Climate is neutral in the sense of impartial or objective, it is not neutral in terms of the affective response elicited from pupils nor in terms of its underlying educational philosophy.

One danger in concentrating on one particular program in this way is that the reader may assume that this program has been selected precisely because it has defects not shared by most educational software. Other programs may well not have Climate's defects, but they will certainly have others. To be fair Climate does have its virtues: it is entirely free of bugs (as far as I am aware); it is very easy to use; the layout of information on the screen is relatively clear. In fact, by present standards, Climate rates highly. One reviewer described it as 'indubitably excellent' (*Computers in Schools*, 1983). Another considered that 'the program represents an intelligent and interesting approach to drill and practice [and is] good value for money' (MUSE, 1983). Yet a third thought that climate showed that 'the standard of software to support [the microcomputer] seems to be improving dramatically' (Day, 1983). Climate was produced by Five Ways, one of the three major centres subsidized under the UK Government's Microelectronics Education Programme (MEP) to produce computer-assisted learning (CAL) material. The director of the MEP (1982) considers that Five Ways gives a 'quick throughput of very high quality programs'.

■ References

Barry R.G. and Chorley R.J., *Atmosphere, Weather and Climate*, 4th edn (Bungay: Methuen, 1982), pp. 366–8.
Comments made during an interview at Plymouth in November 1982.
Computers in Schools, **5**, 4 (1983), p. 121.
Computing, 3 March 1983, p. 32.
Day Joseph, 'A successful science trio', *Educational Computing*, **4**, 9 (1983), p. 17.
Hirst Paul. H., 'What is teaching?', *Journal of Curriculum Studies*, **3**, 1 (1971), 5-18.
MUSE Report No. 4, 'Educational software' (December 1983), p. 18.

Paper 2.3

Computers in the Classroom

Charles Crook

There are many who will argue that computers have a dehumanizing influence on our lives. What is meant by such a claim? Most likely, it will be inspired by the relentless manner in which this technology encroaches upon areas of human work. But to take some particular activity and complain that it has been 'dehumanized' is not just to express concern for those whose labour gets displaced. This will be a complaint bearing on the interests of all those for whom the activity was conceived. The claim of dehumanization identifies a loss in the quality of our participation in some activity.

Of course, technological encroachments need not have such impact: often they may seem quite benign. The challenge, then, is to be alert to ways in which computer technology might be restructuring our experience of familiar exchanges. Perhaps in many such situations we will not feel perturbed by a loss of human contact. But in other circumstances such loss may seem just too great. Surely, this could well apply to an activity with such rich interpersonal characteristics as schooling.

The social organization of instruction is clearly challenged by present extensions of computers into schools. In a way, this is invigorating: it requires both critics and enthusiasts to identify the social dimension of education that they judge to be important. That is a debate which could well be informed by theory and research from developmental psychology, and one purpose of this paper is to highlight how such research may contribute to policy in this area.

First published in Rutkowska, J.C. and Crook, C. (eds.) (1987) *Computers, Cognition and Development.* © John Wiley and Sons, Inc. Reprinted by permission of John Wiley and Sons, Inc. All rights reserved.

The plan of the paper is as follows. First, I shall conceptualize some ways children may interact with computers and consider how such interactions challenge socially organized practices in early education. This analysis invites the suggestion that we stress the computer's potential for supporting collaborative work: two observational studies of such an application will be outlined. I shall then step back and appeal to research in developmental psychology to clarify how interactions among classroom peers could promote cognitive development. The conclusions of this review will highlight the kind of research needed to advance the present conception of peer interaction as a social context for classroom computers.

Two admissions should be made at the outset. Firstly, discussion must be confined to the primary school years. However, this is the period where the anxieties referred to above are greatest. Secondly, it behoves an optimist in these matters to acknowledge that establishing a way in which computer use *could* be developed is no promise regarding how it *will* be developed – but it is a necessary contribution.

■ Characterizing the pupil's interaction with computers

One way of expressing that strong interpersonal quality of school learning is to think of it in terms of various 'partnerships' into which pupils will enter. Successful learning depends on success in establishing and developing such partnerships – with tutors or with collaborators. Thus, the growth of children's understanding is socially mediated in this straightforward sense. In so far as this reflects our general belief, so it follows that we will value the interpersonal dimensions of learning and try to see that the partnerships involved are properly cultivated.

However, such an attitude is not free of complication. It may be argued that one important goal of formal education is to cultivate a capacity to learn independently; in a sense, to find some release from 'learning as partnership'. Now, claims of this sort introduce an element of tension: we wish to develop partnerships for purposes of socially mediated learning, but we also wish to cultivate in the learner a certain autonomy. Of course, tension of aims need not imply conflict of aims. Indeed, far from being in conflict, there may be a necessary developmental relation between socially organized cognitive functioning and that which is 'private' or autonomous to the individual (Vygotsky, 1978). Nevertheless, at the practical level of formulating strategies for teaching, there does remain a tension to be handled. Thus, in practice, one thing teachers must surely consider is how they should manage the learning process in terms of a balance of emphasis between pupil autonomy and interpersonal exchange.

☐ **Two varieties of interaction with school computers**

A claim central to the theme of this chapter is that classroom computers challenge our thinking about this balance and psychological processes relating to it. This requires us to reflect upon the 'social context' of learning in settings where computers play a significant role – to consider how it may disturb the balance of interpersonal processes in the classroom. We should feel some sense of urgency in this challenge, if only to respond to the evident appeal that computer-based activities have for young pupils (Lepper, 1985; Papert, 1980; Turkle, 1984).

Imagine a class of children absorbed in some computer task in much the way that these authors report. How are we to describe their engagement? One account could be in terms of the high degree of apparent autonomy in their learning: perhaps we compare children similarly absorbed in a more familiar task, such as reading or drawing. But a second account could describe their engagement in terms of a kind of partnership: in this case we form a comparison with more socially directed learning and assume the machinery is supporting something that resembles an interpersonal exchange. At first glance, it is not clear which of these two accounts best describes what is actually happening during children's interactions with computers.

In fact, there may be no grounds for unilaterally adopting just one of these possible perspectives. Which is more appropriate will depend on exactly what children are doing in a given situation. So, enthusiasts for the various educational applications of computers may align themselves differently with respect to these two models of computer interaction. For example, Seymour Papert (1980) seems to be expressing the present dichotomy with his much-quoted slogan: 'let the child control the computer not the computer control the child'. Of course, with this plea he is specifically aligning himself with the particular model of computer application that stresses the autonomy it offers the child – it puts the child in charge, it allows learning to occur around the individual's spontaneous activity.

We should not be too rigid about this dichotomy of possibilities for interacting with computers. But if we do prefer something resembling a continuum, then Papert's LOGO environment is surely at one of its extremities. This is self-directed learning; there is no instructional pressure imposed by computers acting as 'partners for dialogue'.

So, what kind of activities will lie towards the other extreme of a possible continuum? Papert himself seems to have in mind drill-and-practice routines reminiscent of the teaching machine tradition. Here the computer's role is usually to prompt children with a sequence of problems and provide suitable feedback for responses. In describing such programs, Papert has popularized a model of computers being 'in control' rather than the cosier view of them being 'in partnership'. This

attitude is contentious: software that denies children maximum autonomy as 'users' includes more than humdrum drill-and-practice
programs. So there is another school of enthusiasts that would develop
programs to draw children into powerful learning dialogues – or
partnerships [see, for example, Brown (1983) on computer-based
coaching or Pea's (1985) discussion of intelligent tutoring systems].

□   **Recovering an interpersonal dimension**

With regard to characterizing the pupil's interaction with computers, the
LOGO tradition and the tradition of intelligent tutoring systems seem to
proceed from different educational philosophies. Yet they do have a
significant common feature: they appear set to dilute an interpersonal
quality in the learning experience. A 'microworld' like LOGO is powerful
if it supports *self*-directed, discovery learning. Tutoring-style systems are
powerful in so far as they promote an instructional dialogue – with the
computer. How this shift of emphasis away from interpersonal processes
will bear on children's intellectual development is a pressing issue. But
suppose we wished to encourage a trend of this kind (say, for reasons of
economics), just how convincingly might we thereby dispense with
teachers' roles in early education?

Confident answers to that question must definitely wait upon
further research, much of it in areas of developmental and educational
psychology. In fact, trends of this kind are more easily discussed in terms
of how desirable, rather than how imminent, they appear. How do we
view models of future classrooms which portray children locked into
sustained but solitary interaction with their computers? This is definitely
not an appealing image. Perhaps it questions a stubborn intuition that
there is something very important about the familiar bustle of primary
school classrooms; that the interpersonal dimension of any learning
partnership is somehow vital. It may help to reflect upon this intuition.

It is probably not just based on a calculated doubt as to whether
technology really can replace particular interpersonal skills of instruction, although research may indeed prove these skills to be precious.
Neither is this intuition necessarily based on a respect for the particular
discourse practices that teachers can organize in their classrooms,
although these too may prove to furnish a precious experience
(Walkerdine, 1982). What may really count is the fact that whether or not
we feel committed to regarding intelligence as necessarily *acquired* in
socially organized contexts, we do acknowledge that it will most often be
exercised in socially organized contexts. What may compel us to protect
the interpersonal quality of early learning is the belief that cognitive
development involves a necessary coordination of our thinking with that
of others – in the interests of various kinds of harmony and in the service
of various kinds of joint activity.

This belief is central to the remainder of this chapter. Unambiguously, it encourages us to attend to the interpersonal dimension of classroom learning. So, we must consider how computer-based activities could be harmonized into an appropriate social context. My own discussion of this problem will not be comprehensive: in fact, it will completely evade the issue of how the role of teachers might evolve. This may appear eccentric but it represents a view that we may begin to define the social context by attending to interactions among the pupils themselves. In short, I wish to focus on the potential of computer-based activities to support a new priority for peer collaboration.

In the present section, discussion has focused on the child's interaction *with* the computer and how it may be conceptualized; what follows, however, really concerns interaction *around* computers. In contrast to socially isolating conceptions of computer use like those discussed above, the technology could function as a 'medium for joint activity'.

In order to develop this idea, it will be necessary to understand exactly what kind of 'medium' the classroom computer might provide for this purpose. As a forum for joint work, will it reveal distinctive properties? I shall approach this question in the next section where two case studies of such collaborative work will be outlined. They raise a number of issues which will prompt brief consideration of relevant theory and research in developmental psychology. However, at this point, some readers might still welcome further persuasion that collaborative work with computers is a social context that deserves to be studied. There is a more straightforward rationale for discovering what kind of joint activity this medium supports: the very scarcity of computers in the classroom obliges teachers to organize their use on a paired or group basis in order to maximize access. Thus, the typical manner in which computers are used makes them a current focus for collaborative work in primary schools. So, research is also needed to explore the consequences of practices which, at least for the present, are well established.

■ Collaborative working at computers: two studies

Hawkins *et al.* (1982) introduced LOGO programing to classrooms of 8–9 and 10–11-year-olds. Joint working arrangements were encouraged. Observers recorded measures of collaboration in LOGO and other class activities before, during and after the 6-week period for which it was available. There are three important findings for us to note. Firstly, the computer activity proved especially potent in facilitating collaborative exchanges. Secondly, post-tests revealed no evidence that this richer collaboration carried over to other classroom work. Thirdly, it emerged that the children had formed strong impressions concerning which of their peers were the experts at LOGO: 50% of them identified the same small group of children as LOGO experts – a much higher consensus than was reached for other areas of classroom expertise.

In short, a valuable study. But its interpretation does require caution. Note that the provision of these computer activities might have been a rather sudden and exciting break from classroom routine. This novelty alone could heighten the children's involvement and even attract their attention towards the achievements of others. Moreover (as the authors note), a lack of carry-over effects might reflect the rather short period of exposure. Such problems of method are difficult to overcome during this early stage of computer use in schools. However, these results do still suggest that computers may prove especially potent in facilitating peer collaboration.

The above remarks imply a special need to look at classrooms where both computer activities and collaborative working are well established. Our second study involves 7–8-year-olds from just such a class. (It was carried out by the present author and is to be reported more fully elsewhere.) In this case, more detailed observations were made (but on fewer children) in order to capture some of the quality of the actual exchanges. The activities studied were several self-contained items of software popular in schools at the time. These activities typically mimic familiar curriculum materials but allow the development of a more interactive experience with the problems they pose.

Twelve pairs of children were observed for at least seven sessions each. For all pairs, analysis was carried out on transcriptions of two of their sessions during which three different problem-solving games were attempted and three further sessions which all involved a narrative adventure activity. The three games were:

(1)   **Maze**, in which a character must be directed along the only possible path through a grid of squares. This route must be composed in advance as a sequence of turns and step instructions.

(2)   **Spot**, in which two numbers in an ascending series of six are given and the four blanks must be filled in by 'spotting' the pattern.

(3)   **Anagram**, in which the jumbled letters of a word must be rearranged; the correct word always being one from a displayed list.

The **Adventure** activity involved finding a number of hidden children; the discoveries depended on solving problems of reasoning or memory embedded in the narrative.

Space does not permit a detailed account of the collaborations. However, it is possible to identify certain general characteristics of these computer activities that appeared relevant to their success as catalysts for collaborative work.

Each of the three problem-solving tasks prompted a strong *turn-taking* approach for controlling the computer keyboard. At least we may say that the children naturally supposed involvement would be shared. However, these sessions were not universally successful as 'collaborations': how children occupied themselves when not taking a turn is revealing in this respect.

With Maze, success depended on distributing attention between the maze itself and the developing sequence of steps being written to traverse it. Most children were reluctant to make this effort at times when they were not keystroking the route instructions themselves. Thus, 'collaboration' on Maze rarely went beyond taking turns at the complete activity. With Anagram, there was greater mutual involvement. However, opportunity for overt, shared discovery remained limited. Often, one child would be slightly swifter in identifying the word and would simply announce it immediately. This could leave one member of a pair merely taking turns at entering (someone else's) solutions.

The number game, Spot, was the most successful of the three. Here, an overall problem is readily perceived at any given moment and does not demand the close concentration of Maze. Neither does its answer involve a single response in quite the same sense as Anagram. The solution is, in fact, a rule – the rule defining the sequence. Thus, the approach to solution in this case may be more differentiated, perhaps prompting discussion of competing hypotheses. To some extent, exchanges of this kind did take place. Certainly, the game accommodated a sharing of keyboard turns, while not encouraging simple announcements of the number that one's less speedy partner might be pondering.

The Adventure game provided the richest forum for discussion. Part of its strength lies in the way written language is used to develop a context and, then, to pose challenging problems within it. However, the central place thereby given to fluent reading could be a limiting factor for certain working pairs. All our children could read the text but in some pairs one child would prove more able. This child would invariably end up taking more responsibility for the total activity. He or she would read aloud and so determine the pace of the task, including the pressing of keys to advance the screen text. This keystroke responsibility seemed to generalize so that these children also took greater responsibility for the more important decision making. Thus, relatively small differences in reading ability may serve to cultivate a more general asymmetry of involvement within a pair. Evidently, this problem may only apply at early stages of reading development and it may be partly circumvented by careful pairing. However, it does draw attention to subtle ways in which dominance may arise and spiral within these working arrangements.

In summary, we may say that in each of the two studies described above there is evidence for involvement and cooperation when young children work together at computer-based tasks. However, the finer-grained account of the second study leaves a mixed impression regarding the actual quality of their collaborations. But this claim only draws attention to an obligation neglected in the discussion so far: how are we to define 'quality' in children's experience of collaboration? Any attempt to highlight joint activity as a social context for using computers would be best grounded in a general theory of how children's development is promoted by collaborative exchanges.

To meet this obligation we should examine established theory and research within developmental psychology. Such a course will be taken up in the next section where studies of peer interaction and cognitive development will be discussed. However, it might be useful, at this point, to pose a more specific challenge for existing theory: how far can it clarify the particular issues that could arise in organizing peer interaction around *computer* tasks? Approaching the literature in this way should help us to identify where new research initiatives need to be made.

How might the design of computer-based activities influence possible collaborations? Consider the studies discussed above: the differences in design of those computer tasks do seem significant. LOGO is an open-ended environment that responds to the user's own initiatives. Considered as a vehicle for collaborative work it is probably more distinctive for the levels of involvement it sustains, not for features that might impose particular structure on collaborations among its users. In contrast, the activities of the second study exemplify a more question-and-answer type of format. Here the machine seems to be 'taking part in' a total interaction – as a kind of partner. This role for the computer does seem more likely to define and organize potential interactions among its users (Laboratory of Comparative Human Cognition, 1982).

In the simplest of designs, a computer may just issue discrete challenges or problems. Yet even these unsophisticated activities are surely structured quite unlike any other that children might do together in the classroom. One characteristic many activities of this general type display is a typically precise feedback on the adequacy of the user's various solutions. This may exemplify one distinctive feature of the computer partnership that could prove significant. In a collaboration where there is real asymmetry in the abilities of the children involved, this feedback may serve to highlight such differences. In fact, both of the studies that have been discussed in this section do make reference to issues of ability differences between collaborators.

Thus, in reviewing the research literature below we should first seek a general rationale for cultivating peer interaction in classroom settings. But we should also seek insights into the specific influences of *computer*-based activities. So, of particular interest will be studies of peer interaction that focus on variables of task structure and design, but also on considerations of ability composition in groups.

■ Peer interaction for learning

It is natural to suppose that experience of interacting with peers will serve to promote an individual's social development. This must have implications for life in schools; for schools are forums in which peer relationships can flourish. Certainly, there is ample research indicating how school experience is significant for social development (Minuchin and Shapiro, 1983). But how far should early education be organized around opportunities for peer interaction? If they are to be cultivated in the classroom, then evidence will be needed to support the (less obvious) claim that peer interactions can also mediate children's *intellectual* development.

Current reviews of research into collaborative learning lead to strong claims for its advantages (Sharan, 1980; Slavin, 1980). Where it is encouraged, it is said to have a favourable impact on children's learning, motivation and attitudes to school. But much of that research merely relates broad classroom strategies to outcome measures; in trying to promote this kind of social context for computer use, we must look for the actual processes that are mediating any effectiveness in peer collaboration.

One possible benefit of peer interaction during classroom activities is that a more expert child may serve as a model for one who is less so. Such learning by observation has been well documented for young children (Kuhn, 1972; Murray, 1972). However, arrangements of this kind are inherently chancy and possible benefits are, of necessity, unevenly distributed within these collaborations. Activities that promote a properly interactive exchange do seem more appealing: perhaps there are characteristics intrinsic to such interactions that will allow all the participants to exceed what they might achieve as individuals. In other words, there might be something truly distinctive in learning mediated by peer interaction. There is now research that seems to suggest this may be so.

This work is roughly organized around three theoretical frameworks. The first derives from sociolinguistic analyses of communication; an important aim being to expose the structure and functions of classroom discourse. A second body of research is in the Piagetian tradition: there the interest has been in how particular coordinations of peer activity could quite directly facilitate the development of cognitive structures. A third, less fully elaborated framework draws upon the Soviet approach to cognitive development exemplified in the work of Vygotsky. These traditions will be considered in turn.

□   **A sociolinguistic framework**

A study reported by Sinclair and Coulthard (1975) provides a seminal analysis of discourse freely recorded during lessons. Mehan (1979) has since amplified that work, revealing some of the implicit rules of classroom communication and how children come to honour them. Research pursuing these initiatives still further has recently been assembled in one useful volume (Wilkinson, 1982). An effect of all this work has been to focus attention on the role of communicative competence in early education (see Cazden, 1972; or Cook-Gumperz and Gumperz, 1982, for development of this point). In so far as the learner's task is one of accessing information via exchange with a teacher, then mastering the rules of classroom discourse is a prime achievement.

It follows that much research in the sociolinguistic tradition does give priority to the study of teacher–child discourse rather than that associated with interactions among peers. This is an appropriately direct strategy: it looks at the most vital situations where communicative skills are being exercised. But it neglects the possibility that cultivation of these skills may occur, in part, during exchanges with peers.

Nevertheless, some analyses of peer communication have been made within this framework. This is fortunate, because any general argument for collaborative working practices must establish young children's straightforward communicative competence with their peers. This is not to deny that there may be value in exchanges involving only minimal verbal communication – as where an able child functions as effective model for one who is less able. But the available research does suggest that even very young children have the capacity for more useful communication around a shared activity. Hence, we may hope to discover within peer interaction something richer than mere observational learning.

Garvey and Hogan (1974) argue that even preschool children have linguistic abilities necessary to sustain the dialogues required in collaborative problem solving. An instructive illustration can be found in Gernishi and Di Paolo's (1982) analysis of organization in young children's spontaneous arguments. They demonstrate how such exchanges could be a rich forum for developing strategies of social influence. When such observations are made in the context of children tackling a defined task, it may be possible to identify particular communicative devices associated with success. Such a study has been reported by Cooper (1980). Pairs of preschool children used a balance to match blocks by weight. Success at this task was associated with the following: greater referential specificity (particularly, use of verbal labels and comparatives), more strategies for focusing a partner's attention, and greater responsiveness to a partner's questions and directives. These represent the kind of communicative skills that may be available to facilitate joint problem solving within the early school years.

A further study by Cooper and colleagues (Cooper *et al*. 1982) considers peer interactions in a school where they are encouraged to take shape spontaneously. The study involved children of 3–7 years; two important findings should be noted. Firstly, this proved a period within which the stability of particular peer groupings became greatly strengthened. Secondly, there were 'striking' individual differences in the extent to which children used peers as classroom resources. Perhaps as a consequence of these differences, there was a tendency for perceived expertise to accrue to individual children. Moreover, Cohen (1984) has shown how children's awareness of these differences can sometimes work to the disadvantage of some members of collaborating groups. Finally, Dickson (1982) has also commented on individual differences of this kind: he shows how, for children in pairs, the stability of such differences is greater within pairs than across the various partners. This implies that communicative competence was located in the dyad rather than the individual.

Our earlier account of collaborative work at computers raised questions both about the process defining effective peer interaction and about the significance of asymmetrics in relationships. Sociolinguistic research does offer one theoretical framework. On the question of process, it gives a central place to communicative competence. Revealing the extent of this competence, it encourages us to recognize that peer interaction can indeed offer more than learning by mere observation. However, the impact of communication within collaborative work tends to be evaluated in terms of two characteristic distractions of the sociolinguistic tradition – control and status. So, this work does reach beyond processes of passive observation, but it tends to encourage instead an emphasis on something more like 'peer tutoring'.

It would surely be more interesting to discover that peer interaction offered something distinctive in itself, rather than depending on the adult-style tutoring of a more able partner. This may prove a matter of emphasis; it remains implicit that participants of equal ability might also gain from collaborating: they might each employ their communicative skills towards the successful coordination of a joint activity. Unfortunately, this literature provides little indication of how typical or how significant such mutual regulations might be.

On the issue of ability differences among collaborators, this research is becoming sensitive to them and would, perhaps, accord them importance – in so far as tutoring-type processes are judged part of effective collaboration. There is some evidence that differences in expertise are salient to young children and that, in group activities, this knowledge can work to the disadvantage of the less able.

☐   **A Piagetian framework**

Piaget (1928) also argued that the value of peer interaction could go beyond passive observation, yet still involve something apart from direct tutoring. The overt disagreements that arise in such interactions may have a special potential for creating cognitive 'disturbances'. He noted how adult–child exchanges must involve asymmetry (in knowledge, authority, and so on), whereas child–child exchanges are more balanced. If other features of early childhood thinking are taken into account (notably an egocentric bias), then problem solving among peers may typically generate some degree of conflict. Piaget claimed a special potency for such conflict. Given the more symmetrical character of peer relationships, the individual is made to recognize the possibility of alternative perspectives. Moreover, this could facilitate more active negotiation of a problem.

Piaget hardly pursued this possibility himself but some recent research has examined the role of conflict in peer interaction. Because of the Piagetian background to this work, the tasks involved tend to call upon the hallmark achievements of operational thinking, particularly conservation and perspective taking. There are advantages to this choice: these are achievements that may be diagnosed in a fairly clear manner; moreover, this diagnosis involves criteria for determining the real depth of any change in a participant's understanding.

Space does not allow a detailed review here (see Glachan and Light, 1982). However, the work of Doise and his colleagues (Doise, 1978; Doise and Mugny, 1984) must be identified as one particularly thorough programme of study. They report broad and stable gains in operational thinking among children allowed to interact around modified Piagetian tasks. Piaget's broad proposal is endorsed: the important experience in peer interaction is disagreement or conflict. This cultivates the child's awareness of responses other than its own and stimulates the elaboration of new cognitive instruments that serve to resolve the disequilibria experienced.

These claims have not been made without controversy. Consider children doing conservation problems together: there is wide agreement that important gains can emerge when a non-conserving child is paired with a conserver. However, Russell (1982) has questioned whether such gains amount to structural change in cognition. He suggests these children's thinking was already, in some sense, 'transitional' and that what their social exchanges influence is the kind of 'propositional attitude' they have towards verbal statements describing dimensional relations. These observations question what it is that is effected by conflict – not the fact that conflict and its resolution are what counts. But Russell urges caution there also. He suggests that real gains through such a mechanism are unlikely when the children involved are both non-conservers. Unlike Doise, he finds that conflict within those dyads would more usually be resolved by social dominance than real coordination of perspectives. Glachan and Light (1982) suggest that differences in research methodology may underly this disagreement, although those authors also describe problem solving characterized by striking social dominance and indicate how it may limit the gains of a less assertive partner.

This Piagetian research identifies conflict as the feature of peer interactions that make them distinctive learning experiences. But, once again, our attention is drawn towards the influence of differences among the individuals comprising a working arrangement. In particular, it remains uncertain whether conflict is only really effective in situations where one participant has a more advanced understanding.

☐   **A framework from Vygotsky**

Recently there has been a revival of interest in the work of the Soviet psychologist Vygotsky (Wertsch, 1985). In this view, the very structure of certain social exchanges can function to promote cognitive development. It is claimed that cognitive strategies may first be encountered within an *inter*-individual context – during various joint activities. A process of internalization is proposed as the mechanism whereby these experiences then become *intra*-individual events.

This account tends to emphasize social interactions in which one partner is, in some way, a more advanced thinker. For it is assumed that the richest encounters involve a more experienced collaborator electing to act as a careful support to the efforts of someone less experienced. This perspective has drawn our attention to how an adult will behave in those activities typically shared between children and parents, or children and teachers. It has been less concerned to show how the structure of interactions among peers might contribute to the internalization process.

While such a process may best flourish in collaborations with skilled and sympathetic partners, could there not still be some gain arising from more symmetrical relationships? Perhaps our uncertainty about this reflects a need for greater specification of the particular social events supposed to be so potent. This must imply more observational research that could highlight the particular ways in which cognition can be embedded in the structures of social exchange (Rogoff and Wertsch, 1984; Wertsch *et al.*, 1980). Observations of peer interaction in this spirit would be especially welcome.

For the present, we can only note that ability differences within collaborating peer groups need not constrain any individual from confronting a partner with 'challenges', 'cautions', 'confirmatory comments', and so on. It seems reasonable to suppose that exposure to these exchanges could structure the thinking of the individuals involved. Moreover, it may be that, by being part of a collaborating group, children are encouraged simply to *declare* their thoughts. Even without any strong communicative intent, this may facilitate and organize the thinking of a partner, but it may also be of benefit to the declarer. Indeed, Scardamalia and Bereiter (1984) have argued the value in encouraging children to 'think aloud' for the very purpose of cultivating reflective awareness of their own cognition.

☐   **Implications for promoting computer-based collaborations**

Recall that our purpose in examining the peer interaction literature was, first, to help identify whatever processes of a general kind might mediate effective peer collaboration and, second, to help anticipate the special features that computers might have as media for collaborative work. Research within each of several frameworks tends to suggest a potential for learning within peer interactions that does go beyond any benefits from simply watching a more able partner. But we find a strong alternative theme of tutorial influences. This is implicit in the sociolinguist's discussion of communicative competence and control. It is encouraged by the traditional formulation of Vygotsky's perspective. Even some of the Piagetian research suggests that gains may be exclusive to interactions in which one participant is more advanced in operational thinking.

If productive peer interaction does depend on such differences among partners, this seems rather constraining. It may demand too much caution in the organization of pairs or groups. However, this conclusion could be too hasty. There remains other Piagetian research suggesting that conflict within well-matched pairs can indeed have an impact. Moreover, the Soviet perspective of Vygotsky – less concerned with conflict – implies that thinking might be enriched by yet other forms of exchange intrinsic to the public nature of peer interaction. The precocious communicative skills described by sociolinguistic research can only serve to encourage exploration of this possibility.

It is disappointing that the processes within peer interaction have not been more fully articulated. Furthermore, available research gives little guidance regarding the potential of computers as specific media for such collaborative work. It is unfortunate that there has been little interest in exploring the effects of different task structures on patterns of peer interaction. The Piagetian work, in particular, has consciously avoided studying the kind of sustained problem solving that typifies real classroom collaborations. The sheer variety of tasks that children may encounter on computers should prompt more systematic research in this direction.

Finally, it is disappointing that so little consideration has been given to individual differences among collaborators, beyond implications for the tutorial roles that children might adopt. A suggestion arising in our earlier discussion of computer-based collaborations was that, when they worked together on this medium, children's attention could be more easily drawn to their own abilities relative to others. This might be particularly so when computers function more as 'partners for learning' and provide very clear feedback about successful choices or decisions. (Although sensitivity to other children's performances was also described above for the very open-ended LOGO activity.) As it happens, there is research indicating that children do become tuned to individual differences of this kind in their early school years (Nicholls, 1983). Unfortunately, there is little indication of how far such awareness might be cultivated within the context of group work or whether it requires cautious management. This does suggests distinctive characteristic of computer-based collaboration; one whose significance cannot easily be determined by references to any existing research.

■ Concluding observations

Any regular visitor to primary school classrooms will be aware of the manner in which computer-based activities can engage even very young children. Two perspectives on the computer's role in such interactions were suggested above. Firstly, the computer may function as an instrument facilitating self-directed discoveries – a source of autonomy in the child's learning. Secondly, the computer may function as a responsive 'partner' in more of a learning dialogue. It was not our purpose to debate the merits of these two applications, but we did note that they each lead to an educational experience in which the interpersonal component seems to be undermined.

We may feel uncomfortable about this. In particular, the inherently social character of our lives seems to suggest that we encourage children to exercise intelligence in an interpersonal context. Fortunately, the two models of computer interaction outlined above allow some elaboration: in this chapter I have argued that a social context for computer use can be constructed around a new potential for collaborative work.

To realize an agenda of this kind, research on peer interaction and early learning must be examined to seek the processes mediating advantages that are claimed for collaborative work. We have done this and found such research somewhat disappointing. This literature offers little insight into the consequences of organizing joint work around the specific medium of computers. There are grounds for thinking that this medium would have distinctive properties. One way to express this is to speculate that the characteristic patterns of interacting *with* computers may serve to organize distinctive patterns of interacting *around* computers. For example, I have drawn attention to one possibility: namely, that the rich level of task feedback that characterizes many such interactions may prompt children to reflect more on their own abilities and achievements relative to their partners'. With this kind of consideration in mind, there is a real need here for research that pays more attention to task structures and the way in which they promote different styles of interaction.

At this point it may be argued that the shortcomings in our knowledge are no cause for alarm: the computer has not yet penetrated classrooms to a degree that represents any serious challenge to their interpersonal dynamics. However, it would be wrong to view the present arguments as simply responding to the threats of technological change – when the pace of such change could indeed be debated. If computers can support greater peer collaboration then we should, in any case, seek to understand how they can be mobilized for that purpose. To reinforce the call for further research in this area, I shall conclude on a reminder that the policy of supporting collaborative learning could well use a new impetus.

Ethnographic accounts of classroom life do convey an impression of early learning as a rather solitary affair (Galton *et al.*, 1980; Kutnick, 1983). Thus, Kutnick (1983) describes the infant school peer group as 'largely an ineffectual gathering of pupils greatly dependent on the parents and the teacher' (p.49). He reports children 'each working for their individual development ... one might say that the children were co-acting (doing the same thing in the same place as others) but not co-operating' (p.75).

So, although the case for group work is strongly made (Sharan, 1980; Slavin, 1980), there remains a discrepancy between theory and practice. Indeed, some academics have openly expressed dismay at the modest impact of their research (Dickson, 1982). Part of the problem here may be the failure of researchers to specify the processes that actually mediate the success of group work. This is a shortcoming already noted above; the same point has been made by Perret-Clermont and Schubaeur-Leoni (1981). They comment that while teachers may strive after joint work, they usually have not been offered formal guidance in how to attend to the structure and function of the groups they create.

A more straightforward reason for the scarcity of effective group work may be the sheer demands of organizing it. Some solutions have involved fairly radical restructuring of classroom routines (Aronson *et al.*, 1978; Cazden, 1979). More cautious enthusiasts might prefer to start from advice on an itinerary of classroom activities that serve as good catalysts for collaborative work. This may be a real stumbling block: it has been hard to identify activities that do serve to sustain and elaborate the involvement of young children working in concert. I would suggest that much computer-based work has just the dynamic properties that may prove potent in this respect. It is, therefore, important to encourage research that draws attention to this possibility.

Thus, cultivating collaborative work with computers is not simply a strategy for grafting back interpersonal contact that we suspect is threatened by the computer trend. The need for group work in primary education is felt quite independently of any view about the development of computers. Enthusiasts for such working practices might therefore be encouraged to view this technology as an important resource for that purpose.

■ Acknowledgements

I am grateful for valuable discussions with members of the Laboratory of Comparative Human Cognition during the preparation of this chapter. My research has been supported by an ESRC grant.

■ References

Aronson, E., Stephan, C., Sikes, J., Blaney, N., and Snapp, M. (1978). *The Jigsaw Classroom*, Sage, Beverly Hills, Calif.

Brown, J.S. (1983). Learning from doing revisited for electronic learning environments. In M. White (ed.), *The Future of Electronic Learning*, Lawrence Erlbaum, Hillsdale, N.J.

Cazden, C. (1972). *Child Language and Education*, Holt, Rinehart & Winston, New York.

Cazden, C.B. (1979). You all goona hafta listen: peer teaching in a primary classroom. In W.A. Collins (ed.), *Children's language and communication: 12th Annual Minnesota Symposium on Child Psychology*, Laurence Erlbaum, Hillsdale, N.J.

Cohen, E.G. (1984). Talking and working together: status, interactions and learning. In P. Peterson, L. Wilkinson and M. Hallinan (eds), *The Social Context of Instruction*, Academic Press, Orlando, Fla.

Cook-Gumperz, J., and Gumperz, J (1982). Communicative competence in educational perspective. In L.C. Wilkinson (ed.), *Communicating in the Classroom*, Academic Press, New York.

Cooper, C.R. (1980). Developmental of collaborative problem solving among preschool children, *Developmental Psychology*, **16**, 433-440.

Cooper, C.R. Marquis, A., and Ayers-Lopez, S. (1982). Peer learning in the classroom tracing developmental patterns and consequences of children's spontaneous interactions. In L.C. Wilkinson (ed.), *Communicating in the Classroom*, Academic Press, New York.

Dickson, W.P. (1982). Creating communication-rich classrooms: insights from the sociolinguistic and referential traditions. In L.C. Wilkinson (ed.), *Communicating in the Classroom*, Academic Press, New York.

Doise, W. (1978). *Groups and Individuals*, Cambridge University Press, Cambridge.

Doise, W., and Mugny, G. (1984). *The Social Development of the Intellect*, Pergamon, Oxford.

Galton, M., Simon, B., and Croll, P. (1980). *Inside the Primary Classroom*, Routledge, London.

Garvey, C., and Hogan, R. (1974). Social speech and social interaction: egocentrism revisited, *Child Development*, 44, 562-568.

Gernishi, C., and Di Paolo, M. (1982). Learning through argument in a preschool. In L.C. Wilkinson (ed.), *Communicating in the Classroom*, Academic Press, New York.

Glachan, M., and Light, P. (1982). Peer interaction and learning: can two wrongs make a right? In G. Butterworth and P. Light (eds.), *Social Cognition*, Harvester Press, Brighton.

Hawkins, J., Sheingold, K., Gearhart, M., and Berger, C. (1982). Microcomputers in schools: impact on the social life of elementary classrooms, *Journal of Applied Development Psychology*, 3, 361-373.

Kuhn, D. (1972). Mechanisms of change in the development of cognitive structures, *Child Development*, 43, 833-844.

Kutnick, P. (1983). *Relating to Learning*, Unwin, London.

Laboratory of Comparative Human Cognition (1982). A model system for the study of learning difficulties, *Quarterly Newsletter of the Laboratory of Comparative Human Cognition*, 4, 39-66.

Lepper, M. (1985). Microcomputers in education, *American Psychologist*, 40, 1-18.

Mehan, H. (1979). *Learning Lessons*, Harvard University Press, Cambridge, Mass.

Minuchin, P.P, and Shapiro, E.K. (1983). The school as a context for social development. In P.H. Mussen (ed.), *Handbook of Child Psychology*, Vol. IV, Wiley, New York.

Murray, F. (1972). Acquisition of conservation through social interaction, *Developmental Psychology*, 13, 236-243.

Nicholls, J. (1983). Conceptions of ability and achievement motivation: a theory and its implications for education. In S. Paris, G. Olson and H. Stevenson (eds), *Learning and Motivation in the Classroom*, Lawrence Erlbaum, Hillsdale, N.J.

Papert, S. (1980). *Mindstorms: Children, Computers, and Powerful Ideas*, Basic Books, New York.

Pea, R. (1985). Integrating human and computer intelligence. In E. Klein (ed.), *Children and Computers*, Jossey Bass, San Francisco.

Perret-Clermont, A-N, and Schubaeur-Leoni, M. (1981). Conflict and cooperation as opportunities for learning. In W.P. Robinson (ed.), *Communication in Development*, Academic Press, London.

Piaget, J. (1928). *Judgement and Reasoning in the Child*, Harcourt Brace, New York.

Rogoff, B., and Wertsch, J.V. (1984). *Children's Learning in the Zone of Proximal Development*. New Directions for Child Development, No. 23, Jossey Bass, San Francisco.

Russell, J. (1982). Propositional attitudes. In M. Beveridge (ed.), *Children Thinking Through Language*, Arnold, London.

Scardamalia, M., and Bereiter, C. (1984). The development of evaluative, diagnostic and remedial capabilities in children's composing. In M. Martlew (ed.), *The Psychology of Written Language*, Wiley, Chichester.

Sharan, S. (1980). Cooperative learning in small groups: recent methods and effects on achievement, attitudes and ethnic relations, *Review of Educational Research*, **50**, 241-271.

Sinclair, J.M., and Coulthard, R.M. (1975). *Towards an Analysis of Discourse*, Oxford University Press, London.

Slavin, R.E. (1980). Cooperative learning in teams: state of the art, *Educational Psychologist*, **15**, 93-111.

Turkle, S. (1984). *The Second Self*, Simon and Shuster, New York.

Vygotsky, L.S. (1978). *Mind in Society*, Harvard University Press, Cambridge, Mass.

Walkerdine, V. (1982). From context to text: a psychosemiotic approach to abstract thought. In M. Beveridge (ed.), *Children Thinking Through Language*, Arnold, London.

Wertsch, J. (1985). *Vygotsky and the Social Formation of Mind*, Harvard University Press, Cambridge, Mass.

Wertsch, J.V., McNamee, G.D., McLane, J.G., and Budwig, N.A. (1980). The adult-child dyad as a problem solving system, *Child Development*, **51**, 1215-1221.

Wilkinson, L.C. (1982). *Communicating in the Classroom*, Academic Press, New York.

Paper 2.4

'I'm the thinkist, you're the typist': The Interaction of Technology and the Social Life of Classrooms

Karen Sheingold, Jan Hawkins and Cynthia Char

[...]Research on technology and the social life of classrooms is in its infancy. Only since microcomputers became widely available some five years ago has it made sense to ask about what microcomputers might mean for students and teachers in classrooms. Now, with several hundred thousand computers in schools and the number growing rapidly (Becker, 1982), the question has become urgent. Just as pressing, however, is the need to reflect on what kinds of questions we should ask about computers and the social life of classrooms, and how we should go about answering them. In this paper we propose a framework for understanding the influence of computers on the social life of classrooms, and we illustrate this framework with examples from several studies we have conducted over the last four years.

■ Questions and methods

The kinds of questions we ask about the incorporation of computers into

First published as Centre for Children and Technology Technical Report No. 27 (1984). Bank Street College, New York. Also published in *Journal of Social Issues* **40**(3), 49–61. Reprinted with permission of the Society for the Psychological Study of Social Issues.

the social environment of classrooms will, to a large extent, dictate our methods for answering them. Three years ago, as part of a program of research, we wanted to know about some of the 'social effects' of using computers in classrooms. The question about effects implied an experimental approach, which we adopted. Having introduced computers for programming work (the 'treatment') into two classrooms, we compared students when they were using computers and when they were doing other classroom work, both early and late in the school year (Hawkins *et al.*, 1983). Comparison of these patterns allowed us to say some things about the effects of technology on different kinds of learning interactions in these particular classrooms. For instance, children engaged in more collaborative talk about their work when they were working with microcomputers than when they were doing other classroom tasks. But this type of study alone was not sufficient to reveal the impact of technology on the life of classrooms. While useful, these time-sampled observational data are limited in scope. They do not provide us with a full picture of what was being done with the technology in the context of everyday classroom practices, nor do they give us information about the meaning of the experience for teachers or students. In order to interpret what happened, it was also necessary to collect information about the day-to-day process of working with technology, and the meaning it had for members of the classroom (Hawkins, 1984b).

Framing questions about technology and the social life of classrooms in terms of 'effects' has particular implications for how we do research. It is problematic for several reasons. To illustrate this, let us do an imaginary 'computer treatment' study. In order to determine the social effects of using computers in classrooms, we first measure social variables of interest in two comparable groups of classrooms, then give computers to one of these groups. We go back and measure these variables again when the computer treatment ends, some few weeks or months later. Differences between the experimental and control groups before and after the treatment will then tell us clearly what the effects are. Or will they?

Our imaginary study is flawed in three critical ways. First, having computers available does not constitute a 'treatment' *per se*. One of the most interesting and, for education, most challenging characteristics of the computer is that it is not a device that can be used only in one way to achieve a single end – it is many devices that can be used in multiple ways to achieve various ends (Sheingold, 1983). While the most common computer uses today are drill-and-practice and programming (Becker, 1982), the range of uses also includes tutorials, simulations and tools (for example, word processing and database management). Each of these uses may have different ways of fitting into and shaping the work of the classroom as well as the patterns of social interaction surrounding that work. For example, while drill-and-practice is generally an activity for an individual child interacting with the computer, programming and word processing afford opportunities for collaboration among students – a form of interaction unusual in most classrooms. We need to ask about particular uses of the technology in order to begin to understand its relation to the social life of classrooms.

Second, even if we study only one use of the computer – let us say, programming – the treatment will not be uniform. With the possible exception of drill-and-practice and the tutorial functions of the computer, most computer uses are flexible. They are open to multiple interpretations and to many different approaches and uses in the classroom. To give but one example, a teacher who introduces her students to LOGO in the classroom, as a way of 'helping students know how computers work', may do very different things from one who introduces LOGO for teaching students specific programming concepts. In the first case, the work is likely to be loosely structured, with the teacher's role one of helping the students use the computers for any LOGO-based activity of interest to them. In the second, the work is likely to be structured around the particular concepts the teacher deems important, with the teacher taking an active role to ensure that those particular concepts are learned and used.

One way to deal with this methodological problem is to train teachers to do exactly the same thing in exactly the same way in their classrooms so we can get a clear notion of the social effects thus generated. But to take this approach would be to engineer out of our research what may be its most important social aspect, namely, the ways in which teachers naturally interpret, work with, and shape this new technology.

The third and final problem with our imaginary study is the assumption that the question about social effects can be answered in a reasonable period of time – a few weeks or months – by a method which looks only at Time 1 (before the treatment) and Time 2 (after the treatment). This snapshot approach to measurement assumes that the effects of computers in classrooms will be clearly observable in a short period of time, that whatever is going to happen will happen quickly. Moreover, it also assumes that comparison of the same measures for Times 1 and 2 will provide sufficient contextual information for interpreting observed differences.

Precisely because the computer is a flexible device, the processes of interpreting it, of adapting to it, and adapting it to the purposes of the classroom are likely to take a long time. Within a few weeks or months, no real end point will be reached, except in the case of the teacher who decides to abandon the machine altogether. And it is only by looking carefully at what happened between Times 1 and 2 that we can gain insight into how this new technology is being shaped by or is facilitating changes in the social life of the classroom.

☐ An alternative view

Let us set aside our concern about the effects of technology and the research methods that follow from this concern, and start instead with the classroom as the social context we are examining. The research questions, then, are about the places and processes of change that may accompany the use of the technology. We need a more specific understanding of *where* to look in the vast territory of social expectations and behavior that constitutes classroom life. This genre of question is certainly not new. It has been repeatedly demonstrated that an understanding of any performance must be embedded in the practices of the particular work setting: cross-culturally (Cole, *et al.*, 1971), in classrooms (Cole *et al.*, 1981), and specifically with respect to children's computer programming efforts (Pea, 1984). Since computers are a new and powerful innovation, the processes of their assimilation into classroom practices require careful attention.

Classrooms are well-established cultures, with social organizations and work-related agendas embodied in long-standing curricula. The core subjects emphasized and the types of activities conducted are features of the formal learning setting constructed over many years. Teachers, students and parents share well-developed expectations about formal learning settings in terms of what is valued, what is taught and learned, and how the work is organized socially.

Microcomputers enter the social context of the classroom and in so doing raise questions for teachers who wish to incorporate the technology effectively. What are computers and different kinds of software good for? How does the hardware fit into the organization of the classroom's social and physical space? What can students learn from computer-based experiences? How should students be accountable for learning? How does technology and the learning it affords relate to traditional areas of the curriculum and to traditional modes of learning?

The teachers' answers to these questions – their interpretations of this new technology – play a central role in how and whether the technology becomes an integral part of the classroom. The technology itself provides many possibilities for new learning activities and interactions. These may or may not be realized. And new activities and forms of classroom organization may well be created by the teachers themselves as they interact with, adapt to, and shape the technology to their own purposes.

This interactive process – between classrooms and particular software-based activities – will happen over a long period of time, with different outcomes depending on factors not yet clearly identified. A research approach that attempts to shed light on this process, at this stage of our knowledge, necessarily entails long-term classroom observation and interviews with teachers.

In the remainder of this paper, we illustrate this framework by further developing what we see as critical elements of the process by which computers are incorporated into the social life of the classroom. First, we consider the teacher's interpretation of what software is for and whether computer-based work is a legitimate part of the learning agenda. Second, we discuss the interactional changes in the classroom that the technology can support, and whether these learning forms are viewed as legitimate.

☐   **The meaning of software**

Standard curriculum subject areas define and separate learning tasks in classrooms: 'I learn these kinds of things for science, and these kinds of facts for social studies'. This conceptual structure helps teachers and students proceed through the school's yearly cycle and accomplish the learning defined as a year's work. Such standard divisions are resistant to change. For example, people experience both conceptual and administrative difficulty in trying to do interdisciplinary work.

Many of the more innovative uses of the technology, however, do not fit neatly into standard curricula niches. There are particular kinds of software that hold significant promise for new learning in classrooms, but which can directly or indirectly challenge what is taught and how it is taught. These include tool software, such as word processors and database management systems, simulations and programming environments such as LOGO. Such uses are now making their way into classrooms. Each of these types of software must be interpreted and shaped by the individual teacher. We have observed how the same type of software, or even the same piece, can be presented through a variety of educational approaches to meet different educational objectives in different classrooms.

> 'They need to recognize that when dealing with information, there is no one right answer; that the process is not linear but schematic ... The research process is hard. Developing probing questions and manipulating information is not easy for them. The data base is a simple way to organize data ... it requires them to pose questions and to be thoughtful about what they want to know.'

Thus, in the above classrooms, we observed fundamentally different ways of viewing and then using the same type of software. Some students were learning that 'this is how computers are used in the world', while others were exposed to new and challenging ways to think about and to conduct social studies research.

In another project we have been developing and studying other types of software, such as data gathering and graphing software, computer models and simulations. All this software is intended to help upper-elementary children learn more about science and mathematics. In a classroom field test of these materials (Char *et al.*, 1983), we noted that teachers' perceptions of science, mathematics and computers proved to be a critical factor in shaping the interpretation and presentation of each piece of software.

A navigation simulation, Rescue Mission, was designed to motivate students to apply mathematical principles to the real-world problem of ocean navigation. The simulation's premise was that a whale was trapped in a fishing trawler's net and that students, as crew members on different ships, were summoned to free the whale. Students received a radio distress call, used simulated navigational instruments such as radar, a radio direction finder and binoculars, and could motor their ship to reach the trawler. Thus, the simulation was intended to provide children with an appealing and functional learning context for general mathematical concepts such as grid coordinates, degrees, angles, vectors, triangulation and speed/time/distance relationships. These concepts are typically presented to students as individual mathematics problems on worksheets, devoid of context.

As with our research on database management systems, the classroom field test of the software demonstrated that different teachers had different interpretations of what the software was about, and therefore how it should be used. Some teachers understood this simulation to be a vehicle for teaching general mathematics skills in the context of navigation problems. These teachers understood how such a program could supplement their mathematics curriculum, albeit in a variety of ways. Children's problems with the software were interpreted as due to difficulty with *mathematical* terms and concepts.

In contrast, other teachers saw navigation as the central topic of the software. These teachers interpreted the software as appropriate for teaching navigation and mapping principles – 'a game about boats and navigation'. They saw little relevant connection with the core skills that were the goals of their curricula. Accordingly, these teachers believed use of the software should be reserved for free periods or for before- and after-school hours. Students' problems with the software were interpreted as due to unfamiliarity with *navigation*, and the fact that many had never been on a boat.

The simulation, unlike the computer and mathematics experiences commonly found in schools, was open to multiple interpretations. It could be relegated to the status of a game about boats or seen as an innovative context for teaching and learning mathematics.

☐   **The legitimacy of software**

When teachers attempt to incorporate computer-based activities into their classrooms, they must consider whether the software is recognizable as curriculum or at least relevant to curricular goals, and whether it is legitimate. These are not independent considerations. For example, the teachers who interpreted the navigation simulation as a game about boats decided it was not a legitimate part of the classroom curriculum. Much innovative software raises the question of legitimacy, precisely because it does not fit neatly and easily into established curricular niches.

One widespread method for dealing with the legitimacy problem is through 'computer literacy'. Almost any computer-based activity can be justified as promoting such literacy, as long as literacy is defined very broadly (for example, feeling comfortable with computers; learning what kinds of things computers can do). Although computer literacy may be a route through which many innovative ideas come into schools, it is not clear that this route leads to substantive changes. As the database management example illustrated, through computer literacy teachers can avoid struggling with how to make the computer a learning tool that can function in different parts of the curriculum. As a separate topic, it can remain vague and unconnected.

Programming is sometimes thought of as computer literacy par excellence. For this reason, it has legitimacy as a separate curricular subject in many schools. In a two-year study conducted in Bank Street classrooms, we were interested in how the programming language LOGO was assimilated into an elementary and middle-school classroom by teachers and students. LOGO is a programming language designed to be accessible to children. The most well-known feature of LOGO is its 'turtle graphics'. Students instruct a 'turtle' to move around the screen, and thus create graphic designs. In the Bank Street study, the primary issues for teachers were what LOGO was for, and whether it was legitimate (for further discussion, see Hawkins, 1984b). Teachers went through a lengthy process of revising their viewpoints about what LOGO was good for, and how they could support this learning:

> 'I have a clear idea of culture such as it is, past culture, of what it means to be an educated person in terms of all different subject areas. In terms of the computer, it's not part of our culture really yet; it's something new, so I don't have clear ideas of what kids should or should not know.' (Sixth-grade teacher)

> 'There were kids who were losing interest. They were receiving a double message. I wanted computers to be a part of their work, yet it was optional. Kids would reach a problem in their work and they would be less inclined to push through it in the way they might with other work, because I didn't make them. Few kids thought about it as a subject like others. They weren't tested in programming, and they know they have tests in other subjects. So when things weren't organized that way, kids dropped out.' (Fourth-grade teacher)

Throughout the two years, both teachers and students struggled with whether the programming work was legitimate as a classroom subject, and for what skills learners should be held accountable. Teachers began with the belief that children would learn general problem-solving skills and 'powerful ideas' through self-guided learning with LOGO (Papert, 1980). Gradually, however, they began to recognize that the children were learning how to achieve specific effects on the screen, without acquiring general programming concepts. Teachers concluded that students required considerable structured guidance from an expert in order to define and achieve programming goals. Thus, the teachers gradually revised their goals, expectations, and methods for incorporating LOGO. The second year was characterized by clearer goals, more modest expectations about what students could achieve, and more structured methods for assuring that all students had experience with a given set of programming concepts. Questions of legitimacy – whether LOGO was a topic in its own right, to be taken as seriously as other classroom subjects; whether or how it could expand students' skills in other areas – had not been clearly resolved by the end of the study.

□   **Summary**

Because computers can be seen as many kinds of learning tools, it is necessary to investigate the meanings of the innovation for teachers and students as we ask questions about change. Studies of classrooms using computers in a variety of ways reveal that teachers grapple with the issue of the technology's legitimate relationship to the traditional learning agenda. The occurrence of this interpretive work by teachers and students is one important aspect of the impact of technology on learning settings, and it defines the context in which other social changes might occur.

■   Organization of interactions

When attempting to understand the process of incorporating micro-computers into the work of classrooms, it is important to look at the kinds of interactions that take place. Just as computer technology can challenge traditional classroom curricula, it can also challenge the organization of learning interactions in classrooms. From the early introduction of microcomputers to classrooms, teachers and researchers noticed that learning interactions in many classrooms were different around the microcomputers than for other activities (Levin and Kareev, 1980; Sheingold et al., 1983). When working with computers, students appeared to be interacting more with each other about learning tasks.

As participants in schools for some years, students and teachers understand the various ways in which information is presented and work gets done (for example, large- and small-group activities, individual and collaborative work, discussion, homework and tests). Students as young as eight are sensitive to the occasions in which different forms of learning are appropriate (Hawkins, 1984a). For example, from interviews with young students, we found that they had clear ideas about when collaborative work was appropriate and when individual work should be done. Overall, collaborative work was good for particular subject areas (for example, doing a play, artwork), when you wanted to have fun, or when you ran into a problem. Individual effort was better for 'serious' work like maths, research, tests, or when you wanted something done efficiently.

The presence of microcomputers can disrupt the framework for the social organization of work in interesting ways. Some of our research suggests that microcomputers can facilitate both collaborative interaction among students (that is, students sharing equally in the interaction) and can increase opportunities for students to act as expert resources for other students (that is, one student providing help to another). Neither of these forms of interaction occurs often in most classrooms. In our classroom programming study, we observed more collaboration among students, more solicitation of help from other students, and more 'dropping in' to make comments or suggestions, in programming than in noncomputer activities in which students were permitted and/or encouraged to work together (Hawkins et al., 1983). The presence of computers in classrooms may be accompanied by increasing salience of interactions among small groups and pairs of learners. These forms of interaction may be uncomfortable for many teachers who are accustomed to students working individually or as a whole class. Many teachers and many students are unsure about the value of collaborative work for legitimate learning (Hawkins, 1984b). Working together may be fun and may teach social skills, but how does individual learning of content material take place? And, if it does, how does the teacher know it has taken place, when the products of such joint activity are themselves collaborative?

Traditional classroom organization positions a single adult as an expert resource for a large group of novices. The presence of micro-computers with challenging software may support the development of a pool of child experts. We have observed that individual students can develop considerable expertise in a particular area – in this case, aspects of programming in LOGO. These students may be more knowledgeable than their teachers, and thus become sources of information for other members of the class. Since it is necessary for most teachers to acquire new skills in order to work with the machines in their classrooms, many are not far ahead of their students. While some teachers are comfortable with the restructuring of expertise in which students can take on some of the burden of instruction, some are not. However, this widely noted phenomenon may be temporary. As the computer becomes a more familiar presence, expertise structures will probably resume traditional patterns in many classrooms.

The potential for emphasizing particular kinds of learning interactions, such as collaboration, raises issues for students as well as teachers. Students have well-developed expectations for what kinds of work they should be doing. They do not necessarily possess good collaborative skills for jointly solving problems (Hawkins, 1984a), nor are they necessarily skilled at making use of human resources other than teachers in their work. One collaborative arrangement adopted by two girls writing a LOGO program was: 'I'm the thinkist, you're the typist.' While this got the work done, it was not a particularly good way of incorporating each other's skills, nor was it an effective interaction for learning. One girl directed, the other typed. There was little exchange of information or argument that would lead either participant to consider alternative courses of action or to recognize misconceptions. The presence of computers may invite new learning interactions, but these must be valued and supported by the overall learning environment in order for important changes to take place in the long run.

Thus, in addition to raising questions about the legitimacy of computer work in the curriculum, the presence of computers raises questions about the legitimacy of the teaching and learning interactions that they seem to afford. While generally valued, collaborative work among students and distributed expertise in classrooms are not always comfortable forms of interaction.

One popular way of dealing with these issues of legitimacy is to remove computers from classrooms and to place them in resource rooms. Computer resource rooms are parallel to computer literacy courses in that they make possible the presence of computers without challenging either the traditional curriculum or forms of interaction in the classroom. Computers in resource rooms then become objects to be used and learned about in structured times and places, but they cannot function as tools to enhance ongoing classroom learning. Resource rooms are generally adopted explicitly to address resource limitations and security issues, but the strategy has the implicit consequence of reducing pressures to incorporate computers, with their potential for change, into the classroom.

■ Conclusion

We are at the beginning of understanding the ways in which computer technology will have an impact on the social life of classrooms. As computers become pervasive tools throughout our culture, their presence in schools offers opportunities for teachers and students to learn new things about and through the technology. Perhaps more important, they also offer the option of rethinking the selection of learning agendas, the design of curricula, and the ways in which learning tasks are done in classrooms. At this early stage of research about technology in the social life of classrooms, we believe that it is important to look not simply for its effects, but for the processes that will shape changes over the next few years.

We have observed that teachers interpret computer materials, and attempt to make them a legitimate part of the classroom work. In the best of circumstances, the availability of computers with high-quality software can facilitate and extend the work of classrooms, and can support teachers in examining the ways in which they organize students' learning. For example, we know of one teacher who introduced a word processor into her writing curriculum. For some students, the tool made it easier and more interesting to engage in the writing process. The teacher reported that the children wrote more and, in some instances, participated in new kinds of collaborative writing with other children and with the teacher. Writing – usually a private affair that is only shared after a draft is complete – could be made public. For the teacher, who had always given high priority to writing, the software provided an occasion for reflection. She began to rethink her writing curriculum and to formulate a new one that could be shared with other teachers. She designed a curriculum that emphasized the process of creating a polished text rather than the product itself. The technology enabled her to require review, feedback and revisions by students of their own and other students' work. The presence of technology extended the traditional activity of writing in new ways, and supported the teacher in considering major changes in the way this area of the curriculum was taught.

Thus, we have observed that technology is not simply a new educational device whose effects on classroom life can be readily measured. Rather, it can provoke teachers (to greater and lesser degrees) to think about both the legitimacy of this work, and the types of learning interactions that occur in their classrooms. Whether this 'provocation' will result in visible changes in how learning occurs in classrooms is not yet clear. What *is* clear is that the use of computers in classrooms provokes us, as researchers, to look anew at the processes of change in the culture of the classroom.

■ References

Becker, H. (1982). *Microcomputers in the classroom: Dreams and realities* (Report No. 319). Baltimore, MD: Johns Hopkins University, Center for Social Organization of Schools.

Char, C., Hawkins, J., Wootten, J., Sheingold, K., & Roberts, T. (1983). *"The Voyage of the Mimi": Classroom case studies of software, video, and print materials.* Report to the U.S. Department of Education. New York: Bank Street College of Education, Center for Children and Technology.

Cole, M., Gay, J., Glick, J., & Sharp, D. (1971). *The cultural context of learning and thinking.* New York: Basic Books.

Cole, M., Hood, L., & McDermott, R. (1981). *Ecological niche picking: Ecological invalidity as an axiom of experimental cognitive psychology.* Unpublished manuscript, Rockefeller University, New York.

Freeman, C., Hawkins, J., & Char, C. (1984). *Information management tools for classrooms: Exploring database management systems* (Tech. Rep.). New York: Bank Street College of Education, Center for Children and Technology.

Hawkins, J. (1984a). *Paired problem solving in a computer context.* Paper presented at the annual meeting of the American Educational Research Association, New Orleans, LA.

Hawkins, J., (1984b). *The interpretation of Logo in practice* (Tech. Rep.). New York: Bank Street College of Education, Center for Children and Technology.

Hawkins, J., Sheingold, K., Gearhart, M., & Berger, C. (1983). Microcomputers in schools: Impact on the social life of elementary classrooms. *Journal of Applied Developmental Psychology, 3,* 361–373.

Levin, J., & Kareev, Y. (1980). *Problem solving in everyday situations.* Unpublished manuscript, University of California, Laboratory of Comparative Human Cognition, San Diego.

Papert, S. (1980). *Mindstorms.* New York: Basic Books.

Pea, R. (1984). Symbol systems and thinking skills: Logo in context. *Proceedings of the Logo 84 Meetings,* MIT, Cambridge, MA.

Sheingold, K. (Chair). (1983). *Chameleon in the classroom: Developing roles for computers.* Symposium conducted at the meeting of the American Educational Research Association, Montreal, Canada.

Sheingold, K., Kane, J., & Endreweit, M. (1983). Microcomputer use in schools: Developing a research agenda. *Harvard Educational Review, 53,* 412 –432.

Paper 2.5

Discourse and the Development of Understanding in the Classroom

Derek Edwards

■ Introduction

Educationists sometimes, though not always optimistically, turn to psychology for help in understanding the processes of teaching and learning. In particular, Piaget's classic studies of the development of children's thinking have helped to shape educational practice. The older, 'traditional' primary classrooms, all chalk and talk, discipline and rote learning, have largely given way to child-centred activity. Children are encouraged to develop their own understandings of things, to work individually or in small groups, learning from their own practical experience, rather than having ready-made conclusions thrust upon their unwilling ears. The legacy of this influence, is a notion of children's learning that is highly individualistic. It stresses the importance of experience and action, playing down the significance of talk, of teaching, and of the ready-made curriculum. [...]

This paper will take an opposing view. It will draw upon some new developments in the social psychology of 'discourse' and 'rhetoric', and in the study of classroom education. It will look at the educational process from a social perspective, taking the view that the development

This is a modified version of the article first published in Rogers, C. and Kutnick, P. (eds) (1990) *Readings in the Social Psychology of the Primary School*. London: Routledge. Reprinted with permission.

of understanding is a communicative accomplishment, embodied in classroom discourse. Education is presented here as the development between teachers and pupils of *shared* understandings, shared experiences and procedures, and a shared conceptual vocabulary. Empirical studies depict classroom discourse as oriented mainly towards the achievement of a *teacher-dominated consensus* of understanding. We shall argue that this embodies an unnecessarily limited sense of shared knowledge. A different emphasis needs to be placed, upon the importance of argument, disagreement, justification and criticism – in other words, a 'rhetorical' approach to shared knowledge. In view of the fact that scientific knowledge is often taken to be the most solid, best established, least vulnerable knowledge that can be taught, we shall concentrate our analysis upon science education, with groups of nine-year-olds working with the computer language LOGO in the classroom.

■ Towards a social psychology of educational knowledge

In the world of education, the currently dominant psychologies of conceptual development are individualistic. Piaget's major legacy has been the assumption that children are learners from experience, actively constructing their own understandings of the world, via how the world responds when it is pushed, pulled, grasped, poured, thrown and generally manipulated. The teacher's role is that of a supervisory provider of suitable materials and learning opportunities. Since the late 1960s, following the recommendations of such influential publications as the Plowden Report (1967), and the Nuffield Mathematics Project (Nuffield Foundation, 1967), the Piagetian notion of individualistic 'learning by doing' has been the major psychological underpinning for the 'progressive' movement in education. The Nuffield recommendation was embodied in the aphorism: 'I hear and I forget. I see and I remember. I do and I understand'. Teachers' words are for hearing and forgetting, unless they relate closely to the real source of understanding – practical activity. Piaget himself had declared, 'Each time one prematurely teaches a child something he could have learned for himself, the child is kept from inventing it and consequently from understanding it completely' (1970, p. 715). Similarly, in the recent educational policy document issued jointly by the Engineering Council and the Standing Conference on Schools' Science and Technology (1985), we are urged to accept that problem-solving projects are particularly well suited to 'the ethos of the primary school', because 'the teaching is usually child centred and many learning experiences guided by the teacher start from activities with which the child is already familiar' (p. 8).

However, in the world of academic psychology, Piaget's conception of the child is no longer predominant. Critiques of the Piagetian orthodoxy have appeared (Donaldson, 1978; Russell, 1978; Butterworth and Light, 1982; Walkerdine, 1982; Carey, 1985; Edwards and Mercer, 1987). The view of the child as a 'lone organism' (Bruner, 1986), constructing a succession of general models of the world as each new stage is mastered, is giving way to two new approaches. One of these is even more individualistic than Piaget's. It derives from the new field of cognitive science, and particularly from the part of cognitive science which, in the wake of Chomsky's innate 'language acquisition device', seeks the innate origins of mind. Gardner (1985) traces the notion back to Plato, and to the rationalist philosophies of Descartes and Kant, that we are endowed with a variety of separate mental structures which are innate in origin, and which determine how we organize our experience of the world. So, for example, Susan Carey (1985, p. 107), in an argument reminiscent of Chomsky, cites the philosopher Jerry Fodor to the effect that: 'Given a hypothesis-testing model of learning, the child cannot possibly learn something he cannot represent' (Fodor, 1972). That is to say, children cannot acquire any conceptual structures that they do not already entertain as 'hypotheses', such that the fundamental structures of mind must therefore be innate. So, as Bullock *et al.* (1982) have argued with regard to causal reasoning in children as young as three years, 'This means that the development of casual understanding is more a process of learning where, when and how to apply the rules of reasoning than figuring out what those rules might be ... ' (cited in Keil, 1986, p. 85).

Of course, our acceptance of such arguments for the innate conceptual structure of individual minds depends very heavily upon our prior acceptance of the 'hypothesis-testing' theory of learning. Like the inductive, experiential model of learning it seeks to replace, it also is based upon the notion of conceptual learning as an essentially individual affair, in which a lone child, armed with whatever sense-making structures nature has endowed, organizes and interprets her experience of the world. While cognitive science lends itself most readily to individualist conceptions of mind, recent developments have begun to address the importance of human–computer interactions, of social context and of the nature of situated action (see, for example, Suchman, 1987). An overlooked source for children's hypotheses and conceptualizations, of especial relevance to education, is children's engagement in ready-made cultural and linguistic practices (Edwards and Mercer, 1987; compare Walkerdine, 1988). This view, in which mental development is seen as part of cultural and communicative practices, is reflected in the second kind of post-Piagetian developmental psychology.

The second 'new' approach is also at least as old as Piaget's, but is only now becoming a major influence in British and American developmental psychology. This is the work of the Soviet psychologist Lev Vygotsky and his followers, which emphasizes the sociocultural, linguistic origins of conceptual thinking, the importance of communicative social interaction in learning, and the roles of education and literacy in shaping what are often assumed to be natural, rational, objectively scientific modes of adult thought. In Vygotsky's perspective (see Vygotsky, 1987; Wertsch, 1985; Wood, 1988) mind is socialized and shaped through teaching and language. Education is formative of conceptual thought, rather than merely a practical context in which psychological theories and findings, derived from the experimental laboratory, can be 'applied'. Conceptual thought is derived from dialogue, and so must follow the rules and categories of discourse, of communicated symbols and written text.

For example, in an extended treatment of this notion, David Olson (1977) has argued (controversially) that it is the invention and widespread use of written forms of language that has resulted in the development of rationality itself, of logical reasoning, of formal education and of scientific thought. And it is the acquisition of literacy that is the key to how individuals and societies, in the modern world, also acquire those powerful modes of thought. The mere fact of having written text available to us for re-reading, and repeated scrutiny, not only facilitates the creation of large cultures of formal knowledge and procedure (science, literature and education), but also encourages an analytic perspective on language and knowledge that differs fundamentally from common sense. We learn to isolate, examine and test statements for the truth value (science and philosophy), and their interrelationships. The form of language dictates the form of thought, such that 'what we call "intelligence" in our culture is little more than a mastery of the forms of literate uses of language' (Olson, 1977, p. 238) – a far cry indeed, from Piaget and practical action.

Clearly, it is the latter, Vygotskian approach which offers the most promise for a social psychology of educational knowledge. However, rather than offering a straightforward Vygotskian account of education, we shall enrich the analysis by drawing upon some recent developments in social psychology itself. There has been in recent years a discernible shift of interest in social psychology towards the study of language, and especially, towards conversational discourse and text (see Potter and Wetherell, 1987; Billig, 1987; Billig *et al.*, 1988). It is argued that much of the traditional subject matter of social psychology may fruitfully be studied in terms of the communicative work that people do in talk and text. Discourse analysis and a concern with rhetoric (argumentation), are also at the heart of the new 'sociology of scientific knowledge' (Latour and Woolgar, 1979; Gilbert and Mulkay, 1984; Woolgar, 1988). These studies examine how scientists work together in laboratories, talk about their work, write about it in scientific journals, argue with each other, and generally 'construct' scientific knowledge as they do so. Scientific knowledge is studied as a socially constructed system of shared (and disputed) assumptions, understandings and procedures. For example, a contrast is often revealed, between the official 'scientific method' version of science, with its impersonal procedures and heroic, prize-winning individuals, and the social practices and communications through which scientific knowledge is created and established. Delamont (1987) has drawn attention to the lack of cross-fertilization between these new insights into the nature and workings of science, and the assumptions about science that prevail in the policies and practices of science education.

Alongside these developments in the analysis of discourse, rhetoric and scientific knowledge, there have been a series of studies of the discourse of classroom education itself (Mehan, 1979; Driver, 1983; Edwards and Mercer, 1986, 1987). Mehan's work is ethnomethodological (see Heritage, 1984), in that its concern is with showing how the practical business of classroom education is accomplished – how the social order of the classroom is created and maintained over time, how teacher and pupils manage the moment-to-moment taking of turns at talking. As linguists have also discovered (Sinclair and Coulthard, 1975), the pattern of classroom talk is highly organized, and even in apparently child-centred, 'progressive' sorts of classrooms, highly teacher dominated. Teachers control the flow of conversation, ask most of the questions, determine who speaks when, and on what, and what the upshot shall be.

Rosalind Driver's studies (1983; Driver and Oldham, 1986; Brook *et al.*, 1988) are concerned more directly with knowledge than with properties of talk, with how children think, how they spontaneously explain things, and how they deal with the sorts of practical experiences out of which, in our modern Piagetian classrooms, children are meant to re-invent for themselves the findings and principles of science. She shows the process to be highly problematical. In the absence of any prior hypothesis or expectation, children simply do not observe what they are supposed to. They also offer reasonable but erroneous explanations: the time taken for a radio's sound to fade away means that there must be a very long piece of wire inside; the higher up something is, the greater the gravitational force exerted upon it; the denser a metal, the harder it should be for heat to penetrate it. Driver argues that it is quite wrong to imagine that children can work out for themselves, merely through observation and induction, what it has taken centuries of scientific research to establish. A better approach, she argues, would be for teachers to take a more active role, 'as mediators between the pupils' experiences and understandings and that of the scientific community' (1983, p. 84), for example, by helping pupils to articulate the significance of their observations. Thus, 'by referring to the ideas and investigations of past scientists, some of the powerful ideas of young children can be explored in a way that treats them with respect' (p. 67).

Valuable as Driver's insights are, they are based upon two assumptions about the relationship between language and thought, which pose difficulties for a social psychology of classroom knowledge. First, there is the assumption of a straightforward relationship between talk and thought. Children's talk is taken as a window upon their individual minds, as revealing how they think, how they solve problems, how they understand the world. Second, the view of science is one that pre-dates the new sociology of scientific knowledge; depicting scientific truth in the classical manner, as established, uncontroversial, arising from the proper application of hypothetico-deductive methods. This has been termed, the 'storybook' account of science (Mitroff, 1974), and has emerged as one among a series of 'repertoires' available to scientists for writing and talking about their work: a *post hoc* way of accounting for a preferred version of scientific truth, rather than an accurate description of how scientists actually talk, think and work (see, for example, Gilbert and Mulkay, 1984; Potter and Mulkay, 1985). So, while we should hardly expect children to re-invent in their classrooms the fruits of centuries of scientific endeavour, we may still be asking too much, that they should conform to an idealized version of scientific history and practice.

In *Common Knowledge* (1987), Edwards and Mercer offer an account of classroom discourse in which, rather than taking the talk as a window upon children's thought processes, they examine it as contextualized dialogue with the teacher. The discourse itself is the educational reality, and the issue becomes that of examining how teacher and children construct a shared account, a common interpretative framework for curriculum knowledge, and for what happens in the classroom. This involves teacher and pupils in the moment-to-moment construction of 'context and continuity', the shared basis of talk and action upon which all subsequent talk and interpretation are built. Typically, this dialogue turns out to be no simple negotiation between equals, but a process that is dominated by the teacher's concerns, aims, expectations and prior knowledge, via the teacher's control of the dialogue.

■ Examining classroom discourse

Investigating shared understandings and how they develop, requires a close examination of classroom discourse. The first three extracts we shall examine are from a transcribed video recording of the last few minutes of a lesson on computer graphics. The teacher is coming to the conclusion of her first lesson on the subject, with a group of nine-year-olds.

They have been shown how to draw straight lines and right angles on the computer screen, using commands from the computer language LOGO. Very briefly, this involves typing into the keyboard, instructions which move a pointer ('arrow') on the screen: 'FORWARD 100' moves the pointer 100 units in the direction it is pointing, drawing a line on the screen as it goes. 'RIGHT 90' makes the pointer turn clockwise through 90°, and a further 'FORWARD 100' would draw the second side of a square. In Extract 1, the teacher ('T') is talking the pupils through how to complete a 180° turn, subtracting 60° to leave 120°. (Normal punctuation is used here, with the addition of slashes for pauses, and some contextual notes italicized in the square brackets.)

Extract 1: Doing a 180° turn

T: You want to point that-a-way. You've got to turn from there/ right round to there. Can you tell me how many degrees?

SUSAN: Measure it.

T: You could measure it. Now how are you going to do that?

SUSAN: With one of these [*Susan picking up a protractor*].

T: Make sure you're measuring the right angle you're going to turn through. What do you turn it through?

SUSAN: Ninety.

T: Umm/ you're going to turn from that way right round to point that-a-way. This is your turn from here to there. Now you've got to measure the turn you're going to make. So what turn is that from there to there?

SUSAN: A hundred and twenty.

T: Now how did you get that? You're right Susan. How did you get a hundred and twenty? Any idea Lara?

LARA: Sixty and sixty.

T: Not sixty and sixty/ no. It's got something to do with the sixty but not quite. If you imagine/ that line's continued/ now that angle's sixty. What do the angles/ what's a straight lined angle? How many degrees in a straight lined angle? If I turn there/ right round/ half turn or straight line angle/ straight angle/ how many degrees have I turned? There's two quarter turns look. That's one. So one quarter turn is how many degrees? What's a quarter turn? [*T rotating her pencil through an angle of 90°, and then 180°*]

LARA: Ninety.

T: Ninety. Make another quarter turn. How many degrees would that be? Another/

LARA: Half turn.

T: It's a half turn but/ the first quarter turn is ninety. How many quarter turns do we need to make that half turn?

LARA: Four.

T: You think about it. We're pointing that way. OK we want to point this way. We want to turn our pencil right round so it's pointing this way/ one quarter turn which is how many degrees?

LARA: Ninety.

T: Again/ which is/ another quarter turn is/

LARA: Ninety degrees.

T: It's another ninety degrees. It's two quarter turns that way. If we do it one/ watch the pencil/ if we do one quarter turn/ it takes us to there. Yes/ that's ninety degrees.

LARA: A hundred and eighty degrees.

T: A hundred and eighty degrees. Right. And that is/ what that measures from there right round to there/ so if to there is sixty degrees what's that? It's hundred and eighty altogether/ and that's sixty so what's that one?

LARA: Forty a hundred and forty.

T: Not a hundred and forty. What are you trying to do?

LARA: Add them together.

T: Not add them together. The whole lot is hundred and eighty. The whole turn/ from there round is a hundred and eighty degrees. Yes/ that part of it is sixty degrees/ so what's that part going to be? Think about that. All right. Success [*T looking at what Lara has written on to the computer screen*]/ OK.

Extract 1 displays several of the features of classroom discourse that we have been discusing, and especially, the issues of *control*, and of the building of a *context of shared understanding*. The teacher is firmly in control, both of the flow of speech, of who takes turns at speaking, and also of its content. She does most of the talking, asks the questions that determine speaker and topic, and defines the points at which each question is satisfactorily answered. Her method is not simply to tell the pupils things; she could easily have told them outright, that a straight line represents 180°, and articulated the rule, for them to learn by heart, that to draw a triangle, you turn the 'arrow' through 180° minus whatever angle you wish to use (in the case of an equilateral triangle, $180° - 60° = 120°$).

Rather than that, she engages in the 'eliciting' style of progressive, child-centred education. She asks questions, and guides the pupils to the required answers by means of how her questions are couched, and by her responses, reactions, pauses, gestures and mimes. The pupils' pursuit of the angle of a straight line is progressively narrowed to working out, via the teacher's prompts and demonstrations with the pencil, what is twice ninety.

It is also a heavily contextualized piece of dialogue. One would need to be there to see what exactly they are talking about; even the video recording does not always reveal what people are looking at or referring to. The point is, of course, that the participants themselves are required to see and understand these things. But simply 'being there' is not enough. It is not merely a physical context that they are working with. The teacher is at pains to ensure that the *significance* of what is done and seen is *understood* by everyone, and can be used as the basis for proceeding with the lesson; the discourse of context and continuity is addressed to matters of shared understanding. So, once Susan comes up with the answer, 120°, the teacher switches to her partner Lara, and makes sure, not only that she also knows the answer, but that she can be guided towards working it out, with however much help, for herself.†

The teacher's questions are not oriented towards finding things out – at least not in the obvious sense. She does not need the pupils to tell her 'answers' that she does not know. Rather, they are oriented towards finding out what the pupils themselves know, serving to establish a commonality of understanding between herself, and the pupils she is teaching. Teachers' questions also *impart* information, as well as requesting it, in that they are devices for introducing the formulations, conceptualizations and links between things that the pupils are meant to adopt ('One *quarter turn* which is how many *degrees*?')

Let us pursue this notion of establishing shared formulations. Extract 2 continues from where Extract 1 leaves off. The teacher, having spent the last few minutes with the girls, now moves them over to where the boys are working at another computer screen. The teacher has already (earlier in the same lesson) worked through, with the boys, what an 'equilateral' triangle is, and how to draw one using LOGO, turning the screen pointer through angles of 120° to draw the required 60° angles.

Extract 2: Talking geometry

T: OK/ will you come over and join this problem 'cause we've got a bit of a problem here/ and it's one I want you to think about for next week. We're going to try and draw a triangle. Now we've decided there's something different about it to what/ we've been doing. What do you think's different?

MARK: The angles.

† There is an intriguing similarity here, between the teacher's elicitation of geometry from these pupils, and the famous sequence in Plato's *Meno*, in which Socrates, in a dialogue with a slave boy, appears to elicit from him a version of Pythagoras's theorem. Socrates claims that the boy must have known the theorem innately. See Billig *et al.* (1988, Ch. 4) for a full discussion of the significance of this parallel, its relevance to modern educational practice, and the doctrines of Piagetian learning and of innate knowledge.

T: The angles are different aren't they.

STUART: Instead of ninety degrees you turn forty-five.

T: Well/ *DO* you?/ OK/ I want you to try for next week/ to draw a
            triangle. Now the girls have got an equilateral triangle here.
            How about you two [*Mark and Stuart*] doing an isosceles
            triangle?

STUART: What's that?

T: To try/ what's an isosceles triangle? Tell him Mark. What's an
            isosceles triangle? [*Mark giggles, as T puts her hand on his
            head*]

MARK: It's one with/ not all equal sides.

T: Not all equal/ are any of them equal?
            Isosceles/ [*T holding up two fingers*]

MARK: Two.

T: Two equal sides/ OK. One's got two equal sides/ that one's got
            three/ so what's that one called?

MARK: Called equal/ [*T begins nodding her head*] equilateral.

T: Equilateral.

The appeal to a continuity of shared understanding, the building
from moment to moment of a context of common knowledge, is quite
explicit in Extract 2. The problem to be solved has a future orientation –
it is one to pay special attention to, because it is to be taken up 'next
week'. The starting point is the immediate past – the context of shared
knowledge that has just been created – '*now we've decided* there's
something different about it ... ' What previously was the explicit, acted-
out and talked-about business of the lesson, is now offered by the
teacher as part of an implicit common understanding, 'what we've been
doing', the 'given' basis upon which new understandings can be built.

The teacher proceeds in the familiar, eliciting style ('What do YOU
think's different?'), together with clues and prompts that signal when the
answer is not the required one ('Well/ *DO* you?'). Then comes the
introduction of new terminology, though again, apparently via elicitation
('What's an isosceles triangle. Tell him Mark'). Through the introduction
of a common vocabulary, a common conceptual currency is established –
joint terms of reference, by which teacher and pupils can express their
common understandings, and also formulate these within the recognized language of geometry. For their part, the pupils appear to understand that, although they are being asked a question, the teacher will
invariably provide them with clues to its answer. The teacher is
understood to be in control of truth and definition. It having been
defined, earlier in the lesson, what an 'equilateral' triangle is, Mark now
offers the safe proposition that an 'isosceles' triangle must be something
other than that – 'It's one with/ not all equal sides'. This is not
acceptable. But rather than simply put him straight, the teacher proceeds

to cue the required response, with words and gesture (the two fingers), and her well-timed nod then helps Mark to recall the term 'equilateral'. We have termed these uses of prompts, gestures, reformulations of questions and other devices 'cued elicitation' (Edwards and Mercer, 1987). They serve, among other things, to maintain the appearance that knowledge and understanding are being elicited from the pupils themselves, rather than being imposed by the teacher. We shall discuss later some educational problems that this subterfuge may create.

Extract 3 is the remainder of the lesson, beginning where Extract 2 leaves off. The teacher is continuing to orient the pupils forward, to what will happen in the next lesson. The capitalized words are LOGO commands.

Extract 3: 'So remember'

T: Equilateral./ What we're going to do for next week is/ you're going to go away and you're going to try and do it on your own/ right. You [*T addressing the girls*] try and do a program for equilateral triangle. You two [*T looking at Mark and Stuart*]/ think about the turns you've got to make/ not the ones you've already got. That's a problem because/ we've gone LEFT NINETY haven't we [*T pointing to the diagram she has drawn on paper*]. FORWARD SEVENTY I think it was. Now we want to turn to point in that direction. We're trying to work out what our turn would be. We know that angle's sixty degrees [*pointing to an internal angle of the triangle*]/ but is that the angle we want to turn?

SUSAN: No.

T: [*Turning to Mark*] Is it?

MARK: No.

T: No. We want to turn from there/ right round to there/ so we've got to decide the angle of turn. So remember that when you're writing your program/ you've got to write down the angle which you want the arrow to turn through/ not any of the turns you've already got. It's what you want it to turn through. So your problem [*T addressing the boys*] is an isosceles triangle/ doesn't matter about the length of the sides/ and yours [*the girls'*] is an equilateral triangle/ OK/ and we'll have a go at that next week/ and perhaps another thing/ if you manage to/ you suss out the triangles/ and we'll try and do our initials or something next week because/ this week you haven't taken the pen off/ the arrow off. What you've done is come backwards if you've needed to go in another direction. Next week I'll show you how to take the pen off/ as if you lift the pen off the paper. [*T gesturing lifting her pen off a sheet of paper*]/ and how to put it back on again. OK/ so that's your problem this week/ equilateral triangles. Think you'll manage that?

MARK: Yes.

T: OK/ fine.

The point about this future orientation of the teacher's talk is that she is not merely providing information, or forward planning, about the next lesson. She is taking the opportunity to recap and reformulate what it is that the pupils are supposed to take away from this lesson, and bring back with them to the next. And it is not merely some homework. It is some shared understanding. 'So we've got to decide the angle of turn/ *so remember* ... you've got to write down the angle which you want the arrow to turn *through* ... it's what you want it to turn through'. The words 'right', 'so', and 'so remember' mark out the upshot of the lesson, the point of it all, the knowledge to take away, think about, bring back and be ready to build upon. The lesson's major point is made and repeated – to draw a triangle on the computer screen, you have to turn the pointer not through the triangle's internal angle, but through its complementary one. In fact, teachers' recaps of what has been 'done' or 'covered' in lessons, are opportunities not only for repeating and reinforcing these shared understandings, but also for tidying them up, redefining them in terms that better fit the teacher's preferred version of the knowledge in question. These 'reconstructive' recaps often occur at the beginnings and ends of lessons, but also during them, at moments when some doubt has arisen, that the required version of events is jointly understood (see Edwards and Mercer, 1987; and in press, for a detailed examination).

■ Discourse, rhetoric and school science

The development of classroom knowledge is the development of a discourse, the creation of a shared conceptual framework, a common language for the interpretation and communication of thought and experience. We have seen that shared understandings are heavily contextualized in terms of the unfolding talk and activity, with the significance of experience and discovery being marked out in the talk, conceptualized, reformulated, and forming the basis for subsequent talk. Despite a superficial reliance upon pupils' own ideas and contributions, it is also very much a teacher-dominated affair. On closer examination, classroom education looks much like socialization, an inculcation of pupils into a predetermined culture of educated knowledge and practice, than some unfolding development of individual cognitions.

We may ask, therefore, what is going on, when teachers seem so much at pains to display education as *e-ducare*, the classic definition, a matter of drawing out, leading out, or eliciting from pupils, thoughts and ideas (cognitions), that are latent within. Why do they overtly elicit everything from the children, while simultaneously gesturing, hinting at, implying and cuing the required answers? This sort of classroom discourse seems oriented towards the accomplishment of consensus, with pupils and teacher coming as soon as possible (if not immediately) to a shared understanding that accords closely with what the teacher already knows. Teacher and pupils appear to collude in this consensus, the content of which, while generally emanating from the teacher, is displayed as if emanating from the children. John Holt (1969) has documented a range of ways in which children learn to fake understanding, seeking to achieve recognized 'right answers', at the expense of any grasp of principle. It is important to emphasize that examining classroom discourse in terms of joint understandings does not mean that we must be solely concerned with consensual agreement. Shared understanding is the issue, not the assumption. We are interested in how teachers and children orient themselves in talk, to the issue of shared understanding, in how it is displayed or accomplished, or fudged, or ignored, or disputed. What we find, in the main, is that teacher and pupils strive to accomplish an appearance of consensus, avoiding unresolved disagreements, and indeed, avoiding disagreements altogether.

Teachers are themselves trained and educated. They learn at college and university, and in teaching practice, the current educational theories and ideologies – the philosophy of *e-ducare*, of Piaget and Plowden, the inadequacy of teaching things to children that they are not ready to learn, that they may learn by rote but not understand. Teachers themselves can articulate the reasons, though not everything that they do is explicitly formulated. But the ideal of elicitation has to be practised against the requirement that the job gets done. There is an overriding practical concern with achieving order and control, both behavioural and cognitive, and with doing the curriculum. They are faced with the dilemma of having to elicit from children, precisely what the curriculum determines shall be taught. (These issues are discussed in more detail, in Edwards and Mercer, 1987, and in Billig *et al.*, 1988.)

Another reason for all the subtle subterfuges may be that educationists are operating with an inadequate notion of the subject to be taught – of what doing 'science' is really like. We argued earlier, that the popular view of science, and the one favoured even by scientists themselves when discussing their own, or some favoured, work is something of a 'storybook' version. The lone scientist constructs knowledge through hypothesis and strict empirical method, the proposed theory being that which must be forced upon any rational mind by the evidence available. Other, 'contingent' repertoires are available for accounting for what are considered to be false beliefs, opposing views and interpretations, misleading research, false trails, and so on (see Gilbert and Mulkay, 1984; Potter and Wetherell, 1987). The point is, that science as it is practised is a social activity, a discourse among scientists that is oriented towards what is taken to be common knowledge. It has the character of a debate, and makes full use of the devices of rhetoric and persuasion (see also Yearley, 1981, 1985).

Classroom science has some of the features of everyday scientific practice. It also is a communal, discursive activity, a construction of shared understanding, publicly communicated and embodied in shared symbolic forms – conversation, writing and text, diagrams, drawings, and so on, with the same concern for establishing a common conceptual framework for the encoding of experience, method, observation and theory. The contrast lies in the lack of debate. Science has no 'teacher', no ultimate power and authority who knows all the answers in advance.
[...]

The notion that pupils may be unable to understand what their individual cognitive development has not yet prepared them for, has an ironic parallel in classroom discourse. Readiness is indeed an issue, but what often occurs is that pupils come up with ideas that the *teacher* is not ready for. In their third lesson on computer graphics (two weeks later), the children decided that it would be a good idea to draw their names or initials on the screen (Extract 4):

Extract 4: 'You can't do curves can you?'

KAREN: (to Lisa) ... the S is going to be a bit difficult/ though. You could just write LC if you wanted to.

T: But you can't do curves can you? You can't do an S. We haven't learnt to do them ...

LARA: We could do that [*finger drawing a boxed S in the air*].

T: That's right ... box writing as long as it's got right angles/ as long as it's not curved/ you're all right. It can do curves/ but we haven't learned how to do them yet. So/ just use what you know. That's the best way.

Again, we have an explicit appeal to a continuity of shared knowledge that encompasses what has already been incorporated into their common understanding, and which extends into the future: '*you* can't do' what '*we* haven't learnt to do [yet]'. But here, it operates also as a constraint. The teacher's 'can you?' superficially elicits, but the teacher's own answer ('you can't') closes down the possibility of Lara's contradicting. Rather than following up the pupils' own thoughts and problem proposals, we have to settle for what, at a point near the scheduled end of the lesson, the teacher has taught so far.

The restrictions of teacher-dominated discourse point to the possibility that pupil–pupil dialogue may be able to offer some compensatory advantages. It was argued earlier, that adult science is more open-ended and uncertain than school science, more argumentative, free-wheeling, open to disputation and reformulation. This suggests a role in the development of educational knowledge, for children to argue things through with each other, without the teacher's constant supervision and control over where the discussion has to lead. Pupils do, of course, engage in such discussions. But one still has to consider what their importance, if any, might be. Pupils' dialogues may help to reveal how individual pupils think (this is the usual use of such materials), but the possibility remains that they may be important also, for the development of dialogical, argumentative forms of thinking. Extract 5 is taken from the end of the third lesson on computer graphics. The teacher has allowed the group to continue 'playing' with the computer, while the researchers were packing up their recording equipment. Stuart and Tracy continued to try to draw their names on the screen. We left the camera running.

Extract 5: Arguing and thinking

TRACY: RIGHT NINETY/ then we'll be there and I don't want to be there.

STUART: RIGHT NINETY/ is just here ... write your columns down here ... It's still not finished yet.

TRACY: Then/ it's/ RIGHT SIXTEEN again. Put RIGHT SIXTEEN.

STUART: Where?

TRACY: We're/there we are. We're facing that way/ we want to go/ RIGHT SIXTEEN.

STUART: Then we want/ FORWARD.

TRACY: No/ we don't want to be there. We're doing a RIGHT. Look. We go down there/ go back up there/ go down there.

STUART: FORWARD.

TRACY: Oh/ come on/ you do it (...)

STUART: F NINETY/ that's your first (...) No that's wrong (...)

TRACY: LEFT NINETY.

STUART: LEFT or RIGHT?

TRACY: LEFT.

STUART: We'd be going that way then.

TRACY: Tell you what/ we could go that way.

STUART: No/ we're going that way.

TRACY: Over there/ you said/ RIGHT NINETY we'd be going that way. He don't know his left and right. NINETY/ so then we'll be facing that way. FORWARD TEN. What's that supposed to be?

STUART: What/ who I mean?

TRACY: TEN then we'll be here/ there then I want to go.

STUART: Miss [*calling to the teacher*]/ what angle do we/ what are we (...) to go back up there again

T: Where are you? You're there/ and you want to turn through that angle there?

STUART: No/ no/ we don't want to do that one Miss. We're going to do one of the smaller ones (...) was it LEFT or RIGHT?

TRACY: See I told you.

T: He's already done it.

It is clear that the children are not merely taking turns at thinking aloud, revealing for an observer's convenience their processes of thought. Rather, they are engaged with each other in joint action and argument, such that what each says and does affects the other's next move. Furthermore, their verbal formulations of thought, are dialogical and argumentative in form, addressed persuasively to the difference between a proposed action or solution, and what the other person thinks or assumes – 'No/ we don't want to be there. We're doing a RIGHT. Look. We go down there.' 'No that's wrong ... we'd be going that way then.' Argument is a form of thought, indeed many and varied forms of thought, irreducible to the mere adding together of individual cognitions that may happen to be put into words (see Billig, 1987, from which the caption for extract 5 is borrowed). As with science proper, once we abandon the notion that there is some higher, pervasive authority that already knows everything, ideas have to be justified against criticism, supported by argument and evidence, against possible refutation. They do not spring from the data, nor from some rigid logic, evident and undeniable. They do not arise merely out of the perception and cognition of individuals, finding form in words only as some final part of the process, for the purposes of teaching them to someone else. The common knowledge of science and of the school classroom is intrinsically social, framed in a common language, dialogical in form and process. [...]

The prevailing emphasis upon individual learning, individual cognitive growth, coupled with the pervasiveness of teacher-dominated dialogue, leads to some of the subterfuges and inadequacies of the sorts of teaching we have examined here. There is a tendency in teachers to keep their educational goals secret; pupils cannot be told too much, but have to work things out for themselves. As Driver also observed,

> 'It is common to see science lessons which end with the clearing up after the practical work is finished. The time for the important discussion of how the important experiences gained relate to the new ideas is missed. Activity by itself is not enough. It is the sense that is made of it that matters.' (1983, p. 49)

We might add that discussion is important throughout the lessons, and that must include discussion between pupils, as well as with the teacher. Our analyses of classroom discourse suggest that teacher–pupil talk and pupil–pupil talk are both important, but often for different reasons. There are overriding asymmetries between teacher and pupil, both cognitive (in terms of knowledge) and interactive (in terms of power), that impose different discursive patterns and functions. The teacher's expertise lends itself to direct explanation and to assisted learning, of the Vygotskian sort, in which the less competent child is helped ('scaffolded' is Jerome Bruner's term), towards increased competence. But we should not ignore what pupils can learn from others who know no more than themselves – the skills of disputation, the notion that all knowledge is questionable, or in need of scrutiny and justification, that we do not always have to agree. It is important that the teacher's knowledge should not be immune from such an approach. Perhaps the most difficult achievement is not to let children argue with each other, but to open up the teacher's own understandings for scrutiny in the classroom – her pre-established plans and assumptions, her aims and methods, her own understandings and conclusions, for disputation, without the whole exercise becoming merely another guessing game of what the teacher wants us all to say. [...]

■ References

Billig M. (1987). *Arguing and Thinking*. Cambridge: Cambridge University Press.

Billig M., Condor S., Edwards D., Gane M., Middleton D.J. and Radley, A.R. (1988). *Ideological Dilemmas: A Social Psychology of Everyday Thinking*. London: Sage.

Brook A., Driver R. and Johnston, K. (1988). Learning processes in science: a classroom perspective. In *Skills and Processes in Science Education: a Critical Analysis* (Wellington J.J., ed.). London: Methuen.

Bruner J.S. (1986). *Actual Minds, Possible Worlds*. London: Harvard University Press.

Bullock M., Gelman R. and Baillargeon, R. (1982). The development of causal reasoning. In *The Developmental Psychology of Time* (Freeman W.F., ed.). New York: Academic Press.

Butterworth G. and Light P. (1982). *Social Cognition: Studies of the Development of Understanding*. Brighton: Harvester Press.

Carey S. (1985). Are children fundamentally different kinds of thinkers and learners than adults? In *Thinking and Learning Skills* (Chipman, S.F. Segal J.W., and Glaser R., eds). Vol. 2, Hillsdale, NJ: Lawrence Erlbaum. Page references are to the reprint in *Cognitive Development to Adolescence* (Richardson K. and Sheldon S. eds).Lawrence Erlbaum and The Open University, Milton Keynes, 1988.

Delamont (1987). Three blind spots? A comment on the sociology of science by a puzzled outsider. *Social Studies of Science*, **17**, 163–70.

Donaldson M. (1978). *Children's Minds*. London: Fontana.

Driver R. (1983). *The Pupil as Scientist?* Milton Keynes: Open University Press.

Driver R. and Oldham V. (1986). A constructivist approach to curriculum development in science. *Studies in Science Education*, **13**, 105–22.

Edwards D. and Mercer N.M. (1986). Context and continuity: classroom discourse and the development of shared knowledge. In *Language Development in the School Years* (Durkin, K., ed.). London: Croom Helm.

Edwards D. and Mercer N.M. (1987). *Common Knowledge: The Development of Understanding in the Classroom*. London: Methuen.

Edwards D. and Mercer N.M. (in press). Reconstructing context: the conventionalization of classroom knowledge. *Discourse Processes*.

Engineering Council and the Standing Conference on Schools' Science and Technology (1985) *Problem Solving: Science and Technology in Primary Schools*. London.

Fodor J.A. (1972). Some reflections on L.S. Vygotsky's thought and language. *Cognition*, **1**(1), 83–95.

Gardner H. (1985). *The Mind's New Science: a History of the Cognitive Revolution*. New York: Basic Books.

Gilbert G.N. and Mulkay M. (1984). *Opening Pandora's Box: a Sociological Analysis of Scientists' Discourse*. Cambridge: Cambridge University Press.

Heritage J. (1984). *Garfinkel and Ethnomethodology*. Cambridge: Polity Press.

Holt J. (1969). *How Children Fail*. Harmondsworth: Penguin.

Keil F.C. (1986). On the structure-dependent nature of stages of cognitive development. In *Stage and Structure: Reopening the Debate* (Levin, I., ed.). New Jersey: Ablex. Page references are to the reprint in *Cognitive Development and Adolescence* (Richardson K. and Sheldon S., eds). Lawrence Erlbaum & Open University Press, Milton Keynes, 1988.

Latour B. and Woolgar S. (1979). *Laboratory Life: the Social Construction of Scientific Facts*. London: Sage.

Mehan H. (1979). Learning Lessons: *Social Organization in the Classroom*. Cambridge, Mass.: Harvard University Press.

Mitroff I.I. (1974). *The Subjective Side of Science*. Amsterdam: Elsevier.

Moscovici S. (1984a). The phenomenon of social representations. In *Social Representations* (Farr R.M. and Moscovici S., eds). Cambridge: Cambridge University Press.

Nuffield Foundation (1967). *Nuffield Maths Projects, I Do and I Understand*. London: W & R Chambers and John Murray.

Olson D.R. (1977). Oral and written language and the cognitive processes of children. *Journal of Communication*, **27**(3), 10–26. Page references are to reprint in *Language Development* (Lock A. and Fisher E., eds). London: Croom Helm/The Open University, 1984.

Piaget J. (1928). *Judgement and Reasoning in the Child*. London: Routledge & Kegan Paul.

Piaget J. (1970). Piaget's theory. In *Carmichael's Manual of Child Psychology* (Mussen P.H., ed.). New York: John Wiley & Sons.

Plowden Report: Central Advisory Council for Education (1967). *Children and Their Primary Schools*. London: HMSO.

Potter J. and Mulkay M. (1985). 'Scientists' interview talk: Interviews as a technique for revealing participants' interpretative practices'. In *The Research Interview: Uses and Approaches* (Brenner M., Brown J. and Canter D., eds). London: Academic Press.

Potter J. and Wetherell M. (1987). *Discourse and Social Psychology*. London: Sage.

Russell J. (1978). *The Acquisition of Knowledge*. London: Macmillan Press.

Sinclair J. McH. and Coulthard R.M. (1975). *Towards an Analysis of Discourse: the English Used by Teachers and Pupils*. London: Oxford University Press.

Suchman L. (1987). *Plans and Situated Actions: the Problem of Human –Machine Interaction*. Cambridge: Cambridge University Press.

Vygotsky L.S. (1962/1987). *Thought and Language*. Cambridge, Mass.: MIT Press.

Walkerdine V. (1982). From context to text: a psychosemiotic approach to abstract thought. *In Children Thinking Through Language* (Beveridge M., ed.). London: Edward Arnold.

Walkerdine V. (1984). Developmental psychology and the child-centred pedagogy: the insertion of Piaget into early education. In *Changing The Subject* (Henriques J., Hollway W., Urwin C., Venn C. and Walkerdine V., eds). London: Methuen.

Walkerdine V. (1988). *The Mastery Of Reason: Cognitive Development and the Production of Rationality*. London: Routledge.

Wertsch, J.V. (1985). *Vygotsky and the Social Formation of Mind*. Cambridge, Mass.: Harvard University Press.

Wetherell M. and Potter J. (1988). Discourse analysis and the identification of interpretative repertoires. *In Analysing Everyday Explanation: a Casebook of Methods* (Antaki C., ed.). London: Sage.

Wood D. (1988). *How Children Think and Learn*. Oxford: Basil Blackwell.

Woolgar S. (1988). *Science: The Very Idea*. Chichester: Ellis Horwood./London: Tavistock.

Yearley S. (1981). Textual persuasion: the role of social accounting in the construction of scientific arguments. *Philosophy of the Social Sciences*, **11**, 409–35.

Yearley, S. (1985). Vocabularies of freedom and resentment: a strawsonian perspective on the nature of argumentation in science and the law. *Social Studies of Science*, **15**, 99–126.

Paper 2.6

Learning Activities and Classroom Roles with and without the Microcomputer

Rosemary Fraser, Hugh Burkhardt, Jon Coupland, Richard Phillips, David Pimm and Jim Ridgway

This paper is concerned with the range and balance of learning activities in the classroom and with elucidating how the various roles assumed by those involved relate to these activities. The analysis is based on records of the detailed observation of 174 mathematics lessons; the use of the microcomputer as a teaching aid in parts of these lessons was a crucial element in the analysis, giving insight through its perturbation of the familiar pattern of roles and activities. This enabled us to develop a taxonomy relating observable classroom activities, inferred learning activities and the roles played by the teacher, the pupils and, when it was in use, the computer. Exemplar lessons are described; they have been chosen to illustrate the taxonomy and the shifting and sharing of roles that we most commonly observed. Among other results, it is shown that the micro is regarded by the pupils as an independent 'personality' and that, suitably programmed, it can temporarily take over some of the roles usually assumed by the teacher in such a way that the teacher adopts other roles, rarely found in the classroom, that are essential to the promotion of higher level learning activities.

First published in Jones, A. and Scrimshaw, P. (eds) (1987) *Computers in Education* and the Journal of Mathematical Behaviour (1988), **6**, 305–38. Reprinted with permission of the ITMA Collaboration.

■ Introduction

[...]

☐ The study

The analysis of the interrelation between visible classroom activities, the learning activities that can be inferred and the roles played at various times by teachers, micro and pupils, forms the content of this paper. This analysis and the resulting classification is primarily based on a systematic study of 174 mathematics lessons taught in the autumn term of 1981 to 17 classes of 12–14-year-old pupils by their teachers, whose individual styles and approaches together covered a wide range. The study is described in detail in a separate paper (Burkhardt *et al.*, in preparation). In summary, the teachers agreed to use a micro in the course of one mathematics lesson per week with the class concerned, choosing freely from a collection of 97 program teaching units supplied to them; each of these lessons was observed and a detailed record compiled containing observational data of three different kinds:

(1)   A few facts recorded in a standard form.

(2)   A structured event-by-event description, using a Systematic Classroom Analysis Notation (SCAN) developed earlier (Beeby *et al.*, 1979), which gives a rich and detailed picture of the pattern of teaching in the lesson.

(3)   Notes by the observer on any important aspects of the lesson not picked up by the more systematic elements (1) and (2).

Discussion with the teacher, and with individual pupils, during the lesson, material used and pupil work are other important elements in the total observation system (Burkhardt *et al.*, 1982). Immediately after the lesson, following discussion with the teacher, the observer summarized the information in a lesson report of a few hundred words. The aim was to provide enough data to enable others not present to analyse the lesson in terms that would prove convincing to the observer; we found that this aim was achieved. Enough cross-observation was undertaken to indicate that disparity between observers was not a serious problem. [...]

While the range of normal teaching style encompassed by the 17 teachers was wide, in some other respects the coverage was narrow. Only a few had extensive experience of using the micro in their teaching; most were using it for first time. By the end of the term all were accustomed to it and the practical handling problems did not generally seem to distort the pattern of classroom interactions seriously, though there are a number of important ergonomic implications that emerge (Phillips *et al.*, in preparation). In almost every case the teachers were using the individual teaching units for the first time so, with a few clearly identifiable exceptions, this was a study of the use of 'unfamiliar' material. It is therefore particularly notable that in their choice of programs to use, teachers mainly went for the richer more complex ones. Substantial amounts of teaching *without* the micro were also observed for each teacher in the course of the term, largely in those parts of each observed lesson when it was not in action. [...]

☐ **This paper**

The structure of this paper is set out as follows. We have chosen to begin at the end, as it were – with the scheme of classification on page 208, we then elucidate its provenance by alternating the description of particular lessons with discussion of the various facets of the taxonomy, before going on to pursue the implications for classroom dynamics in the third section.

In the course of this we describe three lessons using the same program, PIRATES, so that the reader can get some feeling for the analysis given below of the learning activities, and for the roles that pupils, teacher and computer may play in them. The analysis itself is based on the detailed observation of all the lessons, but many of its features are sufficiently general to be seen in the small sample of lessons given. [...]

Table 1   Observable pupil classroom activities

Passive		*Active*
Watching	*Writing*	note taking
Listening		recording
Reading		exercises
'Thinking'		symbolizing
		explaining
Off task		
Dreaming	*Talking*	asking
Fooling		answering
Chatting		describing
		discussing
		explaining
		hypothesizing
		asserting
Mode of classroom activity		
Competition		
Experimenting		
Testing		
Imitating computer or teacher		

■   Analysis of roles and activities

☐   A taxonomy

Out of the observations of this study has grown a classification of roles and activities that provides a framework within which we can discuss the relationship between the roles of the teacher, the pupils and other resources such as the micro, and the learning activities that take place in the classroom. The balance of roles is a crucial factor in the environment within which learning can occur. In this section we explain the classification with lesson exemplars that show how it has arisen.

Table 1(a)

	Passive			Active
*①	Watching	*Writing*	① ②	note taking
①	Listening		① ②	recording
②	Reading		②	exercises
③ ④ ⑤ ⑥	'Thinking'		④ ⑤ ⑥	symbolizing
			④ ⑤ ⑥	explaining
	Off task			
① ③	Dreaming	*Talking*	① ② ③	asking
① ② ③	Fooling		① ② ③	answering
② ③ ④ ⑤ ⑥	Chatting		③ ④ ⑤ ⑥	describing
			③	discussing
			③ ④ ⑤ ⑥	explaining
			③ ④ ⑤	hypothesizing
			③ ④ ⑤ ⑥	asserting
	Mode of classroom activity			
⑥	Competition			
④ ⑤ ⑥	Experimenting			
④ ⑤ ⑥	Testing			
④ ⑤ ⑥	Imitating computer or teacher			

* The numbers indicate the most commonly observed 'Cockcroft' activities that were operational when the particular category shown was noted.

Key to Cockcroft activities paragraph 243 of the Cockcroft Report

① Teacher exposition
② Pupil exercise, consolidation and practice
③ Discussion
④ Investigation
⑤ Applied and/or practical mathematics
⑥ Problem solving

We think it would be helpful to the reader to begin simply by tabulating the resultant taxonomy. The meaning of the terms used will become clearer through their appearance in the lesson descriptions. While there is an inevitable element of arbitrariness in the detail of any such classification scheme, we have found that this one is basically robust. (The reader may like to explore alternatives.)

Table 1 lists the observable 'surface' classroom activities, grouped in a fairly obvious fashion, while Table 1(a) shows them linked to those teaching activities, listed in paragraph 243 of the Cockcroft Report, in which they commonly occurred. These six activities, reordered and numbered, are listed at the bottom of Tables 1(a) and 2(a). Thus, for example, when 'watching' was observed, the activity was frequently exposition. ①, with other categories appearing significantly less often. Conversely, we may conclude that exposition ① and practice ② promote the more commonly observed classroom activities, whereas when the more 'open' activities ④, ⑤ and ⑥ are present, higher level skills are likely to be in use.

Table 2 shows the learning activities that are taking place – some are directly observable (for example symbolizing) while others are inferred from the surface activity pattern. Here the clusterings are less obvious and will be discussed later. The links to the Cockcroft classification are shown in Table 2(a); again ① and ② support the more easily promoted learning activities of a more passive kind, whereas the high

Table 2 Pupil learning activities

d	*didactic*	absorbing
		recalling
		rule following
s	*symbolizing*	using
		translation skills
i	*investigating*	guessing
		checking
		particularizing
p	*problem solving*	technical skills
		tactical skills
		strategic skills
		control skills
h	*higher level skills*	image building
		analysing
		generalizing
		abstracting
		linking
		proving
		reflecting

level activities are more frequent we found when ③, ④, ⑤ and ⑥ are present. This provides a strong objective indication of the reasons for the importance of ③, ④, ⑤ and ⑥, which are rarely found in normal mathematics classrooms (HMI, 1982). The importance of looking for ways of creating a balance of learning activities follows from this; this paper provides a new approach to this problem.

Table 3 gives a corresponding taxonomy of the observed roles that are played at various times by the teacher, the micro and the pupils. The given role is often shared between them in varying proportions. Again the clustering into groups will be of importance in our detailed discussion on page 212. Our central concern will be to link these roles with the learning activities of Table 2 which they help to promote.

Table 2(a)

d	*didactic*	* ① ②	absorbing
		① ②	recalling
		②	rule following
s	*symbolizing*	(all)	using
		③ ④ ⑤ ⑥	translation skills
i	*investigating*	④ ⑥	guessing
		④ ⑤ ⑥	checking
		② ④ ⑤ ⑥	particularizing
p	*problem solving*	④ ⑤ ⑥	technical skills
		④ ⑤ ⑥	tactical skills
		④ ⑥	strategic skills
		④ ⑥	control skills
h	*higher level skills*	④ ⑤ ⑥	image building
		④ ⑤ ⑥	analysing
		④ ⑥	generalizing
		④ ⑥	abstracting
		② ④ ⑥	linking
		② ④ ⑥	proving
		④ ⑥	reflecting

* The numbers indicate the most commonly observed 'Cockcroft' activities when the particular category shown was noted.

Key to Cockcroft activities paragraph 243 of the Cockcroft Report

①   Teacher exposition
②   Pupil exercise, consolidation and practice
③   Discussion
④   Investigation
⑤   Applied and/or practical mathematics
⑥   Problem solving

Lesson 1   Joan with PIRATES

This section gives a description of a lesson by Joan with the PIRATES program. PIRATES is a program about coordinates, set in the context of a problem-solving game. The aim is to find the location of a buried treasure on a rectangular whole-number grid of predetermined size. Each suggestion promotes a clue from the computer, which may be given in the form of a compass direction, a bearing, a vector direction, a distance or as 'warmer–colder' clues, depending on the particular skills that the teacher wants to practise. Thus the teacher defines the type of problem and the type of clue and the program then accepts coordinate pair 'guesses' and responds with clues – all plotting of points is done by the children individually or in group discussion, with or without the teacher. At no time does the computer display the grid; the children are expected to plot their own points and keep a record of the information received. We comment on this aspect of the program design later.

The description is laid out in two columns, the first column describing the lesson as it progresses while the second column comments on the roles and activities involved. To link it to Tables 1, 2 and 3, the observable classroom activities are underlined, the learning activities are classified as *d s i p h* as in Table 2 and the roles are related to Ⓜ Ⓣ Ⓔ Ⓕ Ⓒ Ⓡ as in Table 3. The roles are suffixed to indicate whether teacher t, pupil p or computer c is playing that particular role at that stage – for example, Ⓣᶜ indicates that the computer c is assuming the role of Tasksetter Ⓣ.

She has loaded and tried out PIRATES before the lesson. After a short managerial introduction, she starts straight in – explaining the program, the 0–9 grid, and the compass direction clues.

At this point the computer is a system to *explore* Ⓡᶜ. The screen summarizes the situation – the teacher is in overall control and is *explaining* Ⓔᵗ what's what.

T   Who wants to make the first guess? Richard?

Rd   (5,5)

T   We'll put in (5,5) and see what it says. 'Go South West', Put that down on your grids. What shall we try next, Susan?

Sn   (2,2)

T   (2,2). It says 'Go North West'. Tony?

Ty   (1,3)

T   (1,3). Any other ideas? Gillian?

The teacher is simply *managing* Ⓜᵗ tactical use of the program working in quite traditional roles with a computer providing *task setting* Ⓣᶜ (and a system to *explore* possibly in more flexible ways later).
The learning activities here includes symbolizing *s*, problem solving *p* and other higher level skills *h*.

Table 3   Classroom roles

(M)	Manager (tactical) corrector marker computer operator	(T)	Task setter questioner example setter strategy setter
(E)	Explainer demonstrator scene setter image builder focuser imitator rule giver coach	(C)	Counsellor adviser helper devil's advocate encourager stimulator listener/supporter observer receiver diagnostician problem solver (C)
(F)	Fellow pupil rule applier hypothesizer problem solver (F)	(R)	Resource system to explore giver of information

Gn   (1,4)
T   Which shall we try first? (1,3)?
      Well done, that's it!

In this episode the children have been *watching* and *listening* and *thinking* about the problem, with little sign of off task activity. In drawing and using their grids they are *symbolizing (s)* and *recording*; in playing the game they are *experimenting*, *testing* and *competing*, and probably *hypothesizing (h)*. Those who respond are certainly *hypothesizing* and *answering* – a wide range of activities in one of the 'missing' classroom modes *discussion* ③.

T   Shall we do another?

Ps   Yes ...

      ...

      ...

There followed two more similar successful episodes, with the teacher providing less detailed guidance leaving most of the *tactical managing* (M) ᶜ to the program as the pupils get familiar with it.

T   Can any one say which they think is the best way to find the treasure?
      (Pause)
      What is the best first guess?

The teacher here largely dissociates herself from the *task setting* (T) ᶜ and become a *counsellor* (C) ᵗ on the strategy.

Tony?

Ty (5,5) Miss.

T Why?

Ty Because it's in the middle, so each direction has the same size area *(h)*.

Pt $(4\frac{1}{2},4\frac{1}{2})$ is in the middle, Miss.

T Yes, but we can only have whole numbers. Are there any others as much in the middle as (5,5)?

Ps (4,4) (Pause) What about (4,5)? *(p) (i)*

T Let's try that. It says 'Go east'. What is the best thing to do next?

An Does it mean exactly East, Miss?

T I don't know. What do you think? Does anybody remember what happened before?

Rd Last time it said go South, it has the same first coordinate in the end. *(h)*.

T All right, shall we try that? Where shall we go next?

Sn (5,6)

T It says 'Go East' again. Where next?

Ty (5,7) *(p)*

Gn No. (5,8)

T Why?

Gn Well, it could be at (5,7) (5,8) or (5,9). (Pause) If we try (5,8) we either get it straight away or one step after. If we try (5,7) it could take two more steps if its at (5,9). *(p) (i) (h)*

Some other teachers might explain the strategy of 'binary search', either immediately or after the pupil's less than totally lucid attempt. This would help more pupils to understand the strategy, but prevent their working it out for themselves.

T Shall we do that then?

Ps Yes.

T   (5,8) That's it.
Let's try a different sort of clue – 'Warm' clues tell you if you are getting closer to the treasure or not.
(Pause)
This is harder so we'll change the grid to (0,4) in each direction.
Where shall we start?

Jn   (2,2)

T   (2,2). It says you are cold. Which way shall we go Paul?

P   It doesn't tell you, Miss.

T   No it doesn't. What shall we try?

P   (3,3) Miss. (*i*)

T   Why did you choose that one?

P   (Pause) Don't know, Miss.

T   (3,3) It says you are getting colder.

A controlling decision to leave that strategic domain for a while at least and go on to another more challenging problem, again with an intuitive approach. Note teacher warns it will be harder, which is not obvious to the children at this stage. The teacher begins on a repetition of the search for a strategy for warmth clues (where the 'centre' is seldom the best place to start). More guidance as *counsellor* (C)^t and *fellow pupil* (F)^t, or much more patience may be needed here. The teacher can take these roles because the tactical *management* (M)^c, *task setting* (T)^c and *correction* (M)^c are being handled by the computer.

The reader will have observed how, at times, some of the roles are assumed by the computer, and at other times, by the teacher or pupils. Roles can also be shared – the pupil roles throughout the lesson included Explaining (E)^p and Fellow Pupil (F)^p both of which were also shared by the teacher.

☐   Classification of classroom activities and learning activities

Classroom activities

Table 1 lists major observable classroom activities – these are pupil activities grouped under the headings Passive and Active the latter being subdivided under Writing and Talking. There is also a separate group called Mode of classroom activity, with the headings Competition, Experimenting, Testing and Imitating. The group and subgroup headings were used in analysing lessons both in the lesson descriptions that appear in this paper on pages 217–218 and 220–221, and also in the matrix representation of lessons that appears on pages 224–5. The more detailed labels such as recording, note taking, and so on are included to help the observer classify the large range of observable activities into the groups proposed in this particular taxonomy. We give brief descriptions of the major headings and subheadings and leave the reader to interpret the words describing particular activities, guided by their normal meaning and illustrated by their use in the lesson descriptions.

Passive

This includes all the activities where the child is receiving rather than actively using information. It links very much towards promoting the learning activities of recall, absorbing and rule following which come under the *didactic* heading in Table 2. We include here also the off-task activities of fooling, chatting, and so on, though these don't appear in the matrix analysis in the third section.

Active

This is subdivided into *writing* and *talking*, each with its list of detailed activities.

The following modes of activity have been included; they may also be observed and they are particularly relevant in this study:

- *Competition*, where pupils are placed in some type of competition either among themselves or against the computer.

- *Experimenting* where the children are actually experimenting with ideas or 'apparatus' in the broadest sense.

- *Testing* where the children are testing out certain hypotheses on particular cases.

- *Imitating* where the children are actually imitating the recent roles of computer or teacher. This last category is of special interest as will become apparent from the examplars and the comments on them.

Learning activities

The learning activities are clustered together in groups as shown in Table 2. The headings in order, and in fact in the order that they most commonly occur are:

- *d, didactic* activities are those traditional in classrooms where children are absorbing, recalling, recording and rule following. These were the activities that tend to dominate in classroom according, for example, to the HMI Survey (1982).

- *s, symbolizing* – any activity where the child is employing symbols to represent information in the exercise or problem being studied; the subheadings 'using' and 'translation skills' are given but other headings could also be listed here – we have kept the list deliberately short and its main purpose is to indicate our understanding of this cluster as a group.

- *i, investigating* – this cluster has three subheadings, which could again be expanded, those included again being indicative of the activities that we classify under this heading.

- *p, problem solving* – under this more general heading, the list has been expressed in terms of the skills employed; there is no clear division between this heading and the next one.

- *h, higher level skills* – a long list is given here to help identify activities that fall in this heading.

Tables 1(a) and 2(a) link the taxonomy developed here with paragraph 243 of the Cockcroft Report. This is of interest in that it gives detailed support to the link between the dominance of exposition and practice and a heavy emphasis on the relatively passive learning activities of absorbing and imitative exercising which are characteristic of the didactic approach. In contrast, it shows how the ability both actively to under-stand mathematics and to use it effectively depends on activities related to higher level, more strategic skills. If this is indeed generally true, as seems likely, then it points to two possibilities:

(1)   The teacher is unaware of the need to promote these activities or

(2)   The teacher is aware but finds it too difficult.

There are related difficulties both for the pupil and for the teacher. The standard elements of the didactic approach – the absorption and recall of facts and techniques, and the repetitive practice of imitative exercises based on rule following – are relatively straightforward for teachers and pupils; the latter have clearly defined and unambiguous tasks, while the teacher can pursue a single pedagogical track, explaining, illustrating and, in coaching pupils' working, reiterating the standard technique. Most teachers experienced this approach as pupils and have no compelling reason to change, as the examination system also reflects and encourages a didactic approach to the acquisition of knowledge.

Almost all the other activities require more initiative from the pupil and a more flexible sensitive responsiveness from the teacher; we shall see that these require the teacher to play quite different roles, and in some conflict with the traditional authoritarian ones of the didactic approach. A key strength of the micro seems to be in taking over some of the latter and liberating the teacher to establish a more consultative relationship with the pupil. Evidence of this is shown in the exemplars.

There are some exceptions to this general summary. The activities grouped under symbolizing, which are concerned with translating statements or information from one form to another, depend on skills which can be taught in a similarly didactic way. The separate and explicit teaching of such translation skills has not received much emphasis in

English schools, but this and other research has shown that such teaching is, at least in part, relatively straightforward. Nonetheless, the micro is capable of providing significant assistance in it.

Lesson 2   Jack with PIRATES

In this section we describe a different teacher's lesson with PIRATES.

Jack is concerned with compass points, and the inequality constraints that define regions. Here the computer will set up the situation and produce a statement such as 'The treasure lies in the region $x < 8$ and $y > 2$'. The clues are then given in compass directions as in Lesson 1.

He starts with revision; with a picture drawn on the blackboard, he explains (E)^t the lines x = 4, y = 6 and so on. Pupils appear to *attend (d)* and *absorb (d)*. (7 mins)

He explains (E)^t the program, getting children to *draw (d)* several coordinate grids (0,9; 0,9) in preparation for the 'game' – a straightforward *exercise (d)* on their part. Similarly they draw compass directions (N, NE, E, ...) on tracing paper. (10 mins)

Traditional *didactic (d)* teaching with its well-defined pattern of activities and roles – the teacher *explaining* (E)^t *managing* (M)^t and *task setting* while pupils *attend, absorb (d)* and exercise *(d)*.

Setting the computer to produce inequality constraints, it chooses x < 8, y > 2. the pupils produced guesses (i) and follow clues; successively (3,4) 'Go NE', (6,7) 'Go SE', (5,6) 'Go E', (7,6) finds the treasure.

The computer is now the *task setter* (T)^c and the encourager (C)^c, while the teacher *manages* (M)^t the class.

Three more search episodes follow in similar vein. The teacher *corrects* pupil suggestions not consistent with the constraints, filtering them out rather than letting the computer respond. The possibility of *strategy* is raised ('who can do it in the least number of times?') but not pursued except in the recognition

As the task becomes familiar the computer takes over more of the detailed *management* (M)^c, leaving the teacher freer to take other roles. The teacher, however, does not move outside the usual explainer (E)^t, task setting (T)^t and managerial (M)^t roles, while letting the computer take the major burden of task setting (T)^c

of accumulating evidence ('that's got to be it'). (18 mins)

The teacher, who will be away for the two following class lessons, instructs children to play PIRATES in pairs, taking over in turn the computer role of *task setter* (T)ᵖ and *manager* (M) ᵖ

and detailed management (M) ᶜ. He is content simply to exercise overall control.

For the subsequent lessons, the teacher is handing over to the pupils, subject to the overall *control* consent of the stand-in teacher who will take care of the class.

The children are now asked to imitate the teacher's and computer's roles in their next lesson. They are used to doing initiative exercises but imitating the teacher's and computer's role is only possible because of the clear examples of these roles experienced in this lesson. However, in imitating even this focused role, they are most likely to be drawn into developing high level skills (or something like them).

☐   **The classification of roles**

We now turn to the classification of the roles which may be played by teacher, computer or pupils, and how they may serve the activity objectives. The grouping of these observed roles into the six larger categories is an important element in the construction of this taxonomy; we encourage the reader to consider it critically.

We do not think it would be helpful to attempt a definitional description of what we mean by each of the individual roles; we have tried to use words with their usual, informal meanings to illustrate our interpretation of the headings for the clusters and they are illustrated in our lesson descriptions. It may be worth while however, to comment on the six groups into which we see them as falling.

(M) *Management group* – the more detailed tactical management of the lesson is again usually heavily teacher dominated. These are authoritative roles in the organizational sense and, in allowing the teacher to direct the pupils' learning activities at any level of detail, correspondingly removes responsibility from the pupils for that learning. In open investigative lessons pupils largely carry these roles themselves. Equally, they can be carried by the computer liberating the teacher to do other things.

(T) *Task setting group* – these roles are also related to tactical management but are of such central importance in mathematics (and in some other areas of the curriculum), that it has to form a group on its own. Similar comments apply as with M – normally teacher dominated, with few teachers transferring the responsibility for posing questions to pupils to any significant degree. The micro can easily and usefully assume these common roles (PIRATES, SUBGAME, etc), releasing the teacher for other more subtle ones including 'strategy setter' ('how may we *best* do this, or that?')

(E) *Explanatory group* – these epitomize the teacher's *academic* authority as management does the organizational, with task setting bridging the two domains. The teacher *knows*, and gives knowledge which the pupils receive, and more or less absorb via explanation, demonstration and so on. This is a crucially necessary part of teaching and learning but, because it involves passive constricted learning by pupils, it is not a sufficient way of developing their skills and concepts.

The missing learning activities cannot develop while the teacher remains in the E, T and M roles. Pupils *can* explain to each other in groups of varying size or on paper – but they rarely do; the micro can help stimulate this (for example, EUREKA). The micro itself can contribute a useful explanation in a self-contained or supportive way (indeed, there are still those who talk of the class use of the micro as 'demonstration mode') but, because of its essential pupil passivity, this is not a major contribution to its enhancing pupil learning activities. It can, however, again allow more teacher concentration on other roles including the broader more strategic explanatory ones we call 'scene setting' and 'focusing'.

(C) *Counsellor group* – the consultative roles epitomize a different relationship between teacher and pupils. They are working *together* on common problems, the older more experienced giving *general* help on approaches to tackling them to the younger explorers. The pupils will be more motivated if the teacher, although more knowledgeable in applying skills to the problem, does not appear to know the problem in detail. With the micro as task setter, often using a random element in the particular tasks, this sort of situation can be achieved, apparently naturally. Because the teacher can know the program and thus the essence of the task it is setting, the demands on teacher confidence and competence remain much at the normal level of didactic teaching, and yet, because of the perceived independence of the micro in pupils' eyes, the teacher is able to establish a consultative relationship. This can provide a valuable bridge to the introduction of pupil investigations on more open problems, some of them unfamiliar to the teacher, which place greater demands on all concerned. These extra demands arise in all types of problem solving, including mathematical 'games', from a number of factors including the different stages and approaches of different pupils; the micro can reduce the total demand on the teacher to a tractable level in taking over the task setting and the tactical management of the task-related activity leaving the teacher free for the more important consultative roles. The micro is (pace ELIZA)

(Weizenbaum, 1976) not easily programmed to exercise the skills involved in these high level roles, which are normally best left to the teachers. Pupil–pupil discussion, which is strongly encouraged by the presence of the microcomputer, can allow pupils to help each other in this sort of way.

(F) — in the *Fellow pupil* roles teacher and class are together facing the same challenge, of learning or problem solving say. The teacher is no longer an 'expert', even in a general advisory strategic sense, as in C, but is apparently searching, trying and competing on a more-or-less equal footing. This requires a lot of teacher confidence, which can apparently be built in the well-defined context of a program without damaging credibility on either side.

These roles allow the pupil to see a credible model for themselves in action. The micro can also play or share such roles, when used as a computational device by the pupil in applying rules or models to work out consequences – it does the hard work leaving the pupil free from the technical load to work on the strategic considerations.

(R) — the computer's role as a *resource*, a system to explore, a data store needs little emphasis; indeed we believe it is more difficult to realise in the classroom the undoubted potential in this area than many optimists have implied, the value of the teachers taking on these roles, responding only to specific requests for information from the pupils, needs to be restated. Such roles are more and more accessible alongside those linked to open learning (C and F) than the traditional (M, T, E) didactic approach.

One role that is not listed in those in Table 3 is that of *Controller*, that is, in overall command of the lesson, the topic of study, the general approach and organization and the resources employed. This is and will be the teacher, except in those rare cases where they genuinely allow a class to choose or when control breaks down. Thus we have not considered it as a likely candidate in the discussion of role sharing and shifting.

Lesson 3   Jan with PIRATES

This is yet another PIRATES lesson, illustrating the variety of roles of activities that can occur.

Jan begins by revising compass directions (N, NE, E, and so on) and plotting coordinate points, *explaining* (E)ᵗ and *illustrating* (E)ᵗ clearly on the blackboard to a partly attentive class; she uses a question-and-answer exposition

Traditional *didactic* teaching, with the *explanation* (E)ᵗ roles and *absorption (d)* pupil activities clear.

technique but most pupils are essentially passive *(d)* and the demand is α(recall). (7 mins)

She *explains* (E)ᵗ what PIRATES does and launches into two successive runs – pupils suggesting the next moves, teacher marking each on the blackboard. All are attentive. Some natural development of strategy *(p)* occurs but the teacher plays no part in it here. (8 mins)

She now firmly sets a *strategic task* (T)ᵗ 'This time we must find it in the least possible number of guesses', and soon after, 'Where is the best place to start?' and she *manages* (M)ᵗ a discussion to ensure that all the class gets this new (that is, in SCAN notation (5)) idea of dividing the possible region each time by guessing the middle ('binary search'), 'the middle' (5,5) gives clue 'Go South East'. 'Where next?' (7,3)

'Why'

'Because it's in the middle'. *(p) (b)*

Next the different nature of the clues is explored.

'Go North' (from (7,3)) leads into '(7,5)'

'Why?'

'Because it says go North'.

'What do we know from this clue?'

'That is should not be below three'.

(b)

'Yes, but more than that'.

'It's obviously on the seven line'.

The teacher again *explains* (E)ᵗ to reinforce the point – N, S, E, W clues define lines, while NE, SE, and so on define regions of points.

After *scene setting* (E)ᵗ the teacher, hands over *tactical management* (M)ᶜ and *task setting* (T)ᶜ to the computer; by *marking* guesses on the blackboard herself, she removes a useful technical pupil activity, perhaps to be sure they understand it thoroughly for later.

In all this, pupils use (recording) grids to mark points if they wish; the teacher still puts them on the blackboard. A high level of demand on the pupils, extending their previous knowledge (that is), with guidance that is fairly close (10 mins)

Again Jan is looking for *strategic skills (b) (p)*, minimizing the *technical* load; the computer is *managing* (M)ᶜ and *task setting* (T)ᶜ while she is *manager* (M)ᵗ, counsellor (C)ᵗ and adviser (C)ᵗ on the strategic issue which is established.

Pupils play PIRATES in pairs without the computer, *imitating its roles* without difficulty. Some pairs still show incorrect interpretation of (N, S, E, W) clues but most are good technically and strategically. (15 mins)

The teacher now sets a vaguely related exercise on coordinates from the textbook; all children get involved but with varying understanding of what is needed. Homework is set – 'draw a map, mark on it the position of the treasure and of five separate pirates. Then give each pirate a compass direction to reach the treasure.' These instructions were clearly understood.

Pupils now take over from the computer in *management* (M) P (though rather more weakly) and *task setting* (T) P in turn, while the teacher retains the *counselling* (C) t role – but most pairs lose contact with that. Technical and strategic consolidation takes place. It is notable that pupils, because of the competitive spirit, do not *counsel* each other on *strategies*, though they do play fair *technically (p)*.

Teacher takes over *management* (M) t and *task setting* (T) t roles; *scene setting* is not clear to pupils. Vivid earlier scene setting (E) c by the computer gives a better grasp of the task situation; the *pupils' imitation of the computer role* is easy. The pupils are now back to *exercises (d)* but with some interest in a 'real context'.

☐   **Notes on task setting**

The flow of the task setting role in this lesson was interesting. As always under *overall control* of the teacher, the computer took the main initiative but teacher explanation was an integral part of this phase of *task setting*, extended by the teacher's marking all 'guesses' on the blackboard over the whole 18 mins of class activity. Imitating this model, the pupils take over the *task setting* role.

■   Role shifting and the balance of activities

☐   **Role sharing, role shifting and role imitation**

We have developed in the previous section a taxonomy of roles that the teacher, the pupils or the micro may assume in the classroom. We now examine the possibility of programs' promoting role shifts and whether it is possible to relate this to aspects of program design, its obviously being an aspect of program use.

We took all the lesson reports relating to a particular program and analysed each phase (or Activity in SCAN notation; Beeby *et al.*, 1979) of each lesson, entering the results in a Matrix (although only the PIRATES lessons are discussed here).

The object of the Matrix is to give us an overview of the use of the program by different teachers. In particular we are interested in identifying when the important but less common learning activities occur, and also when the teacher adopts the more demanding roles in an effective way.

The diagram on pp. 224 and 225 shows the Matrix completed for the second and third PIRATES lessons described in the previous section. These are shown in Table 4.

You will notice that each lesson is divided into phases labelled E, W_2, and so on. The time in minutes of each phase is given. This division is the SCAN (Beeby *et al.*, 1979) division of Activities – the Activity is the largest natural unit into which a lesson divides. (E) stands for teacher exposition, W_2 indicates pupils working in groups of two.

In the Matrix, the first set of headings come directly from the observer's record; they also relate to the SCAN notation (Beeby *et al.*, 1979). 'Demand' is the demand on the pupils as perceived by the observer on the following basis:

α = recall of a single fact or carrying out of a single act

β = exercise of a straightforward nature, putting together several facts or acts and

γ = extension of previous work involving new ideas.

'Guidance' is the observer's perception of the level of guidance given to the pupils by the teacher

1 = close guidance, highly structured with a small number of choices

2 = some guidance offered but requires the connection of facts rather than mere selection

3 = minimum guidance in an 'open' style.

The Interest column is a score, out of ten, of the observer's perception of how highly involved the children appeared to be; finally in this section of the Matrix is an indication of the percentage of the class on task in this activity.

The next section of the Matrix concentrates on identifying the roles that are being taken on by the teacher (t), the pupils (p) or the computer (c); it also recognizes the importance of shared roles (t/c, and so on). The headings are the major categories described in the taxonomy

Table 4 Program-in-use Matrix

	Pirates			Pirates				
	1	2	3	1	2	3	4	
Phase	E	E	Next lesson	E	E	W2	W1	Taken from observation records related to SCAN (Beeby et al., 1979)
Time (mins)	16	14	40	7		15	15	
Demand	$\alpha\beta$	$\alpha\beta$	–	α	β	$\alpha\beta$	β	
Guidance	1	2	–	2	2	1.5	1.5	
Interest/10	7	7	–	5	7	7	7	
% on Task	100	100	–	70	95	100	95	
Tactical manager (M)	t	t/c	p	t	t/c	p	t	Roles analysis (pp 208–22)
Task setter (T)	t	c	p	t	c	p	t	
Explainer (E)	t	p	p	t	t			
Counsellor (C)					t	(t)		
Fellow pupil (F)								
System to explore (R)								
Passive	•	•		•				Observable activities (pp 208–22)
Writing	•		•	•	•	•	•	
Talking		•			•	•		
Didactic (d)	•	•		•	•	•	•	Learning activities (pp 208–22)
Symbolizing (s)								
Investigating (i)								
Problem solving (p)					*	*		
High level skills (h)			•		*	*		

224

Table 4 (cont.)

	Pirates (Lesson 2)	Pirates (Lesson 3)
Coordinates	● ● ●	● ●
Plot points	● ●	● ● ●
Shifts		
Compass direction	● ●	● ● ●
Vectors		● ● ●
Distances		
Circles intersect		
Angles		
Bearings		
Lines intersect		
Pythagoras		
Areas		
Regions	● ● ●	
—CONTENT Possible topics—		
Strategy	● ● ●	● ●
Competition	● ● ●	● ●
Abandon		
—Activity—		

Lesson 2   Lesson 3

225

in the previous section. The more common roles are placed first so that the pattern of entries shows clearly when the less common roles are being observed.

In the next section come three headings only, for the observable classroom activities – again these have been selected to cover the more detailed headings of the taxonomy already described. The learning activities follow, categorized in the same way, and again with the commonly observed activities given first. Thus the Matrix contains a Summary of the observation report of the lesson concerned, related to the classification developed in the previous section which is based on the analysis of all the lesson reports.

The final section of the Matrix is peculiar to the particular program teaching unit being used, in that it lists the possible mathematical content or topic areas that the program could be used to support, together with specific classroom or learning activities that we might hope to see (for example, competition, strategy); these also relate back to the taxonomy.

In the body of the Matrix the following notation is used. A cell that has a ● records the occurrence of this item, a cell with * indicates a strong effective use for this category.

The Matrix can be examined for evidence of what happened in the lesson in the framework that we have already established. We are particularly interested when the teacher moves from the traditional authoritarian roles in the (M) tactical management, (T) Task setter and (E) Explainer groups to the less often assumed roles of (C) Counsellor, (F) Fellow pupil or (R) resource or system to explore. We are also interested when pupils appear to adopt roles that have been mainly teacher roles and, of course, to relate these role shifts to the roles that the computer has assumed.

Before commenting on our findings, based on all the lesson observations, we illustrate the line of argument in a discussion of the two records given on the Matrix grid in Table 4.

In the first two phases of Lesson 2 (which has been described in detail) the Matrix highlights the teacher role as it moves from tactical manager and task setter to a position of sharing (M) with the computer, dropping (T) and taking over a counselling role (C). This appears to have occurred because the computer is sharing (M) and taking over (T). The pupil learning activities have moved to more open ones during this change with entries of *h* (higher level skills) and *strategy* appearing on the table in Phase 2. The third phase is unusual in this case, as it actually relates to the subsequent lesson. It is included as the children were explicitly asked to *imitate the roles* of both the computer and the teacher during the next lesson, when the teacher was to be absent.

This highlights the important idea of role imitation, which appeared during these trials as a powerful aid for the teacher to encourage pupils into high level activities. With the computer program, together with the teacher, clearly defining an investigation, the children were often asked to imitate the exercise together in groups, taking it in turns to play the role of the computer; the computer so often appeared to provide the pupils with an effortlessly vivid model of what was intended, which contrasted sharply in its effectiveness with verbal descriptions. Of course, a very great deal of pupil activity in classrooms consists of 'imitative exercises', which aim to promote through practice, low level technical skills; the success of another, richer kind of imitation, involving greater 'transfer', in the promotion of higher level skills is that of imitation both of teacher roles and of computer roles. In this example, the pupils were asked to be in both (M) and (T) roles, but the task was slightly easier. The observer has not noted (b) in this session but strategy continues to be present. As the pupils were without teacher or computer support, this is an encouraging result.

In Lesson 3, the higher level activity of pursuing a strategic approach occurs first when the teacher has moved into (C), is sharing (M) with the computer and is also adopting (E). Secondly strategy occurs when the pupils are again role imitating and assume (M) and (T), working in pairs. [...]

The overall qualitative evidence from the whole of these trials, of which the two above examples are but illustrations, is clear and strong. Programs can be designed which result in teachers working with a potentially wider style range than they would otherwise employ in a way that does not appear to increase the pressure or demands on them; in particular they assume roles in the (C), (F) and (R) groups, and the more open learning activities tend to occur when this happens. The operational style range varied from teacher to teacher and program to program, but the qualitative shift was observed in a large number of lessons; the only exception was provided by two teachers whose style is habitually open, and even here there was a noticeable enhancement of pupil learning activities; indeed, one of these teachers is not surprisingly an exceptionally powerful user of the microcomputer as an aid to his teaching.

Another major outcome was that, when pupils assumed or 'imitated' teacher or computer roles, it led them to take greater responsibility for the learning activity and invariably to move into the higher level skills area.

Since the production of such style shifts has proved a quite intractable problem with all but a few teachers over at least 30 years of enthusiastic advocacy and energetic promotion, this result, if confirmed in general, is of great importance.

An explanation of why the micro can succeed, where other approaches (printed material, for example) have no effect emerges from the observation and is implicit in our discussion so far. It appears that the micro can take on certain roles, particularly the traditional authoritarian teacher roles in the (M), (T) and (E) groups, lifting that demand from the teacher; furthermore, the opportunity to assume the less common roles in the (C), (F) and (R) groups is presented to the teacher in a way that is natural, supportive and unthreatening to their authority, and thus to their confidence – probably because the framework is less 'open' to the teacher than it appears to the pupils, due to the illusory independence of the micro.

Caution is essential in such a difficult area. Although the study was conducted in as realistic a way as possible, with the minimum of special attention to the teachers, circumstances were inevitably not normal in all aspects and there is some evidence that at least one teacher responded to the trial, as well as to the micro with exceptional efforts; we must check that similar results to those reported here pertain when teachers start using micros and material through normal school channels (some informal indications over the year since the trial give hope in this regard). Equally, it is important to see how far the style-broadening effects carry over into other teaching in which the micro is not involved; such transfer would greatly enhance the educational benefit of the very limited amount of good material currently or prospectively available, though it would be surprising if there were a large permanent effect from a restricted experience without follow-up support – further effort and study in this direction are planned. [...]

◼ References

Beeby, T., Burkhardt, H. and Fraser, R. (1979) *Systematic Classroom Analysis Notations*, Shell Centre for Mathematical Education, Nottingham.

Burkhardt, H., Fraser, R. with Clowes, M., Eggleston, J. and Wells, C. (1982) *Design and Development of Programs as Teaching Material*, Council for Educational Technology, London.

Burkhardt, H., Fraser, R., Coupland, J., Pimm, D., Phillips, R. and Ridgway, J. (in preparation) *Microcomputers in the Mathematics Classroom*.

HMI (1982) *Aspects of Secondary Education*. Report of the HMI Secondary Survey, HMSO, London.

Mathematics Counts (1982) Report of the Committee of Inquiry into the teaching of mathematics in schools under the Chairmanship of Dr. W.H. Cockcroft, HMSO; London.

Phillips, R.J., Burkhardt, H., Coupland, J., Fraser, R., Pimm, D. and Ridgway J. (to be published) *Computer-aided Teaching*.

Weizenbaum, J. (1976) *Computer Power and Human Reasoning*, San Francisco, Freeman.

Part 3

Computer Communication for Learning Needs

This third part of the book includes papers on a few specific aspects of computing. These are hypertext systems, computer conferencing, computing for learners with special needs and the use of computer simulation for mathematics and science instruction.

Smith and Weiss (Paper 3.1) describe what is meant by a hypertext document while Yankelovich and colleagues at Brown University (Paper 3.2) discuss how hypertext might be used, and provide a comparison between books and electronic document systems. They use the word hypermedia to denote the functionality of hypertext with additional components such as two- and three-dimensional structured graphics, video, sound and animation. Marchionini and Shneiderman (Paper 3.3) present an information-seeking framework to guide designers of hypertext systems and users who apply them to write and read hypertext documents.

Firminger (Paper 3.4) discusses the way that microtechnology can extend the opportunities for people with disabilities to learn after school. She discusses the Hereward project of study aids and describes the use of micro-based teaching/learning for two years by 37 students at Hereward College, a national college offering a range of further education courses to residential and local day students who have disabilities. She emphasizes that the purpose of the project was to improve student access to the ordinary curriculum using the most efficient means available, not simply to introduce new technology. Middlemas (Paper 3.5) studied 10 students with learning difficulties at Brooklands Technical College.

The third theme in Part 3 combines interface design and the application of artificial intelligence techniques to mathematics and science learning. Hennessy and her colleagues (Paper 3.6) give an account of the development of the 'Shopping on Mars' computer game and the description language which children use to represent some of the procedures they follow in order to perform the calculations they require to achieve the goal of shopping on Mars and eventually escape from the planet Mars. Smith (Paper 3.7) describes the Alternate Reality Kit, an animated environment for creating interactive simulations which has influenced the design of many similar systems.

The last theme in Part 3 is the use of computer conferencing. Mason (Paper 3.8) describes the use of computer conferencing as a tutorial medium in the Open University's course entitled 'An Introduction to Information Technology'. The use of a conferencing system by a large number of Open University students (around 1300 per year) provides some surprising results, for example the relative infrequency of tutor supported dialogues. Although the number of messages varied considerably from group to group, the content of the messages was invariably on the level of information exchange rather than discussion, opinions, comments or critiques of the course material. Graddol (in Paper 3.9) looks more closely at the discourse analysis which might be profitably applied to computer conferencing dialogues. Somekh (in Paper 3.10) discusses the pitfalls of using such systems in the classroom.

This part deals with four very different systems used in educational settings.

Paper 3.1

Hypertext

John Smith and Stephen Weiss

[...]Hypertext is an approach to information management in which data is stored in a network of nodes connected by links. Nodes can contain text, graphics, audio, video, as well as source code or other forms of data. The nodes, and in some systems the network itself, are meant to be viewed through an interactive browser and manipulated through a structure editor.

While the term, hypertext, was coined by Ted Nelson during the 1960s, the concept can be traced to Vannevar Bush's (1945) description of 'the memex'.

> 'A device in which an individual stores his books, records, and communications, and which is mechanized so that it may be consulted with exceeding speed and flexibility. It is an enlarged intimate supplement to his memory.'

What distinguished Bush's concept from other forms of data storage was its associative structure that closely modeled the structure of human memory:

> 'The human mind ... operates by association. With one item in its grasp, it snaps instantly to the next that is suggested by the association of thoughts, in accordance with some intricate web of trails carried by the cells of the brain.
>
> Selection by association, rather than indexing, may yet be mechanized. One cannot hope ... to equal the speed and flexibility with which the mind follows an associative trail, but it should be possible to beat the mind decisively in regard to the permanence and clarity of the items resurrected from storage.'

First published in *Communications of the ACM* (1988), **31**, 7, pp 816–18. Reprinted by permission of the Association for Computing Machinery.

The first serious attempt to build a memex did not take place until 20 years after Bush's description. In 1968, Doug Engelbart, then at Stanford Research Institute, conducted a dramatic live demonstration of his Augment system at the Fall Joint Computer Conference in which he worked collaboratively on a hypertext document with a colleague 500 miles away (Engelbart and English, 1968). During that session, Engelbart also demonstrated two of his other inventions – the mouse and the chord key set. In the 20 years since Engelbart's demonstration, both interest and activity in hypertext have grown steadily.[...]

To understand why hypertext is attracting such attention, one must understand how a hypertext 'document' differs from a conventional paper document.

In most conventional paper documents – such as journal articles, specifications, or novels – physical structure and logical structure are closely related. Physically, the document is a long linear sequence of words that has been divided into lines and pages for convenience. Logically, the document is also linear: words are combined to form sentences, sentences to form paragraphs, paragraphs to form sections, and so on. If the document has a hierarchical logical structure, as do many expository documents such as journal articles, that hierarchy is presented linearly: the abstract or overview of the whole comes first, followed by the introduction, the first section, the second section, and so on, until the conclusion. This linearity is easy to see if one imagines the hierarchical structure represented as an outline, with the sections of the document appearing in the same order as they normally do in the outline. Such documents strongly encourage readers to read them linearly, from beginning to end following the same sequence.

A few conventional paper documents – such as encyclopedias, dictionaries, and other reference works – separate logical structure from physical structure. Physically, these documents are linear sequence of independent units, such as articles on specific topics or entries for individual works. Logically, they are more complex. The reader seldom reads such documents from beginning to end, but rather searches them to locate the article or entry of interest (a form of random access), and then reads that portion sequentially. However, the reader is likely to encounter various cross references to other entries while reading as well as a list of 'see alsos' at the end of an article. To follow those pointers, the reader must locate the appropriate volume, find the appropriate entry, and then the relevant portion. The logical structure of reference and other similar documents is, thus, more complex. They have a sequential structure that aids search, but the logical path of the reader is a network that can criss-cross the entire document or set of documents, from one item to another, to another, and so on. Such documents are more flexible but they are also cumbersome, particularly when they appear in large, multivolume formats.

Hypertext electronic documents provide most of the flexibility of reference works as well as add a number of new features. Earlier, we described a hypertext as a document in which information is stored in nodes connected by links. Each node can be thought of as analogous to a short section of an encyclopedia article or perhaps a graphic image with a brief explanation. The links join these sections to one another to form the article as a whole and the articles to form the encyclopedia. These links are usually shown for each node as a 'from' link pointing to the node just read and a set of 'to' links that indicate the (usual) multiple nodes which one may select to read next.

Many systems also include pointers embedded in the text itself that link a specific portion to some other node or portion of text. Thus, one moves from node to node by selecting the desired 'to' link, an embedded cross-reference link, or the 'from' link to return to the previous node. For many documents, the 'to' links can be thought of as organizational. Collectively, they frequently form a hierarchical structure analogous to the hierarchical logical structure of many conventional documents. From this perspective, the embedded, cross-reference links cross the main organizational structure.

While we can establish a rough analogy between the two, hypertext documents are much more flexible than conventional documents. For example, one can read the hypertext article just as one reads the conventional paper article by first reading the overview node, then the first section node(s), the second section, and so on. However, one can also read the sections in different orders. For example, if the hierarchical structure of the article is viewed as a two-dimensional tree or organization chart instead of as a linear outline, one can easily imagine that if the 'to' links were shown as the children of the current node, selecting the second section before the first or perhaps skipping the first entirely. Hypertext documents are also much more convenient. To follow the cross-references in a modern encyclopedia often means moving among thirty or more (heavy) volumes. Readers do it, but it is a slow, frequently laborious, task.

While hypertext provides greater flexibility and convenience than conventional documents, its power and appeal increase dramatically when it is implemented in computing environments that include net-worked microcomputers and workstations, high-resolution displays, and large on-line storage. While following a cross-reference in a 30-volume encyclopedia can take several minutes, many hypertext systems can deliver the next node in less than a second and from a much larger body of information that might take thousands of volumes in print. While conventional publications are limited to text and graphics, hypertext nodes offer sound, video sequences, animation, even computer programs that begin running when the nodes in which they are stored are selected. While the organizational and cross-reference structures of conventional documents are fixed at the time of printing, hypertext links and nodes can be changed dynamically. Information in individual nodes can be updated, new nodes can be linked into the overall hypertext structure, and new links added to show new relationships. In some systems, users can add their own links to form new organizational structures, creating new documents from old.

Each of these changes represents an incremental difference between hypertext and conventional documents, but when considered together, they are producing a qualitative change in the way some people are conceptualizing information resources. It is this shift in perspective that is creating such excitement and such a wealth of new possibilities in the minds of some.[...]

■ References

Bush, V. As we may think. *Atlantic Monthly 176*, 1 (July 1945), pp. 101–108.

Engelbart, D.C., and English, W.K. A research center for augmenting human intellect. In *Proceedings of the 1968 Fall Joint Computer Conference* (Montvale, N.J., Fall 1968), AFIPS Press, 395–410.

Paper 3.2

Reading and Writing the Electronic Book

Nicole Yankelovich, Norman Meyrowitz and Andries van Dam

[...]

■ Print medium

Scholars, or 'knowledge workers', rely heavily on print media, even though electronic creation and dissemination of information is possible with today's technology. In some cases, this reliance on print is part of a long, ingrained tradition, but in other cases, print is still simply the most appropriate vehicle, either because electronic document systems are impractical to use or because they do not meet a particular objective as well as does paper.

The most important fundamental property of books is that they are static. Once printed, a book cannot be altered except by reprinting, and at no time do readers have the opportunity to change or manipulate its contents. The static nature of books is both their biggest asset and their most serious shortcoming.

A review of the assets and shortcomings of books is helpful in establishing a list of capabilities essential for high-quality electronic document systems (see Table 1).

■ Electronic medium

Electronic document systems have their own advantages and limitations. In some cases they are more powerful or appropriate than paper books

Table 1   Print medium: advantages and disadvantages

Characteristic	Advantages	Disadvantages
Integrity of information	Historical value Never inaccessible because of unreliable hardware	Readers can never alter content Readers cannot customize information Cannot conform to user preferences (type size, margin width)
Physical entities	Portable Allows browsing and exploring Allows annotation and underlining Aesthetically appealing	Limited to 2-D information Limited to static text and graphics Costly to reproduce for quickly outdated information Often hard to locate specific information
Static		Cannot handle sound or motion Difficult to create multiple indices
Advanced technology	Well-defined and accepted standards Typography, graphic design, and photo reproduction refined fields High-resolution print and graphics Easy to read	Joint authorship difficult Rekeying text is error-prone

for meeting the range of information needs of scholars within the university community. In some cases, books are more useful.

☐ Advantages

Theodore Nelson and Douglas Engelbart were among the first to articulate the benefits of electronic document systems (Nelson, 1981; Engelbart and English, 1968). In the early 1960s, they recognized that computers were well suited to helping scholars and others create *connectivity* – webs of related information. In the print medium scholars often mark up books, articles, and papers. When a phrase or illustration sparks a connection to an idea in another book in a scholar's mind, he or she writes that connection, or 'link', down *next to* the phrase or picture that sparked the thought. Providing footnotes, references, and word glosses in books is an author's way of making annotations or explicitly indicating connections between his or her writing and other documents, schools of thought, and definitions. These standard devices provide readers with pointers to additional reading and information sources that will enrich the understanding of the subject matter of books so annotated. Creating webs of information and adding to them are integral to all scholarly work, and in the domain of scholarship these webs are commonly called *literatures*. Nelson defines 'a literature' (as in 'the scientific literature' or a field of discourse) 'as a system of interconnected writings' (Nelson, 1980).

George Landow of Brown University's English Department sees connections and the act of following links as crucial to education. In his teaching, he is particularly interested in helping students see links between the literature they read and such things as art, politics, philosophical thought, and religious doctrine.

Nelson and Landow both stress the importance of *observing existing connections*, which can be done by studying 'the literature', and *making new connections*. Electronic document systems help scholars both create connections and follow those made by others. Because electronic books allow flexible organization of material, they provide authors and readers with a greater degree of freedom than printed books. Explicit connections – 'links' – allowing readers to travel from document to document (as one does with an encyclopedia) or from one place in a document to another in the same document can be made effortlessly by authors, thus fostering the creation of *information webs*. With the electronic medium, readers are not obliged to search through library stacks to look up referenced books and articles; they can quickly follow trails of footnotes without losing their original context.

Linking scholars together – intercommunicability – is an essential aspect of connectivity. Electronic document systems running either on a multiuser, time-shared system or on a series of networked workstations allow authors and readers to communicate with one another in a number of ways. Colleagues can easily view one another's documents (if given permission), send and receive personal electronic messages, and jointly edit the same document without leaving their own workplace. These types of communication capabilities may foster 'on-line communities' (Engelbart and English, 1968; van Dam and Rice, 1970) of researchers or students and enhance the ability of scholars to make meaningful connections.

Perhaps the greatest advantage of electronic documents over paper ones is their ability to handle many more graphic elements. By combining a variety of media, electronic books can provide not only static images, but also dynamics (computer animations and computer-controlled video sequences), interactivity (ability to move objects, change and edit objects, and change states), and sound (computer-generated or audio disk recordings). These features all help in creating better *audiovisualization*. For example, a biology student might be able to rotate and slice a three-dimensional model of a plant cell while reading related material, or a theater arts professor might have students examine video recordings of theatrical productions in parallel with blocking diagrams.

Electronic document systems can be useful tools for visualizing the structure of the information web as well as visualizing the individual concepts or processes contained in that structure. Not only can they allow scholars to make and follow links, but they can also provide a diagrammatic overview of the web of connections. Different 'maps' of information webs can be generated to illustrate the connections that exist in a body of material. Some types of maps, however, are easier to generate than others. For example, it is possible to create a map of a reader's path through a document corpus or a diagram of all possible links from the reader's current position, but as the number of connections and quantity of information increases, so does the difficulty of generating maps of the entire information web. Since most readers cannot readily understand a diagram with hundreds of crisscrossing interconnections, the problem of distilling or summarizing the information must be addressed. In addition, authors may often make circular references, causing even more complexities in graphically representing the web of connections.

The paper medium does not allow a reader to alter the contents of a book. Electronic documents, however, are dynamic in the sense that both authors and readers can customize the material contained within a corpus of documents. For example, in a military setting, an author may want to provide complete access to certain information to those with the appropriate security clearance and only partial access to all others. If working with paper, this author would be forced to publish separate books for each constituency. Readers also may want to 'filter' – limit access to – the information. A literature student, for example, might want to look at only critical commentaries on Shakespeare's plays, while an acting student might be interested in solely the original texts. Filtering permits readers to select only information they consider pertinent. A set of selection criteria or *attributes*, somewhat similar to index terms in the back of a book, can define relationships between information blocks or can identify structural components. For instance, a lawyer might want to apply a filter that would display all cases mentioning the name 'J. Smith', to examine all cases that 'support' a particular decision, or to view the first sentence of every major decision in a given area.[...]

As with hard copy manuscripts, it is possible to preserve multiple versions of a single electronic document. Authors can save a document at any point in the creation process and can produce hard copy renderings of the same information (at least all text and static graphics).

Finally, the electronic medium can aid dramatically in the updating and dissemination of information. In many cases, editing an electronic document (using interactive editors for text, graphics, music, and so on) is far more efficient than making changes to a printed book. In addition, the cost of dissemination (in terms of both money and of natural resources) one day may be greatly reduced by the advent of national networks and high-density storage devices (diskettes, video disks, CD ROMs, and so on).

☐ Disadvantages

A major shortcoming in most electronic document systems developed using current technology is their failure to provide adequate information about where readers are in a document. Readers of paper books can always tell if they are 'at the end of the book' or 'three-quarters through it'. If electronic books were merely linear sequences on a computer screen, then a two-dimensional gauge or a simple numbering scheme would suffice. However, because they are nonsequentially organized and the 'middle' for one reader might be the 'end' for another, a reader can follow link after link and feel disoriented.

Although it is possible to store documents in various stages of revision, the electronic medium does not encourage one to do so. With current text-editing systems, authors must have a sense of history to consciously save 'old' versions of documents created with interactive editors. Even when the versions have been saved, it is difficult to see where changes have been made in a document that always looks 'clean' no matter how drastically it had been revised. Authors working in teams also find it difficult to notice changes made by co-authors when edited versions contain no 'markup' symbols and none of the visual cues offered by color pens and handwriting styles in the print medium.

For those who must rely on hard copy of an electronic document for some purposes, a linking structure can be seen as a disadvantage, as printing a branching document in a linear fashion poses both technical and conceptual problems.

Aside from the issues mentioned so far, there are some disadvantages to electronic document systems that arise from the limitations of hardware. Many people complain about eyestrain from working at a computer, even with high-resolution graphic display screens; others are attached to the 'feel' and aesthetic appeal of bound volumes. Cost is still a major limiting factor to the widespread use of electronic document systems. High-resolution displays and computer systems powerful enough to run the document software are still expensive and not at all portable, especially systems that run on hardware capable of displaying both color graphics and video on the same screen.

In short, electronic document systems using today's hardware and software offer substantial advantages over paper books in providing aids for connectivity, audiovisualization, dynamics, customizability, interactivity, and rapid information retrieval, but also have a number of drawbacks in providing spatial orientation, historical tracing, joint editing, visual clarity, portability, and cost. While these limitations are not intrinsic to the electronic medium, they are problems that must be considered in the development of current and next-generation electronic document systems.

■   Desirable features for multimedia electronic document systems

An analysis of the aforementioned pros and cons suggests a number of design features that will maximize the advantages and minimize the current disadvantages of using the electronic medium for document preparation and presentation. To meet the needs of scholars and other knowledge workers, the minimal set of capabilities incorporated into an electronic document system should include tools for

(1)   promoting connectivity,

(2)   promoting audiovisualization,

(3)   creating and revising documents,

(4)   browsing, searching, customizing, and retrieving information, and

(5)   preserving the historical integrity of information.

These capabilities are explained in detail below and represent capabilities and functions for the current or next-generation electronic document systems. These systems, in effect, are databases composed of text, graphics, dynamics, interactivity, and multimedia components, in contrast to future electronic document systems that will surely be founded on knowledge bases. Stephen Weyer and Alan Borning's Electronic Encyclopedia project represents one interesting example of a prototype knowledge-based system (Weyer and Borning, 1985).

□   Tools to promote connectivity

The first essential capability of a good electronic document system is to provide a means for promoting the connection of ideas and the communication between individual scholars. These capabilities can be conceived of as a set of tools for creating a *hypertext* structure, the underlying framework of all electronic document systems developed or under development at Brown University.[...]

By extension, we use the word *hypermedia* to denote the functionality of hypertext but with additional components such as two- and three-dimensional structured graphics, paint graphics, spreadsheets, video, sound, and animation. With hypermedia, an author can create links to complex diagrams, texts, photographs, video disks, audio recordings, and the like.[...]

To summarize, the basic capabilities implied by the terms *hypertext* and *hypermedia* include linking together discrete *blocks* (word, paragraph, text document, graphical object, spreadsheet cell, and video frame) to form *webs* of information, following different paths through the information webs, and attaching annotations (special types of links) to any block of information. Typically, different information blocks are created using separate *applications or editors*. A hyper*text* document system allows authors to link together only information blocks created with a single application, a text editor, while a hyper*media* document system provides linking capabilities between heterogeneous blocks created with different applications such as a painting program, a chart package, or a music editor. Early systems force the links to be essentially programmed, while newer systems provide interactive link creation as a fundamental component.

Multiuser access to information is another fundamental capability that must be present to promote connectivity. A group of scholars working together should be able to annotate each other's documents. This means that the system must provide multiple users with access to the same *corpus* of documents. At the least, multiple users must have 'read access' to a colleague's documents; at best, they should be allowed to create new links within a colleague's document (either to annotations or to other documents) and to edit the document in a controlled fashion.

The multiuser access problem brings with it extremely complicated issues pertaining to access rights and update consistency. For instance, if user A edits a document and adds a link, do these changes show up immediately in other users' views of this document? Should all users have the ability to add links? Should all users be able to delete links? Can user C delete a document to which other users have linked? Few of the electronic book implementations have tackled this problem on a large scale (Englebart's NLS goes the furthest in providing support over national networks), and it stands as an important research question if electronic books are to be accepted.

To facilitate distribution of documents to a broader audience than a scholar's immediate community, multimedia document systems should provide tools for electronic dissemination. Currently, this would inclu automatic transfer of finished documents to typesetting equipm the incorporation of powerful electronic mail or conferencing systems that make use of national and international networks. In the future, it would be desirable to subsume separate electronic mail or conferencing systems under a powerful hypertext/hypermedia system that allows the linking of documents across long-haul networks and that encourages the creation and exchange of references as opposed to files (Nelson, 1981).

☐   Tools to aid in creating audiovisualization

While a text-editing system with hypertext capabilities is useful, it can be argued that the advantages of a paper book still equal or outweigh the advantages of such computer-based text systems. However, when an author can add visuals and sound – not possible in paper books – the scale clearly begins to tip in favor of the electronic format; tools for creating visual and audio components are equally as important as those for promoting connectivity. The music faculty at Brown, for example, believe that multimedia systems could revolutionize the teaching of music. With present teaching techniques it is hard for music students to make the connection between the written notes and the musical sounds without one-on-one instruction. Integrating a music editor, a piano keyboard, and a synthesizer would allow students to *hear* every note they *see* as they write or play the notes. A text-only document system – which might include many of the essential ingredients for connectivity – does not provide adequate tools for producing visual and aural aids. There is, however, a large continuum between text-only and full multimedia systems. A two-dimensional structured graphics editor (such as MacDraw for the Apple Macintosh) might be adequate for creating simple static illustrations, and a low-level graphics package might be all that is necessary for generating maps of the information web; however, more extensive multimedia capabilities are required to produce dynamic electronic documents.

There is a spectrum of media that can be included in an electronic book. Static text, structured graphics, bitmap images, charts, and graphs fall at the low end of the spectrum. The inclusion of animation, computer-generated sound, and audio and video recordings adds a richness to electronic document systems that is impossible to recreate with paper media. Moreover, each medium in such a system is subject to some level of *interactive control* – methods for readers to move, change, and manipulate the material rather than just view it. For instance, readers may want to manipulate graphical objects [...], or they may want to alter or experiment with animation sequences, seeking answers to 'what if' questions. Readers can even become characters in a dynamic story by influencing the progress of the plot.

As mentioned earlier, it is easy to become disoriented in a complex electronic information web. Authors and readers alike need visual cues that will help them determine where they are in the web of information, and also need graphical means for organizing and reorganizing their material. Tools that promote spatial orientation can include schematics of the information web, maps indicating all possible path options at a given time, and diagrams of specific paths a reader has already taken. For example, MIT's Spatial Database-Management System displays a 'world view', an overview of Dataland with a 'you-are-here' marker (Bolt, 1979).

For maps to be extremely useful and readable, they must be able to represent varying levels of detail. To get a general idea of how a body of information is structured, it is best not to display a detailed 'road map' when a 'globe' is all that is needed. To create global views, document systems must have facilities for summarizing, compacting, and extracting the essence of the stored material. However, once readers are in the midst of the web or already familiar with its overall structure, they will require more detailed road maps that show all the links in a given subsection.

For each reader, the system should always save an encoding of the current position, viewing parameters, and past travelling information – *the document state* – so that each reader of a document may pick up where he or she left off and not be forced to re-create the exact links selected and searches made to return to the current position in the information web.

The effectiveness of visuals, whether in conjuring up concrete images of complex concepts or providing a map of the information web, depends largely on the quality of the final images. Several system features have an impact on the quality of the graphics: tools that promote good graphic design, high-resolution display screens, and color. People who are not professional graphic artists may not be able to produce professional-looking images; however, with features like rulers, gravity grids, automatic justification, alignment, and some simple design rules, they should be able to create reasonable visuals.

☐   **Tools for creating and revising documents**

Since electronic documents are mutable entities that can be interacted with and modified, they must contain tools not only for presenting information, but also for *creating* it. These tools can take many forms, from batch text processors to interactive paint programs, chart packages, or music editors. Most desirable, of course, is a system that provides *direct manipulation*: such systems allow authors to interactively create, edit, and format documents directly in the view in which they will be presented on the screen. This provides the ability to make well-designed documents interactively and is very close to what-you-see-is-what-you-get

(WYSIWYG) editing, which refers to on-screen views that appear as close as possible (given the limitations of screen size and resolution) to the way the document would appear if printed. In these direct manipulation systems, users can be presented with one of two interface paradigms: *procedural* or *declarative*. In the procedural interface, the reader specifies exactly *how* formatting should take place, putting in typeface, margin, line length, and leading information explicitly to arrive at a desired presentation image. In the declarative interface, the user specifies exactly *what* document entities and logical structures are desired (numbered points, chapter headings, indented quotations), and the system automatically formats those entities based upon a separately supplied style sheet specifying formatting rules to be applied interactively. The declarative system removes the responsibility for formatting from the author; all that the author needs to do is specify the document entities. For text and two-dimensional graphics (free-hand structured graphics, charts, diagrams, and so on), direct manipulation editors of both types are commercially available for small computer systems; however, user-level editors for three-dimensional image creation exist only on expensive computer-aided design stations, and those for real-time animation exist only in experimental laboratories.

The creation of data can be handled in substantially different ways. Some systems have separate tools for authoring the document and for presenting it to readers. Many frame-oriented CAI programs fall into this category. Instructors (authors) are given the freedom to create frames of information and link them together sequentially or nonsequentially (by indicating branch points). Students (readers) may have the ability to interact with the lesson and sometimes to browse through the frames, but they are not permitted to alter the links or add their own connections. Furthermore, the systems almost never allow student readers to collaborate, share ideas with other students, or comment on each other's work. In some cases, the authoring tools are resident on large time-shared computers, while the final document is presented on small stand-alone microcomputers. Ideally, authors and readers should have the same set of integrated tools that allow them to browse through other material during the document preparation process and to add annotations and original links as they progress through an information web. In effect, the boundary between author and reader should largely disappear.

It is important to consider not only the quality of the authoring tools, but also how these tools relate to one another. On one end of the *integration* continuum, documents containing different types of information (text, music, spreadsheet) are created with separate application programs, and the 'electronic document' is comprised of many linked documents, each of a single medium. A little farther along on the continuum is the 'cut, copy, paste' paradigm. Here, it is possible to copy bits between heterogeneous applications (for example, paste a spreadsheet into a text document). This paradigm thus provides some integration, but loses important semantic information (all numbers in the spreadsheet are now treated as text strings). The next logical step in the continuum may be called 'reference copy, paste'. At this level of integration, a spreadsheet that is copied and pasted into a text document retains its 'spreadsheetness'. If the original spreadsheet document is updated, all copies, or *instances*, of the spreadsheet are automatically updated (typically today, only data from certain applications can be used in a reference copy action).

At the highest end, a fully-integrated multimedia document system would allow reference copying and pasting of all data types and would include a context-sensitive cursor. As the author moved the cursor over the spreadsheet, all spreadsheet editing functions would be made available; as the cursor moved over some musical notation, all music editing functions would automatically be activated; and so forth. The Macintosh desktop environment (*Inside Macintosh*, 1985) is one example of 'cut, copy, paste' integration, while office systems such as Lotus Jazz offer several special cases of 'reference copy, paste' integration.

It is nearly impossible to retrofit independently written applications into an integrated environment. Achieving the highest degree of integration requires either (1) monolithic applications that understand every type of data structure that one might want to use, (2) a universal data structure (UDS) such that any application can convert between the UDS and its own data structure (an extremely difficult problem that is prone to losing semantic information in the conversion), or (3) attaching functionality not to an application, but to the particular entities that are the focus of attention. In such an object-oriented system, 'objects' are self-contained entities encapsulating information about all possible operations that can be performed on them, thus allowing reference copying between all applications that share the same object library and object memory. The third alternative shows the most promise but is still an open issue, given the difficulty of creating a memory that allows efficient multiuser, concurrent access to very large numbers of objects, not to mention the cultural, sociological and economic problem of getting the programming profession to switch from conventional programming to object-oriented programming.

☐ **Tools for browsing, searching, personalizing, and retrieving information**

Database functions underlie all electronic document systems. Thus a useful document system should take advantage of this underlying structure and provide authors with a set of searching and filtering features, including the ability to search using a single criterion (*simple searching*), to search using multiple criteria (*Boolean searching*), or to customize the presentation in other ways.

The same criteria used for searching can also allow authors to restrict access to documents to specific readers and to groups of readers. Similarly, readers can selectively view the contents of a corpus so as to eliminate material that is not currently relevant. By providing methods for authors to associate *keywords* with any discrete block of information, a document system can filter the information for readers using these terms. Newspeek, a system developed at MIT for creating personalized newspapers, is a good example of information filtering. Readers submit lists of keywords that describe their interests. As stories come over the AP and UPI wires, the system filters stories according to each reader's list and prepares a custom newspaper for each individual (Binder, 1984).

Keywords can also be associated with links to facilitate searching and browsing. A link always represents a relationship between two items. Attaching a keyword (or multiple keywords) to a link allows authors to explicitly name or define the existing relationship. Keywords associated with links might include such terms as 'example' (meaning A is an example of B), 'supports' (meaning A is an argument that supports B), or 'child' (meaning A is the child of B).

Filtering can also be accomplished by associating attributes other than keywords to blocks and links. Different structures within documents can be named so that information can be filtered according to level of detail. An outline illustrates the point best. In NLS and Brown's FRESS system, for example, each level of an outline is identified as a separate structure, allowing readers to expand and contract the outline to see more or less detail. In text documents, sentences, paragraphs, and subject headings can all be identified as separate structures; [...] however, it is considerably more difficult to make such distinctions in other media.

Using keywords and filters for finding specific information, hiding unnecessary detail, or tailoring the format of the material illustrate how the electronic medium allows readers to personalize the presentation of information in ways that are not possible with paper books.

The maps mentioned earlier not only provide a visual summary of the information space, but in fact are critical for browsing and information retrieval. The maps show the connectivity between documents rather than the content of the documents themselves. If these maps are supplemented with capabilities allowing users to travel by pointing to specific sections of the map, the map becomes a convenient way to move quickly through the web via the connections. This travelling can be done with the goal of discovering, for example, an appropriate detailed document or even the pattern of connections between information in the web.

☐   **Tools for preserving historical integrity of information**

An electronic document system should allow authors to preserve a historical record of the creation of a document. Periodically saving versions of the document is one possible option; saving a keystroke/button push record of all updates is another. Finding viable methods for saving each draft version of a document has been one of the major research tasks of the Xanadu project initiated by Nelson (1981). Clearly, allowing authors to print their material at any time is an essential feature, particularly if the author prefers editing on paper.

One method of encouraging electronic editing of documents, particularly if several authors or editors are working together, is to provide *mark-up* tools. Annoland, a hypertext-based system developed by Richard Burton, John Seely Brown, and others at Xerox PARC, includes an option that causes the delete operation to overstrike the target text with x marks rather than removing them from the screen (Brown, 1983). Authors can temporarily 'turn off' the editing symbols and see a clean copy of the document, perhaps with insertions by other individuals appearing in a different font. Editing symbols and edit marks identified by users are two more examples of attributes that can be used for filtering information. Markup features allow an author to immediately pick out the places where changes to a document have been made; these are particularly useful when combined with filtering so that an author can see only one editor's changes at a time (just as one would be able to distinguish different editors' marks by pen color or handwriting). As multimedia document systems become more widely used, markup techniques will have to be developed for editing nontextual information.
[...]

Multimedia electronic documents can be enormously useful adjuncts to the existing teaching, research, and learning tools of scholars, but to do this they must provide facilities that are different from and more powerful than those of paper books. These facilities, which include tools to promote connectivity, enhance audiovisualization, aid in the creation and revision of information, facilitate the search for and retrieval of data and maintain historical integrity of materials, represent the set of features that the electronic document systems developed at Brown aim to encompass. Not all, however, can be accomplished fully with existing technology.

Five areas, in particular, point to the need for further research. The first, concurrent distributed file access over a network, is a problem that must be tackled before sophisticated tools for joint authoring can be included in electronic document systems. The concurrent distributed file access problem is particularly acute in cases when a group of scholars would like the freedom to edit documents in the information web while others are editing, reading, or creating links to and from the same documents. Distributed database techniques will have to be developed and incorporated into multimedia document systems intended for multiple users.

Related to this challenge is the goal of high-level integration of applications. Methods must be found for software developers working separately to create multimedia applications that work together in a consistent user environment. The most promising current technology is that of object-oriented programming.

Third, the art of graphic design for electronic multimedia presentation of information is still young. Today's graphic design specialists concern themselves only with the linear presentation of material, while graphic design for electronic media introduces the elements of change and time. How should a document be presented on the screen if each reader sees a unique sequence of information blocks, and how should multimedia components be combined to present the reader with the pleasing, crisp appearance commonly expected by readers of books?

Fourth, the graphic design issue raises questions of standardization. User interface standards are needed in order to give users a sense of familiarity with the electronic tools, but these standards must, at the same time, be flexible enough to accommodate the full range of applications any one scholar requires.

Last is the problem of interoperability. If the proliferation of hardware and software systems continues, incompatibility may mean that electronic books run the risk of being usable on only a small number of systems. Currently, different readers have available machines with substantially different software, memory, and input and output capabilities. Over the five centuries since the print medium was introduced, a high degree of standardization has been developed that allows books to be used universally. Although it may not take quite so many years to develop a universally accepted format for electronic books, interoperability still looms as a major obstacle to electronic book publishing and dissemination on a wide scale. Until hardware and software become standardized, research and standards in the area of document exchange formats and systems that tailor the electronic document presentation to the type of hardware currently in use are of primary importance.

The pursuit of these goals will be a challenging one. At Brown [University], by separating application-specific components from an application-independent linking structure in Intermedia, we hope to take a first step toward providing a framework for multimedia systems for the knowledge worker. With the current upsurge of high-quality work in this area at other institutions, we expect the remainder of this decade to be a fruitful one for this important field.

■ References

Bender W., 'Imaging and Interactivity,' *Fifteenth Joint Conf. Image Technology*, Tokyo, Nov. 26, 1984.

Bolt R., *Spatial Data-Management*, Architecture Machine Group, M.I.T., Cambridge, Mass., 1979.

Brown J.S., 'Process versus Product: A Perspective on Tools for Communal and Informal Electronic Learning,' in *Education in the Electronic Age: A Report From the Learning Lab*, WNET/Thirteen Learning Lab, New York, 1983, pp. 41-58.

Engelbart D.C. and W.K. English, 'A Research Center for Augmenting Human Intellect,' *Proc. FJCC*, Vol. 33, No.1, AFIPS Press, Montvale, N.J., Fall 1968, pp. 395-410.

Inside Macintosh, Apple Computer, Inc., Cupertino, Calif., 1985.

Nelson T.H., 'Replacing the Printed Word: A Complete Literary System,' *Information Processing 80*, S.H. Lavington (ed.), North-Holland Publishing Co., IFO I980, pp. 1013-1023.

Nelson T.H., *Literary Machines*, Swarthmore, Penn., 1981. Available from author.

van Dam A and D.E. Rice, 'Computers and Publishing: Writing, Editing and Printing,' *Advances in Computers*, Academic Press, New York, 1970.

Weyer S. and A. Borning, 'A Prototype Electronic Encyclopedia,' *ACM Trans. Office Information Systems*, Vol. 3, No. 1, Jan. 1985, pp. 63-88.

Paper 3.3

Finding Facts vs. Browsing Knowledge in Hypertext Systems

Gary Marchionini and Ben Shneiderman

[...]

■ A framework for information seeking

The following framework for information seeking is meant to guide designers of hypertext systems and users who apply them to write and read hypertext documents. Figure 1 presents an overview of these components and their relationships. The interactions of these components determine the overall performance of an information-seeking system.

☐ Setting

The setting within which information seeking takes places constrains the search process. The physical setting (in a user's private office versus in a public place with a line of impatient would-be users nearby) determines physical constraints such as the amount of time allocated, physical accessibility and cost. These act as external mechanisms for the search process.

The setting also determines functional constraints such as the motivation and purpose for conducting the search, whether pleasure, job assignment, or ongoing research interest. The setting actually enables the search task. Thus, the setting helps delimit the task domain

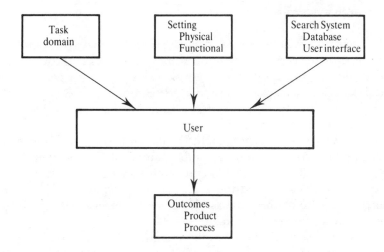

Figure 1   This information-seeking framework helps to identify the determinants of success. Issues include the complexity of the task domain, the physical and functional setting, the search system structure and user interface, and the user's knowledge of each. The outcomes of a search are specific information and the sequence of steps to generate the product.

and motivate the user, and affects the selection and application of the search system.

☐   Task domain

A task domain is a body of knowledge, whether hematology or bridge design, composed of entities and relationships. Task domains vary in complexity (number of entities and relationships), specificity (similarity of the entities and relationships), and evolutionary status (clarity of definition of the entities and relationships, and their rate of growth and change). These characteristics determine the amount of information and level of organization for a task domain.

The amount of information and level of organization vary immensely across task domains. The task domain is critical because it affects the strategies and search systems available. A task domain like hematology offers substantial on-line information from various vendors in various forms, from abstracts to full texts. On the other hand, a task domain like contemporary music offers little on-line information and limited access through such common entry points as subject headings. Furthermore, the type of search system available depends on the task domain. For example, in the humanities the primary vehicle of information is the book, whereas in the physical sciences technical reports and journal articles dominate.

☐   **Search system**

The search system consists of a database and a human–computer interface that allows access and manipulation of the database through a set of search rules. A print encyclopedia consists of words on pages and alphabetical ordering rules for using the index or finding articles by titles. In the case of electronic search systems, some of the rules and structures are embodied in software.

The user's first concern about the database is content – whether it is primary or secondary (pointer) information, full-text or symbolic, and how it matches the task domain and the information problem at hand. Once the user has selected the right database for the task, the organizational structure of the database becomes the primary determinant of information-seeking performance.

The database may be a simple sequence of full-text passages, a set of fixed-length records related through hash coding or b-trees, or a loose web of graphics and text linked through pointers. The organizational scheme chosen by the designer is critical to performance and will influence the interface as well. In turn, physical database organization is influenced by hardware and media. (See Zoellick, 1986, for a discussion of how CD-ROM characteristics affect design.)

The human–computer interface is a communication channel with hardware and software components. The physical input/output devices, selection and feedback mechanisms, and search features determine the power and flexibility of a search system. The search system works because the designer has a view of the typical user when creating the interface. Primitive systems have static internal representations for users; they are controlled by the user and a set of default conditions that reflect the system designer's conceptual view of typical users and their information problems. Information systems that have some adaptive capability enable users to change aspects of the internal representations or the user interface.

The search system is critical because it structures knowledge and defines how it is accessed. The way knowledge is organized and made available affects the strategies used to access this knowledge and thus information-seeking performance.

☐   **User**

Each user is unique, possessing mental representations for task domains. A generic knowledge base of information-seeking experiences includes mental models for various search strategies, dynamic mental models for search systems, and a control mechanism for relating these internal representations to one another and to external entities. Of particular interest for designers is how users develop mental models for new systems and how they apply these mental models when using systems.

A user's mental model for a search system is critical to the search process because it determines expectations for outcomes and the search strategies used. A mental model is active – it 'runs' internally before action takes place. A user's mental model includes both the entities and relationships represented (how knowledge is structured) in the search system and rules for controlling the system.

Users can be classified along three continua: frequency of use, complexity of application, and general range of computer experience. The position of users in a space defined by these dimensions determines how quickly and accurately they will develop a mental model for a system and how effectively they can apply it.

Low-frequency users may develop accurate mental models for what the system can do, but forget the details of system use. These users need menus and on-line reference aides. Frequent users, on the other hand, may prefer commands to expedite their use of the system.

Users who perform only straightforward tasks do not need all the features a system supports and thus need only abbreviated menus. On the other hand, users who push the limits of a system access the complete hierarchy of menus, invoking every system feature.

Users with little computer experience have more to learn and fewer mental models of related systems from which to draw analogies. These users depend more heavily on experience with the system to develop their mental models. Their initial experiences must be simple enough to allow success and continued learning. On the other hand, just as first impressions are socially critical for future interaction among people, initial experiences with a computer system play a critical role in framing a person's emerging mental model for a system. If the initial experiences lead to ambiguous or inaccurate mental models, users will have difficulty extending their use of the system.

Because users vary so much in their individual abilities, experiences, and purposes, designers must struggle with providing an interface that does not frustrate or confuse yet is rich enough to support the eventual appendage of a full set of system features.

□ Outcomes

Outcomes for information seeking include both products and a process. Products of search, from individual facts to complete documents that are interpreted to satisfy the problem condition, provide one basis for evaluating search effectiveness. Typical measures of search products include assessment of relevance or utility by users during or after search, structured or informal subjective evaluations, and examination of the resultant products or artifacts (for example, documents or abstracts). [...]

The behavioral moves made by users and systems during a search – the search process – also help in evaluating performance. Evaluators assume that user behaviours are manifestations of internal information-seeking strategies, which are themselves 'runs' of the user's mental model for the search system.

Although information units retrieved by the system are easily collected for analysis, the analysis of the search process causes more problems. Examination of paths taken and decisions made in jumping to other nodes allow us to make inferences about users' cognitive activity and provide evaluative data on system effectiveness.

Another important aspect of the search process is that the experience itself becomes part of the user's knowledge for dealing with future information problems. Therefore, consistency in design can help support incremental development of users' mental models.[...]

☐   **The Grolier Electronic Encyclopedia**

Another system we examined is the full text of *Grolier's Electronic Encyclopedia* on CD-ROM (see Figure 2). The print version of the encyclopedia occupies 20 volumes. The hypertext version consists of 60 megabytes of text and 50 megabytes of indexes that contain pointers to each occurrence of every word in the encyclopedia, all occupying less than one-fifth of a single CD-ROM disk. The powerful search software for this system provides rapid access to all occurrences of any word or phrase entered by the user. The Boolean connectives AND, OR, and NOT are supported as well as right truncation, character masking, proximity limitations from one to 999 words, and scope limitations for various sections of articles.

One study (Marchionini, in press) examined the information-seeking strategies used by elementary school students. Results demon-strated the tendency of novices to use low cognitive load browsing strategies. The children used the system successfully even though their application of Boolean connectives was weak or incorrect. Their success came from the system itself; results of queries were displayed as alpha-betical lists of titles with frequency of term occurrence. A single keystroke would then retrieve a full article with the query terms high-lighted. This interface facilitated a scan and select strategy. Searchers simply entered a query; scanned the resulting list of articles for titles that were semantically relevant or had high frequency of term occurrence; and then selected the full text of the article and scanned for term occurrences (highlighted in the text) to locate relevant sections. Thus, the hypertext features of the search system compensated for some of the formal search inadequacies of these children.

Follow-up studies (available from the authors) were conducted with high school students to compare print and electronic searches and examine the development of mental models for this system. One study examined the default conditions provide ' by the search software. The results indicate that setting proximity defaults to a paragraph seem optimal for a generic encyclopedia. The default scope condition on searching all categories of the article also proved optimal for this database. These results may not extend to other databases, since the theoretical framework predicts that strategy depends partly on task domain, and some domains may require special default settings. For example, technical documents – typically terse and specific – may require proximity settings that span more than a paragraph.

Another study simulated the effects of adding a controlled vocabulary to the search system. Many novices cannot articulate morphological variations or synonyms for search terms. Three levels of vocabulary control were tested: morphological (using variant forms and endings for terms); synonymic (using synonyms for terms); and semantic (using a hierarchical thesaurus that included broader, narrower, and related terms). Subject searches were reconstructed with these controls applied and analyzed for recall (ratio of relevant items retrieved to total relevant items in the database) and precision (ratio of relevant items retrieved to total number of items retrieved). All levels of control improved recall, but only semantic control improved precision, albeit only slightly. Designers of hypertext systems must decide whether to support vocabulary control of any sort, and then at what levels.

The power of this search system was demonstrated in another study that compared two groups of novice users trained to use different search strategies. One group learned to use a scan and select strategy and the other learned an analytical search strategy (using Boolean connectives and planning complete queries in advance). Subjects who used the analytical strategy performed slightly more efficient searches with respect to time and number of keystrokes, but exhibited no significant differences in effectiveness (success in finding information and quality of essays produced).

Overall, the experiments conducted with this system suggest that novices can successfully apply hypertext by using low cognitive load strategies modeled on existing browsing strategies, and that the power of the system overcomes some of their search inadequacies. However, these successes were accomplished using minimal capabilities of the system (default settings) for tasks appropriate to the users and the database.

Some anticipated problems of menu floundering and disorientation did arise. For example, after finishing with an article many subjects moved back up the menu hierarchy to the query formulation screen and entered the same query again (requiring another CD-ROM access) rather than moving up a single level to the screen of article titles already retrieved for that query. Another common move was to use the backspace key to erase a query rather than using the single keystroke for erasing a query. These subjects also became disoriented within an article because of the way the system put sections of text on the screen. When a user selects an article from the title list, the text of the article is displayed beginning with the first paragraph that contains the query term(s). Many students did not notice that they were in the middle of an article rather than at the beginning.

A similar problem came up with subjects who could not distinguish when they had the beginning or end or an article on the screen. Since the system provided no explicit positional cues, they erroneously continued to page up or down when at the beginning or end, respectively.

In general, the interface actually provided no feedback for queries that yielded no results. It also presented complex and dense screen displays (see Figure 2). We can easily overcome these problems with closer attention to the results from human–machine interface research. This system is currently under revision.

Inaccurate or incorrect mental models of how the system worked were apparent at the general level as well. For example, very young subjects entered queries in sentence or phrase form – they tried to conduct a natural language dialogue with the system. The present system clearly cannot compensate for user's mental models that ascribe intelligence to it. Having little experience with encyclopedias of any kind, these young children modeled use of the computer system on their most common strategy for information-seeking – asking an 'expert'. Older children modeled the electronic encyclopedia on the familiar print versions.

Another common problem was subjects' poor mental models for searching in general. For example, some subjects added terms to queries that yielded no hits and contained ANDed terms. The system could trap such logical errors by pointing out that adding additional terms actually narrows a query (more terms yield fewer hits). Such forms of automatic help and remediation promote accurate mental model development, but if applied too often they may deter beginners from accomplishing immediate tasks and thus discourage continued use.

Perhaps an incremental approach is possible with systems that themselves record histories of use for users, but for hypertext systems like public access encyclopedias, we must find a balance between support for Boolean connectives and automatic adjustment of default conditions. For such systems, we believe that we can achieve significant cognitive advantage by amplifying low cognitive load browsing strategies and making the high cognitive load strategies that require Boolean manipulations and default adjustments transparent to the novice user.

The electronic encyclopedia is much more controlled than other hypertext systems in that jumps from article to article depend on a list of articles retrieved by a query. A user who wants to see an article not on the retrieved list must pose another query or enter a separate mode that allows lookup of single articles by title. On the other hand, the full-text search feature is totally under the control of the user. Problems of

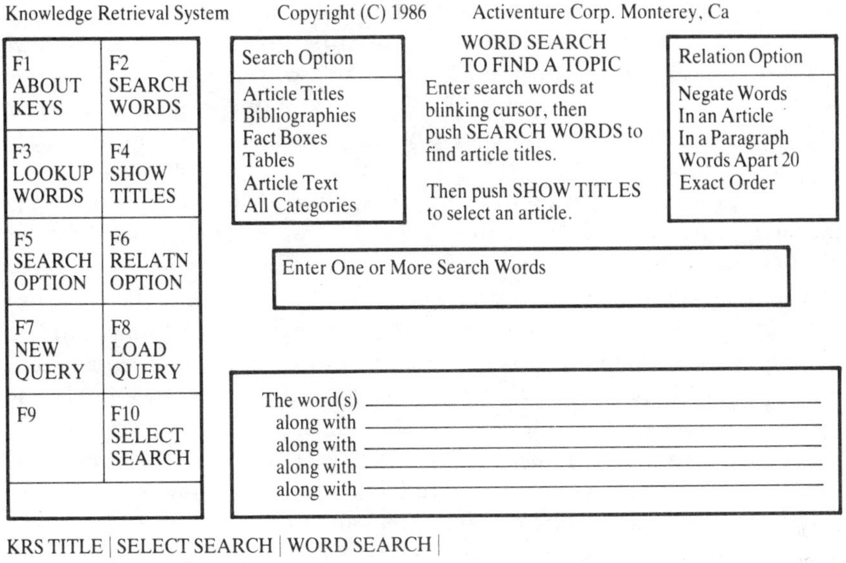

Knowledge Retrieval System   Copyright (C) 1986   Activenture Corp. Monterey, Ca

F1 ABOUT KEYS	F2 SEARCH WORDS
F3 LOOKUP WORDS	F4 SHOW TITLES
F5 SEARCH OPTION	F6 RELATN OPTION
F7 NEW QUERY	F8 LOAD QUERY
F9	F10 SELECT SEARCH

Search Option

Article Titles
Bibliographies
Fact Boxes
Tables
Article Text
All Categories

WORD SEARCH TO FIND A TOPIC

Enter search words at
blinking cursor, then
push SEARCH WORDS to
find article titles.

Then push SHOW TITLES
to select an article.

Relation Option

Negate Words
In an Article
In a Paragraph
Words Apart 20
Exact Order

Enter One or More Search Words

The word(s) _____
along with _____
along with _____
along with _____
along with _____

KRS TITLE | SELECT SEARCH | WORD SEARCH |

Figure 2   This main menu from *Grolier's Electronic Encyclopedia* offers users several search options and information about function key usage.

information overload did occur, but were minimized by the combined effects of the database (a set of generic, highly organized encyclopedia articles) and search rules (easy modification of queries and easy use of the scan and select browsing strategy). Complex, highly specific, or loosely organized databases may require distinct designs.

■ Design issues

Designers of hypertext systems or databases should consider the information-seeking framework (Figure 1). The overall design must attend to the physical system, the conceptual model the system presents (the user interface), and the mental model the user is expected to develop for the system. Design decisions that affect information seeking in hypertext systems are related to defining access points, creating the user interface, and providing search strategy features. These decisions interact in unexpected ways, but thoughtful designs can preserve power and flexibility while reducing complexity of use.

☐ Defining access points

In traditional electronic databases, access points for retrieval include characters, fields, records, and tables or files. Access points may be restricted to selected points, organized in alphabetical or hierarchical sequence, or multiply indexed. Consider the access points typically available in printed books: table of contents, indexes (author, subject, permuted, and so on), glossary, chapter, article (section), physical page, paragraph, footnotes, reference notes, lists, and appendices. Pagination is critical to access in books, since page number is the primary pointer to a field location.

Hypertext databases can support all these access points except physical page. A screenful of text cannot be used as an analog of the physical page in systems that permit control of text window size, scrolling, and stacking or juxtaposing windows. However, since the machine can assist in maintaining pointer information, hypertext systems can link field locations in many other ways, including electronic bookmarks, temporary notepads, graphic maps, backward citation pointers, and pattern matches on characters or words.

Hypertext systems also allow other access points that books do not, such as cumulative record of path, string search, animation, sound, video, or immediate link to related software. (For example, access software for Microsoft's Bookshelf on CD-ROM can be memory resident for immediate use from within another program.) Whether users can take advantage of these features remains to be determined.

A key decision for designers or authors is what access points to define and how to link these points. Users will likely expect access points at least as rich as those available in books. Designers must decide how much more to offer and how much more unrestrained jumping from point to point to allow. Links at every word to every word are clearly not desirable from the perspective of user or system performance. The trade-offs in machine overhead and user cognitive load (in the form of overchoice) must be weighed carefully. Designers should consider the targeted task domains and typical user population in deciding how fine the access points should be and what links among access points should be visible to users.

☐   **Creating the user interface**

An interface enables users to perform their tasks by providing selection mechanisms, feedback mechanisms, and input/output devices. In a book the default sequence is top-down due to the linear nature of the text. The interactive and flexible characteristics of hypertext require users to make more choices (selections) in searching for information. Furthermore, each selection requires appropriate and understandable feedback to maintain a fruitful interaction. Since the organization of the information in hypertext is not linear, mechanisms for selection and feedback are critical to good design.

Results from menu design research offer some guidance, but there are trade-offs to consider. The key issue is one of user control. The extreme cases range from allowing the user to jump anywhere from anywhere (hyperchaos) to forcing the user through a linear sequence of screens with no deviation possible (drill and practice). The degree of user control provided will depend on the user, his or her purpose, and the task domain. Expert users who are specialists in the task domain will welcome great power and control, but novices to the system and the task domain will likely benefit from limited menus and less control.

The direct manipulation approach with embedded menus seems very effective for hypertext applications, but there are many variations on ᛋ the theme. We believe that embedded menus provide meaningful task domain (as opposed to computer domain) terms and concepts, thereby reducing disorientation. However, we need more research to help guide designers in choosing highlighting techniques to indicate selectable text or graphic items without distracting too much from the content.

Similarly, feedback can range from cryptic codes to pseudo-intelligent context-sensitive help. Experts will quickly seek ways to avoid lengthy feedback because it slows down the dialogue and impedes progress toward their goals. On the other hand, too little feedback will frustrate and confuse novices, yet too much can distract them. One approach for hypertext systems in public access settings permits users to specify their level of knowledge of the database content, information-seeking experience and purpose, and previous experience with this and other systems. Feedback settings can then be adjusted accordingly, with the user able to change settings at any point in a session.

Input/output devices affect user information-seeking performance at the behavioral level. Good choices on the part of the system designer can facilitate ease and efficiency of use, but poor choices can lead to user frustration or fatigue. Pointing devices such as touchscreen, mouse, jump-arrow keys, or keyboards need to be refined and evaluated. Improvements in screen readability through proper font design, text/background colour pairs, or higher resolution would benefit users. Increased screen size and multiple window strategies also require investigation. Mapping the proper input/output devices to the system requires consideration of user, setting, and task domain characteristics.

Setting default conditions for these and other issues will depend on how the designer views the typical user. A range of alternative selection mechanisms can then be provided for use by atypical users. Mixed strategies are also possible. For example, a linear 'tour' could be threaded through a complex network to offer new users a guided introduction.

☐ **Providing search strategy features**

Search features like Boolean connectives, string search, proximity limits, scope limits, and truncation facilitate rapid access to information, but cause additional cognitive load on the part of the user and substantial preprocessing of the database itself. Systems that provide only browsing features allow casual, low cognitive load exploration, but are typically inefficient for directed search tasks or fact retrieval. Defining a hybrid system that guides discovery seems an appropriate compromise, but involves a number of trade-off decisions. How deeply the database is indexed, whether some automatic controlled vocabulary is included, and how feedback is summarized and even formatted on the screen affect the strategies users will apply. If every word is indexed, the possibility of information overload increases. Therefore, features for filtering such as frequency of occurrence per node or support for NOT operators must be enhanced. If a controlled vocabulary is included, automatic thresholds must be established, or the user must be prompted to apply the controlled vocabulary or be alerted to its effects. For example, in an encyclopedia, a query that retrieved more than 50 articles could automatically trigger a narrowing function.

Secondary databases (containing pointer information) such as on-line catalogues or bibliographic databases and highly structured primary databases require analytical strategy support. Text or graphic databases seem to invite scan and select browsing strategies, although the size and complexity may warrant some additional indexing to improve user search efficiency. In general, each feature added to a system demands additional machine overhead. Many also add user cognitive load. These effects must be considered in all design decisions.

☐   The flexibility/complexity trade-off

Systems transparent to one user may frustrate and impede others. Flexibility inevitably leads to complexity. Just as printed indexes and directories are organized to facilitate retrieval (nobody reads the phone book), so electronic information systems must be organized to suit the typical purposes of anticipated users. All designers must grapple with the issue of when to stop adding features – they face a law of diminishing returns. Empirical results and the marketplace will determine what the next version of a system should include and how much complexity users can tolerate.

A similar design issue is the tension between the learnability and applicability of a system. A system that is easy to learn may not be easy to apply in full. Results from cognitive science demonstrate that users' mental models will depend on initial training or experience with a system. An incomplete and simple conceptual model used to present the system to new users may limit their understanding of the system and their ability to apply it to future problems.

One approach to this problem, used in systems like Hypercard, is to choose a familiar metaphor (stacks of cards) and provide several levels of application (user preferences), examples and help. The metaphor of the familiar flat index card will surely facilitate initial learnability, but may limit applicability of the multidimensional electronic card. As information systems continue to increase in complexity and power, they will likely become more difficult to learn and apply.

Some designers believe in adaptive systems, in which the computer is programmed to recognize user skills or information needs and then modify the interface or guide the user to the desired destination. Another school concentrates on adaptable systems in which the user is given the power to alter the user interface or is offered a rich variety of traversal methods. Adaptive systems represent an attractive but unproven idea, while adaptable systems place a greater burden on the user even as they provide increased control.

Hypertext systems offer the potential for highly personalized information seeking if designers can apply principles from traditional information systems and the results of empirical studies.

Inevitably, the application of computers as cognitive augmenting agents will improve cognitive performance and change the way we think. An empirical base of evidence is coalescing around research and development on how to create hypertext systems, how to write using hypertext systems, how to read using hypertext systems, and how to find information in hypertext systems.

Our experience suggests that a general information-seeking framework that includes setting, task domain, user, search system, and outcomes aids the design and study of hypertext. Key design issues include

- finding the correct information unit granularity for particular task domains and users;
- presenting interfaces with low cognitive load for selection and feedback mechanisms, and reasonable default conditions; and
- striking a balance between analytical and browsing search strategies.

The general problem of maximizing power and flexibility while minimizing complexity of use must always be attacked.

Although much remains to be learned about how users apply hypertext for information seeking, clearly these systems offer distinct advantages for finding facts, browsing knowledge and – we hope – acquiring wisdom.

■ References

Marchionini G., 'Information-Seeking Strategies of Novices Using a Full-Text Electronic Encyclopedia', *J. Am. Society for Information Science*, in press.
Zoellick W., 'CD-ROM Software Development,' *Byte*, Vol. 11, 1986, pp. 177-188.

Paper 3.4

Microtechnology and Students with Disabilities in Further Education

Janis Firminger

■ Introduction

Hereward College is a national college, offering a range of further education courses to residential and local day students who have disabilities, alongside care, medical and physiotherapy services. Some students follow ordinary FE courses, based at the college or elsewhere in the city-wide consortium. Study and communication difficulties are supported through the work of the Foundation Studies Department and the ACCESS Centre, which grew out of a Department of Trade and Industry funded project at the college between 1983 and 1985. This project was to evaluate the contribution of information technology in increasing students' access to mainstream courses. Today, apart from supporting the third (37) of the Hereward student population who now use micro-based study aids (compared with three in 1982), the centre also offers short courses to non-residential students to help them to manage their studies more effectively in mainstream colleges, using new technology where appropriate. The centre also offers courses and workshops on the use of technology to staff in mainstream colleges. The Keyboard Aids Unit at the centre provides modifications to equipment to improve access to hardware and software.

In this paper, I shall discuss some aspects of our work on the two-year DTI project, particularly our approach to assessment and our students' experience of using technology on their courses and since

First published in Booth, T. and Swann, W., (eds.) (1987). *Including pupils with disabilities*. Milton Keynes: Open University Press. Reprinted with permission.

leaving FE. Later in the paper I shall discuss what is required if new technology is to make a continuing contribution towards students' independence and to their ability to control their own study.

Students involved in the project were following a range of ordinary further education courses, including City and Guilds Foundation, Certificate in Prevocational Education and Training, a Manpower Services Commission Modern Office Skills course, B/Tec Diploma course, GCE 'O' and 'A' levels. The majority had little in the way of formal qualifications when they entered further education. One-third were following City and Guilds Foundation courses.

Students tended to have quite severe disabilities: cerebral palsy was the most common impairment, but also represented were spina bifida, Still's disease, post-operative brain tumour, brain damage, muscular dystrophy, Friedrich's Ataxia, tetraplegia and osteogenesis imperfecta (brittle bones).

During the first year of the project, we equipped 15 students with mobile microcomputer-based workstations for their personal use within Hereward. Their progress was monitored and, in the second year, we extended assessment, awareness and training facilities to students in mainstream colleges. In some cases, equipment was loaned out for periods of up to one year.

For those lecturers initially involved with the project, past experience of innovations and of working with students with more severe disabilities made them highly suspicious of technology as a way of solving educational problems. Everyone involved felt that a critical approach was essential. The work should be not only student centred but also student led. The purpose was to improve students' access to the ordinary curriculum, using the most efficient means available; it was not simply to introduce new technology. To guard against promoting technology as the cure-all, we had to keep three key issues in mind:

(1)   Is technology *relevant* to the student and his/her needs?

(2)   If it is relevant, which configuration would be most *appropriate*?

(3)   What steps will be taken to ensure its continuing *effectiveness*?

■ A critical, student-led approach

Most students with disabilities confess themselves 'assessed' more times than they care to remember. Our aim was not to assess individuals in isolation, but to assess them in the context in which they were studying and to consider the extent to which technology might reduce the handicapping effects of that context. Assessment was not intended to prescribe solutions. It aimed to increase students' and teachers' awareness of difficulties that might arise on a course, and to find ways of overcoming them. In this way we might develop strategies that improve the quality of an individual's FE experience.

There is a considerable temptation in work with students who have more complex difficulties, particularly in their speech, to draw conclusions about their needs based on observation, and not on talking about their needs with them. Conclusions drawn on this basis will often be wrong, and resources wasted trying to solve problems that do not exist. But most important, the value of new technology resides in its potential to increase students' control over their lives. If this is to occur, then people with disabilities need to be fully involved from the outset. In the long term, they will need both the information and confidence to enable them to identify changing requirements, to recognize where technology may be used and to tap the resources available in the community to ensure that the technology remains effective. Unless students participate fully in decisions from an early stage, new technology may come to be regarded as complicated, boring and, ultimately, irrelevant. Like such gadgetry before it, it is welcomed by the professionals and discarded at the earliest opportunity by the users, such as the student who said: 'technology is boring. You don't see what you're creating and it's not personalized ... '

■ The relevance of technology

Attention to the finer points of technology is pointless if other more basic needs are not met. As one student pointed out:

> 'How can we ever become independent if we always have to ask
> people to do things for us? ... Like, you can be stuck on the loo
> and not able to reach the loo roll ... care staff come back and ask if
> you're ready and you have to say, "I couldn't reach the loo roll."
> You feel really stupid.'

A low-tech aid may be all that is required to effect a considerable improvement in students' college lives.

Students' wider expectations of FE also need to be considered. Regardless of the degree of their disability, their perceptions are unlikely to differ significantly from those of any other student. They are likely to value the opportunity to take courses and obtain qualifications, particularly in areas not available at school. Also important is the chance to study in a more adult, less restrictive environment where, 'you get treated more as an equal'. Less emphasis on past achievements and failures, new friendships and greater independence all figure prominently. Many also complain of what they perceive as the 'fussing' they experienced in school. Study support services must take account of student expectations of 'unexceptional' provision. Special provision should not be a barrier to their participation in an ordinary experience. This is the case, for example, if study aids provided are so complicated that lengthy training is required to allow students to use them, if equipment is unreliable, or if proposed modifications will be months, or even years, in development.

It is only worth evaluating the possible contribution of technology to a student's work when you know that he or she is following a relevant course. It is not unusual to find students following courses, not because of any interest in the subjects or because they reflect future goals but rather because more appropriate options were not available. In some instances, for example, computer studies classes were impossible since they were not on the ground floor; typing was not available to students who were unable to use all fingers; modern languages were considered unsuitable for students with speech difficulties; geography was closed to students unable to draw diagrams and science was closed on account of the practical requirements. It is important to establish the right of access to any course, regardless of disability. Students themselves may also need encouragement to overcome their own prejudices about what is possible.

The limited curricula in some special schools may have adversely affected students' ideas about what is possible. Some students are simply not aware of the range of available subjects. They often believe that they need some background in languages, science, arts or commercial subjects to join an FE course. Such misconceptions need to be cleared up by giving students full information about courses and content to enable them to make informed decisions on course choice. New technology may open up subjects where it can provide an alternative means of access. Science experiments, for example, can be computer simulated for students who are unable to handle equipment; courses which use diagrams extensively can be opened up with graphics software. Engineering, an option long considered closed to students with more severe disabilities, has now become a possibility through developments in CAD/CAM (Computer Aided Design/Computer Aided Manufacture). One student, for example, was able to follow a mainstream CAD/CAM course, accessing the system linked to the Keymaster[†] college computer via his footskate[‡] encoding device, developed at the college.

[†] The keymaster is a modular system consisting of a keyboard emulator and a user interface, enabling the user to operate the BBC from a range of input devices. Available from Clwyd Technics Ltd, Antelope Industrial Estate, Rhyddymwyn, Mold, Clwyd, CH7 5JH.
[‡] A footskate is a foot-operated alternative input device (currently offers 2, 4 or 8 switch input). Available from SB Systems, Unit 2D, Jefferson Way, Thame Industrial Estate, Thame OX9 3UJ.

It may also be necessary to check that students are working towards the minimum entry requirements to allow them to follow their chosen career or to go on to higher education. Such matters may be obvious for other students but can be missed for a student with a severe disability. Technology in this context may be particularly effective, as was the case when several students who needed 'O' level English for university entrance were provided with word processing facilities, which enabled them to make corrections, redraft and produce neat copy. This contributed to their eventual success in passing 'O' level six months after obtaining the equipment; for two of them, at their fifth attempt.

Study difficulties we encountered on the project varied considerably, and were not closely related to the students' impairments. They included: slow writing or typing speeds (frequently below 10 w.p.m. and, in some cases, down to 2 w.p.m.); fatigue; problems with legibility; the storage and organization of paper materials; notetaking in lectures and from books; overdependence on memorizing information; difficulty with the production of graphs, diagrams and special symbols; and examinations.

Students who used technology described some of the benefits of micro-based study and communications equipment in overcoming difficulties as: increased enjoyment of the work; quicker and less tiring work; presentation, spelling and grades improved; disk storage was an advantage; and correction and editing facilities which were said to be 'brilliant'.

Some of the remaining difficulties were less obvious, especially where technology was being used with some measure of success. Even though some students doubled their writing speed (in some cases from 4 w.p.m. to 9 w.p.m.), notetaking remained a serious problem for some. We have explored the possibility of using a speed writing system but, as yet, we have not identified a viable method that can be quickly learned and is compatible with use of the standard QWERTY keyboard. In some cases, students have used their own means of abbreviation. One, for example, took 'A' level sociology on the computer using this approach, and was able to increase her output significantly. Other possibilities include the use of word lists stored in the computer, where only one or two characters may be required to access a word from the stored list. A word anticipator program, developed at Dundee University for use on the Epson PX8 portable micro, is also being tried by some students. None of the developments that are currently available, though, seem significantly to affect speed, although the effort required may be less.

A combination of abbreviations and closer attention to the techniques of notetaking may be a better solution. Much notetaking by students in the normal course of events is not only redundant but probably unhelpful as a means of learning. It may be more valuable in the long term to work with students to develop more efficient notetaking techniques so they can use nine words when ninety might otherwise be used than to provide extensive and complex software.

Examinations remain equally difficult for students whose writing is slow. Even where special arrangements have been made, they are a marathon for many students. Alternative means of assessment, particularly course work assessment, can be more appropriate and may give a clearer indication of students' capabilities. Frequently, though, the traditional examinations treadmill remains the only available option. Arrangements need to be assessed carefully with students if they are not to be disadvantaged. It should not be assumed that the computer will be the solution. A number of students involved with the project, particularly from mainstream colleges, had been working to examination arrangements that were wholly inadequate. One student, who had left mainstream school without having had the opportunity to take any examinations, because of his 'learning difficulties', had completed a YTS course and was taking 'O' levels and an 'A' level in computer science at college. His success to date had been in 'O' level computer studies, where he had used a computer, but his performance was marred in other subjects by his illegible script. Five minutes extra time and large print examination papers did not give him an equal chance.

■ What technology is appropriate?

If technology is relevant to a student, the next stage is to decide what equipment is needed. The course requirements, the student's abilities and learning style, their perceptions of, and their attitudes to, technology are all important.

The course may simply require word processing facilities but more may be involved. Maths, science or modern language courses may call for special symbols and presentation. In some subjects, like accounts and business studies, diagrams or graphs may be essential. These needs affect the software or equipment that is required.

Close attention to the effect of a student's physical condition on the mechanics of studying is important. A first priority must be to ensure that the student is comfortably seated for communication and study. The advice of a physiotherapist or seating technician may be needed. In some cases, students may be seated well and have good posture but find that they have to adopt a different position to write or type. Some positions are not viable in some environments. Lying or sitting on the floor or across a desk should be avoided if possible. Before he got a footskate system, one student found that his only viable typing position was to sit on his knees on the floor and to hit the keyboard with a wooden spoon. Another student, with brittle bones, who had taken all her CSE examinations from a prone position in bed, found that sitting in a conventional position at a desk caused acute backache. She was able to overcome this problem by using an adapted microwriter.[†] She has subsequently taken 'O' and 'A' levels, and is studying for a degree with the Open University.

Physical conditions may remain stable or deteriorate. This may be uncertain, as in the case of one 'A' level student with osteoarthritis. Two months after entering further education, she lost the use of her writing hand, as the bones fused, and use of the hand became extremely painful. Within a week of using the other hand to operate a microwriter, she was able to produce neat, printed copy at 14 w.p.m. But by the end of the year her 'microwriting hand' was also deteriorating. Since her condition continues to fluctuate, she is currently keeping three options open: the use both of left- and right-handed microwriters and, on occasions, the use of a pen. She has been able to continue her studies without interruption. This had not been the case in school, where she lost much time. She hopes now to continue to higher education.

Some students are unable to use a keyboard, in which case alternative devices and switching systems will be needed. The number of switches a student can use will determine whether he or she should use a scanning matrix or an encoding device: the more switches, the quicker the writing speed. One of the most efficient input systems available at the college was devised by Patrick Poon at Charlton Park School. This consists of a footskate with the Mac Apple[‡] system for writing. In college, the skate has also been linked with the keymaster for computer programming on the BBC microcomputer. More recently, it has been linked to a computer system in a neighbouring mainstream college, to enable the student to join a computer aided design course there.

It is for the student to decide whether an alternative input device is required. In some cases, students prefer to work with a standard system, even though their speed remains slow. This choice must be respected. Such devices do not always improve speed greatly; it may be more important to make the user more comfortable and reduce the effort needed.

Some students find that, for reasons which cannot fully be explained, they simply do not make progress using computer-based

---

[†] The Microwriter is a portable, rechargeable battery-operated word processor with six keys on the keyboard capable of producing all the characters of a typewriter keyboard, plus additional technical symbols. Available from The Foundation for Communication for the Disabled, 25 High Street, Woking, Surrey, EU2 11BW.

[‡] Mac Apple is a communicator which allows the user to write and make corrections, draw pictures and diagrams on an Apple microcomputer by using switches or a keyboard. Enquiries to Patrick Poon, ACCESS Centre, Hereward College, Bramston Crescent, Tile Hill Lane, Coventry, CV4 9SW.

equipment. Their approach to learning and their individual requirements may be more effectively served by a lightweight electronic
typewriter, with limited correction facilities. On occasions, students find
that a large handwritten scrawl is preferable to any kind of equipment.
One accomplished computer user, for example, said that he preferred his
untidy handwriting any day to the 'anonymous' work created on the
computer.

In a number of cases, even where careful attention has been paid
to assessment and training and where students have persevered with
micro-based aids over some months, these have been abandoned, not
because the system is difficult to use but because the student feels
'further away from the work' or they do not get quick enough feedback
from the machine. The equipment causes some students to feel alienated
from the work. One student with a spinal injury who had learned to
operate an Epson PX 8 portable micro using wrist sticks, apparently very
successfully, abandoned the system after several months for a portable
typewriter. She preferred a low-tech approach and the immediate
printout from the typewriter. The option of a portable printer did not
appeal to her because it still did not give her the immediacy that was
otherwise possible.

Another cause of occasional frustration is the storage of information on disk in environments that are still entrenched in paper-based
method. One student commented that the whole object of using technology to study was defeated by the fact that lecturers marked printouts
and not disks. He could see little purpose in retaining uncorrected
material on disks, so he did not use disks as his main means of storage,
despite severe difficulty in using standard files and in organizing paper.

■ Ensuring technology remains effective

Both students and staff in FE need to be aware of the current applications and the potential of technology. Introductory training is important
to increase their understanding of the role of the equipment and to
ensure that they do not feel at a total loss when something goes wrong.
Students also need to feel that they have staff support. If they are already
struggling with 'unfriendly' manuals, on occasion losing work, meeting
the kind of frustrations involved in learning any skills and at the same
time trying to keep up with coursework, it can be particularly dispiriting
if staff treat the system as, at best, an irrelevance and, at worst, an
invasion.

Some staff in Hereward remain sceptical of the value of microtechnology. Several felt that technology had been imposed without
consultation and regarded it as a hindrance. In their view, students

had coped in the past without hi-tech. Several students remarked on this:

> 'Some lecturers thought I could write perfectly well and asked me not to use the computer. Initially, I used it every day for word processing, then things got more difficult.'
>
> 'The lecturer really hated the computer, wasn't happy about me using it and objected to me bringing it into lectures when I could write.'

In retrospect, staff should have been more involved. The opportunity to make microtechnological aids available to more students when we could already see it working successfully for several seemed too good to miss. We went ahead on the assumption that if it was demonstrably useful then staff in the college would accept it. We did not appreciate how the degree of success could be affected by staff attitudes. Where staff were enthusiastic and encouraging, students were more likely to persevere and succeed, particularly with more complicated equipment.

Mainstream colleges were not very different. Where staff felt involved, then they worked with and supported the student, often putting in extra time. For those less involved, and where the students' difficulties were regarded as an individual rather than an institutional problem, students sometimes felt that they had to tread warily. One commented, with evident relief, that some of the teachers at her comprehensive 'did not mind' her using a microelectronic typewriter in conjunction with a home-based BBC workstation. Throughout her education, this student had had no effective means of producing her own written work. She wrote extremely slowly and had not been able to use a typewriter or a tape recorder in class. A part-time amanuensis had been the main solution for her difficulties. Another student, with hand/eye coordination difficulties, was convinced of the value of a micro-writer but, in practice, did not regard this as a feasible proposition. His school career had been seriously affected by his teachers' lack of understanding. As far as he was concerned, the microwriter could only serve to handicap him further by drawing attention to his difficulties, when his main aim was to be unobtrusive.

So staff need to be acquainted with the use, benefits and pitfalls of technology. Otherwise it may be seen as yet another demand on time that is already limited by the presence of a student with a disability, who runs the risk of being regarded ultimately as a source of disruption in the lecture room.

Students also need a broad awareness and training programme that will extend horizons beyond their immediate needs, and encourage them to explore the use of technology in their future lives. They need to know that equipment provided is not fixed. It can be developed and replaced as needs change. The majority of students who have used equipment expect to continue using it in their future studies or employment. A number have moved on, and are now operating success-fully in new environments. New technology has given some of them a marked boost to their confidence. One student who uses a head pointer and is severely disabled by cerebral palsy, left with an A and B at 'A' level to his credit. He intends to do a Ph.D in computer studies, eventually, and all the indications are that he will succeed. Another student who produced illegible, very slow, hand-written work before she used the microwriter, got a part-time job at the Milk Marketing Board within six months of leaving further education and established her own word processing agency for small businesses. Another was rejected by main-stream further education and spent a year in an Adult Training Centre before arriving at Hereward. She has since used a micro to organize a complicated move to a house in a new area where she lives indepen-dently. She joined a part-time diploma in higher education course and organized all the benefits and services she required. The micro, obtained through the COMET Award Scheme†, carried her progress beyond further education and gave her the impetus she needed to organize her own life. One student with severe cerebral palsy was destined for residential care after further education. He decided not to return to his home area but to work towards becoming self-supporting and independent. After an MSC course in computing, he became involved in the Companies' Training Scheme. Three years later he has become one of the directors of a computer training centre.

A final example is a mature student who learned to type when she was 15, despite 'considerable hostility' from her headmaster at the special school she attended. She has been typing for 25 years. During the last 10 years she has slowly taken GCEs and obtained several Open University credits towards a degree. After moving into residential care, she became demoralized and gave up her studies. She joined the Modern Office Skills course, jointly run by Hereward and the neigh-bouring mainstream college. Within two months of using technology, she had increased her speed from 6 w.p.m. to 10 w.p.m. and intends to double that within the next four months. For the first time in her life, she feels that she can think realistically about finding a job and becoming economically independent. She may also continue her studies, particu-larly as she too has obtained equipment through the COMET Scheme.

† COMET is a bursary scheme which makes awards to people who need microcomputers for studies and training. Organized by the *Sunday Times* and VNU Business Publications. Administered by NBHS, 336 Brixton Road, London, SW9 7AA.

■ The policy and financial framework

The Hereward project was funded through the IT Awareness Programme of the Department of Trade and Industry. This pump-priming strategy meant few administrative controls and more chances to innovate. But there are penalties, not least the lack of permanent funding, although the college is committed to provide resources to allow the work to continue. MSC funding has also enabled complementary activities to develop on the same financial basis. The assessment, training and awareness facilities provided by the ACCESS Centre for people not resident at the college have no regular external sources of funding, although the centre is nominated by the Department of Education and Science to provide assessment and consultancy in the use of new-tech study aids in FE. Fees are charged, but these do not pay for the facilities available nor for the further skills which should be brought into the centre, particularly in electronics, speech therapy and occupational therapy.

The coordination of activities between centres is not formalized in any way. While they are linked informally and share skills and experience, we need resources to consolidate and disseminate our achievements. Exchange between centres is vital for the development of the skills of centre workers and the continued provision of training and awareness courses for staff and students in ordinary colleges and other training agencies. It has also been possible to seek solutions to student difficulties through collaborative work. The University of Warwick has been particularly important in this respect. For example, joint work on the BEN project (the BBC Electronic Notepad) has produced a program for the BBC micro which enables students to carry out several study activities within a single program (Stevens and Pickering, 1984).

A national policy to coordinate current activities and arrangements is needed, to consolidate achievements and to clarify the pattern of services. This policy should include the full involvement of students. Current arrangements for the provision of personal equipment demonstrate the dangers of a prescriptive approach to study and communications support that I discussed earlier. Students who need equipment are obliged to apply through various agencies, including charities, the COMET award scheme, local authorities and the Education Support Grant funding. There is no way to ensure that what is rapidly becoming essential equipment for many people will be made available to them. The success of applications through the various agencies depends less upon individual need than upon access to professionals who are in a position to channel their applications. In the case of Education Support Grant funding, arrangements are such that equipment might be organized for a student without any consultation. There are no controls to ensure that individuals will see the equipment before they receive it, even less have an opportunity to determine what might best meet their needs.

We lack effective evaluation, assessment, training and equipment. The use of new technology to support people with disabilities is still at a relatively primitive stage. If the role of centres like Hereward is to be developed effectively, then future policy needs to take account of this. Facilities available at the ACCESS Centre, for example, depend on the ability to pay. Many people interested in using technology to support their return to education are not eligible even for discretionary grants from local education authorities. Some young people may not be able to persuade their authorities of the value of new technology. In any event, a 'payment by results' system is unnecessarily restrictive and cannot sustain development work in flexible and responsive service. On the contrary, it may encourage a rehashing of the tried and tested and quick, glib solutions to difficulties that need, above all, time and commitment to resolve. We need continued investment to ensure that technology enhances quality of life and creates previously unimagined opportunities for education, training and employment.

■ Reference

Stevens, G. and Pickering, J. 1984. 'The electronic notepad: an integrated tool for writing, drawing and calculating,' in *The Computer as an Aid for Those with Special Needs*, Sheffield Active Conference Proceedings.

■ Further reading

ACE Centre Publications, ACE Centre, Ormerod School, Wayneflete Road, Headington, Oxford.

BARD – British Database on Research into Aids for the Disabled, Handicapped Persons Research Unit, Newcastle-upon-Tyne Polytechnic, No. 1 Coach Lane, Coach Lane Campus, Newcastle-upon-Tyne, NE7 7TW.

CALL Centre Publications, CALL Centre, University of Edinburgh, The Annexe, 4 Buccleuch Place, Edinburgh, EH8 9JT.

Communication Outlook, available from the Artificial Language Laboratory, Michigan State University, 405 Computer Centre, East Lansing, MI 48824-10942, USA.

Hawkridge, D.,Vincent, T. and Hales, G. 1985. *New Information Technology in the Education of Disabled Children and Adults*, London, Croom Helm.

SEMERC (Special Education Microelectronic Research Centre) Newsletters available from:

Bristol SEMERC, Faculty of Education, Bristol Polytechnic, Redland Hill, Bristol, BS6 6U2.

Newcastle SEMERC, Newcastle Polytechnic, Coach Lane Campus, Newcastle-upon-Tyne, NE7 7XA.

Manchester SEMERC, Manchester College of Higher Education, Hathersage Road, Manchester, M13 0JA.

Redbridge SEMERC, Dane Centre, Melbourne Road, Ilford, Essex, IG1 4HT.

With a Little Help from the Chip, BBC TV Publications, 1985.

Paper 3.5

Information Technology for Students with Learning Difficulties: Some Experiences at Brooklands Technical College

Bridget Middlemas

This paper is a selection of extracts from a Dip.Ed. Thesis written by Bridget Middlemas. The study involves 10 students with learning difficulties in the College, and their use of computers for language and literacy work. In drawing conclusions from the study, the implications for staff are considered.

■ The environment at Brooklands College

The Special Needs Section is part of the Department of General Education and Science (GES), the largest department in the College. The section has been in existence for about four years and is still developing its structure. Several courses are run for special needs students, such as YTS, CPVE and a Fountain Course. A student can remain at Brooklands for as long as five years if this is thought to be necessary. Most students join the department in September, although there is some 'roll on/roll off' provision where required.

First published in Vincent, T. (ed.) (1989). *New Technology, Disability and Special Educational Needs: Some Case Studies*. Coventry: Empathy Ltd. Reprinted with permission of The Open University and Empathy Ltd.

All these courses come under the umbrella of CEC, or the Continuing Education Course, which is a course intended for students aged 16–19 (or 21 in some cases) who have been classed as having moderate learning difficulties. There are four classrooms which are used by CEC tutor groups, and good use is made of facilities around the rest of the College whenever possible, to enable the students to be an integral part of the College community.

Most of the IT teaching is carried out in one of these four classrooms, or in the 'Self Teach' area which is in the Science Block. Brooklands also has a number of IT resource rooms elsewhere in the college, as a number of higher level courses are taught, such as BTEC, HND, and various business and secretarial courses.

■ IT equipment used by CEC students

Ten BBC Master computers (in four classrooms) with VIEW and WORDWISE word processing packages, six Epson printers, and four Concept keyboards. Use of Self-Teach area at most times, comprising nine BBC B computers with Wordwise plus Epson printers

■ Staff–student ratios

There are five full-time lecturing staff teaching on the CEC course, and about eight part-time staff. Groups are generally not larger than eight students, with one lecturer per group. There is sometimes a technician available for extra support. Less able groups are usually smaller whenever possible, say four or five to a group, depending on staff commitments elsewhere in the College. There is some double-staffed teaching, for subjects such as home management, literacy and social numeracy. Students sometimes use the computers during these sessions to write up their assignments, or use programs that complement the lessons such as 'Weekly Shopping' or 'Budget'.

■ Student intake on the CEC course at Brooklands

Brooklands is a Technical College catering for approximately 2500 students, most of whom live in the Guildford/Kingston/Woking/Staines/Esher catchment area. There are 40 places for students with special needs on the CEC course, who are referred to the College by the area Special Needs Careers Officer.

Most of the students would be described on their statements as having moderate learning difficulties, although some are quite a lot brighter than this, and some definitely not! There have been problems in recent years with special schools in the Surrey area in that schools are remaining open under the category of MLD schools, whereas in fact many of the more able MLD pupils have been integrated into mainstream provision. Headteachers therefore have occasionally been rather creative in their descriptions of their pupils' abilities, so that students remain in the MLD category rather than have more appropriate provision made for them elsewhere. The students mentioned in this report are a fair cross-section of the course members, but have all experienced particular difficulties with their language skills.

■ The IT provision for special needs students at Brooklands

The students in the report have followed the standard IT course as offered to all the special needs groups, but particular attention has been paid to their language and literacy requirements. The IT course includes options in the following subjects: word processing skills/language/ creative writing skills/desktop publishing/art/design/numeracy/social numeracy/databases/cartoon production programs relating to life skills/ control technology.

Each option includes some word processing, and as the students gain in confidence they are better able to manage their own learning programmes. The students are each initially assessed on the computers, to see what their level of competence is. Sometimes extra aids are required such as a keyguard, or different height of table. Factors such as dexterity, visual problems, past experience, spatial difficulties, and coordination are taken into account before the students are allowed to start work on any of the programs. It is felt to be important that the students do not feel any sense of failure at this early stage, as this may hinder their progress in the future. Many of them will make initial comments such as *'I'm no good at computers'* or *'I had enough of computers at school to last me a lifetime'*, but they are all encouraged to give the subject a fresh try in the new environment at College. After a couple of weeks, they are generally all 'hooked'! There is a great variation in the way that their schools have tackled the teaching of IT (if it has been tackled at all) the result being that some students are keen to further their knowledge as much as possible, and some are absolutely terrified of the equipment and think that they might inadvertently fuse the whole system. However, the advantages of such small teaching groups are tremendous, and there is usually time to meet most of their demands and requirements.

■ The results

□ Introduction

It is not easy to state precisely how much each student has gained from having been exposed to a fairly intensive method of teaching language and literacy, and neither is it really possible to give all of the students an 'end of the year grade' as they have all been struggling to improve their language skills in so many different ways (many of which may not be directly measurable, such as perseverance, enthusiasm or attitude). The students also attend classes with approximately ten other lecturers, not all of whom are in the GES Department, and it has not been feasible to involve all of them in the students' programme of work. The majority of the final comments are therefore only referring to progress that the students have made in their weekly IT classes. It was initially intended to give the group a reading test at the end of the year, such as Schonell or Neale, but as the original conditions of their tests at school must have varied greatly, such an idea was abandoned, as it was not felt that the results would tell anything that was not already known. It has also been thought that some sort of measurement of errors such as spelling errors or crossings out could be incorporated into their assessments, and this would no doubt have been useful in some ways. However, it was felt that as the students seem to fluctuate so much from week to week (depending on how they are feeling, if they are tired from having been on work experience, or if they have other project work in another part of their studies that is taking up a lot of their time), it would be better to form more general observations about how learning word processing has helped them with their language skills.

In the end, it was decided to send them all a simple questionnaire which their parents or family could help them fill in if necessary. A report was also written on each student, and a more general report on the whole group to comment on progress that they had made during the year. How did they feel about themselves and how did they perceive their successes and failures? Did they feel that word processing was a lot of hard work for little reward? Did they feel happier about coping with their literacy problems? In the Autumn term, a small discussion group was also formed, mostly made up from students in the CPVE course, and their report is included elsewhere.

At last the questionnaire was posted ...

■ Questionnaire on using computers for language work

After the end of the summer term (1988), a questionnaire was sent to 10

CEC students to enquire about how they felt they had benefited (or not benefited) by their time spent on the computers. The majority of the questions were deliberately given a positive slant, so that there was no feeling of the questionnaire being some type of 'end of year test'. The response was quick, and all the replies were returned within 10 days. This was encouraging, as less motivated students might not have spent their holiday time on such a task! Ten questions were asked, to which they had to reply true, sometimes, or not true ...

When I use the computer to work on, I think ...

(1)   It makes my work look neater

(2)   It helps me work quicker

(3)   It helps me concentrate

(4)   It's less difficult than handwriting

(5)   It is fun

(6)   It might be useful in the future

(7)   It helps me think clearly

(8)   It gives me a headache

(9)   It makes me a bit nervous

(10) It is a waste of time

The students were also asked how they felt the computers had helped them improve their English ...

They were requested to tick five (positive) points from a choice of ten:

- Fun
- Easy to learn on
- Smart printouts
- Easy to concentrate
- I can work harder
- You can correct mistakes easily
- Easier than writing by hand
- Useful for the future
- Helps me learn spellings better
- I like using different programs

The responses to the questionnaire were encouraging, and it seems that all students benefited from the hard work that they had put in over the last year. The questions have been regrouped according to the replies.

It is a waste of time true 0%, sometimes 0%, not true 100%.

The only question that all the group agreed about, and a pleasing end result to a year's hard work!

It helps me work quicker true 90%, sometimes 10%, not true 0%.

It's less difficult than handwriting true 90%, sometimes 10%, not true 0%.

Most of the group would probably not have answered these two statements in this way when they first arrived at College, but having mastered the basic skills, they did indeed find that they could produce more work in a shorter space of time than if they had handwritten it.

It makes me a bit nervous True 0%, sometimes 20%, not true 80%.

Once again, many of the group were initially very hesitant about using computers to work on, but soon gained in confidence.

It might be useful in the future True 70%, sometimes 30%, not true 0%.

Although most of the group would not consider that using a computer in an office or bank is a viable employment option for them, three of them will be attending IT evening classes next year, and Andrew is hoping to be able to use one of the BBCs at his Adult Literacy class.

It helps me to concentrate True 70%, sometimes 20%, not true 10%.

It makes my work look neater True 60%, sometimes 40%, not true 0%.

These two answers have been grouped together as they seem to complement each other. A student who is able to concentrate on his work without too many distractions should automatically be able to produce neater work. Word processing encourages the student to look at the layout and spacing of a piece of work, and enables the user to check his mistakes before making a final printout.

It helps me think clearly True 40%, sometimes 40%, not true 20%.

It gives me a headache True 20%, sometimes 40%, not true 40%.

It is fun True 30%, sometimes 70%, not true 0%

The last three comments have been grouped together as they show that the group have answered realistically about how they feel towards using computers for language work: 60% say that it gives them a headache 'usually or sometimes', although I suspect that most of them have taken the phrase to mean that they find some of the programs hard work. They are unsure whether using a computer can help them 'think clearly', although a lot of them said that it helps them to work more quickly and concentrate better.

The next part of the questionnaire required the students to state which five factors they felt had most helped them to improve their English. Their answers (in order of popularity) were as follows:

1st – Easier than writing by hand (9 votes). This was a very gratifying result, especially as at the beginning of their time at College they all seemed to feel that the idea of learning word processing was not going to help them improve their written work. The only person who did not tick this option was Lana, who has no real handwriting problems, and generally writes quite neatly and quickly.

2nd – Helps me learn spellings better (7 votes). All the 'poor spellers' ticked this option, Annette, Jerry and Sandra omitting it, as their spellings are nearly always correct. Hopefully, the programs have helped the group to improve upon their spellings, although some of them have very week memories and will need constant practice to maintain their standard of literacy when they leave College.

2nd – I like using different programs (7 votes). The CEC section is fortunate to have a very wide range of programs to suit most levels of ability. The software library contains nearly 200 different programs, many of which can be used for language work, and these were used in conjuction with the programs chosen for the study.

2nd – I can work harder (7 votes). Many of the students are easily distracted, even in the small class sizes that operate within the Special Needs section at Brooklands. Some of the computers are small carrels, so that it is not possible to sit and 'make faces' across the room. Also, the Self Teach Room which is used for much of the IT work is a distance from the main CEC base rooms, and some of the group find that being mixed in with some of the mainstream students tends to have a quietening effect.

2nd – You can correct mistakes easily (7 votes). Although the group all found some of the commands initially confusing, they all soon learnt how to use the delete keys, and were able to correct their work easily when required.

3rd – Useful for the future (5 votes). It was mostly the more able members of the group who ticked this statement, and although only one person (Annette) feels that she might use a computer for word processing in an employment situation, the others would like to maintain their skills which they feel might come in useful at a later date.

4th – Easy to learn on (3 votes). The group soon found that computers are not necessarily easy to learn on, in fact the work is frequently more demanding than other work they might do at College. Lana, Jerry and Steve ticked this option, three students who often find working in a normal classroom situation very distracting.

5th – Smart printouts (2 votes). Sandra and David chose this statement, both of whom have very poor handwriting. Sandra especially has found that handwriting is a real struggle, and much prefers to type whenever she can.

5th – Easy to concentrate (2 votes). The group seemed to accept that if a subject is interesting, it is naturally easy to concentrate, so did not rate this option very highly. David and Andrew ticked this answer, both of whom enjoy working in a peaceful environment.

6th – Fun (1 vote). 'Nasty medicine always does you the most good, doesn't it?' said Andrew one day, referring to his IT class. Only Lana felt that 'fun' would be one of her top five choices, although there has been a lot of good feeling and humour in IT lessons. Many of the group seem to feel that learning should not really be 'fun', and that if they are enjoying themselves, they cannot be learning very much. One of the most frequently heard comments around the Special Needs sections is, 'ooh, but it's not like school!'

■ Progress made during the year – general observations on the whole group

☐ Using equipment

Confidence in setting up the system

Most of the group were initially very hesitant about using the IT equipment and programs, having had very little experience of practical responsibilities during their time at school. For the students that were also in their first year at Brooklands (six of them) there was the added factor of the novelty of being at college, most of them having come from quite small special schools. They were all lacking in confidence as far as setting up the equipment was concerned, being anxious that they might accidentally damage something and get reprimanded for doing so. Having been convinced that the equipment was really quite 'foolproof' they seemed happier to become involved, and were given responsibility for 'switching the machines on and off' which on the whole they responded to well. At school, their teachers did not appear to have given them such tasks, which may partly explain some of their reticence.

Making use of the programs

Once again, they were all initially worried that something might go drastically wrong as a result of their imagined incompetence, such as losing all their work before they had a chance to print it out, or damaging the program disks by incorrect handling. Of course, such things are possible even for the teaching staff, but all the students had a 'code of practice' to follow and were taught to think carefully before making the next move, and to double check their actions with a friend if necessary. Some of the group became leaders in the sense that they picked up the various do's and don'ts fairly quickly, and were pleased to be able to offer advice to the less capable members of their groups.

Keyboard skills – manual dexterity/coordination

Most skills that are regularly practised can be improved upon given time, and throughout the year, the group were all able to say that they had improved their keyboard skills. With the exception of Annette, none of the group had been taught anything about which finger/hands to use for which alphanumeric or function keys, which must have wasted them a fair amount of time. Most of them sat at the computers with one hand firmly placed on their lap, using only one finger from their other hand to carry out a variety of functions.

This had the effect of slowing down the rate at which they could work through the programs, as they also sat as much as two feet away from the screen and keyboard. They seemed anxious to become 'too involved', possibly for fear of having to progress to more difficult programs which they (or their teachers) might not be able to understand.

☐   Using software

Understanding how to run the programs

Some of the less able students with weak memories found problems in remembering from week to week how to work through the programs, and would panic at the beginning of the lessons, feeling unable to get down to work without initial support. Andrew, Gill and David were three such examples, but after regular practice gained more confidence and settled down more quickly, although still requiring to ask a lot more questions than other students, mostly just to reassure themselves that they were on the right track. The CEC course very much encourages the students to take responsibility for their own learning, an idea to which most of the course members respond very well, bearing in mind that they seem to have had little experience of this previously.

Overcoming problems

Although much of the software used was designed especially for use with special needs groups, much of it still required a good amount of explanation and demonstration before the group felt able to use it with confidence.

Individual and group backup materials had to be produced for most of the programs, which was time consuming and should not really have been necessary. However, all the students made good progress with the programs used, becoming more confident as they got to know each program better. The group now feels more confident about tackling new programs which are presented to them, and are quite willing to try and evaluate new programs for use by other students – one of the most useful outcomes of the whole exercise! Some of the more able ones will also produce a 'quiz' on a new program, to help a new user to tackle the problem more effectively. There were no major problems with any of the software used, the main ones being poor graphics, poor instructions (written and on-screen), and unnecessarily complicated methods of producing a printout when required.

☐   Development of language skills

Written language and reading skills

All the students seemed to find it less of an effort to produce a larger volume of written work using a word processor than when writing by hand. Each student will have had his own reason or reasons for this – some found the keyboard easier to use than a pen or pencil; some found it clearer to see what they had written by looking at a screen in front of them as opposed to an exercise book on the table; some made good use of the editing facility and stopped worrying about their poor spelling; some simply enjoyed watching their near perfect work being printed out for all to see, and so on. Their enthusiasm for the written word had not been high at the beginning of the year, most of the group feeling some-what despondent about their literary abilities, and of the opinion that if they had not managed to 'learn English' by the time they left school, there was little point in their continuing in their agony at College. However, many children with learning difficulties have different patterns of learning to normal children, and for many, the age at which they leave school is by no means the age at which they have reached the peak of their academic ability. All the programs required at least a minimal level of reading ability (with the possible exception of CARTOON) and because the group found that they enjoyed using the programs, they felt encouraged to cope with the associated reading required.

Creative thought and spoken language

Roughly 40% of the lesson times was used for group activities, when the classes were encouraged to contribute ideas and discuss projects they were working on. Some of the group, notably Steve and Tony (usually quite shy lads) found it easier to discuss their work and ideas with the computer as a neutral 'third person'. They could talk to the machine instead of the group, yet still gaining valuable practice in public speaking. There was a sense of pride too in tasks well done, and even the more withdrawn members of the group were eager to display their latest work for others to see. In sessions devoted to creative writing activities, it was interesting to watch those students who normally found difficulties expressing themselves adequately on paper. For example, Glenda and Andrew coped far more easily with simple story writing than if they had had to do the same task on a sheet of paper. Andrew explained that he was no longer worried about his spelling as he would be able to correct it later on.

Keyboard skills – editing/criticizing

The group did find a lot of problems at first in coming to terms with the complexities of using a word processing package, albeit a relatively straightforward one. Some of them became anxious at this stage, and felt that they would never be able to remember all the commands that they needed to master the program. Jerry especially showed a lot of frustration, and frequently banged his hands down on the desk, saying he would 'never be able to get the hang of it!' On the whole, the group lacked the powers of concentration and determination that many of their mainstream peers usually possess, feeling that they were entitled to give up and go on to the next subject as soon as they started experiencing any obstacles.

They also found it initially difficult to criticize their own or their friends' work, feeling that this was a rather rude thing to do and might upset someone. However, as the weeks went on, they found this easier, and were able to offer helpful and tactful suggestions to their groups, and to see that their own work nearly always had room for improvements!

At the end of this study, a number of conclusions were reached about the effects of a word processing course on the participants' language development, and also about the effects of the course on their development in other areas (both within and outside of their College life). At the beginning of the study, it was tempting for the sake of simplicity to only try and measure those improvements which could be said to be directly related to their language skills, such as improved spelling, better grammar, faster keyboard speeds or less frequent use of Tipp-Ex.

However it appeared that the group have gained far more than simply having made some progress with the standard of their language work. For example, it was exciting to see that Sandra, Andrew and Gill can produce work up to five times more quickly when they are word processing. Having seen that a word processor can be a useful tool once they had learned to use it competently, they were able to produce more work (and of a better quality) than they might previously have been thought capable of, thus raising their level of self-esteem and appearing in a new light to other students and members of staff. They also gained much more than had originally been envisaged from the group activity sessions using programs such as MYSTERY or CARTOON, and were able to demonstrate confidently these programs to other groups of students. Three of them even appeared on Parents' Evening to do this! In a way, these unmeasurable side-effects have been of far more value than simply having learnt a new skill or improved on an old one.

Rosetta McLeod is an advisory teacher for computer-assisted learning in Scotland, and has carried out a number of studies on the use of computers in the classroom. She has recognized the importance of motivating and encouraging children who possess weak language skills, and writes that: 'Pupils who learn and appreciate that writing is fun gain a tremendous sense of power that motivates them to achieve high standards. Word processors can take over some of the tedious chores of writing, leaving pupils free to concentrate on the ideas, content and organization of their work ... this is not to suggest that all classroom writing should be computer-centered! Computers should be treated not as a threat but simply as one of a number of teaching and learning resources.'

Some of the group did in fact view the computers as somewhat of a threat, challenging them to improve their reading and writing when they themselves did not feel that there was much room for improvement. However, once they have begun to see how they could be helped by some of the programs, they gained in confidence and adopted a more positive attitude towards their studies.

The CEC students at Brooklands were fortunate to have access to a good range of IT equipment and a wide variety of programs, plus, on the whole, families who were supportive and caring. They were aware that if they ran home waving a piece of beautifully word processed text, someone would be interested enough to read it.

■ Main conclusions

Some problems which can be helped by using a computer for language and literacy work:

☐ Poor handwriting

For children who have problems with the mechanical side of hand-writing, word processing can offer a much less frustrating way of getting their thoughts on to paper. Some of these children may have an obvious handicap such as cerebral palsy or spina bifida, or others may have mild brain damage, or perhaps be left handed.

Any factor that inhibits a child from manipulating a pen or pencil will also inhibit his enthusiasm for handwriting, which can be an exhausting struggle: 90% of the group agreed that word processing is easier than handwriting and helps them to work more quickly.

☐   Concentration problems

Some of the students who normally find a lot of problems concentrating on their work in a classroom situation find that they can concentrate better when their work is before them on the screen. Those that have minor sight problems (Andrew and Anita) especially found this to be so, and were able to see their work more easily. 70% of the students replied that working on the computers helped them to concentrate better. This is also true of the CEC students who were not directly involved in the questionnaire, as many of them tend to be very distractible.

☐   Logical thought

Many students with special needs have difficulties thinking in a logical way, and the work on the computers can help them to organize their work in a better way which in turn will help them to 'know what they think and see what they say'. For example, this was especially useful when using CARTOON which involved the groups in a lot of cooperative work. They could all see on the screens very clearly what was being planned, and alter their decisions if required.

☐   Editing and correcting work

With the exception of Sandra and Annetta, the remainder of the group all experience problems with their grammar and spelling, which inhibits them from handwriting too much work which may be inaccurate and need later crossing out/Tipp-Exing or (in some cases, out of sheer frustration) screwing up and throwing in the bin. All the poor spellers agreed that some of the programs are very useful for helping them to learn and practise spellings, although it is very likely they will not retain their knowledge for any longer than spellings learnt by a more traditional method. However, the typing in process required by the programs does reinforce their knowledge in a positive way, and the spellings can be incorporated into other work where appropriate.

■   Implications for staff

☐   Staff training

There are still many staff who are very reluctant to use computers in their classrooms, for a number of reasons. The training available is still virtually non-existent, unless staff are prepared to undertake a course such as the part-time 'RSA Diploma in IT for Teachers' course, which lasts a year. Also older staff are often anxious about using the equipment, suffering, no doubt, from some of the same fears that the children have.

☐   **Cost of equipment and software**

The whole business can be costly, and unless a school or college is prepared to back the member/s of staff involved in teaching IT and word processing skills to the children, the exercise would probably be a somewhat fruitless one.

☐   **Quality control of software**

There is a very daunting array of programs on the market, whose manufacturers are all making claims that the use of the programs will cure a variety of afflictions. Without a member of staff being qualified, it would be necessary for a county adviser to help with choosing initial programs, or to make use of a local teachers' centre. Even so, there are many appalling programs that still seem to 'slip through the net!'

■   Individual experiences – Students at Brooklands Technical College, Weybridge

How Computers are Used on the Continuing Education Course (Moderate Learning Difficulties). An account written by some of the students on the CPVE option.

During the spring term of 1989, students on the CPVE course have brought their views together on various aspects of using computers on their course. A word processor was used by the students to collate these views and present them as a paper for this publication.

☐   **How do you think computers have been most useful to you?**

JE It has given me much more confidence than when I started in the first year of college. I think it will help me in the future when I start work, as I would like to work in a garage.

AN It has given me some idea of how computers can be used in daily life. Using the computers has also given me more confidence, as I now know what other people are talking about.

AD It has made me aware of the uses of the BBC computers in the college with the difference classes. Computers have helped me to write more clearly because people can't understand my handwriting very well.

JA They have helped me to improve my reading and spelling, especially by using the keyboard skills program. I don't enjoy hand writing much, so using the computer suits me better.

TO I found using the computer easier than handwriting as I am left handed and I am slow at writing. It also allows me to erase mistakes more easily. Using the computers has improved my spelling by using some of the spelling programs.

AR I think computers let you learn things more easily and teach you lots of things like how to type and write out programs for the BBC. I enjoyed collecting data for our databases assignment, and making printouts of our work.

JO I am not usually too good at art but the graphics packages have helped me a lot. The 'Keyboard Skills' program has helped me to improve my typing speed, which I am very pleased about!

☐   **How have computers helped you with reading and writing?**

AD When I started college, my reading and writing weren't up to standard. I started to work on a computer using a spelling program and I think it's helped me out a lot. When I go to electronics lessons I use Amstrad 1512s for control technology.

JE My English spelling is not very good, as my first language is German. When I use a computer I can rub out the spellings quicker, so I don't get so frustrated! The spelling programs have given me confidence in spelling English words.

AN Using the computer has enabled me to improve my spelling and punctuation. I found the editing facilities available on Wordwise very helpful.

AR Words printed on the screen are clearer for some people to read, so they don't have so many problems reading. The way that you can type in text is less messy, as when you make a spelling mistake, you can correct it more easily than on paper. I find the instructions clearer to follow than in a book.

CL I have found that the computer has helped me with my assignments for my courses. I mainly do rough outlines for essays in my computer lessons. It is easier to plan my work than on paper.

TO It's easier on the screen to see my handwriting, so I can spot my mistakes more easily. It's also easier to get my spellings correct, because I can see the words more clearly.

☐   **How did you feel when we first started to use computers?**

AN I was excited at the idea of being taught how to use BASIC, and felt quite confident. I managed to write some programs of my own quite easily. I would like to do GCSE Computer Studies next year if this is possible. I expected the IT lessons would be spent playing games on the computers.

AR I thought at first that it would be much harder. I found word processing was easier than I had expected, and I enjoyed seeing what the computer can do.

JE I was excited when I first started using computers at college because at school we always used computers just for games. I thought it would help me when we were set assignments.

TO I was excited when I first used the computers to do written work instead of playing games. I was amazed when I first saw my work being printed out, and felt very proud!

☐   **How do you feel now?**

AD When I went to a computer evening class, I felt much happier about using new programs. I started on different programs and I particularly enjoyed using the art and design program called 'Image'.

AR I feel that computers have shown me lots of different things like art programs and writing out texts. For example, when we use Wordwise, you can create your own texts. It is easy to run through different programs, and the computer shows you the instructions.

AN I feel very confident when asked to work on a computer. I now enjoy writing out and working out my own programs as I can learn so much to improve my knowledge of BASIC.

JA I feel more confident now because I know that what I have learnt will help me to use computers more effectively when I go to work.

CL I feel as though I'm getting along better than I did when I first started using computers.

☐   **What sort of programs do you feel are of most benefit to you?**

CL I think that word processing programs like Wordwise have been beneficial for my course work, in that they have made my work neater and easier to read.

JA I feel that some of the language and typing programs have helped me to improve my spelling. I have also managed to improve my keyboard skills quite a bit.

AR I think the most helpful programs are Wordwise, Folio, and some of the spelling programs which give you clues to the words.

AN Using some of the keyboard skill programs have helped me most, I think. I have also enjoyed working with the creative art and design programs, as I enjoy art anyway!

☐   **What do you think of:**

Word processing?

CL I think it is very useful because it helps my work look neater. It helps me to speed up my writing because I'm left handed, and also I find it difficult to write in a straight line.

AN I found word processing very useful but a little difficult to get to grips with.

AR I think word processing programs are very useful in that you can type out a text without worrying how many words and characters there are. You can change the position of the text if you don't think it is in the correct order or if it makes sense and you can see exactly how the text will be printed out and you can correct any word which is wrong.

CL I am still getting used to where the keys are on the keyboards as I still have to look where certain keys are.

Keyboard skills?

AN I enjoy using Keyboard skill programs as they give me practice on using the Keyboard properly. I also find some of the Keyboard skills' games fun.

AR I think that keyboard skills is useful because you have to find the letters on the keyboard as quick as you can. The keyboard shows you the letter or the word and you type it in under a certain time, plus it is quite like a game so for people with spelling problems find this fun to do.

JE When I used the computer keyboard skills I have to concentrate hard. With some of the games you have to react very quick, which makes you think clearly.

JA When I use the computer keyboard skills program it helps me to type quicker and it also helps me to learn more easily.

Paper 3.6

An Intelligent Tutoring System Approach to Teaching Primary Mathematics

Sara Hennessy, Tim O'Shea, Rick Evertsz and Ann Floyd

■ Introduction

It is becoming increasingly clear that information technology (IT) could potentially make a huge impact on mathematics education in the 1990s. Almost every school in Britain possesses at least one microcomputer, and nearly half of our primary school children have access to a computer at home (Straker, 1985). The advantages of using computers in teaching are numerous: children can progress at their own pace, being given plenty of time and practice to master each task – the computer is infinitely patient; computers can provide direct and immediate feedback, shaping performance and facilitating a progressive build-up of understanding; they can encourage children to solve their own problems and to call on one another (rather than their teacher) for help; finally, computers provide an effective motivator for groupwork and increase the opportunities for cooperative or socially interactive learning.

The introduction of IT to the classroom has overcome earlier fears that social isolation or a reduction of children's social skills would arise. The most up-to-date review of research on the social dimensions of computer-based learning (Light and Blaye, 1989) indicates that work

First published in *Educational Studies in Mathematics* (1989) **20**, 273–92 © 1989 Kluwer Academic Publishers. Reprinted by permission of Kluwer Academic Publishers.

with computers promotes a high level of task-related interaction and that discussion in the context of social interaction, particularly between pairs (Trowbridge, 1987), actually pushes children to achieve more. Various possible reasons for this have been speculated; one interesting finding is that collaborating with others in using a computer can be beneficial for shy children because direct eye contact is not required (Ball, 1986).

Microcomputers obviously have much to offer as tools for teaching mathematics. Yet, most of the existing software for primary arithmetic, at least, is fairly crude, and a recent survey of classroom computer use in England by Jackson *et al.* (1988) shows that drill-and-practice programs are the most commonly used. In our opinion, it is time (a) to invest much more heavily in the development of high-quality educational software for use in everyday classroom situations, and (b) to dispel the prevalent notion that the potential of computer-aided teaching is limited to drill-type activities or to those which simply keep children occupied quietly. With the provision of carefully developed software and backup support, computers could at last begin to make a truly significant contribution to classroom life. The computer might then be viewed – like the calculator – as the valuable resource which it is.

We believe that each such resource has its own important role to play within a wide range of pupil activities that aim to foster the development of mathematical thinking. Some of these activities may be computer based and others not; children might carry them out individually or in small groups. Opportunities for discussing what is happening and for reflection upon what has been experienced are an integral part of the whole enterprise. In this way it is possible for children both to capture particular experiences which may be of subsequent value and to form generalizations about mathematical processes which derive from sets of related experiences. In sum, an educational program, like the one we have developed ourselves, is one of many activities that can play a role in the learning environment of today's classroom.

■ Recent developments in intelligent tutoring systems

A new development in the field of IT and education – the construction of intelligent tutoring systems (ITSs) – further increases the potential value of computers as tools for learning. These systems have the added advantage of being adaptive to the needs and progress of an individual pupil. [...] In this section, we briefly mention some of the work recently carried out in this area that has influenced us.

One key piece of work has been the analysis of the motivational benefits of the 'computer game' format carried out by Malone (1981). An important idea of great generality is the notion that computers can be used to augment human memory capabilities in various ways (some of which are technically 'redundant').

One surprising weakness of most of the ITSs have been constructed to date has been the poor quality of the associated user interfaces. Some of the most celebrated programs in this area have presented the student or pupil via a 'glass teletype'. We have been profoundly influenced by Smith (1986) and his work on ARK, the Alternate Reality Kit. The ARK interface is based on a uniform physical metaphor and all the objects displayed on the screen can be 'directly manipulated' by a simulated hand controlled by a mouse operated by the user. This style makes life very much easier for the user who works out how to operate the displayed objects by treating them as if they were 'real'. We have also been influenced by the work of Foss (1987) who has developed ways of allowing students to express and graphically manipulate the solution paths generated in solving algebra problems.[...]

In common with a number of workers in this area we now do not perceive ourselves as being forced to choose between implementing prescriptive tutors that mimic didactic human teachers and designing non-prescriptive microworlds that effectively force the student to master a new programming language and then reinvent the laws of mathematics or physics. Our belief is that it is possible to construct learning environments which are qualitatively different from both simulated tutors and microworlds. The students should be able to work with attractive user interfaces whose operation they can understand, they should be able to explore and ask for help, and the environment should be able to intervene if appropriate or necessary. Judging appropriateness or necessity depends on some form of student modelling and the help or intervention should be offered in a way that relates sensibly to the user interface. In our system we use the 'Martian shopkeepers'.

Our general views on the current state of the art coincides fairly closely with the recent account given in Wenger's book (1987). Our work can be distinguished by our interface design principles, by our commitment to supporting group work and by our belief in the importance of basing our design on heterogeneous data sources, this includes 'anthropological' data such as that collected by Carraher *et al.* (1988) in their work on 'street arithmetic'.

■ *Shopping on Mars*: An intelligent computer tutor for informal arithmetic

In this section we describe the design of our computer-based educational activity, *Shopping on Mars*. Development of this program is the major outcome of the project, 'An Intelligent Computer Tutor for Arithmetic', whose objective was to carry out research and development work on an adaptive computer tutor for informal arithmetic calculation. As previous work in this field was exclusively concerned with formal methods of arithmetic, *Shopping on Mars* is the first program of its kind. The rationale for our concern with informal mathematics is presented below.

☐   Educational rationale for informal algorithms

It became clear to us in the early stages of the project that our work needed to keep pace with the changing emphasis of arithmetic teaching in the United Kingdom and elsewhere, namely the increased importance of the calculator and the corresponding reduced importance of standard paper-and-pencil algorithms. It is now widely recognized that the standard written methods are frequently not understood – even after many years of endeavour – and are rarely used outside school (Fitzgerald, 1985; French, 1987). Olivier points out that 'it makes little sense for children to spend several hundred hours of precious classroom time on skills that society no longer requires, that the individual can do almost as well without, and that probably drive many pupils away from mathematics altogether' (Olivier, 1988, p. 17). It seems evident that the wide availability of calculators – and increasingly, of computers – should bring about a major change in the way children learn arithmetic. The fact that both adults and children now have access to number-crunching machines which are fast, accurate, easy to use and cheap, has indeed led many researchers in this field (Plunkett, 1979; Shuard, 1986) to conclude that there is little future for the standard written algorithms. We endorse Margaret Brown's view that a combination of reliable mental methods and the ability to use a calculator are probably sufficient for all practical purposes (Brown, 1981).

The advent of the electronic calculator has meant that educators are finally free to replace the traditional curricular focus on practice and memorization with an emphasis on understanding and creative problem solving. We can concentrate on helping children to develop their understanding of number, including the meaning of place value, so that they become mathematical thinkers. While we cannot allow completely open-ended activities, they must be sufficiently unstructured so as to encourage children to build their own models of given problems based on their pre-existing methods of reasoning. These models should represent problems as involving operations on quantities – rather than on formal symbols or on concrete objects, and this entails paying attention to every step of the procedure. One obvious way to facilitate this process is to foster a variety of informal methods of calculation. Learning to execute sophisticated mental techniques and, in particular, shortcuts, necessarily involves reflection upon the procedure itself.

'Informal methods' of arithmetic can include manipulation of concrete aids and non-standard written algorithms as well as mental ones, but we will concentrate on mental methods here. These mostly involve breaking down or 'partitioning' numbers into easy-to-handle parts (typically tens and units), operating on the parts separately, and recombining the partial results. Other common strategies include counting on (in ones or steps of any convenient size), rounding up or down, successive addition or subtraction (often via decimal regrouping), and using known number facts (including ties, commutative or zero facts). Calculations sometimes entail a combination of strategies or operations, and the order of executing steps can vary. Some examples from our data are:

$$22 + 59: 20 + 60 + 2 - 1 = 81$$
$$98 - 29: 98 - 10 = 88, - 10 = 78, - 9 = 69$$
$$7 \times 9: 7 \times 8 = 56, 57, 58 \ldots \text{(counting)} \ldots 63$$

The majority of people naturally invent such methods of calculation for themselves. These personal methods are favoured over standard ones because they are generally simpler, more efficient and more often successful. They are also very flexible – they can be adapted according to the numbers involved – and are more suited to the minds and purposes of the users. Informal methods can even be used by teachers and educators in diagnosing children's understanding of number and of place value. Primary school children's knowledge of place value is known to be very shaky (Bednarz and Janvier, 1982) and the learning of calculation methods that commonly involve breaking down numbers into their base-ten components can be a very fruitful enterprise.

While calculators are becoming increasingly available in mathematics classrooms and detailed curricula based upon their use are being developed (most prominently by the PrIME project team: PrIME, 1988), the advantages of informal arithmetic algorithms have not always been recognized. Many teachers and parents are resistant to any significant deviation from 'proper' written methods. As a result, explicit teaching or fostering of informal methods of calculation is rare, and most mathematics schemes do not undertake this task. Until teachers become confident of the effectiveness of children's spontaneously generated strategies, these personal techniques will remain incompatible with conventional teaching methods. This incompatibility means that school-based mathematical activity is often divorced in the child's mind from the mathematics which is all around us in everyday situations (Harris, 1987).

In sum, to help children learn to use mathematics as a powerful tool for exploring their environment and to solve real-world problems efficiently and with understanding, the primary school curriculum must explicitly promote calculation methods. We have developed an educational computer program, *Shopping on Mars*, which is based on this premise.

□   **Design of *Shopping on Mars***

The overall objective of the Intelligent Arithmetic Tutor project is to help children learn to treat arithmetic as a means for manipulating represen- tations of quantities and to help them learn to formulate shortcuts and efficient methods for problem solving. Our research entails constructing computer-based activities which foster arithmetic principles and which aid us in diagnosing important misunderstandings in relation to those principles. The diagnostic components are used in the development of student models for the computer tutor. We have set up a system in which the computer is an intelligent participant in activities involving small groups of children; the tutor will build up experience enabling it to make sensible judgements. Development of our programs involves close observation of classroom teaching patterns and extensive longitudinal work – examining variation both within and between individuals. This means attempting to characterize the conceptual knowledge underlying children's informal arithmetic procedures and carrying out field trials of the activities with individuals and groups of children.

The research carried out for this project has confirmed that it is possible for children having no prior experience with computers to understand a computer's actions, and for computer not only to keep accurate student records, but to alter its behaviour according to the various knowledge states of different individuals. Our research has in fact broken new ground and overcome come of the shortcomings of earlier work. Specifically, progress has been made towards decomposing a set of commonly used mental algorithms into their subprocedural and concep- tual components. A broad hierarchy of invented strategies in terms of sophistication and efficiency of use in given situations has been constructed. We have started to build a diagnostic system which assesses children's ability on small arithmetic tasks, examines their understanding of basic mathematical concepts, and uses information from the pupils' activities to build a model of their arithmetic skills. The *Shopping on Mars* program requires children to give explicit descriptions of the steps involved in their personal calculation methods. Based on data of this kind, we have evolved a sophisticated description language for child- computer interaction. This language and other components of the *Shopping on Mars* program are described in some detail on pages 300, 301 and 302, but first, an overview is given here.

The activity takes the form of a (non-violent) adventure game and is implemented on the Acorn Archimedes 310 microcomputer. It is aimed at children aged 8–12 and has minimal linguistic content, although children must be familiar with money in order to use it. A range of skills and concepts in primary schools arithmetic instruction are supported. The main purpose of the activity is to help children realize that different types of problems are sometimes best solved using different calculation methods and that the appropriateness of calculation techniques depends on problem structure as well as on the numbers involved. Thus, children obtain practice in using the various calculation methods available and in assessing their relative usefulness.

The tasks presented in *Shopping on Mars* are as similar as possible to those encountered in everyday, 'real world' situations such as shopping. The problems involve addition, subtraction and multiplication of positive whole numbers. The children need to (a) decide which operation is to be performed in each problem situation, (b) choose a computation method and perform the calculation, and (c) report the result using a special language for representing mental algorithms on the computer. (An on-screen calculator can sometimes be used to speed up the second step and eliminate the third; this enables the child's attention to remain on the problem more easily.) A variety of complex skills are involved in the tasks and these may include: describing a procedure in a precise and step-by-step manner; following or using a procedure described by the machine; evaluating and comparing alternative procedures; modifying a procedure to cope with new problem situations; finding and correcting erroneous steps in a procedure.

The *Shopping on Mars* game proceeds as follows. Two players land on Mars in a rocket with no remaining fuel and proceed to cooperate in a series of purchasing tasks. The players' primary aim is to obtain 'fuel' with which to return to Earth. They are represented by astronaut figures who navigate around the Mars landscape in a 'Marsmobile' in search of the fuel shop. Their progress is thwarted by a series of obstacles which may be overcome by buying certain items at nearby shops. While the children act as customers who takes turns in purchasing items and are encouraged to check their change, the computer plays the role of shopkeeper and controls the level of difficulty. It also attempts to make intelligent interventions, acting particularly to encourage the use of efficient calculation tools and informal methods of calculation. The tutor knows all of the common methods, enabling it to obtain information about the intermediate steps in children's invented methods, and to give help where needed. A chronological record is kept of how far individuals have progressed and of their difficulties. Student records are stored on personal disks for access by teachers and pupils. These records are used to construct the current model of the student whenever they use the activity.

Intervention occurs between scenes as well as during shopping transaction. Although there is no rigid path of progression through the game, there is some constraint on the order of movement between shops because a series of simple obstacles arises that have to be overcome. These include physical obstacles which require solution through making certain purchases in certain shops, as well as manipulations of children's choice of calculation method.

Figure 1

☐ **Interface: players' views of the game**

Environmental levels

The child has access to three basic views. The first is a global view of the **Martian landscape** showing the position of the Marsmobile relative to the rocket and Martian shops. External obstacles occur at this level. An example of an obstacle is a landslide which creates a rockfall, automatically cleared after a wheelbarrow and shovel have been purchased. Shops selling appropriate items are situated at various points along a road between the rocket landing site and the fuel shop. The order of the obstacles encountered and thus the route taken between shops in each game is altered for variety.

Where appropriate, screen images are zoomable so that close-up perspectives can be taken. Thus, the **inside of a shop** looms into view automatically upon reaching its door. A replica of the screen image of one inside view can be seen in Figure 1. There is a counter with a till and a sliding tray, a Martian shopkeeper behind the counter, a display of goods labelled with price tags, a shopper with money contained in a zoomable purse in a zoomable shopping bag (clicking on these items enlarges them). This bag is worn by either shopper and acts as a container for their purchases. Items for sale may include a decoy item or a working calculator, which can be used twice before its batteries run out. The control panels show whose turn it is at any one time via colour-coded name labels; the active child's name is highlighted. Finally, when the shopper moves up to the **counter**, it zooms into close-up view so that maximum space is available for the purchasing transaction. The purse, calculator, money and objects to be bought can then be easily manipulated.

The activity's interface was designed around the theme of direct manipulation (Shneiderman, 1983). Thus, all objects on the screen are controlled using a (single-button) mouse-driven cursor: a grabbing hand. This feature pre-empts the difficulties caused by children's very limited keyboard skills (the latter are known to impose severe limitations on computer-based instruction; Crook, 1986). In using the direct manipulation interface, children learn to map mouse operations on to simple 'metaphorical' physical activities such as picking up change and opening the purse. Moreover, the conventions for entering and exiting shops, opening and closing tills, and so on reduce the screen clutter.

Going shopping

Having encountered an obstacle, the shoppers drive to a shop in order to purchase an item with which to overcome the obstacle. Once inside the shop, the active shopper acts by clicking on objects it wishes to buy and taking them to the counter. Additional tasks entail finding the total cost of two items with different prices, subtraction involves calculating what a discounted item will cost, and multiplication involves calculating how much x items at y pence would cost. After calculating the total cost, the players have to hand over to the Martian shopkeeper the correct amount of money (from the zoomable purse), and check their change, if any.

Instructions and help are given to the children by the shopkeeper at various points during the game; they are spoken and simultaneously printed on the screen in a message box. In particular, children are encouraged to check their change after each transaction and to indicate that it is right or wrong. The shopkeeper sometimes shortchanges the child blatantly. Occasionally, players will be asked to demonstrate how they worked out the total cost; they then enter an account of their method using our special description language (see page 301).

Finally, we believe that in order to derive most benefit from the activity, extensive experience with it will probably be necessary. Children and teachers will have the choice of engaging with a short, medium or long version, the latter with most tasks to be completed. This is separate from intervention according to ability, whereby the difficulty of the tasks given varies according to what is known about the pupils.

Implementation

Shopping on Mars is programmed in C. The base machine is the Archimedes 310, which is very fast, has high-quality colour graphics and a large screen, and is subsidized by the British government for use in schools. A Dolphin 'Apollo' speech synthesizer is used as an optional extra for presenting instructions and making interventions. Development of the description language, student modelling and the instructional architecture took place using a Xerox 1109 artificial intelligence workstation, which runs Lisp. This prototyping saved a lot of time since it enabled us to make simple changes quickly.

☐   *Protocol collection and 'intelligent' interventions*

The instructional architecture

The program's overall goal is to foster the development of a flexible repertoire of mental arithmetic algorithms, coupled with the ability to select the most appropriate one for a given problem. Appropriateness depends of course on the individual student; the tutor's control structure involves first ascertaining what calculation-specific concepts and methods the child already possesses, and then selecting a new method to teach the child. The method chosen is constrained by the child's understanding of arithmetic.

The program consists of a set of tutorial rules (the 'Executive'), which encode heuristic information about what action to take next: for example, whether to teach, to model a child's problem-solving behaviour, or to alter the level of problem difficulty. The system's two other main components are a diagnostic module (for modelling calculation methods and inferring the conditions constraining the child's use of a rule), and a problem generator which can set up a problem for the child, based on the constraints imposed by the Executive. It is not normally possible to ascertain what mental arithmetic algorithm the child has used on the basis of answer data alone; intermediate step information is indispensable. A special graphical description language was created to meet this need; it also serves to reduce considerably the huge space of rules which must be searched.

The description language

In developing a tutor for this domain, we were faced with the problem of designing a language for describing mental arithmetic which is both rich enough to encompass the diverse processes used by children, sufficiently simple to be easily learned and used, and suitable for demonstrating new algorithms to the child (that is, the language used for exemplar presentation should be the same as that used to obtain student protocols). To this end, we have developed the Graphical Arithmetic Description Language (GADL). It again embodies the principle of direct manipulation and is based on the simple metaphor that numbers and arithmetical expressions are objects which can be manipulated by arithmetical tools (Evertsz *et al.*, 1988). The mouse operations and movement conventions are carried over from the 'shopping' interface.

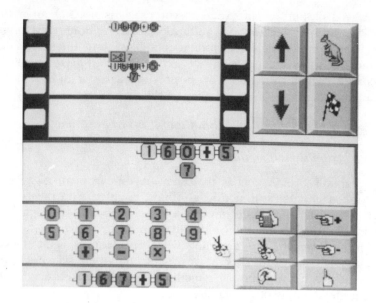

Figure 2

The GADL interface (see Figure 2) consists of a number of objects, and six on-screen tools for manipulating them. Objects comprise encircled numerals and arithmetic operation symbols which can be hooked together (a **2** joined to a **6** forms **26**). Tools include incrementing and decrementing tools (which take arguments), a deletion tool and a number fact one. There is also a 'partitioning tool' for splitting up a number or the terms of a problem. Both objects and tools are accessed via a mouse-driven grabbing hand. The screen is scrollable so that the child can access and return to previous steps. It is important to note that GADL is not a calculation device; the child has already solved the problem mentally and is now retrospectively describing what he or she did. Although this description often takes longer than the original calculation, the graphical representation reduces working memory load since all of the child's solution steps are explicitly available on the screen (Bonar and Cunningham, 1986). This feature is just as important when the shopkeeper demonstrates solutions through the medium of GADL.

The description language influences children's development of informal methods through encouraging the use of certain ways of operating with number and certain representations of the steps involved in a mental calculation, and through limiting other means of representation. For instance, a common error is partitioning one instead of ten – the GADL interface forces children to work with tens and hopefully to realize their significance. We have also deliberately excluded mental calculation which mimics the conventional column-by-column written algorithms. Due to lack of resources (memory constraints), erroneous calculator algorithms, money-counting algorithms, and multiplication carried out using a division operation are uncapturable too.

Strategies for intervention

Our general strategies involve intervening whenever a 'new' kind of problem is presented which causes difficulties, particularly if the child has made an inappropriate choice of problem-solving method. A useful technique for intervening in the first instance is to rephrase the question or problem. This has proved successful during field trials because children do not always grasp immediately what is required of them. Ultimately, the shopkeeper may have to offer some help or present a new subgoal. If the child is still stuck, the second child can be consulted.

Some further kinds of 'intelligent' interventions we have included are as follows. Prices and the range of goods available in the shops are adjusted if the arithmetic involved is proving too easy or too difficult for an individual. We can also alter the calculation tools allowed and enforce the use of mental calculation. The program comments on accuracy as well as continually providing exemplars of efficient informal methods and incentives to use them. If a child's algorithm has too many arduous steps, a similar problem is set and an alternative, shorter method is suggested for solving it. We try to get children to draw on prior solutions and strategies where relevant. Our suggestions are made on the basis of a previously determined hierarchy of efficient strategies for given situations. By way of example, methods involving partitioning both numbers into their units, tens and hundreds components are most efficient in many problem situations.

☐ Preliminary field trials

Interface and intervention

We have tested the *Shopping on Mars* program extensively in two local primary schools; so far, 120 children aged 8-12 have taken part in the field trials. The methods we have used comprised clinical interviews and protocol collection, coupled with videotaping and analysis of child–computer interactions. The collection of video data (in conjunction with an experimenter's note-taking) provided a very effective and accurate record of the children's problem solving during testing and the children showed no adverse reaction whatsoever to being filmed. Most of the time, we recorded the screen image – in conjunction with the children's verbal interaction on the soundtrack – so that the detail of their work with the system could be analysed. This type of video was felt to be more valuable during development work than filming the children themselves.

In order to iron out at an early stage any obvious problems arising with the interface, a cardboard version of the game was used before programming on the Archimedes was completed. We constructed a simulated Martian shop, employing plastic money and cardboard materials. One experimenter acted as the shopkeeper during the game, setting tasks according to the perceived ability of each pair of subjects, and another experimenter made interventions and recorded the children's responses (on paper, audio tape, and occasionally on video). Interviewing individuals in this context and requiring them to make the steps of their algorithms explicit, allowed us to gather a significant amount of data on how children calculate mentally. Their actual preferred methods were compared with known common ones and found to be very similar. All of the (correct) informal methods obtained during the fieldwork were specified as rules and entered into the tutor's production system.

The *Shopping on Mars* activity was tested during all stages of its development on the Archimedes microcomputer and many iterations were required to make the system usable. (Much of the iterative work related to *simplifying* the interface and *improving* the system's response time.) The activity proved very successful with children in this age group (8-12). With only one or two exceptions, all of the children tested could (a) quickly and easily learn to use the mouse-driven cursor to drag objects, (b) use the direct manipulation interface to carry out shopping transactions involving manipulation of screen money, (c) operate an on-screen calculator and (d) understand the notion of containers. The activity was very popular with the children and we believe that the effort spent on good quality graphics was repaid by their positive response. The adventure game format, known to promote the richest form of discussion between children working with computers (Crook, 1987), also proved to be highly motivating. However, we do not yet have evidence concerning whether children can generalize from the fantasy context of Mars to real-world problem-solving situations. We also tested our strategies for intervention and refined them continually according to their perceived success with the children until an extensive tutorial specification was obtained. We observed that the program does encourage children to reflect upon their problem solving, and that this reflection frequently results in the detection of an error or the use of an improved informal method of calculation. Again, however, the studies reported here were preliminary, and we plan to do some intensive testing of the program to see if it actually helps to promote change in children's strategies over time.

Description language

One aim of the fieldwork was to measure the success of our description language as a medium for two-way communication of informal algorithms. We found that the children were usually able to achieve a reasonable grasp of all the tools and functions of the GADL within a half-hour session. The skills they could demonstrate included (a) forming numerical strings and expressions, (b) using a variety of tools to transform number and (c) operating a scrolling bar enabling them to review an arithmetic procedure. Fifteen of our subjects were given a second session with GADL after time periods ranging from 1-11 weeks. We observed that after a few minutes of recap by the experimenter, most (nine) of the children could recall the interface sufficiently well to be able to use it again to communicate their informal algorithms to the computer, with minimal prompting from the experimenter. This was true even after the longest time periods.

We have also tried using the GADL to teach children new informal methods for addition, subtraction and multiplication. Those methods were of similar or greater complexity than the ones we had previously observed the children using. They consisted of alternative – usually more efficient – strategies for solving problems similar to or harder than those which the children had successfully solved before. Twelve of our previous subjects (aged 9-12) took part in a preliminary study. The experimenter used the GADL and a limited verbal description (of the kind we later represented using a dialogue box and synthesized speech) to demonstrate algorithms for the various operations. Each individual was shown algorithms which we had not previously observed them using. We found that in 94% of cases ($n = 34$), the children could pick up a new method from the GADL description and could apply it to a new problem. In four of the successful cases, it was first necessary for the experimenter to repeat the new method once.

The results indicate that the GADL has a great deal of potential as a means for communicating sophisticated mental arithmetic algorithms to children. The majority of children relate easily to the metaphor of numbers as manipulable objects and quickly acquire skill at using the interface; direct manipulation works here because of the success of this metaphor. A spin-off from the data resulting from these studies was the specification of a diverse set of common mental methods.

■ Role of the activity in the classroom and its educational outcomes

The specific educational intentions of *Shopping on Mars* are as follows. To begin with, it makes children aware of a variety of tools for calculation through providing practice in using those technologies and it helps them to make sensible choices between more and less efficient means of calculation. Furthermore, children are engaged in modelling real-world situations and are building upon methods that they themselves have devised previously, so that their mathematics is rooted in first-hand experience. They also externalize and track their own working, which has the virtue of facilitating reflection on the procedures they are following and of enabling the other participants to comment upon them. Checking skills are fostered too, both as a means of raising the likelihood of accuracy and in order to help children learn when and how to estimate. Finally, and overarching all the above, the activity is designed to be a rich and cooperative learning experience in which children help each other with choice of technology, with deciding on procedures to be followed, with 'explaining' their procedures to the computer tutor, and with checking.

Shopping on Mars encourages collaboration between two players through its requirement that they cooperate to reach a common goal. Inherent in the program's design is the notion of turn-taking. While control alternates between the two players, the children or computer can summon help from the non-active player when necessary. Field trials have shown that this design was successful in making *Shopping on Mars* a very interactive activity. In sum, we have attempted to construct a *three-way activity* in which the participants are two children and the computer tutor. We have tried to capitalize on the very distinct strengths of the three participants. The children are able to listen to each other's ideas and to check each other's calculations. The computer tutor can alter the parameters of the tasks in hand, build up models of the children's informal methods and act as a role model for procedures which the children have not yet developed. It can also furnish the teacher with valuable information about the children's progress and levels of understanding which he or she can then use either simply as a record of achievement, or as a means of deciding on future activities for the children concerned. It may be that some quite different activity is deemed appropriate for one or other of the children, or that more productive pairing of children is possible, or both.

Shopping on Mars has been designed to enable children to engage productively with it without the need for frequent teacher intervention. This has to be an essential characteristic of any small group activity in any typical classroom. The teacher is thereby enabled to deploy his or her talents wherever they are most needed in the classroom. Sometimes this will be working alongside the children working on *Shopping on Mars*, of course, but there will be many other demands on the teacher arising from the needs of all the other children in the class, and these will require his or her presence elsewhere. *Shopping on Mars* will all the time be building up information on the progress of individual children, which the teacher can consult at any point in order to guide future plans. Because of these twin features of constructive use independent of teacher presence, and its information building facility, it seems to us that the activity has the potential to play a valuable role in the reality of today's classrooms.

■ Conclusion

A great deal of time and effort has been put into the development of the activity *Shopping on Mars*. We consider that the time is well spent because the outcome potentially includes a general structure which will facilitate the development of further activities in which the computer tutor is an 'intelligent participant'. Three broad characteristics of this general structure are clear. First, the activity's direct manipulation interface provided a uniquely high degree of both interaction with the child and realism of the manipulations involved in the activity. Secondly, we have developed a 'description language' which can be used in many other contexts to enable children to communicate their procedures, both to each other and to the computer tutor. Thirdly, we are beginning to evolve an approach to ICAI which concerns a three-way interaction, rather than the more usual one-to-one model; we will thereby have gained insights into how we can capitalize upon the fact that another child is always present and can play an intelligent role throughout. In addition, we have produced, but not yet implemented, a simple specification allowing the program to take account of both players' known mathematical capabilities in devising its tutorial strategies. However, the task of getting the modeller to cope with the interaction between two students proved too complex for the scope of this project.

We consider that development of an innovative medium for child–computer communication was an extremely worthwhile pursuit and one which has useful implications for future programs. The graphical description language provides us with a unique and effective means of both capturing informal calculation methods and communicating new methods to the child. However, we are interested in exploring other potential means of child–computer communication and the possibility of overcoming some inevitable shortcomings of our initial prototype. The language sometimes takes a long time to use when a child is mid-transaction (this can lead to forgetting or losing one's place in the game). Moreover, some less common algorithms can only be expressed clumsily in GADL and some unusual behaviours cannot be expressed at all (such as methods based on the visualization of pointers moving up and down an imaginary number line); this is the classic trade-off between the simplicity and expressivity of a language. It is improbable that GADL could be extended to encompass such visual algorithms – rather, we envisage such a need being fulfilled by a separate number line interface. Similarly, GADL cannot cope with finger counting. Another omission is mental counting errors (since incrementing and decrementing operations are performed automatically by the computer). We hope that other researchers will continue our work in this area and that a description language which overcomes some of these drawbacks will eventually emerge.

There is considerable scope for further development of the *Shopping on Mars* program. We have designed a series of sophisticated refinements to the interface and to our strategies for diagnosis and intervention, which, it is hoped, will one day be implemented. One example of our ideal refinements would be to provide the users with explicit reasons for using the calculation strategies demonstrated by the program and to describe clearly the conditions under which they are most appropriately used. Simon *et al.*'s (1987) study of the significant factors in learning with microcomputers indicates that these provisions enable children to continue using newly learned strategies when they are faced with new or possibly more complex situations.

■ Acknowledgements

The authors are indebted to three other members of their project team at the Open University, namely Roshni Devi, Mike Fox, and Dave Perry, for their invaluable assistance with many aspects of the research. We carried out our work in conjunction with a commercial software house, System Applied Technology Ltd, and would like to express sincere thanks to Phil Black, Rob Brown, Dave Ellis, and Bourne Hurst for contributing their ideas and their considerable programming expertise.

We are grateful to the staff and pupils of Springfield School and Simpson School in Milton Keynes for their kind cooperation during our fieldwork phases.

This research was funded by the Science and Engineering Research Council through the UK 'Alvey' programme of advanced information technology research.

■ References

Ball, D.: 1986, *Microcomputers in Maths Teaching*, Hutchinson, London.

Bednarz, N. and Janvier, B.: 1982, 'The understanding of numeration in primary school', *Educational Studies in Mathematics* **13**, 39-57.

Bonar, J. and Cunningham, R.: 1986, *Bridge: An Intelligent Tutor for Thinking About Programming*, Learning Research and Development Center technical report, University of Pittsburgh.

Brown, M.: 1981, 'Number operations', in K. Hart (ed.), *Children's Understanding of Mathematics*: 11 to 16, John Murray, p. 47.

Carraher, T., Schlieman, A. and Carraher, D.: 1988, 'Mathematical Concepts in Everyday Life', in G. Saxe and M. Gearhart (eds.), *Children's Mathematics*, Jossey-Bass, San Francisco.

Crook, C.: 1986, 'The use of wordprocessing to support writing as a joint activity', *Second European Developmental Psychology Conference*, Rome.

Crook, C.: 1987, 'Computers in the classroom: defining a social context', in J. Rutkowska and C. Crook (eds), *Computers, Cognition and Development*, Wiley, Chichester.

Evertsz, R., Hennessy, S. and Devi, R.: 1988, *GADL: A Graphical Interface for Mental Arithmetic Algorithms*, CITE technical report no. 49, Open University.

Fitzgerald, A.: 1985, *New Technology and Mathematics in Employment*, Dept. of Curriculum Studies, University of Birmingham.

Foss, C.: 1987, *AlgebraLand*, Psychology Ph.D Thesis, Stanford University.

French, D.: 1979, 'Mental methods in mathematics', *Mathematics in Schools*, 8(2), 39-41.

Harris, M.: 1987, 'Mathematics in work', *Institute of Education Research Seminar*, University of London.

Hennessy, S., Evertsz, R., Ellis, D., Black, P., O'Shea, T. and Floyd, A.: 1988 *Design Specification for 'Shopping on Mars', a Computer-based Educational Activity*, CITE technical report no. 29, Open University.

Jackson, A., Fletcher, B. and Messer, D.J.: 1988, 'Effects of experience on microcomputer use in primary schools: Results of a second survey', *Journal of Computer Assisted Learning* 4, 214–226.

Light, P. and Blaye, A.: 1989, 'Computer-based learning: The social dimensions', in H. Foot, M. Morgan and R. Shute (eds.), *Children Helping Children*, Wilely, Chichester.

Malone, T. W.: 1981, Towards a theory of intrinsically motivating games', *Cognitive Science* 4, 333–369.

Olivier, A.: 1988, 'The future of pencil-and-paper algorithms in the arithmetic curriculum', *Pythagoras* 17, 11–16.

Plunkett, S.: 1979, 'Decomposition and all that rot', *Mathematics in Schools* 8(3), 2–7.

PrIME Project: 1988, 'One year of CAN', Homerton College, Cambridge.

Shneiderman, B.: 1983, 'Direct manipulation: A step beyond programming languages', *IEEE Computer* 16(8), 57–69.

Shuard, H.: 'Primary mathematics towards 2000', *Mathematical Gazette* 70, 175–185.

Simon, T., McShane, J. and Radley, S.: 1987, 'Learning with microcomputers: Training primary school children on a problem-solving program', *Applied Cognitive Psychology* 1, 35–44.

Smith, R.B.: 1986, 'The Alternate Reality Kit: an animated environment for creating interactive simulations', *Proceedings of IEEE Computer Society Workshop on Visual Programming*, pp. 99–106, Dallas, Texas. [See also Paper 3.7 of this volume]

Straker, A.: 1985, 'Another look at primary mathematics with a micro', *Micromath* 1(2), 13–15 and 26.

Trowbridge, D.: 1987, 'An investigation of groups working at the computer', in D.E. Berger, K. Pezdek and W.P. Banks (eds.), *Application of Cognitive Psychology: Problem Solving, Education and Computing*, Erlbaum, Hillsdale, pp. 47–58.

Wenger, E.: 1987, *Artificial Intelligence and Tutoring Systems*, Kaufmann, Los Altos.

Paper 3.7

The Alternate Reality Kit: An Animated Environment for Creating Interactive Simulations

Randall B. Smith

[...]

■ Introduction

[...] The designer of a system for use by novices can gain great advantage by basing the interface on a known metaphor. If the computer behaves in a way analogous to a system already understood by the user, the learning time will be greatly reduced. Interface features that are true to the designer's metaphor might be called *literal*. The learnability of literalism makes it a good thing.

However, the designer can always provide the user with enhanced capabilities at the price of breaking out of the metaphor. These features might allow the user to do wonderful things that are far beyond the mundane capabilities of literal features. Capabilities that violate the metaphor in order to provide enhanced functionality might be called *magical*. The power of magic makes it a good thing.

There is a tradeoff between the learnability of literalism and the power of magic. I employ this tension as a way to present my experiences in designing and observing users of the Alternate Reality Kit, a metaphor-based system being developed for non-expert computer users.

The Alternate Reality Kit (ARK) is intended to allow users to play in and create their own simulated worlds. ARK is based on a strong analogy to the physical world. Many of the important capabilities of ARK are *literal*: they are transcriptions into the computer of physical world behavior. Even though the system is designed for use by inexperienced users, ARK has certain magical characteristics. Observations of users suggest that ARK demonstrates that even metaphor-based systems designed for novices can benefit from a small amount of magic. Although each magical feature requires a brief explanation, the basic functionality can still be taught in a few minutes.

This paper is about the Alternate Reality Kit: it is a brief introduction to the ARK user interface in terms of the magic-literalism dimension. For more complete description of the functionality and philosophy behind ARK see Smith (1986). I will not attempt much in the way of a general discussion of the tension between magic and literalism: I simply employ this tension as a useful way of analyzing the central features of ARK's interface. However, ARK does serve as an example of a magic vs. literalism tradeoff which I believe to be present in all user interfaces that are firmly grounded in a single metaphor. In the conclusion I will present some questions raised by the magical–literal view of this kind of user interface.

■ Literalism vs. magic in ARK

The Alternate Reality Kit (ARK) (Smith, 1986) is a system for creating interactive animated simulations. ARK simulations are intended to enable the development of intuitive understanding of the simulation's interaction rules by making these rules appear as accessible physical objects. ARK is also intended to support the modification and creation of new simulations from within the animated ARK environment.

The interface is quite faithful to a physical world metaphor: all objects have a visual image, a position, a velocity, and can experience forces. One of the objects is a hand, which the user controls with a mouse. With the hand, the user can carry objects about, throw them, press buttons and operate slider switches (see Figure 1). The environment is animated – as in the real world, many things are happening simultaneously. The intent is to have the user conclude very quickly that the screen depicts a physical world, and that the user is directly manipulating physical objects. This is the advantage of *literalism* – interfaces strongly based on a well-known metaphor require very little explanation to novice users (Gentner, 1980; Carroll and Thomas, 1980).

However, sticking completely to a metaphor can cripple a system's functionality (Halasz and Moran (1982)). For example, an ARK user may

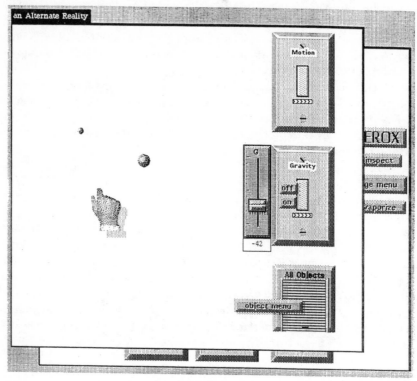

Figure 1

wish to connect a simulated pushbutton to some ARK device, perhaps for turning the device on and off. Both the button and the device are depicted as physical objects that can be directly manipulated with the hand. Should the user be required to connect the button by drilling a hole in the device and cutting into metaphorical electrical work? Something like this would be required if ARK were perfectly analogous to the everyday physical world. In the design of ARK, I considered perfectly literal ways of connecting buttons to be too tedious. I decided to allow the ARK user to connect the button simply by dropping it on to the device. Buttons have the message they send stamped on the surface – if the device does not understand the button's message, the button will fall right through the object (see Figure 2). If the button's message is meaningful, it will stick to the surface of the object. An invisible connection is established automatically, and the button is immediately functional. Features like these are called *magical* because they enable the user to do powerful things that are outside of the possibilities of the metaphor.

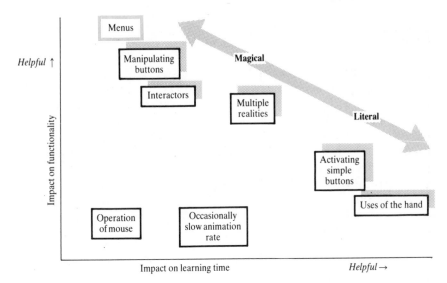

Figure 2   Various aspects of the ARK interface are represented on a graph in which easier to learn things are to the right, and very useful things are toward the top. Interface aspects tend to lie on a line with magical features in the upper left, and literal features in the lower right. The existence of a void in the upper right is a sign of the fundamental tension between literalism and magic: interface designers can always provide more powerful functionality at the price of violating the metaphor. Sometimes a broken metaphor is not particularly enabling, as evidenced by ARK's occasionally slow animation rate and use of the mouse. (Menus have been included here even though they have not yet been used as part of the user experiments with the system.)

Admittedly, literalism and magic are not part of conventional computer science parlance. However, I find them to be particularly appropriate for discussing ARK, where even the name 'Alternate Reality Kit' suggests both the real (literal) and the ability to choose between or modify realities (magic).

Although ARK is more literal than most systems, it does contain certain magical features which are useful where the literalism can be limiting. But one of the lessons of ARK is that the literal aspects of the interface are often obvious while magical capabilities are harder to learn. In ARK, the time to explain the basics is actually measured in seconds. Every piece of added magic is relatively 'expensive' because it requires its own explanation: it does not 'come for free' as it does when the user realizes there is a physical metaphor. In designing ARK, I am therefore faced with a tension between the *limitations* imposed by literalism and the *obscurity* of magic. Or, in positive terms, between the *power* of magic, and the *learnability* of literalism.

■   Overview of ARK

ARK is a project under development in the System Concepts Laboratory of the Xerox Palo Alto Research Center: it is being implemented in the Smalltalk-80* programming environment (Goldberg and Robson, 1983). The system described here has already evolved under the influence of user feedback, and will continue to do so. [...]

The system consists of a collection of 'physical' objects that can be manipulated with a simulated hand. Except for rare use of the keyboard for typing text, the hand is the user's sole means of interacting with the system. The ARK user can do three kinds of things with the hand: directly change an object's position or velocity (by carrying or throwing), send objects messages (by pressing buttons) and introduce new objects and buttons into the environment (by selecting from 'pop-up' menus). [...]

■   Types of ARK user

ARK, like some other visual programming environments (Borning, 1982; Gould and Finzer, 1984), is intended to have more than one kind of user. The *applications-level* user might typically be a student carrying out a simulated lab. At a lower level, the *simulation builder* is the creator of a particular application. There may be a role for another layer below that, populated by individuals who create tools for use by simulation builders. [...]

■   Limitation of the magic–literalism analogy: external factors in ARK

This presentation of the Alternate Reality Kit depicts the designer as only violating a metaphor in order to provide enhanced functionality (magic). But sometimes designers face factors beyond their control. Input devices, computer performance limitations, or other constraints can cause the metaphor to be violated in a way that does not necessarily enhance functionality. These fixed requirements are called *external* factors, because they are imposed upon the designer. That is not to say that external factors are unimportant – successfully presenting external factors to the user can be absolutely crucial.

I have found external factors difficult to present as either literal features or magical enhancements to the ARK interface. In ARK, external factors typically degrade learnability without necessarily enhancing functionality: I consider such features to be neither literal nor magical.

For example, when an alternate reality contains a very large number of strongly interacting objects, the animation rate (frames per second) drops, and it can become noticeably harder to grab and throw objects. The 'jerky' motion of objects makes them look less like real-world things, and makes them harder to interact with. This external factor has broken the metaphor in a way that degrades functionality. This behavior is clearly not literal. And even though it is outside the real-world's behavior, I prefer not to use a sense-of-wonder term like 'magic' for this odd and annoying visual phenomenon.

A second example is the mouse, which is used to operate the hand. The use of an indirect input device like the mouse breaks the real-world metaphor without providing enhance functionality. As a pointing device, the mouse is known to take a small but finite amount of time to learn (Card *et al.*, 1983). Furthermore, one mouse button is used to make the hand grab objects, another to make the hand activate the simulated buttons – every observed user has at some point confused these two functions (Bewly *et al.*, 1983; Price and Cordova, 1983). Not only does the mouse take a while to learn, it does not even enable users to do things within the capability of their physical world hand.

Observations of the system's users indicate that these external factors are the most troubling aspects of the system. As indicated in Figure 2, the operation of the mouse and the occasionally slow animation rate are neither enhancements to the functionality nor aids to ARK's learnability. The ideal system would be one in which everything, including external factors, fits along the magical–literal spectrum. But due to unfortunate constraints, I believe that metaphor-based interfaces will usually have some features that are neither literal nor magical.

■ Selected interface aspects

This section describes in greater detail some of the aspects of the interface which have been used by applications-level users. For each feature listed, I evaluate the magic content, discuss the power vs. learnability tradeoff, and note user experiences. The more literal aspects are listed first. This section is summarized in Figure 2.

☐ Use of the hand

With the simulated hand, the user can pick up any object. As the grasped object is carried about, it casts a shadow on the alternate reality beneath it. When a grasped object is released, it falls back into the alternate reality and maintains any velocity imparted by the hand's motion. In this way the user playing in the gravity simulation depicted in Figure 1, for example, can literally throw the moon into orbit around the planet.

Magic vs. Literalism: Literal

Power vs. Learnability: The hand has only limited abilities. It enables users to change position and velocity of objects, and establish physical contact relationships between objects. However, it contributes quite a bit to the user's understanding of the system's basics. Users need only be told 'This mouse moves the hand on the screen: The left mouse-button enables you to grab hold of an object', and 'Try throwing something'. Some of this is about the mouse. The remainder of this brief explanation is about the use of the hand, from which most users infer the following:

- The objects on the screen are physical entities.

- Physical proximity has semantic content. (Only one user has asked if it was necessary for the hand to be over an object in order to pick it up.)

- The hand can carry an object and drop it at a new location, thus changing its position.

- The hand can change an object's velocity. (After being invited to throw an object, some users ask how throwing is done. When asked to go ahead and guess, most of these users have guessed correctly: start the hand moving and release the held object.)

- The use of shadow to indicate that an object is 'above' the reality has only been moderately successful. A few users have assumed that the grasped object is in the same plane as other objects within the simulation. The shadows are either not noticed or not interpreted as intended. For these users, an additional sentence or two of explanation is required. ('See the shadow? That indicates the object in the hand is hovering *over* the objects in the window.')

☐   **Activation of [...] buttons**

A user playing in the planetary orbit simulation of Figure 1 may wish to suspend gravity temporarily. On the right side of the figure there is a kind of controller device labeled 'Gravity' with an *off* button on its surface. All buttons have the name of the message they send stamped on them. The user activates a simulated button by positioning the hand over it and pressing the middle mouse button.

Magic vs. Literalism: Literal

Power vs. Learnability: Buttons are moderately useful. They enable users to send a message to an object. They are fairly easy to explain: users seem to understand immediately what buttons are for. The only training time is spent in pointing out to the user the characteristic visual presence of a button. The idea that an object responds to a button press in a way suggested by the name stamped on the button is simply assumed. Thus, without explicit instruction, the user adopts a model consistent with the picture of a button as a thing that 'sends a message'. The button builds on the importance of physical contact in establishing relationships between objects.

☐   Manipulating buttons

A simulated button can be picked up from the surface of an object and put down anywhere, even on top of certain other objects. A button will stick to the surface of any object that can respond to its message. If a button is dropped on an object that does not understand its message, the button will 'fall through' the object, failing to stick to its surface. Many buttons can be simultaneously attached to an object. Sometimes a button will be larger than the object upon which it rests. It is not uncommon for an object to have a button 'hanging off the edge', or even completely covering the object upon which it rests.

Magic vs. Literalism: Moderately magical

Power vs. Learnability: The fact that buttons are easily connected and removed enables the user to communicate with objects in a flexible way. It is not uncommon to have several generally useful buttons laying about. The 'selective sticking' of buttons prevents a certain class of semantic errors. (As an example, sending some text the message *cube root* would result in such an error.)

While the manipulability of the buttons is useful, these aspects require a few sentences of explanation. The fact that buttons 'stick to' or 'fall through' an object depending on the object's ability to respond to the button's message is a bit of a tale. Uninformed users have sometimes discovered accidentally that buttons can be picked up from an object, and are slightly startled. Some of these users wonder if a button will still work when removed from the surface of an object and dropped off to the side. Some have dropped the button on to the surface of a large, non-understanding object, only to have the button 'disappear'. (Actually, the button is lying underneath the object, having fallen through.) [...]

■   Conclusions and questions

I have used the magic–literalism tension to discuss some of the central features of the Alternate Reality Kit because it serves as a useful way to analyze some of ARK's design issues and user experiences. In particular, because a large portion of ARK is at the literalism end of the spectrum, much of the important aspects do not need to be explicitly explained. Furthermore, although each magical aspect requires its own explanation, limited use of magic in ARK keeps the total teaching time quite low. User experiences indicate that applications-level functionality can be taught in a few minutes. Features that are neither magical enhancements nor literal adherents to the metaphor are the most troubling in ARK.

The magic vs. literalism tradeoff may be an interesting perspective on other systems whose interfaces are centered about a single metaphor (such as other graphical programming environments or desktop-like window systems). Some general questions phrased in magic–literalism language 'How does the designer decide when to implement a capability magically instead of literally?' [...] What is the minimum set of magical capabilities that allow users to build their own magic spells? Is it possible to find a metaphor that puts all external factors along the literalism–magic spectrum? Questions like these can lead to interesting discussions of ways to enable controlled release of the magic latent in computers.

■ References

W.L. Bewly, T.L. Roberts, D. Schroit, and W.L. Verplank, *Human Factors Testing in the design of Xerox's 8010 'Star' Office Workstation*. Proceedings of the Conference on Human Factors in Computer Systems. Boston, December, 1983, pp. 72–77.

Borning, A.H., The Programming Language Aspects of ThingLab, a Constraint-Oriented Simulation Laboratory. *ACM Transactions on Programming Languages and Systems* 3(4): 353–387, October 1982.

Card, Moran, and Newell, *The Psychology of Human-Computer Interaction*. Hillsdale, New Jersey: Lawrence Erlbaum Associates, 1983.

Carroll, J.M. and Thomas, J.C., *Metaphor and the cognitive representation of computing systems*. Yorktown Heights, N.T.: IBM Watson Research Center technical report no. RC 8302. (1980).

Gentner, D., *The structure of analogical models in science*. Report 4451, Bolt, Beranek, and Newman, July 1980

Goldberg, A.J., and Robson, D., *Smalltalk-80: The Language and its Implementation*. Reading , MA: Addison-Wesley, 1983.

Gould, L., and Finzer. W., *Programming by Rehearsal*. Technical Report SCL-84-1, Xerox Palo Alto Research Center, May 1984. A short version appears in Byte Magazine, Vol. 9 No. 6, June 1984.

Halasz, F., and Moran, T.P., *Analogy Considered Harmful*. Proceedings of the Conference on Human Factors in Computer Systems. Gaithersburg, Maryland, March 1982.

Price, L.A., and Cordova, C.A., *Use of Mouse Buttons*. Proceedings of the Conference on Human Factors in Computer Systems. Boston, December, 1983, pp. 262–266.

Smith, R.B., *The Alternate Reality Kit: An Animated Environment for Creating Interactive Simulations*. Proceedings of the 1986 IEEE Computer Society Workshop on Visual Languages, Dallas, Texas, June 1986, pp. 99–106.

Paper 3.8

Refining the Use of Computer Conferencing in Distance Education

Robin Mason

For a medium which is not much over 10 years old, the number of computer conferencing applications described in the literature is truly impressive. Studies range from single isolated experiments (for example, Phillips *et al.*, 1988; Upton, 1987; Roberts, 1988; Gray 1989), to long-term, wide-ranging analyses using rigorous, replicable methods (for example, studies carried out by the Institute for the Future in five volumes: Vallee *et al.*, 1974, 1975, 1978; Johansen *et al.*, 1978) and the extensive writings of Hiltz (for example, 1984, 1989).

The various educational applications of computer conferencing can be subdivided initially into uses at 'place-based' institutions (primary and secondary schools, and traditional higher education campuses) and distance education institutions (graduate schools, distance programmes at campus-based universities, and dedicated distance learning establishments such as the Open University).

Even within distance education, there are a variety of ways of using computer conferencing. These are distinguished by the degree to which computer conferencing 'delivers' the course material: mostly online, adjunct mode, or tutorial support (see Figure 1).

- *Mostly online* Online courses at the Ontario Institute for Studies in Education and at Connected Education are delivered more or less entirely through computer conferencing. Students may be sent hard copy of assigned readings, but otherwise, the content of the course is conveyed in the discussions, guest lectures and cooperative work carried out online. Most students of Connected Education never meet either the teacher or each other.

- *Adjunct mode* Computer conferencing has also been used in

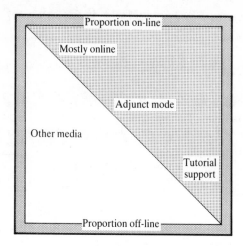

Figure 1   Proportion of the online element of a course

combination with traditional delivery media – face-to-face
meetings, print, assignments and readings. Graduate students at
the University of Strathclyde have used computer conferencing on
a local area network to produce an electronic journal (Baird and
Forer, 1987), and Saunders and Heyl (1988) describe a two-year
graduate-level professional health care programme which drew
together electronically students from six major Western
universities.

- *Tutorial support* As a means of providing tutorial support,
  computer conferencing is particularly useful to large-scale distance
  teaching institutions. The New York Institute of Technology uses
  computer conferencing in its distance education programme to
  increase student contact with teachers. As this institution has a
  'rolling enrolment', the opportunities for students to discuss
  course issues with other students are limited. Nevertheless, many
  advantages are reported for remote students (Richards, 1987):
  asking questions, submitting homework assignments, 'meeting'
  other students, reading notes and exchanging information.

The educational use of computer conferencing when used as the
main delivery medium is quite different from its use as a small, tutoring
element in a full credit course. The preparation and conception of the
course will be different; the role of the online tutor will be different and
the motivation and participation of the students will be different.

This paper aims to evaluate the use of computer conferencing as a
medium for tutorial support in the 1988 Open University application.

■ The Open University's first use of computer conferencing

In 1988 the Open University embarked on the use of computer conferencing primarily for tutorial support. However, unlike other such uses – The New York Institute of Technology, the NKI College of Computer Science in Norway, and the Jutland Open University in Denmark – the Open University was the first to exploit computer conferencing on a mass scale. Each year, 1300 students and over 65 tutors use conferencing for tutorial support on one OU course.

The course *An Introduction to Information Technology: Social and Technological Issues* (called DT200), is a second level undergraduate course which explores some of the issues arising from the advent of information technology. The course consists of seven 'blocks' of printed material, a course reader, audio and broadcast media and other supplementary materials. In addition to these 'standard' presentation media, this course sets aside 20% of the study time for practical work in order that students should gain direct experience of the social and technological issues discussed in the written material. Four software packages are introduced on the course; some are commercial: word processing, database management and spreadsheet analysis, and one was specially developed at the OU: computer communications. The communications element, therefore, forms a very small part of the whole course.

In conjunction with the start of this course, the OU decided upon its Home Computing Policy. It defined an approved specification (an IBM PC compatible) and purchased with the aid of a £2.25 million grant from the Department of Trade and Industry, a stock of these which students could rent. In addition, it made arrangements for students to buy their own machines through mail order, and offered a discount on course fees, to bring the cost of rental down to below £100, and to encourage purchase. For the communications element of DT200, a pool of modems was purchased by the University to lend to all students and tutors studying the course.

☐ Integrating the communications medium

A number of steps were taken to prevent the small communications element of the course from being perceived by students as an optional extra, which could be ignored if necessary. In the first place, the communications package has to be understood, experienced and mastered like the other software on the course, as well as being used for tutorial support. The 14 hours of tutor contact allocated to the course were divided approximately in half with three face-to-face meetings during the course, and tutor support on the conferencing system throughout the course, especially before the due dates of each of the seven assignments.

The second integrating feature of the communications element in the course was the design of the project, in effect, a double weighted essay which would assess all the practical elements of the course. The subject of the project is an evaluation of computer-mediated communication, based on the student's experience of it during the course, the textual material presented in the units and readings, and the reactions of fellow students. The latter information can be gathered directly from conferencing messages, but is mainly drawn from a database formed by all students uploading answers to two detailed questionnaires concerning their reactions and use of the conferencing system during the course, supplemented by questions on their own personal and educational background. Students are expected to download data and combinations of data from this remote database, present it in graphs and tables using the various software packages and write an assessment of some aspect – social, educational or technological – of computer-mediated communications.

☐ The conferencing system

In 1986, the OU purchased the conferencing system, CoSy, from the University of Guelph, Ontario. This system provides three areas for different kinds of communication: electronic mail for one-to-one communication; a conversation area for unstructured, informal group discussions; and a conference area designed with many more facilities to allow interchange among any number of participants.

Each tutor on the course was moderator of a conference for his or her tutorial group of up to 25 students, thus forming an online classroom to discuss the assignments, practical work and course issues. These conferences were closed to other users in order to create a contained discussion area where students, having met at face-to-face tutorials, would feel confident to participate.

A read-only conference was set up for the course team to provide up-to-date information, stop press announcements and fixes for software bugs. Students could read these messages but not add comments.

Tutors were given a closed conference, which was a private space for them to discuss tutoring issues among themselves and provide feedback to the course team on the course generally and conferencing in particular. Students, likewise, were given a conference for socializing, a place to 'meet' others on the course with similar interests, to moan about course problems and to chat with other students.

Rather at the last moment, a forum conference was added where course issues could be discussed by all students, tutors and staff. Topics for each of the seven blocks were created, as well as for the project, practical work, errata and gremlins.

Although the conferences for the course were all prefixed with DT200, which is the number designated by the administration for the course, all of the open conferences on the system were available to students. The university does not operate separate systems for staff and students, so all staff with IDs on CoSy are contactable by students.

☐   **The interface to CoSy**

The conferencing system CoSy was originally designed for access by on-campus terminals, with no connect charges for students – a different situation from the distance learning environment of OU students. The course team felt that this remote access by students required an interface which would provide automated log on facilities and an offline editor for the preparation of messages and reduction of connect charges.

Most applications of computer conferencing to date have placed great importance on an initial face-to-face meeting where users can be introduced to the basics of electronic communication and to the particular conferencing software. As this kind of hands-on experience would not be possible, a third facility was introduced to the interface – an optional menubar to help new users remember the commands and available activities.

This 'front-end' to CoSy, called OUCom, was designed and produced at the OU for use with the Pace Linnet Modem, which was sent to all students. The interface consisted of an automatic dial-up and connection through to CoSy with a few key strokes, an offline editor and an optional menubar when online.

■ Use of CoSy in 1988

In its role as a piece of software for students to master, CoSy was clearly a 'compulsory' part of the course. In its role as a substitute for face-to-face tutorials, it was technically optional. Although this was never made explicit, the data shows without a doubt that students picked it up implicitly: over 95% logged on at least once and responded to the course team's welcome message, while only a third participated in sending conference messages. Add to this third the number who read conference messages and the statistic are roughly in line with the 40–50% attendance at one post-foundation tutorial per year within the OU system.

A number of tutors questioned whether computer conferencing would always be a 'selective' medium, which some students would never find compatible. As a selective medium, however, CoSy seemed to advantage the verbal and wealthier students – those who were articulate or who had enough money to pay the telephone costs of extensive connections to CoSy.

☐   The tutor group conferences

By far the most significant and unexpected outcome of the use of CoSy in the first year was the lack of academic discussion and activity in the 65 tutor conferences and the nature and amount of activity in the 'national' conference, Forum. The help topic of this conference was the most heavily used, with over 500 messages in the first two months of the course. The topic on the fourth block of the course, which was guided and stimulated by the course team member responsible for the corresponding text material, had the second highest activity. Discussion of later blocks towards the end of the course was very sparse, but the messages in the practical and project topics picked up as the deadline for submission of the project approached.

The tutor group conference was envisaged as the area in which tutors would conduct online tutorials. Topics were pre-set for each block of the course and tutors were given written advice about how to moderate educational discussions. However, although the number of messages varied considerably from one tutor group to another, the content of the messages was invariably on the level of information exchange, rather than of discussion, opinions, comments or critiques of the course material. Most tutors reported that the number of active participants was about five students, though some conferences 'died' completely and others had as many as 15 students who put in one or more messages.

What was surprising to the course team, and indeed to tutors and students, was not the low level of participation – this is standard in face-to-face tutorials and in viewing rates of broadcasts – but the inability of even the most diligent and enthusiastic tutors to stimulate sustained interactive discussion in the tutor group conferences.

The reasons for this are partly related to the nature of this application – too small a use of a very powerful medium on an already full course, and partly related to the limitations of the medium itself, in its present stage of development.

☐   Nature of the application

Tutors who tried to engage their students in discussing a particular topic found that there was never a critical mass of participants to carry this kind of interchange. Lack of time to participate was one of the main reasons given by students in the extensive evaluations of the course. The course was heavily loaded with text and reading material, as well as new practical applications to master each month. Furthermore, the cost of accessing CoSy deterred many students. Though half the students could reach the OU's dial-up network at local call rates, the other half were obliged to pay *a* and *b* band rates, which are many times more expensive.

When used in a largely optional mode, many of the inherent advantages of the medium are lost: if tutors cannot be sure of reaching all their students electronically, conferencing adds to, rather than reduces their workload. Lack of use by others can lead to considerable frustration and disappointment – that other students are not contributing thoughts and ideas, that discussions do not take off and that questions lie unanswered.

Despite these negative features, many students did benefit from the use of conferencing, and many more remained enthusiastic about its potential. The Forum conference did act as a focus for students and tutors to offer or seek advice on technical problems, to give opinions and personal reactions, to engage in light-hearted interchanges, or simply to read what others were saying. The creation of this kind of 'virtual community' for isolated learners is almost unprecedented in distance eduction. A DT200 student, quoted in Mason and Kaye (1989, p. ix) said:

> 'CMC has tremendous potential in creating impromptu tutorials and this course has been the first one to make me feel that the OU has a campus like the conventional Universities. DT200 in a way has spoilt me – I am going to sorely miss active discussion whenever I like for the remainder of my courses – it will be like losing my right arm or a friend!'

CoSy was also used effectively by some tutors for the general administrative and information exchange aspects of their duties:

> 'The most appreciated value of CoSy on DT200, as far as the majority of staff and students were concerned, was the new speed and ease of getting and sending crucial administrative types of information in all directions. Some examples were: warning students about late dispatch of course materials and revising assignment submission dates; notifying tutorial meetings and examination dates; reporting on errors in course material, software and audio-tapes as soon as they were identified.' (Castro, 1988, p. 8)

The 'remedial' function of the tutorial was another successful aspect of the use of CoSy. Apart from the help topic on Forum, the project and tma topics both at the tutor group level and the national level acted as a place for students to air their difficulties with assignments. Other students as well as tutors gave advice, opinions and fixes for software problems.

> 'I have found electronic conferencing and email to be a very effective means of obtaining help with course difficulties. I have also felt constantly "in touch" with both tutors and students throughout and the wealth and variety of experience, knowledge, information and friendship available without the barrier of distance or time has proved limitless.' (from a DT200 student project)

> 'I found that whenever there was something puzzling me, particularly involving the practical side of the course, I invariably "logged on" to find that someone else has already asked the question and received the answer. (student project)

One of the less commonly acknowledged functions of tutorials is as a platform for students to air grievances, to let off steam and generally express the emotional element in learning. CoSy rose to this challenge admirably. In fact, it is well known that computer conferencing seems to attract emotional outbursts. There were many examples in 1988 of students expressing their pent up frustrations with the course, with studying and with coping with the OU:

> 'Whoever allowed this course to be given the title DT should be shot, it should have been entitled DDDDDDDT. The number of marks given in TMAs to the technological content are laughable. I feel that I have been conned into taking this course, I had been hoping to progress and complete a good Honours degree. The only way that I can now do this is if I can strike this fiasco from my record. Before I get too personal towards members of staff, maybe I had better quit.' (CoSy message, 1988)

Interestingly, this 'flaming' message was picked up by another student and turned around:

> 'I think this course is brilliant. It's about INFORMATION TECHNOLOGY and the course title fairly reflects the course content. How can you learn about the social implications without knowing some of the technical aspects. It all depends where you are coming from. The person who feels they are wasting a year should have applied for a Computer course – there are plenty on offer. Information Technology is all about the application of computers and telecommunications – not necessarily about programming.' (CoSy message, 1988)

☐ Limitations of the medium

Many of the negative features of this application of computer conferencing can be overcome – by avoiding them in new applications, and even by adjustments to this application. The following negative features, however, are limitations of the medium itself, and most will only be overcome with further development of conferencing software:

- *Quantity of messages in conferences* For all but the very frequent and regular users of the system, the volume of messages was very difficulty to manage. The tools within CoSy to cope with large conferences – the *skip* command, *list headers* command, *read by reference* and so on – really do not address the problem of the infrequent user wanting to get information efficiently, let alone contribute to a discussion.

- *Peripheral nature of comments* The nature of the messages in the main discussion topics on the whole offered a broader, rather than a deeper understanding of the course issues. Students with considerable expertise in certain areas of information technology contributed sometimes long and complex messages which gave a wider perspective on many areas of the subject, but relatively few messages tackled specific course issues in depth.†

- *Loss of spontaneity working offline* The need to read and/or compose messages offline for reasons of cost, transforms communication into a tedious and unspontaneous activity for many people.

- *Lack of impetus to contribute* The disadvantage of the medium's flexibility to allow users to reflect on messages and a possible response, often leads to their not making a response at all. Face-to-face communication carries a much higher obligation to respond.

- *Proliferation of 'irrelevant' messages* The definition of an irrelevant message is ultimately a personal one, but there is no doubt that many users were put off by the number of 'junk' messages on the system.

- *Technical difficulties* The nature and extent of the technical difficulties experienced by students in the first year were rather lower than some course team members anticipated and pilot tests had indicated. Nevertheless, the bugs in OUCom, complaints about the network, totally inexplicable technical failures and odd snags in CoSy due to the large number of users, were hard to handle in the first two months of the course.

---

† Although this factor seems to relate to the nature of the users rather than the medium, it is my experience with many educational uses of computer conferencing, that the medium tends to encourage personal digression, asides, peripheral comments and tangential contributions, rather than focused discussion of issues. I therefore consider it a characteristic of the medium which in this case is limiting.

The following selections from various data sources – student projects (P), interviews (I) and survey questionnaires (SQ) – demonstrate the initial enthusiasm and the combination of limitations which often led to disappointment with the reality of conferencing:

'CoSy is wonderful in theory but there were too many options/ conferences available and too many frivolous messages.' (SQ)

'Many conferences were full of unrelated comments. I tried to follow the flow but got disheartened and gave up on main conferences. I tended to stick to news and our tutor conference, but found other students also fed up so tutor conference also died.' (SQ)

'I found that the time required to engage in useful CMC out-weighed the benefits and therefore I didn't use it very much.' (SQ)

'Like most of the students starting the DT200 course, I brought a genuine degree of enthusiasm for the opportunity of being able to use CMC within the course ... In practice I found that the messages I did send were short because I was aware of the cost of drafting online, whilst I found the operations involved in preparing text offline tedious and guaranteed to destroy spontaneity ... I know you can skip backwards and forwards in reading messages – but you are making the decisions blind. Quite often I jump to the last 10 messages, but I don't know what I have missed. There might have been something really important or really interesting ... In my own case then, technical, economic and psychological factors meant that I was unable, or unwilling, to use the medium in any comprehensive fashion.' (P)

'I found the early messages in Forum a bit high-flown. I wasn't really sure what they were getting at and what relevance it was. It was in the category of "nice to know". It might be quite useful to pick something off there and include it in your assignment. I don't know – to get the full picture you need the comments on the message because that is where the discussion takes place. It can actually take quite a while to get the complete picture and put things in perspective.' (I)

Question: 'How would you compare conferencing with face-to-face tutorials?'

Answer: 'Well I think there is a difference in the sense that the contributions might be the same, but face-to-face you do feel you ought to make a contribution. There is no compulsion like that online. So you aren't getting a "full" discussion really.' (I)

None of these factors is unique to the OU application. Some of them were identified by the Institute for the Future 15 years ago (op cit.) – reduced obligation to respond, lack of focused discussion and, of course, technical difficulties. Improvements in the hardware and network equipment promise to overcome some of these limitations, and the next generation of computer conferencing software with transparent on- and offline working, non-linear storing of messages and greater personal tailoring capabilities, may well overcome the other limitations. In the meantime, it is important that any application capitalizes on the positive features of the medium and tries to minimize its limitations.

■ Conclusions

This paper has looked at the applicability of computer conferencing as a tutorial support on a mass distance education course. (For a fuller treatment of this application see Mason, 1989 and 1990.) The following conclusions can be drawn from the discussion:

- As a vehicle for discussing course issues, it is useful for broadening peripheral perspectives. It is much more difficult, though potentially possible, to provoke sustained, interactive analysis of specific course material.
- As a method for exchanging information and conducting administrative duties, it is very efficient and effective.
- As a means of providing practical support to students, particularly on technical matters, it is an effective use of tutor expertise.
- The social atmosphere created through computer conferencing for learning, for overcoming isolation and for expressing emotions, is very positive for some, though by no means all students.
- There may be a gap between the expectations raised by the medium and the actuality of using it.
- Use of the medium in an optional or self-selected mode renders many of these functions less effective, as it increases tutor workload and reduces the necessary critical mass of participants.
- In the 1988 application, the medium tends to disadvantage the weaker, less affluent or less verbal students.

■ References

Baird P. and Forer B. (1987). An experiment in computer conferencing using a local area network. *Electronic Library*, 5(3), 162–9.
Castro A. (1989). Critical reflections on the introduction of computer-mediated communication into a distance-teaching institution. The Open University, Milton Keynes. Mimeo.

Gray R. (1989). CMC for in-service training. In *Mindweave: Communication, Computers and Distance Education* (Mason R. and Kaye A.R., eds). Oxford: Pergamon.

Hiltz S.R. (1984). *OnLine Communities: a case study of the office of the future.* New Jersey: Ablex.

Hiltz S.R. (1989). *Learning in a Virtual Classroom. Final Evaluation Report.* Research Report 25. Computerized Conferencing and Communications Center, New Jersey Institute of Technology.

Johansen R., DeGrasse R. and Wilson T. (1978). *Group Communication Through Computers,* Vol. 5: *Effects on Working Patterns.* Menlo Park, CA: Institute for the Future.

Mason R. (1989). An evaluation of CoSy on an Open University course. In *Mindweave: Communication, Computers and Distance Education* (Mason R. and Kaye A.R. eds). Oxford: Pergamon.

Mason R. (1990). Case Study of the Use of Computer Conferencing at the Open University. Unpublished doctoral thesis. Centre for information Technology in Education, Open University.

Mason R. and Kaye A.R. (eds) (1989). *Mindweave: Communication, Computers and Distance Education.* Oxford: Pergamon.

Phillips A.F. and Pease P. (1987). Computer conferencing and education: complementary or contradictory concepts? *The American Journal of Distance Education,* 1(2), 44–52.

Richards A. (1988). A community of learners: computer conferencing and distance education. Supplement to *Proceedings of the Second Guelph Symposium on Computer Conferencing.* University of Guelph, Ontario.

Roberts L. (1988). Computer conferencing: a classroom for distance learning. *ICDE Bulletin,* **18**, 35–40.

Saunders C. and Heyl J. (1988). Evaluating educational computer conferencing. *Systems Managements,* April, 33–7.

Upton E. (1987). Computer conferencing: a tool for hospitality professionals. *Proceedings of the Second Guelph Symposium on Computer Conferencing.* University of Guelph, Ontario.

Vallee J., Johansen R., Randolph R. and Hastings A. (1974). *Group Communication Through Computers,* Vol. 2: *A Study of Social Effects.* Menlo Park, CA: Institute for the Future.

Vallee J., Johansen R., Lupinski H., Spangler K. and Wilson T. (1975). *Group Communication Through Computers,* Vol. 3: *Pragmatics and Dynamics,* Menlo Park, CA: Institute for the Future.

Vallee J., Johansen R., Lupinski H. and Wilson T. (1978). *Group Communication Through Computers,* Vol. 4: *Social, Managerial, and Economic Issues.* Menlo Park, CA: Institute for the Future.

Paper 3.9

Some CMC Discourse Properties and their Educational Significance

David Graddol

Users of computer conferencing systems often claim that although the medium involves written language it possesses a number of features which are more like speech. Many computer conferences are much like conversations; that is, they are informal turn-taking activities. The cause of such informality, which seems to be a tendency on all CoSy conferences, is not clear. Does it relate, for instance, to properties of the software (which encourages certain behaviours and inhibits others) or to the psychology of interpersonal communication? It is also unclear whether the tendency is to be regarded as a weakness of computer-mediated communication or a strength. Usually, it is regarded as a problem, and the informal discourse which results is dismissively referred to as 'chat', 'unstructured', or 'off-topic'. Such conferences are imagined to provide a poor context for students' learning; contributions are said to lack substance, to provide an obstacle to students through their bulk and lack of relevance, and so on. This paper presents an opposing view: that informal talk is highly structured and represents a valuable context for learning, and that a close examination of the discourse structure on some conferences on the Open University's CoSy conferencing system reveals certain properties which are not found in either written or spoken language, but which have special implications for the participation of students who may be marginalized in conventional educational settings.

■ The structure of teacher-mediated discourse

Traditional classroom discourse is controlled by a teacher with whom the students are in an unequal power relation. This relationship is often supported by the physical arrangement of the class; by various non-verbal asymmetries (the teacher may be standing and free to move whereas the class may be seated and confined); by the teacher's role in evaluating and grading students' written work; in the teacher's ability to resort to institutional sanctions and penalties in order to control behaviour. One gross effect of this power asymmetry is that a teacher in class usually talks far more than all the students put together. Flanders, in a well-known study of USA schools, proposed the 'two-thirds rule' which suggests that two-thirds of classroom talk is by the teacher, and only one-third pupil talk. This figure has proved a conservative estimate, but such inequality in talk is found in educational settings in all age groups, including adult classes. This inequality in talk derives from specific features of discourse structure. The teacher, for example, has privileged speaking rights and controls the turns of other speakers. That is, rather like a chair in a formal meeting, the teacher has responsibility for selecting the next person who will speak and this ensures that the teacher will take a turn after each other speaker – twice as many turns as all other participants together. The teacher's role in evaluating or giving feedback on each student turn gives rise to a turn structure peculiar to classrooms, sometimes called 'initiation, response, follow-up' (Sinclair and Coulthard, 1975). The IRF pattern allows the teacher to control the flow of the topic by rejecting turns until a suitable one is found.

Such institutionalized power relations are not just reflected in talk, they are also in part established through talk. The IRF pattern, for example, is a powerful way in which a teacher can establish a claim to rights over controlling the discourse and determining what is to be regarded as legitimate knowledge. However, we can note that the mechanism depends on every other turn being taken by the teacher who must be able to respond to a student contribution before any further contribution is made. Such teacher-mediated discourse is often an inefficient environment for learning: students have very little opportunity to talk themselves; most questions are asked by the teacher, rather than the learner; learners are given no opportunity to define and articulate their own needs and problems; and so on. The learner has little control over either the curriculum or the mode and pace of learning.

■   Characteristics of informal talk

Since the early 1960s a great emphasis has been placed by educators in Britain and many other countries on the role of informal talk between pupils. Pupils could only learn, it was argued, if they were able to talk freely. The rationale was twofold: first, the act of planning and uttering was regarded as psychologically beneficial to thinking and problem solving. Second, it allowed the joint negotiation of knowledge, and cooperative learning. Even talk which appears to be off the topic may provide a vital forum for adventitious learning (see Phillips, 1987). 'It is as talkers, questioners, arguers, gossips, chatterboxes, that our pupils do much of their important learning' claimed one of the leading exponents of this approach (Harold Rosen in Barnes *et al.*, 1971).

The primary curriculum has long been structured according to this student centred view of learning-through-language, with extensive use of small group work, especially in the science curriculum (see Barnes and Todd, 1977) and it is fast becoming an orthodoxy among teachers of older pupils and adults. It forms, for example, a principle method of face-to-face teaching at Open University Summer Schools, at both foundation and post-graduate level.

Although conversation and chat is often regarded as unstructured and chaotic, conversation analysts have documented the orderliness that informal multi-party discourse displays, and how such order is maintained by the participants. Participants do have to work to maintain such order. For example, in order to ensure a smooth change of speaker, the person finishing a turn gives out signals which allow the new speaker to synchronize their entry. Each new turn must be topically tied, usually to the immediately foregoing turn, so that the conversation maintains a coherent thread. There are many examples of the way in which the meaning or function of a statement depends crucially on how it is placed in relation to other turns. As a simple example, 'Hello' means something different if said at the beginning of a telephone conversation rather than in the middle. Informal talk can, in this way, be shown to be a highly structured activity, in which the format and ordering of turns is conventional and understood by all participants. The coherence of a conversation relies on the way each turn is closely bound to the foregoing turn in various ways (see Graddol *et al.*, 1987, for a fuller discussion of turn exchange mechanisms and discourse structure).

The dynamics of face-to-face talk allow for many inequalities, however. The turn-taking mechanism is such that successful participation in conversation is often a competitive business requiring speed and confidence: a maxim of 'first in gets the floor' seems to operate; one person can interrupt another and prevent them from taking or completing a turn. The need for contributions to be topically tied to the current topic means that those who cannot or do not wish to participate in that topic have limited powers to change the topic to another. There is, instead, a continuous thread in which current participants have more control than those listening and a current speaker has first rights to select the next speaker.

In summary, research shows that both talk mediated by a teacher and informal peer group talk is highly structured, but that both suffer from inequalities which may have educational significance. For example, boys and men routinely get to say much more than girls or women; within each gender group there will also be great differences in the participation rates of individual learners (see, for example, Swann and Graddol, 1988).

■ CoSy discourse

Such research raises several interesting questions with regard to how computer-mediated communication can best be used to provide a context for student learning. What kind of 'work' has to be done by participants in a CoSy discourse and how is this different from face to face? CMC still requires a certain burden of social maintenance, both in terms of meta-linguistic comments that organize the flow of the discourse and in terms of maintaining a sense of community and belonging among participants. Much of this is done through non-verbal communication (NVC) in ordinary talk and the lack of NVC on computer conferencing has both advantages and disadvantages. Some of the 'idle gossip' which characterized the conferences analysed for this paper probably serves purposes which would otherwise be handled by NVC. For example, the gender of a speaker is normally apparent in face-to-face interaction, and participants' gender identities may be continuously apparent through the different styles of speech used by women and men (see Graddol and Swann, forthcoming, for a review of such differences); in CoSy discourse participants' gender is not immediately apparent from their usernames. Nevertheless, some women have complained that men often indicate their gender through what they say, with phrases such as 'now, lads' and so on. However, the lack of NVC may make it difficult to maintain and negotiate power differentials, since the usual technology of accent, dress, location of speaker and so on, is missing.

However, it is in terms of the discourse structure and the dynamics of turn taking and topic development that interaction on CoSy differs most from other media. Below are listed a number of such observed differences.

☐ Turn taking

Turn taking on CoSy does not require skills or special management in the same way as in face-to-face interaction. There is no such thing as an interruption and there is no way in which one participant can prevent another from taking a turn (other than by a moderator 'withdrawing' a contribution after it has been made).

The maxim of 'first in gets the floor' which operates in both teacher-mediated discourse and informal conversation does not apply on CoSy. In an ordinary conversation, the first person to respond also determines the topic flow of the discourse, and the requirement for coherence between adjacent contributions means that it soon becomes too late to say something different. Not so on CoSy, where the complaint 'someone beat me to it' means someone else said what I wanted to say and deprived me of the credit.

On CoSy, unlike conversation, the current speaker has no special rights to select the next speaker. A clique of participants cannot bounce the conversation between themselves and, in principle, any person can always contribute next. One person may take several turns in sequence, taking up points made by a variety of earlier contributors or dealing with both the assertions and the assumptions made by an earlier contributor. In face-to-face discourse, such multiple turns are usually a feature only of very formal situations, where a contributor has been called upon to speak and given special local speaking rights.

☐ Topic development

In ordinary discourse if a question is not answered or a topic not taken up in the very next turn, then it is unlikely ever to be so. The close bound nature of 'chat' means that a convention of 'relevance' must be satisfied in the very next turn. Not so in CoSy where a contribution can be commented upon days later. Cohesion between adjacent contributions is broken down in favour of a more complex cohesion pattern that extends over a longer discourse domain. This cohesion is supported by the 'comment' function within CoSy which marks a contribution as tied to a particular earlier one, but many of the shorter, apparently vacuous messages may also serve to maintain this pattern of cohesion.

Because of the irregular pattern of logging on, later arrivals will scan all subsequent contributions in one go and will take up for further comment those that seem of interest and substance rather than whichever happened to be last. Where mean time between log-ons is small, one can expect that adjacent entries will be more closely tied, topic development will be less dispersed, entries will begin to feel out of date faster (the discourse has 'moved on') and fewer topics will be handled simultaneously. Hence the stochastic behaviour of students logging on to the system is likely to have far reaching effects on the discourse structure.

The lack of the requirement for close tying with the foregoing turn means that CoSy is able to handle simultaneous topic flows. The ability to take multiple turns means that each participant can engage with as many of these topics as desired. Participants cannot be disenfranchised by a particular topic dominating.

■   Some educational implications

Formulating contributions in text, off line, may be a better aid to learning even than talk. The conversational nature of CoSy also discourages too great a polish from contributors which would lead to more of a set piece debate and thereby lose the interactional and 'joint negotiation' of learning that CoSy engenders.

Such learning is often adventitious and divergent, so many apparent digressions from a set topic can be expected. However, such digressions are not nearly so injurious to a CoSy conference as they would be in a formal classroom. The loose bound cohesion of CMC not only encourages divergent talk but also supports it. Hence one can argue that CoSy is uniquely equipped to provide a context for adventitious learning.

☐   Support of minority topics

The ability of CoSy discourse to maintain several topics simultaneously means that minority interests can be represented within the mainstream community. For example, women and disabled students have been able to draw out specific implications of contributions without appearing to divert the flow of the discourse. Women have also been able to make meta-linguistic comments, pointing out, for example, the sexist assumptions or language used by a contributor. Such comment would appear hostile and damaging in a discourse where strong ties existed between adjacent contributions and where a contributor could only take one turn before yielding the floor to another speaker.

☐   Support of late arrivals and lurkers

All discourse, to be successful, requires certain assumptions to be made about shared knowledge. The start of many conferences shows participants negotiating a shared or usable social reality. The flow of discourse also needs participants to be able to build on and tie to earlier contributions. A latecomer to a face-to-face interaction, whether a classroom or a chat, is in an unprivileged position compared with existing members and this may create a power inequality which can take a long time to repair. This inequality manifests itself in the restricted ability of the newcomer to contribute, or in the ability of existing members to give put downs such as 'yeah, we've been through all that weeks ago'.

Most conferences contain a very large number of lurkers. A lurker may only log on occasionally to a particular conference, nevertheless such a person is able to scan through the history of the discourse and contribute as a fully experienced participant who knows all the protagonists and their histories, and is a full party to shared knowledge.

☐ Discourse genres on CoSy

I have assumed that there exists a single style of computer discourse but this, not surprisingly, is a simplification. Already we can see several 'genres' developing within CoSy. Users are typically not familiar with the subtleties of such genres; CMC represents a new cultural context for which they need to develop a new communicative competence. In this respect the architectural metaphors used to describe the areas on CoSy may not help. Traditional registers of talk do not always map on those found in CoSy, and the metaphors of 'common room' or 'tutorial' suggest too much of a continuity between familiar discourse styles and CMC. An ordinary speaker who knows how and when to be 'formal' or 'informal', encouraging or hostile, and so on, in speech does not necessarily know how and when to do these things appropriately in CoSy. Both the dynamics and structure of CoSy discourse differ from those found in more familiar kinds of written or oral interaction.

■ References

Barnes, D., Britton, J. and Rosen, H. (1971) Language the learner and the school. Penguin, Harmondsworth.

Barnes, D and Todd, F. (1977) Communication and learning in small groups. Routledge and Kegan Paul, London.

Graddol, D., Cheshire, C. and Swann, J. (1987) Describing Language. Open University Press. Milton Keynes.

Graddol, D and Swann, J (forthcoming) Gender Voices. Blackwell, Oxford.

Phillips, T. (1987) 'On a related matter: why successful group talk depends on NOT keeping to the point', Paper presented at the International Oracy Convention, University of East Anglia.

Sinclair, J.McH. and Coulthard, R.M. (1975) Towards an analysis of Discourse. Oxford University Press, London.

Swann, J. and Graddol, D. (1988) 'Gender inequalities in classroom discourse'. English in Education, 22, pp. 48–65.

Paper 3.10

The Human Interface: Hidden Issues in CMC Affecting Use in Schools

Bridget Somekh

The experience so far gained of CMC, at least in Britain, suggests that one of the main problems lies in getting people to use it. This paper is about that part of CMC which constitutes the relationship of people to the machine. The term 'human interface' is used as a metaphor for that relationship, a metaphor which suggests a techno-human hybrid, because that is how many people *feel* about CMC. The paper reflects on this human interface as I have observed it, drawing on my research with the UK/USA Communications Project during 1986–87 and my continuing experience of using CMC in the course of my work (for a full account of the former see Somekh and Groundwater-Smith, 1988, and National Union of Teachers, 1988). The purpose of the paper is to open up discussion about how people approach CMC in order to capitalize more fully on the opportunities it provides for human communication.

The key factor in establishing an individual as a user of CMC seems to be the social context which surrounds its use. The social context is considered here under two headings: (i) the individual and (ii) the institutional, with particular emphasis in the case of the latter, on British schools.

■ CMC and the individual

CMC is a tool for people to use. Just like the telephone, CMC can bring people closer together. Yet, the majority don't see it like that before they use it. For many, using a computer itself does not fit their self-image; for others who are computer users the notion of communicating via a computer seems to be perverse, since communication is about human relationships in which they can see no place for a machine.

Much of human behaviour is ritualistic. We sleep on the same side of the bed, dry our bodies bit by bit in the same order after taking a bath or shower ... Rituals simplify life so that departing from them takes thought and reduces time for other things. More fundamentally, though, these rituals are closely bound to our personal self-image; they symbolize the way we present ourselves to ourselves and the world. It is not just convenient to have our desk arranged in a particular way, it also indicates our acceptance or rejection of order, and some undercurrents of attitude to our work. Those few people who refuse to own cars or television sets are making proud statements about themselves and their attitude to life. So too are those who reject the very notion of using CMC. It would cut across the familiar rituals of their daily life on two counts: first it would be more time consuming (yes, it would at first) and less familiar than the telephone or letters; secondly it would cut across their self-image as non-technology people – they would not feel good about using it. What becomes crucial is that their concepts of themselves as non-technology people prevents them trying out CMC; whereas only through use can they establish new rituals which make CMC integral to the social context (as has happened with radio and television).

For some whose self-image is strongly non-technological the barrier can be broken down. If the terminal literally becomes 'part of the furniture' on someone's desk it loses its cold technological aura. Then, going on-line is endowed with feelings much like those we experience when lifting mail from door mat or pigeon hole. Once over the initial barrier, with the system beginning to feel familiar, it is possible for individuals to reach a decision about the usefulness or otherwise of CMC. Until that time any rational decision may be impossible.

There is some confirmation of the importance of this human interface in acting as a barrier to use of CMC in the difference between the ways in which email and fax have been adopted. It seems that, almost accidentally, different patterns of use make fax fit more easily than email into existing behaviour rituals. A fax machine is often dealt with by a specialist operator, and becomes a magic device for transporting pieces of paper produced in the normal way. Email and computer conferencing by contrast are not normally filtered through operators – they demand an intimate 'hands on' relationship with the machine so that side-stepping the human interface is not possible.

In order to establish the use of CMC we need, therefore, to provide access to on-line facilities on every desk to create an environment in which individuals can adapt the machine easily to their own self-image and personal rituals. This goes further than the usual notion of 'user friendliness' and involves looking at the machine in the context of the whole personal work space. Far from reaching this ideal, CMC as it now operates in Britain, almost perversely caters to the prejudices of the non-technology self-image. We still have to key in a 20 digit series of code in order to use JANET internationally; and we generally use systems which are command rather than menu driven, in small print, without colour, and without the support of a good on-line HELP service.

■ CMC in the context of British schools

When introducing CMC to a school, there is a further series of institutional assumptions and expectations which strongly affect its use.

☐ The siting of CMC equipment

Apart from the obvious and important consideration of ease of access, there seem to be two main factors about CMC which strongly affect the siting of equipment: the link with the telephone and the high prestige value of computer hardware.

Telephones are strongly linked to emotions in British schools. They tend to be in short supply, and access to a telephone is a status symbol for teachers, as well as considerably easing administrative task. Telephone bills are relatively high and difficult to justify as value for money: so, telephones represent one of the items of expenditure which it is felt can and must be controlled. Siting a telephone line in a classroom, and/or giving students access to it, is, therefore, contrary to accepted institutional norms. Computer hardware is expensive and has high prestige value in terms of the school's public relations with parents, local industry and the community. In this context, security considerations and the perceived opportunities to enhance prestige can play a large part in deciding where to site CMC equipment.

☐ Issues of autonomy and control

The need for teachers to establish control over their students is embedded in the culture of British schools, particularly in the secondary age range. This, together with attitudes to the use of telephones, may account for the assumption made by many teachers that they should retain responsibility for the use of CMC – by spooling their students' word-processed files, transmitting them to other schools and downloading incoming files. This results in a considerable extra work load for teachers which can only be handled out of school hours. In consequence, it results in major blocks in the chain of communications and loss of the vital spontaneity offered by CMC. It seems that initially teachers want to use CMC in privacy after school, so that they do not risk loss of authority and control by exposing their lack of expertise in front of students. However, a significant factor may be the ritualistic quality of their pattern of control. Once having done the 'work' by writing the word-processed files, the students 'give it in' and the teachers have the responsibility of sending it off as part of the usual 'marking' procedures. Thus new technology is simply being fitted into existing rituals of behaviour in which the teachers habitually assume a controlling role through the setting and marking of work.

☐   **Assumptions about the nature of email communications**

Email can be used in two different ways:

- for short on-line messages; and
- for the exchange of lengthier word-processed pieces.

These two types of use have considerable bearing on the nature of the communications and, although there are variations of the first pattern with software capable of downloading mail and transmitting mail in batches, these two types of communication remain quite distinct from each other. Short on-line messages tend to be written without formal patterns of addressing or signing off, without careful attention to spelling or punctuation and with an immediacy and informality half way between a memo and a phone conversation. Whereas, word-processed pieces are no different from any other form of writing and adopt style and form appropriate to their purpose and audience in the normal way.

Within schools the assumption tends to be made that communications will always be of word-processed files. Partly, this is because of the nexus of control and cost implications outlined above, but another significant factor may be institutional attitudes to students' work.

Writing is the main constituent of a student's classroom activity in Britain. Despite the importance of reading, listening and talking there is overwhelming evidence (see for example Bullock, 1975) that students spend an inordinate proportion of their time on writing. There is an assumption that a carefully constructed piece of prose is of more 'worth' for assessment purposes than a memo, a jotting, or a short message. Consequently, teachers can see a piece of word-processed writing sent electronically as purposeful and therefore part of the curriculum. They may feel much more uncomfortable about letting a student loose to write brief notes and 'chat' on-line.

☐   **Communicating within the curriculum – issues of classroom interaction**

In using email to communicate between classrooms a strong influence seems to be the nature of internal classroom interactions. Despite many ideas for joint projects, the most successful communications are often pen pal letters, 'relay stories' (in which one group begins a story, the next continues it and so on), and communications with an 'outside adult', perhaps taking a mystery role of some kind. In each of these examples there is little in-built conflict of purpose. Writing pen pal letters leaves students at both ends entirely free to write as they wish. The task becomes one of interesting the unknown partner (which is not an easy one, but the parameters of pen pal letters are familiar and students know exactly what is expected). Similarly, continuing the writing of a story begun by someone else is relatively straightforward – there may be problems of unmatched interest, but with sufficient ingenuity even an entirely unpalatable plot and characters can be subverted to a new purpose. Similarly, too, one outside adult is likely to be very responsive to students' interests.

Other tasks prove much more problematic. The stated curricula of different schools do not match, making it hard to carry out joint work on the same curriculum content. Even at the simplest level a recurring problem is delay or straight failure to reply. I have written elsewhere (op. cit.) of my realization that classrooms are not structured around the notion of communicating interactively with others. They are closed boxes from which information can be published or into which information can be drawn, but they are not able to interact spontaneously with other closed boxes. CMC between two classrooms is a complex business – in effect team teaching at a distance – and requires extensive and detailed planning between the teachers concerned.

I should like here to elaborate on this a little. Within a typical classroom the teacher will nominally control the curriculum and activities by selecting the topics for study, planning the activities, giving out the books and resources, setting the tasks and assessing the work done. However, in reality a great deal of negotiation goes on between the teacher and students as to the level of noise, the time spent on task, and even the nature of classroom tasks and activities. The work of Doyle (1979) and others has shown that students engage in an 'exchange of grades for compliance' in which they negotiate the level of difficulty of each task. Within this context, only the most careful planning of collaborative CMC can involve the students in both classes so that there is a real commonality of priorities for the teachers concerned. Even quite careful planning is likely to fall by the wayside if an uninvolved class doesn't like the look of the communications when they arrive. No teacher can put a responsibility to other students and another teacher in a remote classroom before the interests of those for whom he or she has a specific responsibility. It will never be worth risking violation to the fragile balance of the negotiated curriculum.

☐ **Collaborating at a distance – the human end of the human interface**

In the end, even when individuals and schools come to terms with CMC and use it successfully, there remains a remoteness which makes collaboration difficult. If there is a shared purpose, as with colleagues working for the same company or on the same research project, or between a student working at a distance and his or her tutor, CMC will be an excellent addition to other available means of communication. Conversely, when there is no shared purpose at all there may be a sense of adventure in ranging across the mailboxes and making unexpected friends – let's see who's out there to 'chat' to (a kind of 'ham radio' phenomenon). For those like teachers and their students whose purposes are neither urgent nor serendipitous there is the very human problem of depending heavily on other people. On reflecting why it is that I have sometimes been so badly let down by others over CMC links between schools, I realize that it is not an uncommon experience except in that the consequences have been more serious because my reliance has been greater than normal! It is human to promise, with good intentions, to do something and sometimes to fail. With the colleagues we work with from day to day we know them well enough to gauge their dependability and will pick up the job for ourselves when we judge it will not be done after all in any other way. At a distance we do not have the same personal knowledge of colleagues and cannot gauge when our priority is slipping beneath the weight of another's work load. It has nothing to do with technology, only a human failing masquerading as part of the human interface.

■ Conclusion

Establishing the use of CMC is a complex process involving changes to the personal and social context of daily life. For many there is a barrier to the use of CMC in their self-image as non-technology people. Within schools, there are further institutional assumptions and rituals of behaviour which create an extra layer of complexity. Following the government initiatives which have introduced CMC equipment into British schools there are considerable opportunities to enhance learning, and it is hoped that this paper may give some insights which will enable teachers to overcome problems and capitalize on these opportunities.

■ References

Bullock Report (1975) *A Language for Life*. HMSO, London.

Doyle, W. (1979) *The tasks of teaching and learning in classrooms*. R and D Report, No 4103. North Texas State University.

National Union of Teachers (1988). *We did it our way*. Tape no.2 Video, Focus in Education Ltd, Middlesex.

Somekh, B. and Groundwater-Smith, S. (1988). *Take a balloon and a piece of string*. In: *New Technologies and Professional Communications in Education* (D. Smith, ed.) Occasional paper 13, National Council for Educational Technology.

Index